Indigenous Mestizos

A book in the series

Latin America Otherwise: Languages, Empires, Nations

Series editors:

Walter D. Mignolo, Duke University

Irene Silverblatt, Duke University

Sonia Saldívar-Hull, University of California

at Los Angeles

MARISOL DE LA CADENA

Indigenous Mestizos

The Politics of Race

and Culture in Cuzco,

Peru, 1919–1991

DUKE UNIVERSITY PRESS

Durham & London

2000

2nd printing, 2003

© 2000 Duke University Press

All rights reserved

Printed in the United States of America on acid-free paper ∞

Designed by C. H. Westmoreland

Typeset in Sabon by Keystone Typesetting, Inc.

Library of Congress Cataloging-in-Publication Data appear
on the last printed page of this book.

Contents

About the Series

Latin America Otherwise: Languages, Empires, Nations is a critical series. It aims to explore the emergence and consequences of concepts used to define "Latin America" while at the same time exploring the broad interplay of political, economic, and cultural practices that have shaped Latin American worlds. Latin America, at the crossroads of competing imperial designs and local responses, has been construed as a geocultural and geopolitical entity since the nineteenth century. This series provides a starting point to redefine Latin America as a configuration of political, linguistic, cultural, and economic intersections that demand a continuous reappraisal of the role of the Americas in history, and of the ongoing process of globalization and the relocation of people and cultures that have characterized Latin America's experience. *Latin America Otherwise: Languages, Empires, Nations* is a forum that confronts established geocultural constructions, that rethinks area studies and disciplinary boundaries, that assesses convictions of the academy and of public policy, and that, correspondingly, demands that the practices through which we produce knowledge and understanding about and from Latin America be subject to rigorous and critical scrutiny.

Racial discourses, often crucial to the development of nationalist ideologies, have shaped much of Latin American history since independence. Marisol de la Cadena explores the dynamic of racial and cultural discourses in Peru throughout most of this century and places them within the broader swirl of modernization and state-building.

With careful attention to the regional strains generated by the push toward "modernity," de la Cadena focuses on the intellectuals of Cuzco, once the capital of the Inca Empire, and helps us see how the clash between this region and Lima, Peru's capital since colonial times, produced a regional ideology that emphasized culture over biological notions of human difference while giving racial categories a strong moral content. In this context, definitions of "Indio" and "Mestizo" took on special weight, often becoming the focus of clashes over the assessment of human worth and political identity. One of this book's great contributions is to make us aware of the complex ideological struggles behind hegemonic racial categories and so remind us that the powerful do not have the only, or the last, word.

Constantly moving between the Latin American Studies tradition in the United States, and the political engagement of intellectuals living and working in Latin America, Marisol de la Cadena builds a strong argument about her own country at the intersection of disciplinary norms and political concerns.

Walter D. Mignolo, *Duke University*
Irene Silverblatt, *Duke University*
Sonia Saldívar-Hull, *University of Southern California*

Acknowledgments

I had not returned to Cuzco since I finished my last fieldwork season in October 1992. In September of that same year, we had celebrated the capture of the Shining Path's highest leader. Like most Peruvians, I too began to see the light at the end of the very dark tunnel created by the twelve-year war waged by that group against all who opposed them. Terrorist and military violence had not hit the city of Cuzco — at least not in the magnitude that it had swept over Ayacucho, the Mantaro region, and Lima — and the most visible consequence of the conflict was the general absence of tourists. During 1991 and 1992, when I was doing the fieldwork that led to this book, only Cuzqueños and Cuzqueñas busily crossed the Plaza de Armas or cozily sat on one of its benches to get warm under the morning sun. With few foreigners, I imagined that the city looked like it probably did in the 1930s when the Cuzqueño tourist industry was only just beginning.

In June 1999 I finally went back to Cuzco. On my way from the airport to the city I was struck by the sight of an immense statue, which the taxi driver identified as Pachacutec, the most legendary of all Incas. *No matter what, Cuzqueñismo — that pride of belonging to the region that had cradled the Inca Empire — never dies,* I thought (not without some aesthetic arrogance) as the taxi driver explained that the monument had been built with foreign funds channeled through the municipal council. But monuments to Incas were not the only changes I observed. During the seven years that I had been absent, peace returned to the country and tourism had resumed in Cuzco. New hotels and restaurants had been built, many of which represented investments of transnational corporations. I learned that one of these had even mutilated an impressive Inca wall by carving an entrance through it to provide easier access to a five-star hotel. Meanwhile, the local cultural authorities had offered little resistance. This was big news indeed. Partially destroying an Incan antiquity with the acquiescence of Cuzqueño politicians would have been inconceivable in the early 1990s. At that time, cultural authorities hotly contested even alterations to the spelling of regional Quechua words. That cultural authorities now accommodated the requests of foreign investment interests surprised me; yet it also made me realize that my initial reaction to Cuzqueñismo had perhaps been too simple. Although it had not receded, the power of authorities to build statues in the name of Cuzqueñismo required them to introduce changes in the regionalist ideology that would accommodate a larger global economic system and ideology. After all, isn't flexibility an attribute of ideologies that remain hegemonic? Why wouldn't Cuzqueñismo change? It had constantly done so throughout the century, yet it had remained strong. This time, however, the transformation was induced by the free market—demonstrated by the fact that the fate of Inca relics can be determined not only by tradition, but also by a high bid—which may be able to absorb Cuzqueñismo into its own global hegemony. What happens next remains to be seen. For the time being, the Plaza de Armas was once again teeming with tourists. Many of them, and many Cuzqueños too, paid a dollar an hour to communicate beyond Cuzco via the "Cabinas Internet," privately owned small stores located all over the city and packed with computers connected to the World Wide Web.

I wondered how these changes had affected the two Cuzqueños I wanted to see the most and whom I consider crucial to my analysis: Lucrecia Carmandona and Alejandro Condori. Would I even find them? Back in 1991, when I first met Lucrecia, a mestiza woman and political leader, she was a market vendor. Alejandro, a dance choreographer of Capac Qolla, earned his living as a street vendor of cosmetics. Fortunately, I found them in the same places: Lucrecia was sitting in her market stall, where she still sells potatoes and yucca; when I saw Alejandro he was there, in the same street, busy choosing the right lipstick for a customer. Except for a few pounds less or more and a few more wrinkles, they showed no signs of the passage of time. Of course they asked me about the book. It gave me great satisfaction (and relief!) to tell them it was done and an enormous pleasure to thank both of them personally. Lucrecia and Alejandro gave me all the information I asked from them, sat endless hours answering my queries, walked with me through the steep Cuzco streets, introduced me to their friends and relatives, and shared with me intimacies that helped me understand their lives and emotions. But most important, both Alejandro and Lucrecia — who do not know each other — shared with me a life wisdom to which I still turn in my own difficult moments. Many other Cuzqueños helped me. Although I cannot list them all, I want to thank Delia Vidal de Milla, Juan Bravo Vizcarra, Ricardo Castro Pinto, Timotea Gamarra, Lucho Carhuamán, Vicky Mojonero, and Paulino Chihuantito. All of them gave me access to their rich personal archives, which provided texture to my insights. Georgina Mendívil and the late Manuel Velasco Quintanilla were also great sources of local knowledge and very generous with their time.

Since 1991 this book has traveled many places and gone through many stages; during all of them I have been surrounded by wonderful friends and colleagues. I could not have survived the combination of pregnancy and fieldwork in Cuzco without them. Kathryn Burns took loving care of me in the house we shared in Calle Suecia. Ever since she has remained one of my chosen readers, always making the subtle editorial change that enhanced my argument theoretically. Chuck Walker and Thomas Kruggeler helped me through my days as a novice historian — I will never forget their unusual combination of immense kindness and sarcastic jokes that eased many long hours in the archives. Their comments have improved my ideas from the earliest days when I had only a dissertation proposal. Zoila Mendoza generously introduced me to the analysis of dance troupes, for which I will be forever grateful. Cesar Itier opened the world of Inca Theater to me and generously shared material with me that he had gathered. Margarita Castro, Margaret Najarro, and Patricia Vivanco were excellent assistants in the archives. Fernando Pancorbo and Teófila Huamán assisted with my fieldwork and contributed their insights. The cariño of Pilar Zevallos, Luis Nieto, Adelma Benavente, Miki Suzuki, Gabriela Martínez, and Norma Neira helped me weather the cold Cuzco days. Zully Grandillet helped me care for my daughter Manuela, who was still a nursing baby. I would not have trusted Manuela to anybody else but Zully. My sister, Aroma de la Cadena, came to Cuzco on several occasions and was able to help me in many ways.

In Madison, Frank Salomon, Florencia Mallon, and Steve Stern inspired, nurtured, and challenged me in the manuscript's early stages. Frank's comments — long pages replete with shrewd ideas, exquisite knowledge, and extremely demanding questions — always made me return to my writing with deeper insights. Florencia shared with me her unique, strong analytical intuition, and somehow, Steve Stern always discovered the exact point where I had stopped thinking and pushed me further. As if this were not enough, the two anonymous readers chosen by Duke University Press made invaluable comments. Once I knew their names, Brooke Larson and Deborah Poole, I felt an even stronger need to respond to their suggestions for more rigor and creativity. Although I have to confess there were moments when I did not enjoy it, I also have to admit that I could not have asked for a better dissertation committee, a better team of readers, a better group of Andeanists, and a better group of friends, both within and outside U.S. academia.

In the last four years, while physically in Chapel Hill and officially a "resident alien" in the United States, I have straddled this country and Peru, and in both places friends have continued to shower me with insights, criticism, and encouragement. I have struggled with Sinclair Thomson's sharp, critical, and inspiring comments on issues of representation; with Penelope Harvey's unmatchable ethnographic talent; and with Orin Starn's exigencies to generalize beyond my self-imposed limits. Carlos Aguirre encouraged me when I doubted my skill for historical analysis. Hortencia Muñoz obliged me to refine my arguments about elite Peruvian culture, and my analysis of indigenous social movements is filled with images inspired by Eloy Neira's relentless quest for human equality. Long, deep, and memorable personal and academic conversations with Eileen Findlay and passionate discussions with Marisa Remy deeply affected my writing. Mercedes Niño Murcia does not know it, but she was very inspiring and stimulating. Carlos Iván Degregori and Gonzalo Portocarrero, as politically engaged intellectuals, have been the best role models. Dorothy Holland, Donald Nonini, and Jim Peacock were among my first readers at the Department of Anthropology at the University of North Carolina; they read the manuscript when it was still a dissertation, and their comments framed my rewriting process considerably. During the last stages I was blessed by Judith Farquhar's invitation to join an extraordinary writing group. Here I used Judy's shrewd analytical skills, learned from her intellectual generosity, and profited from the editorial and theoretical comments of Jane Danielewicz, Megan Matchinske, Laurie Langbauer, and Joy Kasson.

Still, a book needs more than ideas. Valerie Millholland from Duke University Press was a wonderful editor, always ready to assuage my anxieties; Mather George, Marsha Michie, and Amy Mortensen, graduate students of anthropology at UNC, assisted me in the final details of the manuscript. I must thank Paul Leslie, who as associate chair of the Department of Anthropology always accepted my requests for research assistants. I also had a good copyeditor. As a nonnative speaker, I have a style all my own, and Maura High was respectful of it yet daring enough to change it when my invented syntax or vocabulary made no sense. Finally, the research that led to this book was funded by the Social Science Research Council and the Wenner Gren Foundation Predoctoral Grants. To write the dissertation I received grants from the Graduate School of the University of Wisconsin—Madison, the School of American Research, and the Harry Frank Guggenheim Foundation. The National Endowment for the Humanities, the Richard Hunt Fellowship from the Wenner Gren Foundation, and the Institute for Research in Social Sciences at the University of North Carolina financed the last writing period.

Steve Boucher, my partner, and our daughter, Manuela Boucher–de la Cadena, have not read a word of this last version. However, they have been the most important presence in my life since the early fieldwork days until now, when I am finally writing the acknowledgments. They left me alone to think, write, and read, but most of all, they have given me enormous amounts of happiness and restored the sense of reality that I always lost after hours of tinkering with ideas. Thanks, Steve, for encouraging me when I got stuck and for cooking wonderful meals, doing the laundry, and buying flowers. Thanks, Manuela, for staying near me and not letting me shoo you away when I was busy writing. I owe both of you so much.

Past Dialogues about Race:

An Introduction to the Present

La violencia étnica existe en todas las sociedades que como la nuestra albergan culturas y tradiciones diferentes. (Ethnic violence exists in any society which, like ours, harbors different cultures and traditions.) — MARIO VARGAS LLOSA, 1990

Indian peasants live in such a primitive way that communication is practically impossible. It is only when they move to the cities that they have the opportunity to mingle with the other Peru. The price they must pay for integration is high — renunciation of their culture, their language, their beliefs, their traditions, and customs, and the adoption of the culture of their ancient masters. After one generation they become mestizos. They are no longer Indians.
— MARIO VARGAS LLOSA, 1990

En nuestro país la raza ya no manda, ahora manda la inteligencia, la educación, la cultura. (In our country, race does not rule anymore; instead, intelligence, education, and culture do.)
— ADRIANA B., CUZCO, 1992

In Peru everyone accepts that social discrimination is pervasive, and almost everybody would explain and even justify such practices in terms of "cultural differences." Apparently innocuous and incidental, this social convention is at the heart of the Peruvian racial formation (Omi and Winant, 1986; Winant, 1994). Peruvian modern discourses that acquit racist practices and even legitimize them by appealing to *culture* are integral to the political process through

Map 1. Peru

race not seen as biological / Culture linked to race

which in Peru—to borrow Robert Young's words—race was culturally constructed and, significantly, culture was racially defined (1995:54). These exculpations of racism are embedded in a definition of *race* rhetorically silenced by the historical subordination of phenotype to *culture* as a marker of difference. In other words, Peruvians think their discriminatory practices are not racist because they do not connote innate biological differences, but cultural ones. What goes unnoticed in this way of thinking is that since the early part of the twentieth century, Peruvians (intellectuals and nonintellectuals) have tended to define race with allusions to culture, the soul, and the spirit, which were thought to be more important than skin color or any other bodily attribute in determining the behavior of groups of people, that is, their race. All the above phrases implicitly share this culturalist definition of race while also containing some disagreements that in turn, reflect the social position of their authors, their conventions, their desires, and their social anxieties. These differences, which are as politically important as the agreements, reflect discrepancies in the ways of thinking and practicing the relationship between "race" and "culture" in Peru.

The first two epigraphs to this introduction are from Mario Vargas Llosa, who thought that the war waged by the Shining Path terrorist movement in Peru (1980–1992) was the inevitable result of cultural differences between the Indians and "the rest" of the country. Implicit in the phrasing of his first statement is a notion of culture that echoes some nineteenth-century racial thinkers who, like Gobineau (1915:30), explained that the relationship among different human groups inevitably resulted in violence because it was governed by natural laws of repulsion or of attraction. The second statement implies that the different cultures of Peru represent different stages in the development of reason; this uneven development explains — and indeed justifies — the hierarchies that structure the nation's political and economic inequalities. Against the cultural roots of inequalities — and, indeed, to deter ethnic violence — Vargas Llosa proposes "integration," which he envisions as the process through which Indians shed "their culture" and become mestizos, subordinate participants in the dominant culture. Vargas Llosa's logic is very simple and ahistorical: since "the Andean tradition" and "modern Peru" are incompatible, the former has to be sacrificed, because the latter is, obviously, rationally superior.

The third epigraph comes from Adriana B., a university student whom I met in Cuzco, a region in southern Peru that tourism has made famous as the capital of the pre-Hispanic Inca Empire. Adriana self-identifies as *mestiza*, yet (contradicting Vargas Llosa's definition of *mestizos*) she honors her indigenous origins. She demonstrates this pride by dancing in an urban folk troupe representing "the people of the highlands," as she elliptically refers to the people Vargas Llosa calls Indians. She considers the word "Indian" contemptuous and criticizes its usage. Yet, like Vargas Llosa, she also appeals to culture to approve social hierarchies and believes that discrimination is legitimate if it is based on differences in formal education. She argues eloquently, however, against using race to justify social hierarchies.

Adriana's and Vargas Llosa's discriminatory views and practices concur in that they both use culture to mark and justify social differences. However, their views also conflict conceptually and, indeed, politically, and this conflict derives from the different meanings that they attach to culture. The position Vargas Llosa represents, as a privileged, educated, well-known male writer — one that he has articulated in several publications and interviews — deems cultural specificities as innate and as determining of cleavages among groups of people, who surmount their differences through the gradual process of group evolution.[1] Adriana may also perceive culture as innate. But — as a woman and a student who aspires to the privileges of education — she subordinates this notion to an alternative one, which she defines as personal achievement rather than group evolution; she uses education to mark differences within this individualized idea of culture. Adriana does not imagine that cultural differences among groups preclude cultural similarities among individuals. Instead, crucially, she considers that individuals who are different in some cultural aspects can share other cultural traits. "People can be [culturally] different and similar at the same time. I practice indigenous culture but I am not an Indian," she explained.

In Cuzco, the site of my research and the place that this book is about, Adriana's words taught me to understand how she — and many other *cuzqueños* like her — challenge a definition of cultures as vessels of immanent inequalities of reason that legitimate — and naturalize — hierarchies among human groups. This is the belief that Vargas Llosa represents and that I consider an expression of Peruvian dominant racism, which I define as the discriminatory practices that derive from a belief in the unquestionable intellectual and moral superiority of one group of Peruvians over the rest. This way of thinking, which does not resort to racial terminology, is a version of what some authors identify as "new racism" (Barker, 1982), "racism without race" (Gilroy, 1987; Balibar, 1988), or "cultural fundamentalism" (Stolcke, 1995). Yet I also learned that when Adriana (and others) challenge race as the mark of differences, or critique essentialist notions of culture, they can still make discriminations. Although Adriana and her peers stress that culture is achievable, and that education is a legitimate source of social differentiation, in doing so they may converge with dominant racism by appealing to hierarchies of reason to legitimate discrimination. While it would be too simplistic to consider them "racists," it would be more of a mistake to disregard their participation in the dominant forms of discrimination while only documenting their resistance to it.

Neither institutionalized hypocrisy, nor self-deception, nor inferiority complexes undergirds these subaltern forms of discrimination; rather, I think that the explanation lies in the complexities of contradictory consciousness: "the co-existence in individual minds of two conceptions of the world" (Gramsci, 1987:326). In Peru, contradictory consciousness leads individuals like Adriana to deny the existence of insurmountable hierarchies and immanent cultural differences—those that would place "them" in absolute inferior positions—and at the same time acquiesce to the legitimacy of social differences created by educational achievements. This contradiction, by converging with dominant forms of racism, contributes to its hegemony. Intriguingly, culture—either the innate attributes of a group that correlate with stages in the development of reason (as Vargas Llosa understands it) or "formal education" and individual achievement (as Adriana defines it)—is the arena where racism and the challenge to it meet in the compromise arrangement that enables dominant forms of discrimination to prevail. Yet in the contradictory consciousness of subordinate groups, culture as achievement constitutes an effective challenge to racism. The notion that culture/education is achievable, together with the perception that cultural differences among groups do not preclude similarities among individuals, has enabled cuzqueños like Adriana to transform the dominant meanings of the "mestizo" and "Indian" racial labels.

The second of Vargas Llosa's statements illustrates the current dominant usage of the term "mestizo": a Spanish and Indian racialized cultural mixture, evolving from "primitive" Indianness into a more "civilized" stage, and eventually incompatible with indigenous ways. Working-class indigenous cuzqueños give the word an

alternative meaning: they use "mestizo" to identify literate and economically successful people who share indigenous cultural practices
yet do not perceive themselves as miserable, a condition that they
consider "Indian." Far from equating "indigenous culture" with
"being Indian" — a label that carries a historical stigma of colonized
inferiority — they perceive Indianness as a social condition that reflects an individual's failure to achieve educational improvement. As
a result of this redefinition, "indigenous culture" — or Andean culture, to be more specific — exceeds the scope of Indianness; it broadly
includes cuzqueño commoners who are proud of their rural origins
and claim indigenous cultural heritage, yet refuse to be labeled Indians. They proudly call themselves "mestizo."

This process, which I call de-Indianization, lies at the heart of
my book. The process is a complex one, which goes well beyond
the simple view that when Indians become mestizos they adopt
"the culture of their ancient masters" (Vargas Llosa, 1990b). De-
Indianization is the process through which working-class cuzqueños
have both reproduced and contested racism. Conceived as such, de-
Indianization is not the shedding of indigenous culture and subsequent "integrating" that Vargas Llosa envisioned as the solution
to violence in Peru. Neither does it mean "assimilating," and thus
disappearing culturally, as some anthropologists have presented it
(Bonfil Batalla, 1996; Friedlander, 1975). Rather, it is through active
de-Indianization that subaltern cuzqueños have redefined essentialist notions of culture. They accomplish this by replacing regional
beliefs in fixed identities with infinite degrees of fluid Indianness or
mestizoness. They measure these degrees relationally, by considering, for example, the levels of literacy of the persons involved in an
interaction, or their relative success in urban jobs; the individual
who shows greater achievement in the aforementioned activities is
perceived as less Indian, and therefore the mestizo in the interaction. In this alternative and relational view, Indians and mestizos
emerge from interactions and not from evolution. Although de-
Indianization legitimates subaltern cuzqueños' own discriminatory
behavior, by moving away from the dominant perspective it includes
an antievolutionary impetus as it opens up the possibility to ascend
socially without shedding indigenous ways. Rooted in a political

concept of culture and of self — one that takes power into account — de-Indianization emphasizes the difference between indigenous culture as a postcolonial phenomenon and "Indianness" as a colonized, inferior social condition. The discourse of de-Indianization allows grassroots intellectuals to reinvent indigenous culture stripped of the stigmatized Indianness that the elites assigned it since colonial times. However, since this liberating process itself continues to define Indianness as the utmost inferior condition in the region, it leaves room for racism to persist.

Recently some scholars have argued that "race" is a political category, whose meanings are shaped through struggle (Omi and Winant, 1986; Gilroy, 1987; Goldberg, 1993). Building on these ideas, and considering the almost inseparable bond between race and culture in Peru, I include de-Indianization among the dialogic struggles through which subordinate cuzqueños have inserted liveable meanings into the racial-cultural identity labels that elites have produced. Because "race" is present on both intellectual and daily life discourses, the dialogic struggles have occurred in and across academic and everyday spheres. In this book, the protagonists in the conflict-ridden process to define race (and later ethnicity) are the cuzqueño elite as well as grassroots intellectuals. The latter are usually working-class people, and (following Gramsci) I define them as nonacademic thinkers who, by organizing and engaging in persuasive activities, contribute to bringing into being new modes of thought shaped after their own particular conception of the world and conscious line of moral conduct (Gramsci, 1987:8–10). Grassroots intellectuals, unlike intellectuals as they have been traditionally defined, are also peasants (as in Feierman, 1990) or, as in the cases I will describe, dancers, market women, and street vendors. In turn-of-the-century Cuzco, their counterparts were the *indigenistas,* members of an elite intellectual movement that strove for country-wide recognition, using arguments about their authentic nationalism and profound knowledge of Peru.

Although this book is about Cuzco, the interregional dialogical racial struggle has always been part of broader Peruvian politics, and most importantly, nation building and state policy making. At the turn of the century, cuzqueño struggles were linked to the processes that defined race in terms of culture. This connection between race and culture in Peru has a much longer history, one that can be traced back to colonial beliefs about "purity of blood" (referring to Christian descent) (Gose, 1996; Schwartz and Salomon, forthcoming; Burns, 1999). Yet my particular story begins with a turn-of-the-century dialogue between Peruvian elite intellectuals and European thinkers about the racial character of Peru, a sensitive point during a period in which Latin American leaders were formulating their national projects. In this process Peruvian intellectuals and politicians (for reasons that will become clear) juggled with an imprecise notion of race in which the "spirit" prevailed over (but did not cancel out) the physical aspects of race. Many Peruvian male intellectuals (and a few very vocal women) offered a culturalist definition of race, which could include — though not necessarily — some biological features, randomly subordinated to the superior powers of morality. Morality was deemed to be innate; however, education could instill more virtues in an individual.[2] Cuzqueño elite intellectuals were highly influential in these dialogues with Europeans over the national racial character. Several of them were particularly decisive in the historical and academic formulation of what I see as a "culturalist" definition of race. Their ideas (which they propagated in newspapers, books, and speeches in their capacity as university professors, members of regional judiciary courts and municipalities, or as congress representatives or state ministers) included both an adamant rejection of biological determinism and the naturalization of hierarchies that, nominally at least, derived from essential moral/cultural differences. Élite intellectuals from Cuzco were not alone in this project, nor did their work go uncontested. Throughout this century, in various arenas ranging from direct political confrontations to daily life, even including ritualistic manifestations, grassroots cuzqueño intellectuals both contested and complied with the classificatory systems and the identity labels that the dominant intelligentsia, progressive and conservative, proposed. But subordinate groups embraced educational differences as legitimating social hierarchies, as did the elites, thus allowing dominant racism to leak into their alternative practices. Thus, shielded by the concessions made to Indian-looking individuals *if* they were "educated," dominant sectors acquitted themselves from racism while they overtly continued to discriminate against noneducated groups and, indeed, claimed a difference of skin color, regardless of whether any real difference existed or not. Elites and commoners eventually came to share beliefs in the power of education and "culture" to legitimate discrimination and thus silence denunciations of racism, rendering racism hegemonic and eloquently illustrating that "hegemony at its most effective is mute" (Comaroff and Comaroff, 1991:24).

There are myriad definitions of hegemony, but I envision it as denoting an ambiguously defined dialogic field shared by elites and subordinates, where a dynamic of power struggle characterized by constant agreements and disputes, and by domination and insubordination, produces a conflict-laden consensus, usually narrow, yet politically crucial.[3] In the case of Peruvian racism, the consensus that makes its hegemony possible is the idea that "education" — meaning schooling in its different degrees — creates legitimate hierarchies. Although beyond it the disputes start, the agreement (based on ideas that education is potentially achievable and cancels original inferiorities) induces self-identification, a condition that Raymond Williams sees as decisive of hegemony (Williams, 1977:118). In Peru, and most specifically in Cuzco, this identification was made possible by a modern definition of race that included the possibility of subordinating one's phenotype and emphasizing instead one's intelligence and morality, if these had been exposed to the corrective power of "education." This definition was certainly replete with legacies of discriminatory colonial discourses. However, at the turn of the century they were made legitimate by liberal ideals about equality. Moreover, the taxonomy deriving from a definition of race that subordinated phenotype was peculiarly ductile, as it included both the perception of rigid hierarchies and an unequivocal fluidity to position individuals within it. Thus, although the ranking of racial groups was consensually accepted and class-related, the definition of what label adhered to which person left room for negotiation. Such negotiation was expected to be positive, in the sense that the individual could be placed in the highest ranking position possible, but if that could not be done, the resolution would "rest on a resigned recognition of the inevitable and the necessary" (Williams, 1977:118). Currently in Cuzco, what sustains the negotiation, and eventually makes racism hegemonic, is the implicit agreement that "whiteness" — in its local, not necessarily phenotypical, version — is ultimately superior and Indianness represents absolute inferiority. Ambiguously situated between both terms, upper- and middle-class brown-skinned cuzqueños struggle to approach an elusive yet possible social whiteness; when class and gender (and the cultural perceptions of both) intervene to prevent this achievement, or even thoughts about it, individuals avoid Indianness by settling on being mestizos, albeit of different sorts.

Crucial to my notion of hegemony — and my analysis of hegemonic racism — is a Bakhtinian notion of dialogue: not as face-to-face exchanges but as historically grounded encounters among competing discourses about "culture" (glossed as race, ethnicity, or class) that circulate in cuzqueño social and academic spheres.[4] I assume that these dialogic encounters are articulated by relationships that occur across multilayered links of power, and thus, the dominant side in one instance may be the subordinate side in another. Identifying multilayered links of power allows me to view a panorama of subordinate practices that defy a higher level of domination while acting as the dominant side of another chain of power and subordinating "others" defined as inferior.[5] I can thus treat "top" and "bottom" — as Herzfeld has suggested (1997:3) — as two of a host of refractions in a broadly shared and disputed cultural engagement, which in this case involves discourses that intertwine race and culture. This perspective also opens up the possibility of scrutinizing the common ground between "elites" and "ordinary people" — the ground that makes hegemonic forms possible — while avoiding simplistic references to those categories as merely oppositional. I analyze this multilayered view of the ways in which cuzqueños act out their daily lives in light of the recognition that identities are always and constantly crossed by issues of race, ethnicity, geography, class, gender, and generation (Laclau and Mouffe, 1985; Hall, 1992).

Dialogically constructed, the racial/cultural labels that cuzqueños currently use are intimately entangled with formal education, as Adriana B. argued. Located on the edge of racist hegemony, Adriana self-identifies as mestiza *and* uses indigenous cultural discourses, thus avoiding and defying rigid Indian/mestizo evolutionary dichotomies, but her views of the "less educated" (who also form the vast majority of the underprivileged working classes) are similar to those of the elites. Therefore, although beliefs like hers represent a rupture with evolutionist and racialized notions of culture, the idea that education legitimates social hierarchies condones discrimination, intersecting with turn-of-the-century dominant racial thought in Peru, and the images of class difference it bequeathed.

This perception of race as linked to education (and therefore to class and gender) leads me to address—if briefly—how my own identity has shaped my research. I am a brown-skinned, middle-class, intellectual from Lima. As a result of my background—and, crucially, of my academic training—I belong to Peruvian elite intellectual circles where "whites" predominate, and where, as a result of implicit racialized feelings, people either politely ignore my skin color or consider me white. I think that most less-privileged Peruvians would not make a crucial distinction between me and individuals considered white by North American standards. Some provincial university students (like Adriana), who are aware of racial and cultural identities as concepts, would accept in a conversation that I am *mestiza* (because of my brown skin), but they would at the same time consider me *limeña* and, given the geographical construction of race in Peru, socially white. All this contrasts sharply with the perception that my U.S. friends have of me, particularly those who first met me in this country and not in Peru. For them, I am a Latina, therefore inevitably and overtly marked as a woman of color, as a friend of mine recently said (to my surprise, so much had I internalized my Peruvian colorlessness, and therefore, my whiteness!). These experiences have molded my reflections about the Peruvian "whitening" processes and their linkages with class, gender, geography, and with what being an intellectual meant. Memories of my elderly grandmother constantly reminding me that I was *una señorita muy decente* (a very decent young lady) called my attention to the fact that, although I look like Adriana, neither my *limeño* intellectual peers nor my grandmother were willing to consider me a mestiza. Telling me that I was "a very decent young lady," my grandmother was deflecting attention from my skin color and instructing me on the social construction of whiteness, and like any other average middle-class limeña, she was also expressing her culturally ingrained dislike of mestizos. This racial category is not as related to skin color as it is to a combination of class distinction and education, which is what the social category of decency indicates. Obviously, it was not my grandmother's dislike of mestizos that prevented my identification as one; rather, as I explain in the following pages, it was the historical intellectual and political itinerary of *mestizaje* as a nation-building model for Peru that had this effect. Initially embraced in the nineteenth century, mestizaje has not been a central nationalist ideal of state policies and intellectuals since the mid-twentieth century, though it was mildly revived by Vargas Llosa in the 1990s as part of his ephemeral and disastrous political career. Relegated to official oblivion and subdued by everyday elite rejection, mestizaje has nevertheless been claimed and redefined by the working classes as an empowering alternative that does not imply a rejection of indigenous culture yet distances them from Indianness.

Turn-of-the-Century Racial Dialogues about Hybridity
Constructive Mestizaje versus Degeneration

The influence of race in the destiny of peoples appears plainly in the history of the perpetual revolutions of the Spanish republics in South America. Composed of individuals whose diverse heredities have dissociated their ancestral characteristics, these populations have no national soul and therefore no stability. A people of half-castes is often ungovernable. — GUSTAVE LE BON, 1912

Since when do revolutions announce decrepitude and death? None of the Latin American nations currently presents the political and social misery that reigned in feudal Europe; but the feudal era is considered an evolutionary stage, while the Hispanoamerican revolutions are deemed as a terminal definitive state. We could say that Le Bon mistakes a child's skin rash for the geriatric gangrene of a ninety-year-old, or the sudden outbursts of a teenager for the homicidal insanity of a senile person. — MANUEL GONZALEZ PRADA, 1904

In a recent article, the historian George Stocking stated that at the turn of the century, widespread confusion about the definition of race was the most immediately evident characteristic of racial thought (1994:7).[6] We can picture race as a historically specific concept that attaches to theoretical and social discourses to establish the meanings it assumes at any historical moment (Goldberg, 1993:74). Furthermore, because race is a powerful yet empty concept, debates that have sought to define it have been (and still are) shaped by the specific "structure of feelings" (Williams, 1977) that underpins the relations between the groups or individuals who participate in racial discussions or are touched by racial discourses at any given historical period. As a "discourse of vacillations" (cf. Foucault),[7] the treatment of race (and by the same token of ethnicity) has manifested "characteristic elements of impulse, restraint, and tone; specifically affective elements of consciousness and relationships: not feeling against thought, but thought as felt and feeling as thought: practical consciousness of a present kind, in a living and inter-relating community" (Williams, 1977:132). Because race manifested social experiences still in process, its popularity among turn-of-the-century Peruvian elites, I want to argue, derived from its ability to express feelings of superiority while scientifically legitimating these emotions. This allowed them to distribute power based on the structure of their feelings, thus imperceptibly connecting intimate spheres with official realms. Race was simultaneously a scientific and political notion and an officially legitimate, emotion-laden term. Of course, the elites were not a homogeneous pack, yet the conceptual emptiness of race licensed celebrities of all stripes to shape the notion in accord with their divergent feelings.[8]

"Mestizaje," the regional, nineteenth-century word used in debates about the perils or benefits of hybridity, was the epicenter of the racialized structure of feelings of this region of Latin America. As Brooke Larson put it, mestizaje was "a vexed and multivalent metaphor upon which elites hung their hopes, hatreds, and fears upon the future of the race and the nation" (1998:377). Their fears had been provoked by European arguments that saw in Latin America hybridity's degenerative effects. Robert Knox specifically used Mexico, Peru, and Central America to prove that "the hybrid was a degradation of humanity and was rejected by nature."[9] Paul Broca, a polygynist who believed in the benefits of eugenic racial-crossing, claimed that the mixture between races as distant as the Iberian colonizers and the Indians was the origin of the disgraces of Latin America (1864:33). Herbert Spencer held a similar view regarding Mexico (quoted in Brading, 1984). As illustrated by Le Bon, these beliefs had not ebbed by the turn of the century and continued to cast doubt on Latin America's ability to construct nations, and to block any stable superior identity for regional elites. A frequent reaction to the problem of potential hybrid degeneration was what Nancy Leys Stepan (1991) has called "constructive miscegenation," which reversed arguments against mestizaje by praising the benefits of racial crossing. The pioneering nationalist mestizaje project was launched by Mexican indigenistas after the Revolution. Championed by Andrés Molina Enríquez and Justo Sierra earlier in the nineteenth century, it was promoted again by José Vasconcelos and Manuel Gamio in the 1920s. Its goal was to produce a bronze-colored people, one that could boast the refinement of both European and Aztec civilizations (Knight, 1990). Nineteenth-century Colombian intellectuals and Brazilians in the 1920s expressed a similar pride concerning racial mixture, although their goal was to produce a white national race (Wade, 1993; Skidmore, 1993; Larson, forthcoming).

Many important Peruvian nation-builders proposed constructive miscegenation as an alternative to the country's racial problem. In the late 1860s, Manuel Atanasio Fuentes, a leading historian, alluding to the pervasive racial mixture Peru appeared to include, described Lima—the capital city—as a "multicolored garden" and linked this characteristic to the progressive nature of the city (Poole, 1997). He also thought that the country's nonwhite races were the cause for the backwardness of certain regions, because they were "pure." He wrote: "In Lima, even those men who are immediately descended from the European race have a *trigueño* color [literally 'like wheat,' light brown] which is pale and yellowed" (Fuentes, 1867:104; quoted in Poole, 1997:159). Trained in physiognomic methods—which read facial features as reflecting signs of personal moral character—Fuentes also surveyed Limeños' morality and intellectual capacity, which he found diverse. While extolling the intellectual and aesthetic refinement of the upper classes, he derided the chronic vagrancy of the underclass of blacks, *zambos, cholos,* and the rest of the lower-class population (Gootenberg, 1993:67; Oliart, 1994). Fuentes was writing at the same time as Europeans who feared the degenerative effects of hybridity.[10] However, for Fuentes the immorality of the lower classes did not result from miscegenation but from enduring negative aspects of their original "pure" races. From his perspective, the mixed racial inheritance that character- ized the limeño upper classes was a far cry from the degenera- tion that Broca, Knox, or Spencer imputed to all Latin Americans. Fuentes wrote during a mid-century economic export boom, which, according to economic historian Paul Gootenberg, made Peru the richest regime of Latin America (1993:58). The wealth benefited mostly Lima, and most specifically its upper classes, while failing to reach the rest of the country, and seriously aggravated the hard- ships of limeño working classes. The gains also boosted the intellec- tual lifestyles of Lima's elites, which even before the mid-century economic expansion were fairly sophisticated (Gootenberg, 1993; Poole, 1997). In an era when racial thought was pervasive, it comes as no surprise that Fuentes attributed the success of limeños to their racial make-up. Also, the notably successful lives of the upper classes belied the judgments of Europeans who doomed hybrid Latin Ameri- cans — including the affluent oligarchies — to failure. Not surpris- ingly, Fuentes constructs an opposing image: miscegenation led to progress, and Lima's multicolored leading classes proved it; more- over, they were as informed and sophisticated as any European.

This economic bonanza and political stability came to a sudden end when Peru lost territorial possessions to neighboring Chile in what came to be known as the War of the Pacific (1879–1884). Political instability prevailed from then until 1895. That year saw the advent of the political leadership of the *civilistas* — members of the Peruvian oligarchy, which included bankers, *hacendados,* and traders with modern approaches to economy. This elite, called civil- istas after their antimilitary politics, inaugurated a long rule (1895– 1919) that came to be known as the República Aristocrática (Basa- dre, 1964). During the period, the rulers were blessed by another economic surge, this one resulting from the new international market that followed World War I. As in the preceding boom, export products — wool, sugar, cotton, rubber, oil, and minerals — funded the economic expansion (Klaren, 1986). If, during the 1860s, the elites rejected the idea of degeneration by boasting of their sophisticated erudition and intellectual capacity, at the turn of the century when politicians championed the twin ideologies of liberalism and progress, education occupied central stage as a nation-building and race-homogenizing tool. In the face of European racial theories, education became the quintessential instrument of the limeños' project for constructive miscegenation. In this respect, their ideas clashed once again with those of European intellectuals like Gustave Le Bon. "One of the greatest illusions of democracy is to imagine that instruction equalizes men. It often serves only to emphasize their differentiation," he had written (1979:289). Obviously this thinker did not lack followers among limeños, but they represented an extreme conservatism that modernizing liberals and iconoclastic radicals derided as "racial pessimism."[11]

Instead, optimistic ideas asserting the power of education to uplift individuals racially were far-reaching among limeño elites of assorted tendencies. "Thanks to education man can today transform the physical milieu and even the race. It is his most glorious triumph," asserted the aristocrat Javier Prado (1909:52), the leader of Peruvian philosophic positivism and Comtean sociology and rector of San Marcos, the most important university in the country. Prado, like Le Bon, also favored interbreeding between "compatible races," and supported state policies promoting the immigration of Europeans aimed at solving the Peruvian racial predicament. However, he rejected Le Bon's racial pessimism, and he was not alone in so doing. Like Prado, the modernizing oligarchic government that ruled the country from 1893 to 1919 also endorsed beliefs in the redemptive power of education. Through the minister of justice and education, Jorge Polar, the ruling group declared in 1905: "Luckily it has been proved that no race exists that cannot be molded by education: clearly, ours can be so molded, even in the remotest regions of our territory. The myth that the Indian does not want to abandon its miserable condition is rapidly falling into discredit" (1905:xxxviii, quoted in Contreras, 1996:6).

A conspicuous rebuttal of Le Bon came from Manuel Gonzales Prada, as the second epigraph to this section suggests.[12] Granted, there were inferior races in Latin America, but they did not express continental racial degeneration. And as the minister of justice and education had stated, Gonzales Prada also believed that education could improve even the most inferior of all, the Indian race. Gonzales Prada wrote "whenever the Indian receives instruction in schools or becomes educated simply through contact with civilized individuals, he acquires the same moral and cultural level as the descendants of Spaniards" (1904:179–180). Racial pessimism did not have a broad appeal among the country's intellectuals and politicians, at least publicly. Policies regarding the immigration of superior races for eugenic schemes were issued along with propositions that envisioned educational programs as the solution to improve the racial configuration of the country. A conservative intellectual, Francisco Graña (1908) even coined the term *autogenia,* which can be interpreted as an alternative to *eugenesia,* eugenics.[13] Rather than improving races through cross-breeding, autogenia represented the attempt to improve the Peruvian race internally, by raising health and nutritional standards and by improving the educational level of groups deemed inferior.

Undoubtedly, prevalent liberalism swayed the country's elites to envision education as the "racial homogenizer" and therefore a key nation-building element. However, their self-perception both as capable intellectuals and as *trigueños* (from Sp. *trigo* [wheat]; it refers to a type of white, but, crucially, not a European one), and therefore as "mixed" and potentially inferior, was a powerful component of their agenda. Reflecting this feeling, a conservative intellectual announced: "Do not allow copper skin to be a source of social shame and shrinking. Let us destroy once and for all that inferiority complex" (García Calderón, 1986:576). Not surprisingly, intellectuals denied the existence of pure races in Peru and even ridiculed those who presented themselves as purely white.[14] "En el Perú, quien no tiene de inga, tiene de mandinga" was a popular saying in which "Inga" stood for Inca, and "mandinga" for black Africans. A translation of it would be: "The individual who does not have inga [Indian heritage] has mandinga [black heritage]," alluding to crossings among Spanish, indigenous, and African races. This self-awareness of skin color might have inclined them to minimize the relevance of phenotype and privilege instead intellectual merit as they pondered racial hierarchies. On a more conceptual level, this attitude was wrapped in a racial discourse that rejected totalitarian determinisms — the ill-fated racial pessimism — in favor of optimistic ideas favoring racial improvement through education. Francisco García Calderón, a lawyer and major ideologue of the aristocratic Civilista Party, spoke of the need in Peru for a strong leadership from a cultivated, unified progressive oligarchy that would move to capitalize the economy, centralize and modernize the state, and gradually incorporate the Indian masses into the nation by way of a system of universal education (Klaren, 1986). Beliefs in the power of education to racially redeem the country were compatible with mestizaje, which was foundational to their projects, as expressed in the following thought: "The viable Peru is and will be the one which harmoniously integrates the ancient musical stridencies which reverberate sometimes in our blood and which naturally resound like a surprising cacophony combining the Spanish guitar, the indigenous flute, and the funerary drum" (García Calderón, 1986:577).

A feature of this type of optimistic limeño racial thinking was that — as the above quote illustrates — blood was a "synecdoche of culture" (Williams, 1989:431).[15] Explaining an analogous turn-of-the-century expression by a North American, Stocking argued that at the time, " 'blood' — and by extension 'race' — included numerous elements that we would today call cultural." Linking this to the generalized confusion that colored racial thinking, the same author remarked that "there was no clear line between cultural and physical elements or between social and biological heredity." American academics, he continued, used race as a "catchall that might be applied to various human groups whose sensible similarities of appearance, of manner and of speech persisted over time, and therefore were to them, evidently hereditary" (1994:6–7). The same could be said about limeños' racial ideas, which did not only contest but were also influenced by European thinkers. Local references to the "racial soul" or to the "spirit of the race" might have been borrowed from Romantic historiography, which spoke of race when referring to a people developing over time and distinct from others by language, religion, or geography (Brading, 1984). Likewise, inspired by Hippolyte Taine's historical sense of race and by French physiognomists, limeños tended to look beneath the surface of observable traits for the "elemental moral state" of a people (C. A. Hale, 1986:397; Poole 1997). Drawing on some aspects of Spencerianism, limeño racial thinkers commonly believed that hereditary transmissions applied to psychical peculiarities as well as to physical ones (Stocking, 1968:240; Luna, 1913:14). These ideas were connected by Lamarckism, the theory that acquired characteristics can be inherited, which was current in nineteenth-century popular wisdom (Stocking, 1968: 242; S. Gould, 1996:401).[16] Beliefs in the inheritance of acquired traits suited the intellectuals' hopes in the redemptive power of education, and indeed promoted a definition of race ambiguously connected to biology, overtly interested in a historical "spirit," and predisposed to subordinate external phenotypic markers to internal racial characteristics such as intelligence and morality.

Race could be biology, but it could also be the soul of the people; it was also their culture, their spirit, their language. Debates about the "Peruvian race" and its future were colored by the tension between its spiritual and biological aspects. For example, Javier Prado combined in his racial thinking a concern for "the spirit" and the "moral world" with organicist references to intelligence and physiology. Positivist philosophy, he argued, "studies the genesis of intellectual faculties, the influence of the nervous system in psychological life; in a word the development and the complexities of the spiritual phenomena in living beings, conditioned directly by the organism and the physical milieu" (1891:159). Generally, however, there was a tendency to reject the biological aspects of race without rejecting the notion itself. The influential Francisco García Calderón, for example, noted that the idea of race "persisted as a synthesis of the diverse elements of a defined civilization," but he also felt that biology as the basis of race was losing prestige (quoted in Hale, 1986:419). This tendency would eventually favor a culturalist definition of race in which biology was either subordinated to the cultural aspects of race or, as in the socialist thought of José Carlos Mariátegui, dismissed as a fiction (1968:34) and instead circumscribed race within culture. Key figures in formulating these views were the group of cuzqueño intellectuals known as indigenistas, whom I discuss in the next section.

Indigenista Contribution to Cultural Race
Mestizaje as Degeneration and as a Racial-Class Fact

Cuzco and Lima are, in the nature of things, two opposing hubs of our nationality. Cuzco represents the millenary maternal cultural heritage that the Incas bequeathed to us. Lima is the yearning for adaptation to European culture. And this is because Cuzco already existed when the Conqueror arrived, and Lima was created by him ex nihilo. There is nothing strange in Lima's being foreign-inclined, Hispanophile, imitator of exoticisms, Europeanized, and Cuzco being vernacular, nationalistic, and pure, portraying the hoary pride of legitimate American aristocratic ancestry.
— LUIS EDUARDO VALCÁRCEL, 1978

The economic bonanza that benefited Peru during the first decade of the century did not result in evenly distributed national progress. While oil production and plantation agriculture technologically modernized the coastal areas and transformed its working classes from indentured workers into wage laborers, the increase of wool exports—a commodity produced in highland haciendas—did not modernize the sierra. Lacking basic urban infrastructure, highland cities were actually large rural towns, inhabited by absentee landlords of large haciendas who lived in large mansions teeming with indigenous male and female servants. Completing the image of backwardness, servitude was the main labor relationship in the large and medium-sized countryside properties, although there were also free peasant members of indigenous communities, or *ayllus*. Aggravating these circumstances, but in accordance with the above image, the limeño elite looked abroad for its cultural references and was scornful of much that was *serrano* (Klaren 1986:610).[17] Not surprisingly, Lima was the stage for the political decisions of the liberal oligarchic state; from the dominant viewpoint, this state of affairs had racial causes.

Probably influenced by popular nineteenth-century Lamarckism and environmentalism, the definition of "Peruvian races" matched geographic images of transects that ranged from the Pacific coast to the Amazonian tropics.[18] To the image of the coast as the historical site of colonial culture corresponded the idea that it was the natural environment of Spaniards or their *criollo* descendants. Since the nineteenth century, they have been labeled "whites," regardless of their color (Barragán, 1998). In the same picture, Indians were the natural inhabitants of the sierra, the highland region where the Inca Empire had flourished. Lastly, the Amazonian tropical forest, known as "the jungle," was associated with "primitive," "savage" tribes, imagined as a different indigenous breed who, unlike the Inca descendants, had never produced any contribution to Peruvian history. Mestizos, those ambiguous individuals of all kinds, could live anywhere in the highlands or on the coast. Blacks were considered a foreign race, and therefore lacked a specific place of origin in the national geography; yet as a "tropical people" they were deemed to adapt to the hot coastal areas.

Significantly, modern Peruvian race-making paralleled a political process of place-making as it assigned races to spaces and evaluated these within evolutionary temporal schemes (Gupta and Ferguson, 1992; Fabian, 1983). Reflecting tropes of progress, integration, and obstacle (Orlove, 1993b), the modernized spaces of the coast ranked higher than the highlands. Illustrating this enduring and pervasive belief, José de la Riva Agüero, one of Peru's best known thinkers and one of the few limeño intellectuals who ventured to the highlands as early as the 1910s, recorded in his travel log: "The coast has represented innovation, swiftness, joy, and pleasure; the highlands, have symbolized an almost backward conservationism, a seriousness that approaches sadness, a discipline that approximates servility and an endurance leading virtually to torpidness" (1995:225). Following this racialization of geography, people were ranked according to their surroundings: the higher the geographical elevation, the lower the social status of its inhabitants. This implied that, regardless of their social origins, highland dwellers (contemptuously called serranos) were considered inferior to coastal inhabitants, and among the coastal peoples, the most elevated were the limeños.

Of all serrano cities at the turn of the century, Cuzco, the pre-

colonial capital of the Inca Empire, might be expected to have occupied the lowest rank as the symbolic center of Indianness. Although elite cuzqueños acknowledged the unprogressive nature of
the countryside, they also countered limeños' perception of Cuzco as
backward and inferior to Lima. Moreover, competing with coastal
"gentlemen" for national leadership, as the epigraph opening this
section illustrates, cuzqueño elites used national racialized geography to emphasize Lima's inherent hispanophilia. By contrast, they
boasted about the authenticity of their nationalism, seeing it as geographically and historically legitimated by the rank of their city as
the capital of the Inca Empire. This practice eventually produced
cuzqueñismo, or the pride to be cuzqueños, heirs of a quintessen-
tially national historical legacy.[19] Initially shaped as *regionalismo* (a
political doctrine promoted by provincial politicians in general), cuzqueñismo, as Benedict Anderson has said of nationalism, "belonged
with religion or kinship, rather than with liberalism or fascism"
(1993:5). Thus, like nationalism it accommodated the variegated political and academic tendencies of its champions, whose consensually
shared feelings of regional pride limited the significance of their political disagreements. Launched at the turn of the century, this sort of
regional nationalism began as an elite political-intellectual project to
counter the view of cuzqueños as racially inferior serranos and to
compete politically with limeños. From the beginning, cuzqueñismo
asserted its place in the nation by drawing from the pre-Hispanic tradition: enactments of Inca history, regional dances, and research into
the indigenous past and present through archaeological and ethnological studies have aimed to show the past eminence of Cuzco and
therefore its entitlement to equal (or even superior) standing related
to Lima. Initially the brainchild of elite intellectuals, all these activities converged in the 1920s in the modern political-intellectual formation known as indigenismo, the academic face of cuzqueñismo.[20]

A salient feature of modern indigenismo, and one that would influence the Peruvian nation-building process for years to come, was the
way it sharpened the culturalist definition of race already latent
among other non-cuzqueño thinkers and, more specifically, in dominant limeño racial thought. One of its most prolific and influential
representatives, Luis Eduardo Valcárcel, was particularly explicit in

this respect: "This universal relationship between human beings and the natural world is resolved through culture. We are the offspring, that is, the heirs, of a being that has been shaped by the interaction of Nature and Culture. Thus, our minds reject spontaneous generation, mutation, or any life without history [La generación espontánea, la mutación, la vida, sin historia, repugnan pues a nuestra mente]" (1927:109). Intertwining history and human life, Valcárcel aimed at discrediting extreme Social Darwinists and at rejecting the idea that the progress of human races could be reduced to biological struggles, which he phrased as "mutation" and "spontaneous generation." These were only biology, which was different from "Nature" because unlike the latter, biology was void of "Culture." Intensely historicist (although still from an evolutionary perspective), Valcárcel denied the significance of biology in shaping races, while attributing to culture the power to do so. He thus claimed "Conocemos, pensamos, sentimos según el conocer, el pensar y el sentir de la propia cultura" (We know, think, and feel in the manner of knowing and feeling proper to our own culture) (1927:109), thus implying — like W. E. B. DuBois in the "Souls of Black Folk" and "The Conservation of Races" (1996) — that culture and history, and not biology, constitute the core of human races and determine their differences.[21] Perhaps an early version of today's "cultural fundamentalism," this position represented in the 1920s an articulate challenge to European racial pessimisms inasmuch as it questioned the power of biological inheritance to rule human destiny. However, none of this eliminated race or hierarchical racial feelings.

A distinctive feature of cuzqueño indigenismo was its repudiation of mestizos, and the view that promestizo opinions were anti-Indian. Moreover, cuzqueños judged that limeños' mestizaje project expressed Hispanophilia and rejected the Inca legacy, which to them was the pillar of Peruvian nationalism. Reacting against promestizo arguments, leading indigenistas borrowed from Europeans and North American racial thinkers the idea that races degenerated if they were removed from their proper places. For example, Luis E. Valcárcel, whose abhorrence of biological determinism was paired with his strong scorn of mestizaje, wrote in his *Tempestad en los Andes:* "Every personality, every group *is born* within a culture *and can only live within it,*" implying that individuals or groups degenerate when they abandon their original places or cultures (1927:109; emphasis added). In this, Valcárcel coincided with those European racial thinkers he otherwise despised, specifically those who thought that the fate of races when they transgressed their boundaries was degeneration, and even racial extinction (Stepan, 1985:99).[22] According to him, "El mestizaje de las culturas no produce sino deformidades" (Cultural miscegenation only yields deformities) (1927:111).[23] Mestizaje was a degenerative process, initially the result of colonial displacements, and as Valcárcel perceived it, during his time the product of indigenous migration to cities. But as we shall see, embedded in a culturalist definition of race and supported by an elite class perspective, this mestizaje rather than being biological, came to be defined in moral terms.

Valcárcel's position on this point was influential, swaying ardent pro-Indian champions beyond Cuzco. Those who argued influentially against the unremediable inferiority of "the Indian race" employed his indigenista ideas about the proper places of the races and the degenerative effects of transgressing them via mestizaje. In this vein, the leftist José Carlos Mariátegui, wrote: "In his native environment, as long as migration does not deform him, [the Indian] has nothing to envy in the mestizo." The mestizo, radiated "imprecision and hybridism . . . resulting from the obscure prevalence of negative sediments in a state of morbid and sordid stagnation" (1981:34). In neither Mariátegui's or Valcárcel's view were mestizos necessarily defined as *biological* hybrids as in European depictions of U.S. or African mulattoes (Stepan, 1985). Rather, mestizos were Indians (monolingual Quechua-speaking agriculturalists) who had "abandoned" their proper natural/cultural environment and migrated to the cities, where they degenerated morally, as reflected by their deviant sexuality. "The impure Indian woman finds refuge in the city. Flesh of the whorehouse, one day she will die in the hospital" (Valcárcel, 1927:78). According to cultural/racial purists, the salient characteristic of female Indians' sexuality was their rejection of "foreignness," an aversion that had however guaranteed the "purity of the Indian race." This racial xenophobia supposedly inherent in indigenous female sexuality was central in culturalist definitions of race and allowed some elite thinkers to define hybrids as immoral, and primarily *sexually* so. Indian female impurity resulted from transgressing the xenophobic quality of their sexuality. From this perspective mestizaje was a moral problem, the result of rape or deviant female sexual behavior. Hybridity thus represented not biological but moral degeneration.

Articulated through morality (with sexual behavior as its index), the antibiological and culturalist theories of race of the indigenistas were compatible with discriminatory beliefs against mestizaje. Ultimately, mestizaje emerged in a class discourse that marked nonprivileged social sectors as immoral because they lacked "proper" education. Intellectuals were by extension excluded from such a stain: they were members of the proper class, had the right education, lived in their proper places, and maintained appropriate sexual behavior. In the 1920s the sophistication and social refinement of cuzqueño intellectuals was able to dissolve, or at least limit, the fact of their skin color. In this they were different from other racially subordinate intellectuals, such as Franz Fanon, whose intellectual sophistication, he declared, did not remove the derogatory fact of his black skin: "No exception was made for my refined manners, or my knowledge of literature, or my understanding of the quantum theory" (1968:117). Instead, the cuzqueño intellectual community, and even the limeño one, did not self-identify as mestizos nor were they seen as such by their class peers. They were *gente decente,* people of worth. Unlike the fact of blackness described by Fanon, being mestizo in Peru was not of necessity related to skin color; rather (and redundantly), it was a hybrid fact of race and class together. It did not necessarily coincide with the European perception of mestizaje as biological hybridity, thus allowing Peruvian elites to amend the European perception of them as hybrids.

Analysts of the new European version of racism ("racism without race") (Barker, 1982; Gilroy, 1987; Balibar, 1988; Taguieff, 1987 and 1990) explain that it is a culturalist rhetoric of exclusion resulting from the reformulation of former biologically based discriminatory procedures, and that they arise from a postwar discrediting of biological notions of race. From the viewpoint of these scholars, European and neoracist discriminatory rhetoric presuppose that the peoples of the world are separated by unsurmountable, essential cultural differences. From a slightly different position Verena Stolcke (1995:4) proposes the concept of "cultural fundamentalism." The new rhetoric of exclusion is different from racism, she argues, in that rather than asserting different endowments of human races, it assumes the propensity of human nature to reject strangers, which explains the inevitability of hostile relations among different "cultures." Thus, for example, from Stolcke's viewpoint, Mario Vargas Llosa's statement about cultural diversity producing violence in Peru expresses cultural fundamentalism and should not be analyzed as being racist as it does not proceed from a biological notion of race. Rather than postulating the existence of biological hierarchies, cultural fundamentalism presupposes that the impenetrability of cultural boundaries naturally produces xenophobic reactions among groups, which engage in violent actions, thus canceling the possibility of harmonic cohabitation of different cultural groups.

The historical study of racial discourse in twentieth-century Peru shows that the concepts of race and culture were thoroughly intertwined. The version of racism expressed by Vargas Llosa had an antecedent in a fundamentalist notion of culture that was not aimed at moving away from race. Rather, Valcárcel, Mariátegui, and others — including conservative Peruvian thinkers like Victor Andrés Belaúnde — retained the idea of race while opposing European racial pessimisms and biological determinisms.[24] The early culturalist definition did not intend to replace race as a notion but to advance an optimistic idea: that races could surmount inferiority. Their historical contribution consisted in emphasizing the "spiritual" aspects of races, and to privilege "culture" over "biology." This emphasis was not unique to Peruvians. Nancy Leys Stepan (1991:148) describes how some Mexican thinkers, specifically José Vasconcelos's project for constructive miscegenation, highlighted the "spiritual" qualities of Aztec and Spanish civilizations. In a similar vein, Rigoberto Paredes, a contemporary of Valcárcel writing in neighboring La Paz (Bolivia), proposed that changing the Indians' clothing would contribute to improving their race (Thomson, 1988). In the United States, W. E. B. DuBois (1897, 1903) also emphasized the cultural aspects of race and developed optimistic ideas about racial redemption via education.

Certainly not every influential North or South American racial optimist subscribed to cultural definitions of race. At the risk of being interpreted as reductionist, I want to suggest that this tendency might have been stronger among subordinate intellectuals, like Du-Bois and Valcárcel, whose social status derived from their "inferior" racial identities vis-à-vis the dominant "white" world of all kinds. Whatever the reason, there were other thinkers whose projects for "constructive miscegenation" implied biological eugenics. The Guatemalan man of letters and indigenista, Miguel Angel Asturias, is a brutal example. In 1923 he proclaimed: "Do with the Indian what you do with other animal species when they show symptoms of degeneration: new blood, that's the answer!" (Asturias, 1923, quoted in Cojtí Cuxil, 1997:49).

The historical contrast between Asturias and the culturalist alternative makes evident the contestatory dimension of the latter. Racial culturalism, however, was still confined within the explanatory domain of race and sheltered unequivocally discriminatory beliefs shaped by class, gender, or even geographic feelings. Consistent with their emphasis on the power of education to transform race, the tendency among Peruvian racial thinkers was to condemn those individuals who, from their viewpoint, lacked education, thus implicitly denouncing their lack of class distinction. Gonzales Prada, reputed as a nineteenth-century iconoclast, contemptuously called them *encastados* (lower class individuals) and Mariátegui, the paramount Peruvian socialist, following Valcárcel, despised them as mestizos. At the turn of the century, racial optimists believed that education could become a racial/cultural acquired attribute that could be passed down, in Lamarckian fashion, to improve the Peruvian race. Adriana's remarks shocked me into the realization that education in Cuzco — and I would venture to generalize, in all Peru — has retained both its contestatory edge and its discriminatory potential. Formal education may not preclude or replace indigenous culture (a view that counters racialized conceptions that indigenous culture is unsurmountably archaic and incompatible), but it does play a legitimated discriminatory role.

Unveiling the discriminatory potential of culture and its historical embeddedness in Peruvian racial thought is important; it can shed light on Peruvian cultural fundamentalism as a form of racism that is neither exclusive to rightist politicians like Vargas Llosa nor limited to academia. On the contrary, cultural fundamentalism in Peru is a widespread, racialized way of explaining social differences, the peculiarity of which does not derive, as analysts of new European racisms contend, from its having replaced biological definitions of race. Rather, Peruvian cultural forms of discrimination — including "cultural fundamentalism" — emerge from a historical matrix of racial ideology. Working within it, early twentieth-century intellectuals elaborated a culturalist definition of race that rejected the power of biology to determine the essence of the peoples. The international reaction against race — which started in the 1930s and which repudiated *race as biology* (Stepan, 1991; Barkan, 1992; Stolcke, 1993; Harrison, 1995) — did not question the discriminatory potential of culture. Significantly for my purposes, in the case of Peru — and probably elsewhere — it did not unveil the ways in which culture had been racially constructed. Thus, the original culturalist tendency to explain and legitimate hierarchies lost its original contestatory thrust while preserving its authority as a rhetoric of exclusion, discrimination, and dominance embedded in the apparent egalitarianism of culture talk. As in Europe, it became cultural fundamentalism, but of a very specific version, in which race has been only rhetorically silenced.

The academic repudiation of biological notions of race was significant for anthropology, as it meant the emergence of the concept of "ethnic groups" to explain human differences. As Stolcke (1993) has suggested, it implied the reification of culture, which thus potentially prolonged the naturalization of sociohistorical differences earlier contained in the European notion of biological race. In Peru a similar shift from race to culture began in the early 1930s, and as in Europe it was grounded in the desire to denounce Nazi racial crimes. Unlike Europe however, in Peru the shift unfolded from prevalent images of essential culture undergirding antibiological definitions of race. Thus, while former dominant ways of imagining differences continued, overt references to race were silenced by culture now bearing its own conceptual right to mark differences. Along with this shift, and simultaneous with its rejection by intellectuals and politicians, the Peruvian definition of race acquired overt biological and phenotypical connotations, while expelling culture from its sphere of meaning. Yet, given the historical antecedents, the independence of the notion of culture from race was never total, either conceptually or politically. This implicit intertwinement was highly consequential for the present hegemony of racism: shielded by culture, former essentialisms were acquitted from racism, as they joined the international chorus to condemn biological determinisms.

Seventy Years Later

Indigenous Mestizos and Subordinate Mestizaje

The academic ethnic taxonomies that emerged in the 1950s projected images of the superiority of literate, rational Western tradition, and defined culture as traditional and therefore as the opposite of (formal) education. Hence they did not include "educated" Peruvians in their classification systems and implicitly whitened them — or, at least, subordinated their phenotype to their "knowledge" — and recognized their privilege to be unnamed (cf. Frankenberg, 1993; Williams, 1989). Blacks — who during the previous period were considered a foreign race and thus dispensable in most Peruvian nationalist projects — were excluded from scholarly produced ethnic taxonomies, thus continuing as a race, and a clearly inferior one at that. Ethnic taxonomies thus functioned to distinguish Indians — the putative contemporary descendants of the original precolonial civilizations — from mestizos — former Indians, but not whites yet. These taxonomies measured the evolution of Peruvians considered indigenous in terms of their level of literacy and urbanity. Indians were conceived of as illiterate agriculturalists, possessing vestiges of precolonial culture. Mestizos were conceived of as incompletely educated highlanders, residents of cities or rural towns, and petty merchants. Both groups allegedly lacked the cultural capital to enter rational, lettered society and were subordinate to the unmarked possessors of education. From this perspective, mestizaje was the gradual process by which Indians gradually became literate and acquired urban skills and naturally, as in a metamorphosis, discarded their original culture. The process implied, it was said, acculturation: changing cultures; its consequence was assimilation: disappearing into the dominant cultural formation.[25]

Having been trained in this tradition, I was not surprised when the individuals I talked to in the course of my fieldwork — cuzqueño commoners with recent or remote peasant background — commonly defined themselves as mestizos and, indeed, as non-Indians. Contradicting my academic knowledge, however, I gradually found out that they asserted mestizo identity as a social condition with room *both* for literacy and urban education *and* for the continuation of regional *costumbres,* the customs that they call authentic or *neto* and that I term "indigenous" for lack of a better word. By this I mean those aspects of the regional cuzqueño culture in which the dominant sectors of the local society do not participate (at least publicly) and which are consensually perceived as subordinated to the national cultural formation. For working-class cuzqueños self-identification as mestizos implies changing social conditions, *but* not cultures, as I had been used to thinking. De-Indianization as explained to me by indigenous cuzqueños means indeed shedding the markers that indicate the social condition of Indianness, such as walking barefoot or with *ojotas* (handmade rubber sandals) and lacking urban skills in general. Thus it means progressing, in the most usual term of the word. Yet it is a far cry from the evolutionary conventions implied in dominant ethnic taxonomies, according to which formal education and urban life, as superior forms of development, are considered to naturally replace indigenous culture.[26] Within this process, a de-Indianizing individual can be mestizo and indigenous at the same time. This individual (the indigenous mestizo) considers herself neto and thus familiar with practices deemed extraneous to the dominant culture — and at the same time understands practices that are perceived as belonging to the dominant national formation.

Adriana Belén and Isabel Sánchez, two young university students whom I befriended, were among the first to alert me to this (to me) totally unusual meaning of "mestizo." They danced in a folk troupe called Pasña Coyacha, in part, they told me, because of their proud identification with regional indigenous culture. Since they were university students, one of their problems was to accommodate their course schedules with the regional ritual calendar, which became

Isabel and her sister dressed in their P'asña Coyacha
outfits during a break in the ritual to celebrate a
mayordomía in the atrium of the Almudena church,
1992. Photograph by author.

particularly difficult in June and July. "We have to make special
arrangements with the professors particularly because July is an
exam month, but June is also difficult because both Coyllur Rit'i and
Corpus Christi are so important to us, but they take the whole month
and we miss so many classes, but some professors are *comprensivos*
[understanding] and let us go." This conversation alerted me to an
alternative possibility of combining Western education with "An-

dean knowledge," which did not mean literal acculturation (or the shedding of indigenous ways). Therefore I began to redefine academic notions of what being mestizo meant. Adriana and Isabel guided me through this nonacademic process of the making of regional ethnicity.

Their dance represented the people of the highlands (*la gente de las alturas*), individuals regionally identified as Indians. Since I was aware of the stigma Indianness carried among Cuzco urbanites, one day while we were chatting at the university cafeteria I asked them if they had problems performing the dance. Their response and the ensuing conversation merit being quoted at length:

Isabel: Last year we had a problem with one young man. He did not want to dance because they had insulted him as *cholo* Indian. We told him not to pay attention. I said: "After all, you're acting. The fact that they see you in those clothes doesn't mean that you are *entirely that way.* Out of ignorance they have insulted you. In Cuzco race does not govern any more. Instead intelligence and education does."

Marisol: Why did you tell him that he was "not entirely that way?" Is he "a little" that way?

Adriana: Well you see, Marisol, in Cuzco, *el pueblo,* we can all be Indians, and some Indians are also mestizos. Like us. *We are not entirely Indians, but we are indigenous, aborigines,* whatever you want to call us, because we are not like, for example, you.

Marisol: What do you mean you are not like me? We are all university students, we have the same skin color, the same kind of hair, we are speaking in Spanish.

Isabel and Adriana (alternating): Yes but you don't believe in the things we do. You may go to Coyllur Rit'i, but you don't really care about it. Besides you don't even know the ritual. We go like the people of the highlands [Indians] do, and we follow their example, but I say that we are not entirely that way because they are not educated, they are ignorant and *toscos.* We respect them, but we are not entirely like them. We follow many, some, of their beliefs, but we wear shoes and not *ojotas* [rubber sandals], we sleep in beds, we eat properly, right? We are different and alike, do you understand? Like you and we are, you may say you are mestiza because of your race, we are all mestizos in Cuzco. Nobody is pure anymore. But some mestizos like us are also indigenous, aborigines, *oriundos,* because of our beliefs. Others are only mestizos like you.

Marisol: So are the gente de las alturas also mestizos?

Isabel: No, they are only Indians, but we don't use the word any-more — only ignorant people do. We call them other things, like *aborígenes, netos, compañeros, oriundos, indígenas, campesinos,* right Adriana?

Adriana: Yes, only ignorant people call them Indians. We respect our costumbres, we don't insult the people from whom we learn them. Our parents perhaps were like that [Indian]. We never know, *quién sabe,* that is why we don't use that word. They came here and changed their clothes; they learned to wear shoes, to be civilized, that is what living in the city teaches. With people of the highlands, it's not their fault to be like they are [Indian] — that is their way, they live in the alturas, they don't need anything else. When they come to the city they learn, and they become educated. That is what our parents or our grandparents did.

Listening to my tapes, remembering their faces, and looking at the pictures of Adriana, Isabel, and many others from whom I elicited responses during many months, it became obvious to me that the way in which I had been culturally caught up in dominant binarisms and racial classifications had blinded me to historical heteroglossic possibilities of notions such as Indian, mestizo, and mestizaje. Adri-ana's and Isabel's recorded voices made me consider the possible ways in which subaltern cuzqueños have lived, practiced, and cre-ated alternative meanings of mestizaje and have crucially redefined the term "mestizo." Goldberg's idea that "in the shift from imposi-tion to self-interpretation, received terms are rarely if ever entirely synonymous with self-assumed ones" seems highly pertinent here (1993:9).

Many among the urban working-class cuzqueños with whom I lived and worked self-identify as mestizo to emphasize their urban education *and* their pride in earnestly practicing "authentic cus-toms." As such they refer to those practices and beliefs that dominant ethnic discourses have termed indigenous, presuming that mestizos will shed them in the process of assimilating into dominant Western culture. Adriana and Isabel, contradicting these ideas while at the same time negating their Indianness, did not assimilate: being mestizas did not mean that they would gradually become like me, as my culturally ingrained utilization of racial/cultural categories had led me to believe. Adriana and Isabel, and many cuzqueños like them, did not simply yield to the dominant taxonomies; they reformulated them, and in so doing they did not necessarily abandon the practices and beliefs that, as they clearly stated, they do not share with other kinds of mestizos, that is limeños like me or other cuzqueños.

The alternative taxonomy has not absolutely displaced the dominant one. In a given social formation there can coexist, sometimes conflictually, sometimes not, more than one classificatory system. Which one prevails, and which markers are enforced, depend on power relationships. In this sense, ethnicity (the current way to identify cultural differences), like race, does not exist by itself. Rather, it acquires its meanings through political struggle, as individuals reinvent themselves and respond to wider politics and economics (Comaroff, 1987; Clifford, 1988). If, resulting from political struggles, ethnicity becomes a significant component of life, it can have the same discriminatory potential of race, even if it does not reproduce racial discourses per se. This is the case in Peru, and more specifically Cuzco, where the alternative ethnic discourse defines culture as achievable, yet still considers discrimination legitimate if it responds to differences in formal education.

An Overview of the City of Cuzco

Although cuzqueñismo began as a doctrine and an exclusively elite feeling, it is currently shared by working-class sectors as well. Its official inauguration as a shared ideology dates back to the 1930s, when Cuzco celebrated the fourth centennial of its Spanish foundation. Since the 1960s the upsurge of tourism has contributed to the magnificence of cuzqueñista festivals and stimulated creative cultural activity ranging from folk dance troupes to elite official repre-

sentations of Inca history, as well as the production of religious rituals. Because cuzqueñismo offers the opportunity to demonstrate
regional expressive culture publicly, it is the arena where elite and
grassroots intellectuals meet. The popular culture so expressed is not
restricted, as in usual definitions, to beliefs or practices of rural and
urban working classes, or subordinate groups that actively or pas-
sively oppose official culture (García Canclini, 1993, 1995; Rowe
and Schelling, 1991).[27] Rather than an arena where either grassroots
or elite intellectuals prevail, cuzqueñismo is a shared dialogic field,
the cultural expressive space from which both groups draw inspiration, the sphere where they compete for influence, and an important
public arena in which to dispute the meanings of identity labels.

The small size of the city and the design of the dwellings has kept
elite and plebeian groups physically together and has contributed to
the cultural sharing of cuzqueñismo. At the turn of the century,
the city of Cuzco was the dwelling place of hacendados (owners of
large wool-producing estates or medium and even small agricultural
properties), indigenous servants, and teeming plebeian merchant
groups, indigenous and nonindigenous. The outermost urban neighborhoods were located in the hills that surrounded the city, which
were rural then and supposedly inhabited mostly by Indians. The
center of the city was the main square, the Plaza de Armas, perceived
as the aristocratic portion of the city and therefore where the "best"
cuzqueños lived. Then came the neighborhoods of San Blas, San
Cristóbal, and Santa Ana, which occupied the areas between the
"best" and the "worst" sections of the city and were identified as the
dwelling place of artisans — a very broad, stratified, and ambiguous
occupational category in Cuzco, including tailors, seamstresses,
shoemakers, bakers, barbers, tanners, and carpenters, among others.[28] Cattle slaughterers, chicheras (corn-beer female vendors), and
market women, considered gente del pueblo and the scourge of the
city lived in San Pedro, which was therefore viewed as the coarsest
among plebeian districts. Although along with Belén and Santiago,
two colonial Indian barrios, San Pedro was considered to be on the
outskirts, in fact it was only a couple of blocks away from the Plaza
de Armas.

Along with this image of spatial social distance, every barrio had

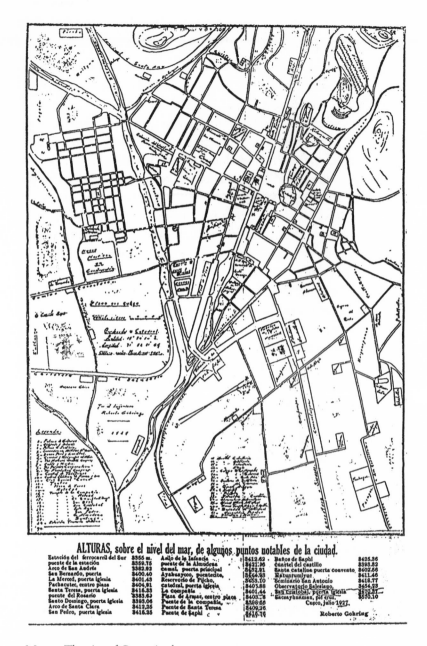

ALTURAS, sobre el nivel del mar, de algunos puntos notables de la ciudad.

Estación del ferrocarril del Sur	3355 m.	Asilo de la Infancia	3412.62	Baños de Saphi	3425.36
puente de la estación	3359.75	puente de la Almudena	3421.96	Cuartel del castillo	3393.82
Arco de San Andrés	3382.93	Camal, puerta principal	3452.91	Santa catalina puerta convento	3402.56
San Bernardo, puerta	3400.40	Ayahuayco, puertecita,	3464.93	Matunrumiyuc	3411.46
La Merced, puerta iglesia	3401.43	Reservorio de Pijcho,	3653.10	Seminario San Antonio	3418.77
Pachacutec, centro plaza	3404.91	catedral, puerta iglesia	3405.88	Observatorio Salesiano	3454.23
Santa Teresa, puerta iglesia	3416.33	La compañía	3401.44	San Cristobal, puerta iglesia	3470.81
puente del Rosario	3583.63	Plaza de Armas, centro plaza	3403.78	Sacsayhuaman, pie cruz,	3570.10
Santo Domingo, puerta iglesia	3393.06	Puente de la compañía,	3398.60	Cuzco, julio 1927.	
Arco de Santa Clara	3412.25	Puente de Santa Teresa	3409.26		
San Pedro, puerta iglesia	3416.25	Puente de Saphi	3449.79	Roberto Gohring	

Map 2. The city of Cuzco in the 1920s

its ill-reputed streets where "indecent" urbanites lived and where the worst *chicherías* (plebeian corn-beer bars), *teterías* (another type of working-class bar where tea with *pisco* [a grape liquor] was served), and brothels were located. The streets of Tullumayo and Limac-pampa in the parish of San Blas, for example, lodged *manaderos,* men and women who bought and slaughtered cattle from nearby rural areas.[29] *Alcanzadores,* produce-brokers between peasants and market women, infamous among the elite because they allegedly abused the Indian sellers (giving them low prices) and the decent folk (selling the produce at high prices), lived in Calle Meloc in the Santa Ana barrio.[30] Nueva Alta street, also in Santa Ana, was renowned for its infamous chicherías, as was the famous Calle Suecia (Sweden Street), located only one block away from the Plaza de Armas, which present day cuzqueños recall as Calle Sucia, Dirty Street. Other streets such as Procuradores and Plaza de las Nazarenas were also stigmatized, the former because of its teterías and the latter because, besides being dirty, it housed a brothel. Yet these last two places fell well within the elite zone of the city.

Colonial houses, *casas de vecindad* (multifamily houses)[31] shared by people from all walks of life, still occupy these streets. Currently these buildings still have two or three internal patios, surrounded by living areas. In the early decades of the century, the first area was usually the domain of the property-owning family, while the other two sections lodged tenants. In addition to renting a living space, tenants frequently leased small rooms in the front of the house where they operated small stores. It was (and still is) usual for plebeian women (the mestizas) to establish chicherías in their rented rooms. Their social positions set landlords and tenants apart. However, because daily gatherings took place at the few water faucets and inter-connecting patios of the house, the tenants and proprietors (or their servants), could not remain secluded. In such conditions, daily life was a far cry from private. This housing system has been gradually changing since 1950, when an earthquake destroyed many of the multifamily colonial houses and accelerated an urbanization process that was already in progress. Yet the modern apartment complexes built in the new urban areas continued to have spaces shared by cuzqueños of assorted social backgrounds. "El sitio no hace a la gente sino la gente al sitio, así decimos en Cuzco" (The place does not make people, it's people who make the place, that's what we say here in Cuzco) was the explanation Señora Polar, an elite lady, gave me when I asked her how she managed to share spaces with the people she deemed inferior. Given the small geographic and social scale of the setting, spatial segregation was impossible to achieve, and physical distance was more a result of social gesture than of geographical distance. The shared concrete spaces have served as arenas where elites and plebeians debate life's daily beliefs, the basic components of popular culture.

"Years ago in Cuzco everybody was acquainted with everyone; now not so much, but still . . . ," Señora Polar also told me, as she explained to me how different social classes could live together. As a result of changes in the regional economy and society (the tourism boom, the expansion of small-scale urban commerce, and agrarian reform), migrants from the countryside have settled in the city in vast numbers, changing the urban layout. Former rural areas (like those behind the Almudena church) were urbanized and three new marketplaces were inaugurated. The urban population increased from a little over forty thousand in 1940 to almost 200,000 in 1981 (Tauro, 1988). During these fifty years Cuzco went through major changes. In the 1950s, the countryside was afflicted by a prolonged drought that impoverished the peasants and sent migrants to the city. This natural catastrophe did not exactly cause but was nevertheless followed by innumerable peasant seizures of hacienda lands, which eventually climaxed in an important nationwide agrarian reform. Launched by a progressive populist military government in 1969, the agrarian reform transformed haciendas into state-owned agricultural cooperatives and, significantly for my purposes, eradicated the label "Indian," officially replacing it with the term "peasant." Parallel to these changes in the agrarian structure was a surge of tourism, which began in the 1960s and peaked in the 1970s and which favored the increase of commerce for both the elites and working classes. All these events affected the demography of the region and modified significantly the physiognomy of the city. Affected by the agrarian reform, former hacendados left Cuzco for Lima, and peasants began to commute more intensively between the city and the

A street bordering the central market place, 1992. Photograph by author.
The inscription "Viva el Perú!" in the background was made by migrants
hoping to avoid being evicted from the hacienda lands they seized to build
their houses.

countryside, and eventually built urban houses and sent their children to be educated or to work in the capital of their region. The
1993 census showed a population of 255,568 cuzqueño urbanites
who, according to the same source, work mostly in commerce, industry, public administration, and, significantly, in education (INEI,
1994).[32]

In spite of this population increase and economic diversification,
the city occupies a relatively small area.[33] In 1991, I lived in Calle
Suecia, a block from the Plaza de Armas, on the southeastern border
of the city. From there I would walk ten minutes to get to the Mercado de San Pedro. From there, walking through the Calle Avenida
and then Calle Hospital, I would arrive in fifteen minutes at the
Almudena church, which is located at the northwestern edge of urban Cuzco. After three or four months of fieldwork, when I walked
along these streets, I greeted many people whom I had met during the
first ritual season I spent in Cuzco: market and street vendors, chi-

cheras, restaurant and hotel owners, university students, workers from nongovernmental organizations, priests, elite ladies, even a few gentlemen. My rapid familiarity with the socially assorted protagonists of cuzqueñismo was facilitated by the scale of the city and by the routine nature of its urban activities. The market place and the Plaza de Armas, traditional convening points, continue to function as such for many cuzqueños who, therefore, like Señora Polar, are able to assert that although Cuzco has grown people still are acquainted with one another. Even if, as she told me, "ya no tanto" (not so much anymore).

An Overview of the Chapters

As is by now evident, the period I analyze stretches from the early twentieth century to 1992. In the first chapter of this book I analyze the prolegomena to today's silent racism by presenting the contribution of indigenistas (a group of cuzqueño lawyers and self-taught historians active during the 1920s), to the Peruvian culturalist definition of race. Specifically, I present the ideology of *decencia,* briefly, a new elaboration of colonial honor codes through the lens of political liberalism. I then discuss how decencia went beyond daily life, to influence intellectual formulations about the supremacy of racial/cultural purity, specifically defined as moral/sexual proper behavior. Mestizos were different from gente decente, in spite of their identical phenotype, because the former were ignorant and therefore sexually promiscuous while the latter were educated and therefore sexually proper and refined.

Indigenistas defined Indians as a racially deformed group, the evolution of which had been hampered by four hundred years of colonialism. Yet the fact that Indians had been a great race in the past made them redeemable, provided they maintained their cultural purity in the present. This made of Indian redemption a scientific process, to be led by experts in indigenous race/culture. In the second chapter, I analyze how, guided by these beliefs, leading liberal indigenistas from Cuzco defeated a radical grassroots project which sought to obtain indigenous citizenship by implementing literacy campaigns. Implicit in this project was a different definition of Indianness, which rather than solely emphasizing cultural purity advocated for political self-representation. The victory of liberal indigenismo confirmed for modernity that Indians were an inferior racial/cultural type undeserving of Peruvian citizenship, whose relationship with the state had to be mediated either by experts or by laws that acknowledged their "inferior" condition. After their early defeat, the proponents of alternative Indianness abandoned race and — inspired by worldwide tendencies — shifted to class, a category they used to style their political identity as peasants.

During the years that preceded and succeeded World War II, in Peru, as in other parts of the world, traditional academics and politicians, motivated by anti-Nazi feelings, engaged in a historical struggle to disqualify the concept of race and to replace it with more allegedly accurate conceptual categories to account for social differences.[34] In Peru this antiracist struggle only intensified the culturalist, essentialist rhetoric that was already present in the earlier contestatory definition of race. In the sixties, discrediting racial taxonomies became the banner of a thriving group of leftist activists in their quest to install class struggle as the dominant explanation for all things social. Class was finally superseded by ethnicity in the 1980s, following the international collapse of the power structures of the Cold War, the national breakdown of leftist political parties, and the emergence of the Shining Path. In chapters 3 and 4 I analyze how this period unfolded in Cuzco by presenting the academic and political dialogues through which elite intellectuals recast race in different classificatory language, namely culture, class, and ethnicity, each in its turn. In chapter 3 I explain how, coinciding with the conceptual shift from race to culture, around the 1930s, pro-Indian cuzqueños intellectuals renamed themselves neoindianistas. They also shifted from claims of racial purity to clamors for mestizaje, cultural miscegenation. To express their political alternative they actively used art and most specifically folklore and a local dramatic genre, Inca theater, which had also been employed by indigenistas earlier. Using both, neoindianistas engaged in the production of neo-Inca tradition, the underpinning of which was the exaltation of the cholo, whom these intellectuals described as the male plebeian figure that incarnated the highest expression of regional virility. Along with this male figure, the most salient symbol of neoindianista elite tradition was the public presentation of a reinvented Inca ritual, the Inti Raymi, or Feast of the Sun.

In chapter 4 I specifically focus on mestiza market women's contestation and reformulation of dominant classifications, both in the indigenista and neoindianista versions. Their unclear class position (they were neither workers nor peasants) shielded them from the dominant tendency to efface regional racial labels. They conserved their name as mestizas, thus offering me the entry point to analyze the subordinates' reformulation of dominant taxonomies. Mestizas' taxonomies emphasize not decencia, but *respeto* (respect). Respect is not about "proper" sexual behavior; rather, it involves striving fearlessly to achieve relative economic and educational success. Subordinate cuzqueños use the notion of respect to free the indigenous mestizo identity from connotations of immorality, which they redefine as laziness and cowardice.

Struggling to win respect, working-class cuzqueños have dismissed the moral/cultural implications of the elites' social taxonomy while championing de-Indianization. I continue this analysis in chapters 5 and 6, by presenting grassroots performances of expressive culture. In chapter 5 I describe Corpus Christi as one of the arenas in which mestizas, empowered by respect, display their identities. If the marketplace is the economic realm of mestizas, the annual celebration of the religious celebration of this religious festival is their ritual sphere. Like Inti Raymi, Corpus Christi has become an icon of cuzqueñismo. Unlike Inti Raymi, however, the elites do not control its script. Instead, powerful mestiza market women do. Through mayordomías — a central ritual of Corpus, and of tourist folklore — mestizas and their husbands appropriate the celebration and dauntlessly show "inappropriate" behavior, thus defying elite rules of decencia. Mayordomías are the quintessential stage for the performance of de-Indianized indigenous identity, for as mestizas acknowledge "neither *los decentes* nor poor Indians are apt to be mayordomos." Dances — indigenous folklore — are a central feature of successful mayordomías. In chapter 6 I show how grassroots intellectuals use dances as autoethnographic devices in which they express their de-Indianized — "refined" they say — indigenous culture.[35] Through dances, indigenous mestizo choreographers affirm their "authenticity" by simultaneously claiming rural origins and deploying what they consider urban manners. They thus express their version of indigenous culture, which shatters the rural-urban dichotomy traditionally used to distinguish indigenous from nonindigenous culture and to imagine Indians and mestizos as discrete identities.

To gather the data — more than I could have ever possibly used — I resided in Cuzco for a total of sixteen months during the years of 1991 and 1992. During that period I spent most of my time in the Almudena neighborhood, and in the Mercado Central (central market) de San Pedro, where I conducted one hundred and twenty-one open-ended interviews. The duration of these interviews varied from twenty-two hours to one hour. In addition to these, which were all recorded, I conversed with people in the neighborhood and during the celebration of fiestas. I also conducted and taped interviews with elite people: eleven intellectuals (one woman) and nine nonintellectuals (four men and five women). As an in-law relative of a cuzqueño lady, in whose house I lived during the second stage of my fieldwork, I was invited to elite houses and parties. I (of course) recorded in my diary the informal conversations I held at these parties with guests, hosts, and domestic workers.

The residents of the Almudena neighborhood and mestizas in the marketplace, who have authorized me to use their names, also facilitated many connections that allowed me to review very intimate records such as the *libros de actas* (minutes) of the neighborhood institutions, which registered information about the history of the mayordomías. This documentation convinced me of the necessity of undertaking a historical investigation of the academic ideas and daily life aspects underlying the notions of race and ethnicity in Cuzco. Hence, I also worked in two public archives (the Archivo Municipal del Cuzco and the Archivo Departamental del Cuzco), in the archives of the newspaper *Diario El Sol,* and in the library of the Centro de Estudios Regionales Andinos Bartolomé de Las Casas. Additionally, the families of some elite intellectuals generously offered me access to their private collections. Grassroots intellectuals also kept records — minutes of their associations, photographs, pamphlets that circulated for the celebration of mayordomías — which they enthusiastically shared with me.[36]

I

Decency in 1920 Urban Cuzco

The Cradle of the Indigenistas

The race that has produced a Leibneitz and a Newton is
inferior to none. — PAUL BROCA, 1864

Recibir un título profesional es una dignificación que borra los
estigmas de la procedencia. (Receiving a professional degree is a
dignity that erases stigmas of origin.) — LUIS E. VALCÁRCEL, 1914

In 1912, when a team of professors and students from the University
of Cuzco conducted an unofficial census of their city, they found it
difficult to assign the residents an "accurate" racial identity. Among
the methodological problems that the director of the census reported was that "the tendency both of the interviewer and of the interviewed, is and will always be to prefer the superior classification. This means that the mestizo will try to be included as white,
and many Indians [will choose] to be [considered] mestizos." Since
"whites" occupied the apex of the Cuzco racial hierarchy, with Indians at the bottom, the cuzqueño population made efforts to whiten
themselves. To avoid misrepresentations in the numerical reports,
the census director felt compelled to train the census interviewers
to identify the race of the residents. Later he corrected some data
that he considered inaccurate (Giesecke, 1913:26). This episode illustrates the conflicts that surrounded racial definitions in Cuzco,
conflicts that were already several centuries old at the time of the
1912 census.[1] However, this census was unique because it revealed
the efforts of its North American director, Albert Giesecke, to implement a scientifically defined concept of race to rectify what he
considered to be the "self-misrepresentations" of the cuzqueño
populace.

At the turn of the century, however, it was not only the racial identities of commoners that were at stake. Latin American elites in general at that time were wrestling with the relatively new European scientific definition of race, which placed them in a subordinate position vis-à-vis their European peers. "To a large extent the educated classes of Latin America shared the misgivings of the Europeans. They wished they were white and feared they were not," writes Nancy L. Stepan (1991:45). The cuzqueño elite was in a particularly difficult racial situation. Starting in early nineteenth century, influential Peruvian thinkers, drawing on notions of environmental determinism, produced a picture of Peru in which Indians were anchored to the Andes (the sierra) but were rhetorically absent from the coast, purportedly populated by mestizos and whites (Orlove, 1993b:324). Similarly, they identified the sierra as retrograde, while the coast was associated with progress. The cuzqueño elite status as serranos (highlanders) potentially lumped them with the images of regression associated with the mountains, and subordinated them to the coastal politicians, and more specifically to the limeño elite, who were perceived as the more advanced racial group.

Like other Latin American elites, cuzqueños contested subordinating classifications. At the turn of the century, the racial-geographical debate between the highland and coastal elites was part of a political debate known as *regionalismo* versus *centralismo*. Regionalists claimed direct participation in the administration of their regions, and accused limeños — the centralists — of concentrating political functions and economic benefits in Lima. Although regionalism represented provincials (in general), it was the serrano politicians that engaged in the struggle against limeños. In Cuzco elites labeled regionalism as cuzqueñismo. In the mid-1920s regionalism intertwined with indigenismo, to become the modern academic and political doctrine that represented the aspirations of cuzqueño politicians. Indigenistas of diverse tendencies thrived during President Augusto B. Leguía's eleven years' mandate (1919–1930). A modernizing and initially populist ruler, Leguía began his second presidential period by seeking intellectual and political allies for his struggle against the aristocratic regimes that had preceded him and which he identified as retrograde. The president included the regionalist-versus-centralist debate in his political agenda, and he found in indigenismo a political proposal that was favorable to the claims of and thus appealing to provincial regionalists. A pliable intellectual and political project, indigenismo (and cuzqueñismo, its local version) was also used by the regionalist serrano elite, both pro- and anti-Leguía, to carve their distinctive place as intellectuals on the central political stage of the nation. In an era when intellectual achievements allegedly determined racial hierarchies and status (as suggested in the epigraphs to this chapter), indigenismo, as an originally serrano doctrine, had an important effect: it proved that highland politicians were as capable as their limeño peers, and therefore, racially equal rather than subordinate.

Additionally, indigenismo articulated a historical argument to define mestizos and Indians as moral (rather than biological) racial others, who were different from the brown-skinned elites. This distinguished the elites from Indians and, most important, from "hybrids," a label that cuzqueño indigenistas fastened onto regional mestizos. Mestizos had been identified as blemished characters since colonial times (Gose, 1996; Schwartz and Salomon, forthcoming). Thus, skirting around their own phenotype, cuzqueños joined limeños in contesting European thinkers who scorned brown-skinned South Americans. Yet in defining themselves as nonmestizo, they rejected the limeño proposal that miscegenation was the racial future of the Peruvian nation. At a time when national attention was focused on the centralism-regionalism debate under the academic leadership of Luis E. Valcárcel, cuzqueño indigenismo in the 1920s proposed racial purity as a national aspiration.[2]

In a country where hybridity (defined from a European viewpoint) was only too obvious, cuzqueño purists backed their position with a conceptual formula that combined European idealism and romanticism — specifically, vague allusions to "language" and "culture" as delineating the "soul of peoples" (Young, 1995) — with theories of racial degeneration. Although their academic alchemy concerning race was rooted in Peru, it was facilitated by the worldwide intellectual tendency to use inchoate definitions of race (Goldberg, 1993; Poole, 1997). As in other places, in Cuzco "race" was primarily a strong sentiment, with political undertones, motivated by a desire for distinctions (Gilroy, 1987; Stolcke, 1993; B. Williams, 1989). In Cuzco itself, discourses of decencia underpinned the local, academic definition of race. As I argue in this chapter, decency was a sexualized moral class discourse that defined the racial identities of the region. By stressing moral/sexual purity it distinguished gente decente from gente del pueblo (Indians and mestizos), notwithstanding their phenotypic similarities. Decencia allowed brown-skinned elites to appear in the censuses as *blancos* and underlay descriptions of individuals "having Indian features without being an Indian" (Valcárcel, 1981:68). Gente del pueblo certainly contested decency, but this is an issue I shall treat in later chapters. In this chapter I limit my interpretation to the elites.

Cuzqueño Decency
A Moral Definition of Race

Decency was a flexible norm of conduct for daily life, one that allowed a belief in the preeminence of ascribed status to coexist with an acceptance of the liberal definition of social equality.[3] Decency, which was a reformulation of colonial codes of honor, was primarily considered as an "innate high morality." However, since the most basic liberal ideas were premised on the possibility of social mobility, Cuzco liberal intellectuals contended that high moral standards were not only present at birth but could be acquired by individuals if they received appropriate training. Education, as one intellectual put it, "imprints upon the individual's psyche the concept of the moral and the immoral, of justice and injustice, of what is licit and illicit, determining the orientations of the feelings" (Mariscal, 1918:12). And an influential politician proposed, "Educative disciplines can combat and modify inherited tendencies because education is the true hygiene that purifies the soul" (Luna, 1919:25).

As the conduit of education and morality, the biological family was a central component of decency. "The family is the first social element which notably modifies an individual's inherent tendencies, inclining him to good or evil, depending on the parental habits displayed at home" (Luna, 1919:31). The expression "Individuals acquire education and morality in the cradle," a common saying among cuzqueño gente decente, echoed the elite sentiment that moral propriety and class origins were coterminous. Because of this emphasis on "the family" — defined as the blood-related nucleus of parents and offspring — decency did not replace ascribed status (Stolcke, 1993). Yet, by stressing the power of education to gradually amend the lack of morality, "cradle ascription" intersected with later achievement, thus allowing modernizing politicians to combine their need for social distinctions with liberal notions of equality.

Implicitly — yet not necessarily — associated with whiteness, decency was a class discourse the elite used to distinguish racial categories culturally and morally in a society where phenotype was useless to define social boundaries. Putative lineages of gente decente were those in which moral purity — or cradle education, as the elites referred to it — had been inherited through generations. The accrued impeccability of moral standards among the gente decente resonated with the concept of *pureza de sangre* — purity of blood (Gose, 1996; Schwartz and Salomon, forthcoming) — which referred to the religious purity that distinguished Christian family lineages from those with Jewish or Muslim ancestors. Latin American regimes, like other colonial administrations, wielded moral purity as a powerful signifier for the production of difference (Callaway, 1993:32). In Cuzco, pureza de sangre outlived the colonial period, and the morality that religious purity had entailed became a racialized modern principle acquired through (cradle) education instead of being a status ascribed at birth. As a modern principle based on a cultural feature it could supersede somatic hybridity and "purify" elites' spirit and thus their race. Conversely, the moral impurity of the gente del pueblo (the antithesis of gente decente) indicated their racial impurity and even degeneration, which allegedly resulted from lack of education and was passed down through the generations. As one intellectual wrote, "The son of the people [*el hijo del pueblo*] will direct its steps to the path of evil" (Luna, 1919:31). Another added, "The child of a poor individual [who] lacks the restraint of education . . . easily slides into the path of perversion" (Mariscal, 1918:12). Mestizos were identified as a dangerous class, an identity that in colonial times was deemed the opposite of *castizo*, a Spanish idiom designating a chaste individual (Schwartz and Salomon, forthcoming).

Grounded in inherited morality and education, decency also allowed elites to formulate liberal conceptions of social hierarchies while minimizing the relevance of wealth to identify social cleavages. This fostered the continuity of colonial cultural features and the reproduction of a status quo that honored the economically decayed elite, those whom the local crème de la crème called *familias pobres, pero decentes* (poor but decent families) and discriminated against the working classes, the mestizos, among which were economically thriving families. Unfit to be wealthy because they had not been cleansed by education, prosperous subordinates were considered gente del pueblo, obviously mestizos, and implicitly associated with "the poor" regardless of their actual economic standing. Reflecting the beliefs of his times, Valcárcel wrote, "A professional title cleanses stigmas of origin" (1914). The flip side of this phrase was that well-off common folk who lacked the symbolic capital that a university degree represented did not have access to the social status that their high income could have otherwise granted them.

By means of decency, the dominant classes of cuzqueño postcolonial modernity kept up selected colonial discourses through which the old status quo endured. Thus, although income was an ingredient of decency, it was not definitive. According to a document dated 1906, the top economic group of the city was composed of fewer than twenty families.[4] Within this upper echelon (comprising foreign merchants, hacendados, and non-cuzqueño Peruvian merchants and moneylenders), the declared annual income ranged from about six hundred to one thousand soles. These were considered the "most decent" group within cuzqueño society. However, decency and income did not coincide for the group at the next economic level, where individuals declared an average annual income of three hundred soles. Within this group there were men and women who held both the most prestigious and the most despised occupations. Among the latter were a middleman for local produce (*rescatista*) and a cattle slaughterer (*manadero*) who claimed four hundred soles as their annual income, while three tailors and a leather worker (*talabartero*) reported three hundred. This income was greater or equal to that of the most eminent lawyers, whose annual declared income ranged between two and three hundred soles. Other professionals such as physicians, engineers, and notaries, reported a similar annual income.[5]

Although the economic distance between these middle-income professional families and their working-class counterparts was trivial or nil, social distance did exist. Constructed upon the notion of decency, it created a chasm within this economic group: even if a slaughterer earned more money than a lawyer, the lawyer was considered more decent.

Underlying this distinction was a lingering colonial stratification of occupations according to their purported cleanliness and degree of physical effort. "The harsh law of work [*la ruda ley del trabajo*] impoverishes and consumes the creature," was how this principle was given its modern expression by a physician in the 1930s.[6] The more strenuous the occupation, the lower the status of the individual. *Manaderos* (cattle slaughterers) and market women occupied the lowest end of the spectrum; the elites deemed them the most immoral members of broken families, although economically they represented powerful working-class cuzqueños. Chicheras were another "unclean" group; gente decente linked them to single motherhood and prostitution.

At the other end of the spectrum, intellectual achievements defined a male individual's *cultura* (culture) and allowed for differentiation among gente decente. Luis E. Valcárcel, an influential indigenista, distinguished two cuzqueño hacendado families with the remark "The Lunas were . . . a bold and adventurous family; they were bold and pugnacious. . . . The Pachecos were refined people, some of them even became university professors" (1981:29). "Refined" (*refinado*) was the adjective used to refer to someone considered *culto*, having culture. Diametrically opposed to ignorance, and yet more significant, to coarseness and immorality, having culture implied being erudite, having delicate manners, and behaving according to the principles prescribed by the Catholic religion. "The more ignorant a man is, the more he approximates the animal, in that the savage instincts manifest themselves through bloody and violent acts" (Luna, 1919:2). Instead, culture domesticated the instincts, and was the reason why gente decente allegedly "did not abuse" their inferiors, but on the contrary treated them properly. Since to be decent was equivalent to being just, decency defined the boundaries beyond which the realm of injustice and illegitimacy began. It demarcated the limits beyond which, as Félix Cosio wrote in the early 1900s, "transgressions against the legitimate expectations of the subordinate" began (1916:5).

The quotidian idiom of gente decente formally translated in legal language as *personas perfectas* (perfect persons). A judicial notion used to calibrate the degree of responsibility of an individual for legal purposes, the perfect person combined physical as well as moral characteristics. Perfect persons were "those that have reached a greater physical as well as psychic development, those who have completed their total evolution, [thus] possessing the culture required to promote social happiness" (Vega Centeno, 1925:9–12; see also Cosio, 1916:22–5). Because the gente decente had developed their discernment, the elites considered their authority as legitimate, and the punishment they inflicted on their subordinates as necessary and just.

The story of Doña Juliana Garmendia is an example of how the gente decente used their power to punish subordinates. It eloquently illustrates decency's symbolic violence — that invisible form which is rarely recognized as violence and instead coded as loyalty, confidence, obligation, piety, and gratitude (Bourdieu, 1993:192). Doña Juliana Garmendia, considered among the elite a very decent cuzqueña *matrona* (matron), owned and administered her family's rural properties, including the very productive hacienda Ccapana. She lived in a mansion in the center of the city of Cuzco while a manager (*administrador*) administered the hacienda. As the hacienda was very large, several foremen (*mayordomos*) helped the manager and worked under his orders. On the hacienda there lived both peons and sharecroppers, who, according to the letters that Doña Juliana and the manager exchanged, were very "rebellious." To control them she had explicitly ordered him to whip "the hacienda Indians" (the peons and sharecroppers) if necessary. However, she warned him against violating her orders by beating them excessively. She also cautioned him not to delegate too much authority to his subordinate foremen, "those abusive *mozos*," because of their inclination to steal the Indians' belongings.[7] Although Doña Juliana was the owner of the hacienda and responsible for its productivity, and therefore could and should punish rebellious workers when necessary, because of her education she understood there was a humane limit beyond which the workers should not be punished. However, Doña Juliana apparently did not believe that the manager understood this, even less the mayordomos. To refer to them, she used the term *mozo*, the local word for a hacienda worker. Their upbringing in the countryside, aggravated by their lack of education, inclined them (she assumed) to abuse their subordinates, the Indians. Doña Juliana's behavior is an example of how, unrecognized as violence and even cloaked in benevolence, the ideology of decency dictated what working-class individuals could legitimately expect; overstepping these graciously granted chances was considered a transgression, a hindrance to progress; it was an *abuso*. Abuses were the immoral acts of racially defined subalterns, whose undomesticated instincts impelled them to mistreat the defenseless. They were considered "imperfect persons," people who had not achieved full development because of moral and psychological deficiencies (Vega Centeno, 1925:10).

The Gendered Qualities of Decency
Making Perfect Gentlemen

According to the historian of Europe George Mosse, "Just as modern nationalism emerged in the eighteenth century, so the ideal of respectability and its definition of sexuality fell into place at the same time" (1985:1). Similarly, in Cuzco, the modern definition of decency overlapped cuzqueñismo, the regionalist discourse with many of the features of nationalism. Cuzqueño elites, like their European counterparts, also evaluated individuals' moral standards in terms of their sexual behavior. The racial categories that decency identified in the region were gendered and distinctively sexualized. "Gente decente" alluded to the sexual virtue of *damas* (ladies) and the responsible sexuality of *caballeros* (gentlemen). These qualities guaranteed the moral well-being of families, and in the modernizing era, they also vouched for progress. Contrasting with this image, mestizos were considered sexually promiscuous and retrograde. Uncontrollable lust characterized the women, while the men were considered unreliable fathers and consorts. Because of its supposed sexual immorality, this social group was thought to contain broken families. The indigenous population, according to this ideology, comprised sexually violent *indios* and frigid *indias*.

Verena Stolcke (1993) explains that in nineteenth-century Europe, sexuality was coupled with race through the idea of the "blood-related" modern family, thus tightly binding race and gender. In Cuzco, it was believed that sexuality differed according to race, and so naturally fostered endogamy among sexually compatible groups. Early in the 1910s an intellectual pronounced:

> The feeling of love is directly related to the mental state of the individual. We can distinguish three stages in the psychological evolution in reference to love: the first comprises only the instinct, and as we know perfectly well, the supreme director of the inferior sociological classes is the instinct; the second stage of love is the emotional stage; and the third is the intellectualized stage. . . . These three evolutionary periods of love also correspond to the three phases of knowledge. Love in the Indian unfolds between the first and the second phases of the general evolution of love, this difference of degree being determined by lack of education. (Flores Ayala, 1913:27–28)

Because among members of the upper echelons of society love allegedly had an intellectual—rather than instinctive—component, the resulting sophisticated sensuality characteristic of gentlemen inclined them to ladies, whose commitment to personal beauty was a sensual feature that suited the refined sexuality of the male elite. Beautiful ladies, therefore, would not attract uncivilized Indians, who lacked aesthetic feelings. Endogamy among gente decente was considered a natural fact grounded on the racially developed feeling of love (Flores Ayala, 1913; Escalante, 1910; Luna, 1919). Of course, these considerations did not prevent gentlemen from experimenting sexually outside from their group. The rule, however, was "discretion" and matrimonial (not sexual) endogamy.[8]

The most prominent indigenista, Luis E. Valcárcel, in his *Memorias* revealed intimate details about his own love life, which illustrate the sexual principles of decency. In his youth he had an affair with a fatherless woman, whose mother ran a small shop in the neighborhood of San Blas (1981:189). The liaison lasted two years, and they had a son. Valcárcel behaved like a sexually responsible gentleman. He kept his relationship clandestine, and when the boy was born he admitted he was the child's father and economically supported his illegitimate child. Yet, maintaining the decency of his paternal family, and respecting his mother's desires, he did not marry his lover but instead a decent woman who belonged to a prominent landowning family. He thus pleased his family and cuzqueño elite in general. A gentleman's manliness (*hombría*) accrued with his erotic adventures outside his racial-moral group; yet he could maintain his status only if he respected the endogamy of the group. The basis to this social norm was the racial belief that only the refinement of a lady could fully satisfy a gentleman's sexual needs, which, because of his intellectual sophistication, went beyond carnal desires.

Indeed, during this period racialized sexuality formed part of a lay and academic elite discourse not just among cuzqueños (see Callaway, 1993; Stoler, 1989 and 1995; McClintock, 1995). Yet in Cuzco these beliefs intertwined with arguments about the "superior intelligence" of morally and sexually proper groups. "Only the offspring of love are endowed with superior physical and moral qualities," a local leader asserted (Escalante, 1910:10). Moreover, beliefs in the racial superiority of individuals who demonstrated their higher intelligence through a university degree secured the position of cuzqueño intellectuals in leading circles countrywide and, in turn, downplayed their serrano origin. Years later—roughly by mid-century—promoted by populist ideologies, the same belief would facilitate the social mobility of nonelite intellectuals into selected circles. Eventually this created a dynamic in which being an intellectual led to social ascent, and, although it did not necessarily secure an adequate income, it did ensure the continuance of hierarchies.

The superior intelligence that distinguished brown-skinned gentlemen from the plebs (who were equally brown-skinned) also solidified their position as rulers of the city. Legitimized by their indisputable preeminence, gentlemen selected individuals from their own rank for positions of power in the high court (*corte superior*), the university, the municipality, and the official state charitable trust (*beneficencia pública*). These were the most esteemed institutions of the city. A cuzqueño elite man would spend his life working as a judge, professor, city administrator, or manager of charitable funds, where he was supposed to display the wisdom necessary to enhance the region. He was a flawless and complete individual; no aspect of his life was reprehensible. As the patriarchs of decent families the most refined cuzqueño men were well known yet not necessarily wealthy members of society, whose marriage into relatively affluent families allowed them to combine a nostalgically aristocratic lifestyle with the liberal tenets of regional modernization.

The values of decency for gentlemen were conveyed to all of urban society through two frequent street rituals: funerals and duels. These public performances confirmed that gentlemen held a high place in Cuzco society. The 1924 funeral of Romualdo Aguilar is an example. Aguilar was the owner of a large hacienda, a professor at the university of San Antonio Abad, and an attorney in the local court. He was eulogized by Albert Giesecke, José Uriel García, and Luis E. Valcárcel. Giesecke had been rector at the local university, while García and Valcárcel were at the time prominent local intellectuals and the main proponents of modern indigenismo. As a prime example of endogamy among the Cuzco elite, Valcárcel was married to Romualdo Aguilar's sister. The orators described the comfort of Romualdo Aguilar's residence in Chiñicara, where he personally directed the tasks that "his team of Indian workers [*sus indiadas*] performed." They stressed his "culture and gentleness," "austerity, tried-and-true honesty [*acrisolada honestidad*], and patriotic love," "erudition, integrity and justice," and "voluntary service on behalf of others" (*servidumbre voluntaria hacia los demás*).[9] In the eyes of local society, the economic stability of this man's family guaranteed his honesty. Last, but not least, his trips to the United States and Europe accompanying archaeological commissions had earned him recognition as a worldly intellectual.

Besides functioning as manifestations of grief, such funerals were rites of passage in which the deceased was publicly recognized as a selfless modern intellectual who had promoted the moral well-being and progress of all cuzqueños. Although women participated in the funeral parade, it was a male-dominated ceremony. Local authorities, prominent citizens, and male relatives of the dead man led the way. Newspapers, testimonial *coronas fúnebres* (pamphlets specially printed for the occasion), and obituaries in academic journals, described the route of the funeral parade through the main streets of the city, stopping at buildings where the deceased had held an office, and finally arriving in the cemetery.[10] These processions were open to cuzqueños of all social sectors, and were thus, a manner of educating the populace about the qualities of decency: the generosity to serve the collectivity "beyond personal interests," the honesty to do so, and the sense of justice necessary to guard the precepts of society.

Funerals of elite men contrasted with the public silence that cloaked elite ladies' services. Newspaper items describing them were common only in the cases of matronas (matrons), relatively wealthy widows who had a public function in society. The death of a married, decent woman was mourned "in private" (*en privado*), a colloquial idiom that captures the domestic inflection of the ritual.[11]

Duels were the other public display used by elite men to defend and emphasize their honor. The contests provided an opportunity for men to prove that bravery and manliness were compatible with rules of gentlemanly behavior (*caballerosidad*). Ruled by the Code of the Marqués de Cabrignana, duels usually resulted from verbal or physical aggression in which the dignity of one gentleman had been affronted by the other. Offenses involved political, economic, and familial matters. Although the transgressor was publicly challenged by the offended party — normally through a notice in the newspaper that would also inform the literate cuzqueño community — the cause of the duel was generally kept secret to guard the honor of the offended. Supposedly, only the parties involved in the duel knew its origins. The official witnesses of the duel included two sponsors (*padrinos*) and a physician for each combatant, all of them prominent and wealthy cuzqueños, "reliable and knowledgeable in matters of honor." The confrontation was open to the public and outcomes of duels varied. Some ended with only a slight injury for one or both combatants, but others caused death. Such was the case of the journalist Juan Pablo Tresierra, who died in 1914 in a duel fought with pistols against another intellectual, Demetrio Corazao. As a result of this event, Corazao acquired a reputation for bravery and for being "a man"; his fame lasted until his death. In 1936, twenty years after the incident, he answered a judicial claimant with the phrase, "I dare him who considers himself a man to challenge me." No challengers came forward (Aragón, 1983:92–123).

Depending on the nature of the offense, the importance of the parties involved, and the political conjuncture, duels could attract a large audience. They were a vehicle in which private offenses were publicly repaired and honor became a public affair. The male figures involved in such combat obtained public acceptance, which in turn could result in political or social revenue.[12] Thus, if funerals stressed the high moral standards of cuzqueño elite men — namely their nobility, generosity, and sexual and economic honesty — through duels gentlemen cleansed their stained honor, by parading their manly boldness. Both rites signified the public exposure of the qualities of gentlemen beyond the walls of their homes.

Given the public importance of the moral behavior of patriarchs, their adversaries could profit from revealing their private misdeeds. In 1921, a married member of the city council (*municipalidad*) shot and killed his mistress in a bar, where she was drinking with two male friends. The murderer held a high governmental position and was politically prominent. When the woman died, enemies of the city council member published a letter in a local newspaper accusing him of killing the woman and abusing her when they lived together. The murderer's older brother answered the denunciation. In his written response he said that being older, the woman had seduced his brother into their love affair. His brother had shot her in self-defense, responding to the offenses she had proffered against the virtue of his "saintly mother and that of my brother's wife as well."[13]

As this vignette shows, a gentleman's alleged flawlessness allowed him to represent himself as a "victim" of ill-fated circumstances provoked by his subordinates.[14] Flawlessness and its flip side, "victimization," protected gentlemen even vis-à-vis state representatives. In 1923 Juan Lomellini, the owner of a textile factory in Cuzco, received a fine after transgressing a decree from the *prefectura*. Protesting the fee, he went to the prefect's office and verbally and physically injured him. The prefect imprisoned Lomellini. The following day, the chamber of commerce officially protested the prefect's "mistake" and the gentleman was liberated.[15]

The Gendered Qualities of Decency
Domestic Ladies

Unlike the gentlemen, who were destined to public life and politics, ladies were deemed unqualified to exercise political power or to publicly defend family honor. During the first decades of the century, the most advanced legal thinkers — in challenge to the status quo — held that women could hold political positions provided they acquire special instruction and training and that they remain single. Political life was incompatible with a woman's duties as a mother and a wife (Cosio, 1916:31–33). Those who challenged these ideas asserted that domesticity was not an innate female characteristic but a product of the social division of labor, which due to laws of social evolution had become part of women's constitution (Cosio, 1916; Luna, 1919). Natural laws of inheritance had imbued tenderness in female feelings: "Chained to the household and dedicated to domestic chores since the most remote times, the woman has developed affective tendencies and a delicate character, qualities that she has transmitted to her sex from generation through generation, producing since her very early years the cuddling feelings that she expresses as the love for her dolls" (Luna, 1919:21).

Elite women who challenged this pattern risked harsh social sanctions. Relegated to the deviant side of society, disobedient elite women had their sexuality questioned and usually had the reputation of being mannish (*machonas*) or dissolute and base. To their close relatives, a disobedient sister or daughter was a source of humiliation. In the rest of society they provoked an ambivalent response, a combination of repugnance and admiration. Such was the case of a woman lawyer, one of the few female intellectuals of the time, who was also affiliated with the incipient local communist party. Memories of her public declarations that her determination never to marry would not prevent her from having children, still lingered in 1992.[16] But few women were as daring; improper relations jeopardized an elite woman's standing, as she would be left defenseless were she to be deceived by her lover. Some ended as victims of their own transgressions. The daughter of a respected lawyer and president of the superior court of justice, for example, committed suicide by poisoning herself after her father had "paternally admonished her for her amorous misconduct" (*su conducta de desliz amoroso*).[17]

Although ladies were publicly presented as subordinate to ruling gentlemen, wealthy women's domestic power helped maintain decency. As in Valcárcel's case, mothers were the enforcers of matrimonial endogamy. They were gatekeepers of privacy, their performance constrained within domestic circles. Although they could reveal things that could have public impact, they usually performed as ornamental figures, called upon to sponsor inaugurations of public buildings or other urban infrastructures (*obras públicas*), to whose construction their families contributed financially. Young single daughters from crème de la crème families were "beauty queens" in the yearly celebrations of Carnival, thus reasserting rather than questioning the status quo. On such occasions, receptions would be offered at the leading ladies' houses, where elite women displayed their worldly knowledge of the art of hostessing by serving "French champagne, Russian caviar, and hors d'oeuvres."[18] These rituals were publicized in the newspapers as "complying with the most aristocratic norms, and the standards of parties held in Lima, the capital of the country." The "beauty, grace, and elegance of cuzqueño women" were the center of the celebration. Held at the ladies' inherited paternal mansions, the parties were attended by governmental officials and visitors from Lima, as well as foreign ambassadors and local authorities.

A crucial rule of female decency was that women undertook their public activities under the tutelage of a suitable male figure. Alone, women could not venture far from the walls of their homes without provoking scandal. In the early months of 1921, the city newspapers were occupied for several days with the story of a single woman who, looking for economic opportunities had, "ventured into the recently colonized jungle of Madre de Dios on a miserable trip in which she was exposed to dreadful conditions." By leaving the protection of her family and home to independently seek her livelihood in an utterly uncivilized jungle area, this woman had broken the rules of decency and humiliated her family. Her male relatives were so embarrassed that they "were the first to condemn her acts, even in shame for their besmirched family name, [and] rejected their kin ties."[19] Independent public appearances were proscribed for "decent" women, as was earning a living on their own. Matronas, wealthy women who administered their own riches, were exceptions to this rule, because of the absence of a qualified male provider among their immediate family. Doña Juliana Garmendia, for example, was one of these locally respected matrons.

Active and direct engagement in an economic activity was reserved for women of the lower echelons of society. Allegedly lacking a male figure to protect them, they were marked as deviant. In his analysis of European women, George Mosse remarked that those who did not live up to the ideal of respectability were perceived as a menace to society, a threat to established order (1985:90). In Cuzco, following the precepts of decency, the elite identified local mestizas as the epitome of a similar female deviance. They were working women, market vendors, known as *placeras* because they sold in plazas, before marketplaces were built, chicheras, and *alcanzadoras,* brokers of agricultural produce. As important suppliers of consumer items, they were a nightmare for city rulers who considered restraining these mestizas a difficult task. To the elite, the coarseness of these women's jobs and the fact that they thrived coping with them only confirmed the unruly moral nature of gente del pueblo. The lives of mestizas blatantly contradicted elite norms of sheltered femaleness, one of the pillars of decency. Given the specific gendered quality of decency, it was these urban working women — and not their male counterparts — who separated the decent ladies and gentlemen from immoral classes. However, decency had even broader signification, in that it formed a component of indigenismo, the academic and political discourse that confirmed (male) cuzqueños' status as national intellectuals.

Modern Indigenismo
Public Politics Meet Decency

Viscount Laurent de Saint Cricq, an elite Frenchman, visited Cuzco in the late nineteenth century. Probably persuaded by European beliefs about the inferiority of South Americans, he mockingly wrote (under the pseudonym of Paul Marcoy) about the intellectual pursuits of the cuzqueño elite: "All the men study with great interest the subjects of theology, the philosophy of natural law and human rights, civil rights, and canon law. The natural sciences, dead and living languages, and the arts of recreation appear to be unworthy of a virile education to these men. . . . They know that a lawyer can aspire to anything" (quoted in Porras Barrenechea, 1961:243). Saint Cricq had correctly perceived the central place that a university position and particularly a law degree held in cuzqueño elite life. However, two decades later, he would have perhaps been surprised at the modernizing impetus that characterized the university in Cuzco. In 1909, echoing the political preaching of modernizing intellectuals and reacting to a pervasive national crisis, decent cuzqueño students and some professors engaged in a struggle to transform an obsolete curriculum and replace a retrograde academic aristocracy.[20]

One pioneer of the university reforms was the physician Antonio Lorena, who graduated in Lima in the late 1880s and returned to Cuzco, where he became a university professor. According to one of his contemporaries, Lorena was a disciple and close friend of Alphonse Bertillon, the French inventor of criminal photography (Poole, 1997). He also taught "the novel ideas of the anthropologist Topinard" and the "basic principles of biology and evolutionary theory as proposed by Lamarck and Darwin."[21] Crucially for the later development of the cuzqueño intelligentsia, Lorena inaugurated courses in anthropology, legal medicine, and physiognomic techniques in 1899. Many years later, one of his students remembered him as a "witty Voltairianist, who exhibited a scientificist [sic] and positivist rhetoric" (Saavedra, 1967:82). Trained in the methods of the French mathematician and philosopher Auguste Comte and in positivist notions of social health, Lorena proposed the sociological study of reality as the first step toward changing the backwardness of local society.[22] Under his leadership the Faculty of Natural Sciences awoke from its lethargy, and became highly active, with classes in ethnology, anthropology, human anatomy, physiology and paleontology, along with chemistry, physics, mineralogy, and zoology.

The intellectual reforms of 1909 signified the official beginning of cuzqueño scientific politics. Scientific politics had swayed Latin

American intellectuals since the nineteenth century; it held that the methods of science could be applied to solve national problems (Hale, 1986:387). As Angel Rama explains: "At the turn of the twentieth century, the fact of their enlightenment alone *fated* [intellectuals] to take leading roles in societies that had, as yet, barely initiated the practice of democracy" (1996:83). In Peru, scientific politics swayed intellectuals of all parties, who considered it their duty to intervene in the administration of the country and deter the chaos provoked by civil and military *caudillos*. Liberals, radicals, idealists, and positivists all felt obliged to combine their academic and political activities. In Cuzco, the tendency had started the previous decade through the creation of the Centro Científico del Cuzco (the Science Center of Cuzco), organized by hacendados imbued with a desire to modernize (Rénique, 1991:47). In the early twentieth century, scientific politics expanded to include cuzqueño historians, lawyers, and artists, some of whom were influenced by nineteenth-century European idealism or romanticism (Poole, 1997). These historians, lawyers, and artists (whom I will call the culturalists) often questioned the physiological methods of the natural scientists (whom I will call the organicists) and proposed instead that knowing the local cultures was crucial to solve the regional problems. These challenges were important because many of those who made them were politically influential in Cuzco.

In Cuzco, Albert Giesecke (a U.S. citizen, and a Harvard-trained economist) joined Antonio Lorena in leading scientific politics in the Andes from a positivist, organicist viewpoint. Giesecke arrived in Cuzco at the turn of the century with a government appointment as the rector of the local university and was invaluable in transforming the university's teaching methods. Early in his career, Luis E. Valcárcel wrote about Albert Giesecke: "His political economy classes are not limited to pontifications about the great philosophical theories. [Instead] he uses knowledge to our benefit, and applies all his doctrine to the study of Cuzco. It is only then that we open our eyes and understand why we study such science. In the current academic year, the students have studied many of our local economic problems; and in the trip Dr. Giesecke led to the valleys in July, students collected good information, and gained fruitful knowledge" (1914:31–32).

The son of a prosperous merchant and an immigrant from the southern department of Moquegua, Luis E. Valcárcel was himself a university-trained lawyer and self-taught archaeologist and ethnologist "por una necesidad primordial de orden científico y de orden patriótico" [Because I feel a primordial need to do so, which is both patriotic and scientific] (Valcárcel, 1937:118). This man, who so admired Giesecke's teachings, became the indisputable champion of the 1920s version of cuzqueño indigenismo, which he defined "as the science which will help us understand Perú" (1937). He was also the most eloquent proponent of a culturalist scientific definition of race that rejected biological determinism. Instead, he believed that human races resulted from the historical evolution of culture in its interaction with the environment.

The proximity of these intellectuals to the cuzqueño "reality" initiated under Giesecke's stimulus, along with Lorena's teachings of physical anthropology and the official unearthing of Inca ruins in 1913, revitalized colonial and early Republican cuzqueño indigenismo.[23] Built on broad premises, modern indigenismo was far from monolithic. Instead, it was a ductile intellectual formation adopted by gentlemen from many different political and academic positions—the organicists and the culturalists among others—harmonized by their practice of decency and their cuzqueñista feelings. Conforming with dominant social and political trends, indigenismo capitalized on its wide-ranging potential appeal to become a doctrine of politically plural regionalist ideology that united cuzqueños against dominant limeño centralism. Under the impetus of scientificism, it became in the 1920s a modern intellectual, moral, and political nationalist movement of countrywide scope, which sought to root the image of Peru in its pre-Hispanic Incan tradition. Politically, regionalist intellectuals assumed indigenismo to be their response to centralist national projects. One of the central issues in this debate was racial mixture (or mestizaje) versus racial purity.

Since the nineteenth century limeños had adamantly projected an image of their city as multicolored and therefore mestiza, and inclined to progress.[24] Whereas their position signified a contestation to European and North American theories about the degeneration of hybrid races, it implied that cultural elimination of "Indians," allegedly a pure race located in the Andes and identified with the past, which leading limeño thinkers considered retrograde and pagan (Belaúnde, 1962; Riva Aguero, 1995). By virtue of their association with the Andes, promestizo limeños dismissed highland cuzqueños as retrograde — regardless of their social status — and racially inferior to the allegedly progress-inclined costeños. This was an image that liberal serrano intellectuals had challenged since the early Republican period (Gootenberg, 1993). In the 1920s, when scientific politics loomed large, indigenistas contested this relationship, deploying their regionalist discourse against the dominant centralists. Cuzqueñista exaltation of "the Inca race" and the past history of the country, as endorsed by scientific archaeological studies, represented a challenge to limeño modernizers, who identified the past with racial purity and backwardness and the future with mestizaje and progress.

Decency and moral scorn of mestizos provided a basis for the cuzqueño agreement among diverse indigenistas, regardless of their intellectual identification with the culturalist or organicist tendencies. Cuzqueño intellectual elites, as we have seen, self-identified as nonmestizos, though they would have looked mestizo — or even Indian — to noncuzqueños.[25] Judging from their self-perception, cuzqueño indigenistas used selected ideas from those European racial thinkers who, like Hippolyte Taine for example, emphasized the need to seek beneath the surface of observable human traits (Hale, 1986:397–398). Also, European mentors of cuzqueños, like Alphonse Bertillon, said to have trained Lorena, might have provided some basis of consensus. Bertillon's work on criminal identification systems resonated with the popular science of physionomy (Poole, 1997) and might have moved even the organicist Lorena to appreciate the idea of searching for moral traits under the surface of phenotypic features. Along with this implicit — unconscious and self-reflective — agreement about the precedence of inward traits over phenotype, indigenista intellectuals used degeneration theories that assigned races to geographical environments and held that racial types declined when they abandoned their racially proper places (Stepan, 1985). Local intellectuals modified the European theory by stressing moral over biological degeneration, and thus were able to remove themselves from the mestizo sphere of identity. Generally, indigenistas defined mestizos as former Indians who had decayed morally after leaving the haven of their agricultural community. From the culturalist indigenista perspective, mestizos were cultural/moral hybrids rather than biological hybrids, and antimestizo organicists would have agreed, as disagreeing would have ejected them from the sanctuary that the racial/moral category gente decente offered. Wielding notions of decency and a compatible — if blurred and mixed — scientific racial knowledge, purist indigenistas modified the Europeans' conclusions about the general degeneracy of the Latin race, removing gente decente from it and limiting it to gente del pueblo, the populace. Valcárcel described mestizos in the following terms: "Rickety, with turbid, sluggish, and reddened eyes, they look at city things with stupid expression. They spend every cent that results from their cattle or harvest sales. To them, decency means the prodigal consumption of beer and liquor" (1925:40). And Luis Felipe Aguilar, a lawyer, and an outspoken indigenista (who was also Valcárcel's brother-in-law) wrote this about countryside mestizos or mozos:

[He] has degenerated physically and morally. He is slightly more educated than the pure Indian, but he does not use this education for individual or social improvement; instead he uses it to position himself in an unreal superior condition vis-à-vis his surroundings, and moreover brags about it. He is as conceited and insolent with those inferior to him, as he is subservient, servile and abject with his superiors. He has an invincible tendency to laziness and alcoholism. He works only if motivated by material needs, rather than moved by material ambitions or to satisfy noble ideals; if he has what he needs to survive today, he is oblivious about tomorrow, and therefore ignores the idea of savings. (1922:109)

In their disdain for mestizos, academic indigenistas were no different than some other Latin American racial thinkers (such as the Argentinean Bunge, author of *Nuestra América* (1903); the Bolivians Rigoberto Paredes and Alcides Arguedas, writers of *Provincia de Inquisivi* (1903) and *Pueblo Enfermo* (1912) respectively; or the Brazilian Euclides da Cunha author of *Os Sertões* (1902).[26] Yet unlike these writers, leading cuzqueño indigenistas did not see European immigration as the key to national racial redemption. Instead, they sought racial regeneration in the revival of the "soul" of the Inca race. The trend was to assert that the spirit of the Inca race (hazily equated with moral characteristics) had persevered unchanged, reproducing a harmonious historical relationship between environment and culture, in spite of the exterior, physical degeneration of Indians. "It can be an Empire today and tomorrow a bundle of slaves. It does not matter. The race remains identical to itself," wrote Valcárcel (1927:21). And since the Incas had been a "race of agriculturalists," the solution to the national conundrum that Indians represented was to dignify their identity as agriculturalists. Rather than civilizing Indians through urbanizing education (that is, rather than transforming them into mestizos as limeños proposed), indigenistas believed that Indians had to be remade in their racial proper places. It was in the rural, agricultural *ayllus* that the Indians should be taught, by *educadores de la raza* (educators of the race), because "the Indian teacher knows exactly what to teach the offsprings of his race, and whatever he teaches he does so lovingly, using the ideal of rehabilitation as the light of Sirius that illuminates the darkness of the Indian's pedagogic unconsciousness" (Valcárcel, 1927:87).

Along with their belief in the redemptive power of education, their veneration of Inca memory was a ground of agreement between politically and philosophically diverse indigenistas. When Peruvian president José Pardo visited Cuzco in 1905, Antonio Lorena compared their city with Rome and Alexandria, yet presented the region as "the center of an advanced civilization, extinct today." As Francisco Javier de Clavigero (and others) had argued in the eighteenth century, to produce *neoaztequismo* for the Mexican elites (Fowler, 1987; Pagden, 1992; Brading, 1991), Lorena explained that the conquest and colonialism had altered the normal path of evolution of the pre-Hispanic race, thus immersing Indians "in a deep well of indolence" (1905). Lorena had arrived at this conclusion about the deterioration of the Indians through his scientific study of craniometry, a technique that indigenistas, who hoped to establish the evolution of races via history and culture, might had disavowed. However, Lorena also exalted the "high degree of development reached by Inca culture," specifically, its technological advances like Inca techniques of cranial trepanations (Lorena, 1931:135). Thus, although cultural-ist indigenistas — might have denied the utility of craniometry, they concurred with Lorena's appraisal of Inca civilization and on the negative effects of the Spanish Conquest on the Inca race. For the culturalist the centuries of colonial domination, rather than deform-ing Indians biologically, had affected their historical memory and made them analogous to "anacronitic primates" (humans whose natural evolution had stopped), who were "unable to emancipate themselves from ancestral fears" (Valcárcel, 1975). Neither organi-cist nor culturalist indigenistas thought the Indian condition was terminal. Indians could be cured from their amnesia, and the race could be revitalized and reequipped with their former abilities, said Valcárcel.[27] He thus concurred with Lorena and Giesecke, who be-lieved in the organic regeneration of Indians if surrounded by a fa-vorable environment. Cuzqueño past greatness and contemporary national prevalence of Inca history, as well as the possibility of re-generating Indians and modernizing their region, all combined to unite these gentlemen.

In the 1920s, Cuzco indigenismo housed numerous political and intellectual compromises — and unresolved discussions — among cuzqueño elite politicians. Above all they were eager to achieve a cherished political goal: to launch Cuzco as a nationally relevant political center and themselves as legitimate politicians like their limeño counterparts. At the conceptual level the agreement was facil-itated by the generalized haziness of racial thought, nationally and internationally. At the more quotidian level agreement was made possible by the elite endogamous social life so eloquently reflected in their marriages. Félix Cosio, the lawyer who believed that women had to remain single to participate in politics, married Leonor Gue-vara (ironically, one of the few women to attend the university in the 1910s); Cosme Pacheco, a liberal professor, married Luisa Garmen-dia, a relative of Doña Juliana, the matron who warned the foreman of her hacienda against whipping the Indians. After the marriage his mother prescribed, Luis E. Valcárcel became the brother-in-law of Luis Felipe Aguilar, the vocal lawyer and pro-Indian champion, whose racial definition of mozos was quoted above. Endogamic elite marriages fostered endogamic intellectual routines and practices, which minimized the significance of political or philosophical discrepancies. Decency was the implicit underpinning of social endogamy, as importantly, in the 1920s it also underpinned the indigenistas' purist national quest.

Modernizing a Decent City (and Cleaning up the Marketplace)

In addition to modernizing colonial indigenismo, the renovating intellectual thrust of scientific politics yielded a peculiar generation of city rulers. Botanists, physicians, lawyers, and self-taught archaeologists, they ventured beyond the walls of their studies and laboratories to apply the premises of their sciences in modernizing the city (Giesecke, 1912, 1913, 1915, 1917). The link between material and moral purity that formed the foundation of decency led them first to clean up the city. The opinion of illustrious foreigners like Hiram Bingham, who called Cuzco "the dirtiest city in the world" only confirmed this need.[28] Lacking an adequate sewage system, the streets were constantly filthy and chronic epidemics ravaged the region.[29] Concerned about the "hygiene and orderliness of the population," successive city governments launched sanitary campaigns. In 1917, for example, resulting from this desire to cleanse and modernize, a new marketplace and slaughterhouse were built and a new sewage system was inaugurated. That year, the city administration included as aldermen the prominent intellectuals Albert Giesecke, Luis E. Valcárcel, Humberto Luna, Cosme Pacheco, and a nationally renowned botanist, Fortunato L. Herrera (Frisancho, 1918).

The cleansing efforts assumed that the populace's ignorance of basic notions of hygiene threatened the city's infrastructure and explained the high rate of infant mortality (Giesecke, 1913; Luna, 1919; Roca, 1922). "Servants and cooks," explained Giesecke, suffered "from fevers, pneumonia, and angina as a consequence of their ignorance and unhealthy sanitary conditions" (1913:25). So, in addition to infrastructure changes, sanitary campaigns entailed the education and surveillance of the "hygienic habits" (*hábitos de higiene*) of the populace.

A leading figure in the sanitation crusade, and adamant enforcer of hygienic habits among the urban populace, was Luis A. Arguedas, a wealthy physician who had studied in Lima. A member of the local aristocracy, he was connected to the most prominent intellectuals of the time both in Lima and in Cuzco, where he taught chemistry at the university. He was respected by his intellectual associates, including his colleagues at the university and in the city council, Luis E. Valcárcel and Alberto Giesecke, who chose Arguedas as his *padrino de matrimonio,* the best man in his wedding. He was also acquainted with aristocrats from Lima, such as José de la Riva Agüero y Osma and the relatives of President Leguía who, on their visits to Cuzco, were guests at Arguedas's mansion. Dr. Arguedas's clinic was located in the Plaza de Armas, where he treated "ladies' diseases, venereal diseases, and syphilis," his specialties. Like most of his peers, he played a prominent role in politics. He held such positions as vice president of the local branch of the Liberal Party, mayor of the city, and president of the Sociedad de Beneficencia.[30] In 1927, as a member of the modernizing party led by Augusto B. Leguía, he served as a representative in the national Congress. His most active position, however, might have been that of *médico sanitario departamental* (health inspector of Cuzco), a government post that Arguedas held during the twenties.

Although he was a liberal, Dr. Arguedas was not an indigenista. Actually, he was one of the few writers who ranked humans on a "zoological scale": the "white race" at the apex, followed by the "American race" (Indians and mestizos), then African Negroes, and finally Asians or the "yellow race" (Arguedas, 1930:146). His concerns with Cuzco's hygiene went hand in hand with a mandate to protect, increase, and enhance the national population through biological means, including eugenic cross-breeding. A clean city and country would invigorate "our own American race" and attract the immigration of superior human groups (Arguedas, 1928). As health inspector, he supported the construction of a city sewage system and called for the destruction of the waste dumps on the outskirts of the city. Like his peers, Arguedas coupled filth with indecency, and thus his cleansing efforts also targeted gente del pueblo for moral rehabilitation. Under his lead, sanitary campaigns policed the sexual behavior of the lower classes, because the high incidence of syphilis that then afflicted Cuzco would persist, as he explained, until the "populace [was] instructed in the prophylactic rules of venereal diseases that were dangerously affecting soldiers and policemen." Unless female prostitution was exercised under the conditions of hygiene that he, as the official physician of the state determined, it was considered unlawful. Along with the city police he organized a civic campaign for "clean prostitution."[31]

Hunting prostitutes was not only a cuzqueño practice: other Latin American cities also produced the same kind of sexual policing (Findlay, 2000; Guy, 1991). The salient feature of cuzqueño sanitary campaigns was that it reached beyond prostitution to include working women (the mestizas) and urban Indians in this aura of filth and immorality. This was not a coincidence: working in the marketplace, mestizas already transgressed images of female decency. Likewise, urban Indians contradicted their definition as a "race of agriculturalists," and trespassed beyond their "racial proper place," the countryside. Because Indians did not belong to the city, Arguedas ordered the eradication of their dwellings which he considered *focos de infección*, hubs from where germs spread out to infect the population.[32] Additionally, he modernized the supply of water by installing more than one thousand private sources of water, thus eliminating Indian water carriers, whose hands he considered filthy and unhealthy.[33]

But Arguedas's greater concern was the poor infrastructure and lack of cleanliness of the "new marketplace," *el mercado nuevo* constructed by the modernizing group of aldermen mentioned above. He constantly sent notices to the city mayor describing the inadequacy of the locale, which he deemed "subversive against urban culture" and "shameful." The conditions were certainly deplorable: the lack of running water turned the bathrooms, and the entire marketplace into a source of contagious diseases. The most critical sections were the "meat, fruit, and vegetable stalls, which attract enormous amounts of flies carrying millions of germs." Last but not least, Arguedas was particularly worried about the female vendors' appearance and their *vestido de castilla*, the typical mestiza dress, made of hand-woven wool. As the "favorite nesting material for bugs and filth [*inmundicias*] of all sorts, and as a permanent carrier of bacteria" it should be covered by white, body-length aprons. The white fabric would facilitate the supervision of mestiza cleanliness. Additionally the long braids of the market women should be cut, and mestizas should be obliged to have short hair. Their long hair touched and infected the produce they sold.[34] To implement the hygiene measures, he recommended that the municipality increase the number of market guards and replace the feeble ones with energetic persons with modern notions of hygiene.[35] Confirming the gentlemen's belief that controlling mestizas was not simple, Arguedas's recommendations encountered market vendors' resistance as the following account from a Cuzco newspaper reported:

> Yesterday a woman called Rosa Pumayalli, a meat seller, set off a serious disturbance in the marketplace because the guard . . . informed her she had to wear her apron and clean her belongings in conformity with the orders from the mayor's office. That was enough for Pumayalli, whose Quechua name means vanquisher of tigers [*pumas*]. She tried to attack the guard and chased him brandishing a knife and showering him with insults from her well-supplied repertoire. This was enough to encourage the rest of the sellers to rebel against the municipal decree concerning tidiness and cleanliness. . . . It would not be strange if one day we had an armed strike in the marketplace, in which there is an abundance of dirty and indecent Pumas who do not want to remove their secular filth.[36]

Chicherías, the popular bars also run by mestizas, represented another source of concern. They were required to have a nearby source of running water and, to safeguard morality, chicherías located in decent neighborhoods had to operate in inside patios. This would spare honest neighbors from witnessing scandalous scenes. Establishments that did not fulfill the sanitary conditions had to pay fees or were closed.[37] Undeniably, by applying their knowledge to construct a modern city, the intellectuals controlled people's lives. Decency (and its antimestizo class feeling) was the moral force that connected the public and private lives of scientific politicians and organized a modernizing consensus between indigenistas and nonindigenistas, just as it had organized the consensus between culturalist and organicist indigenistas. No indigenista would have opposed Arguedas's measures to control marketplace mestizas. Likewise, no indigenista would have protested the eradication of Indian water carriers and their replacement with household faucets. They all agreed that modernization and moralization should respect the racial proper place of individuals.

Teatro Incaico
Performing the Past and Presenting Racial Purity

By what token would the latter-day Greeks portray themselves as the true descendants of the ancient Hellenes? Even if they were able to do so, had several centuries of unenlightened Ottoman rule not affected on their intellectual and moral condition? Were they still in any sense that an educated European could grasp the same as the Greeks of old? — MICHAEL HERZFELD, 1986

One of the tasks the urban rulers assumed as essential to cuzqueñismo and in accordance with their regional political quest was that of casting the image of their city as the center of national culture. Cuzco was historically eligible for this status, as the capital of the Inca Empire and as an important colonial site; it was "the only city of America where all time periods and civilizations coexist" (Valcárcel, 1925:115). Backed by their growing archaeological scholarship, several intellectuals wrote tourist guides (*guías turísticas*) depicting the Inca and colonial monuments. The pragmatic rector, Albert Giesecke (who accurately foresaw in tourism a successful cuzqueño industry of the future), jointly edited *Guía histórica y artística del Cuzco* with Uriel García, the man who would years later replace the indigenista Valcárcel as a leader in Cuzco. Published in 1925, the guide remarks on the uniqueness of Cuzco and compared it to "the great Oriental cities of Antiquity" (1925:5).

The Incaism of the cuzqueño elites was not limited to the monuments of their city. Since colonial times local upper classes had glorified the Quechuas' memory by representing Inca dramas written and enacted by elite gentlemen.[38] The new generation continued the legacy, using Inca theater to enact their cuzqueñista emotions and to present the accurate versions of Inca history. It was also the vehicle by which cuzqueño elites portrayed themselves as the true descendants of the ancient Incas. Promoted foremostly, but not exclusively, by indigenista intellectuals, Inca theater was extremely important in taking their specific discourse beyond intellectual and political activists and spreading their nationalist influence among the decent spheres of society, individuals accustomed to theatrical performances by foreign troupes, of foreign genres.

Reviving and preserving the past was an academic "mission" as Félix Cosio, a lawyer, asserted: "The university of a people [de un pueblo] whose only heritage is the memory of its past [should be] the focal point for reviving this [past] through an intelligent evocation" (1922:4). When Luis E. Valcárcel inaugurated the Instituto Histórico del Cuzco in 1914, he mentioned the necessity of "always representing the great dramas of ancient provenance, such as Ollantay, Usca Paucar, because they enliven the memory of past glories."[39] Both were colonial dramas depicting the bounty and wisdom of Incas and were written in Quechua. The versatile Luis E. Valcárcel, one of the main scholars of the Inca past, was among the leaders of dramaturgical activities in Cuzco. In addition to teaching at the university, he directed an artistic group called the Compañía Peruana de Arte Incaico (Peruvian Company of Inca Art), famous for its tour of Buenos Aires (Argentina) and La Paz (Bolivia). In those two South American countries, the Peruvian troupe deepened professional links with local intellectuals who, like the indigenistas, delved into their pre-Hispanic past in pursuit of Americanism as a fundamental piece of their national identity. Valcárcel molded the performances according to his scholarly conceptions of the Inca Empire, which he felt was the greatest of the original regional cultures and whose enlightened sages had led those cultures to civilization.

Jean François Marmontel, in his eighteenth-century novel Les Incas, drew inspiration from the colonial cuzqueño writer Inca Garcilaso de la Vega to portray Incas as models for perfect righteous men (Gerbi 1988:124; Poole, 1997). Similarly, Valcárcel (also inspired by Garcilaso and perhaps also having read Les Incas) thought of the Inca as a benevolent patriarch, "a great paterfamilias who presided at the domestic banquet and the liturgical acts of his chosen clan"

(1925:95). Using this frame (not coincidentally reminiscent of the social deportment required from local gentlemen), two famous dramas — *Yawar Waqaq* by Jose Silva and *Washkar* by Luis Ochoa Guevara (Itier, 1995:35) — explained that a particular Inca defeat was the result of the deviations in conduct of Atahualpa, a bad ruler. In *Yawar Waqaq*, Atahualpa was a son who ignored the advice of his father, Yawar Waqaq, to govern his people with love and generosity became instead a greedy and cruel governor. In the second play, Atahualpa was again represented as a bad Inca, an intractable, bohemian character who defeated his brother Washkar (Itier, 1990:114–5).

Citing the same virtues that backed indigenistas as national politicians and certified their racial status as gente decente, Valcárcel attributed to the Incas "culture and high intellectual refinement" (1925). These qualities colored pre-Hispanic cuzqueño agrarianism, which transcended the usual images of rural societies as coarse and retrograde. To illustrate Inca sophistication, the central performance piece of the Compañía Peruana de Arte Incaico featured aspects of Inca nobility. In *Coro y canto al Cuzco* (Chorus and Chant to Cuzco), the theme was the significance of the main urban center; in *Himno al sol* (Hymn to the Sun), the company represented religious sophistication of the Incas; and in *Escena culminante del drama Ollantay* (The Decisive Scene of the Ollantay Drama), they highlighted the elevated sense of morality and family values of the noble Quechuas. Accompanying these main pieces, the group performed several "scenes from everyday Inca life," which presented a people involved in pastoral, agricultural, and weaving occupations, and a few "Inca dances" that implied that the well-being and happiness of the Inca domain was the product of a civilization that harmoniously combined festivals with work.[40] The Argentine and Bolivian press referred to the tour as the "Inca artistic resurgence."[41]

The Compañía Peruana included members of other elite cuzqueño families besides Valcárcel. Among them was photographer and painter Manuel Figueroa Aznar, as stage director, and the lawyer Luis Ochoa Guevara, as "costume and Quechua literature director." Both belonged to regional landowning families. "The prestigious writer" Luis Velasco Aragón, who owned real estate in the city, also formed part of the company.[42] Because of local norms of decency,

"What the Traveler Dreamed." Photograph by Figueroa Aznar. Courtesy of the U.S. Library of Congress, Milhollen Collection, LC–USZ62–90226. Indigenista staging of Inca theater, ca. 1917.

female participation was discreet, and actresses were not named. Yet, as in French Inca operas (Poole, 1997), the Sun Virgins were important female characters in several pieces that the company performed. However, during this period and particularly under the lead of Valcárcel, the cuzqueño performances lacked the sexual and sensual undertones that characterized the French operatic plots and its female characters. Chastity, innocence, and light happiness were instead the Sun Virgins' main features, traits that were also desirable in "decent ladies." Most important, however, in the quest for racial/ cultural purity was sexual chastity (I elaborate on the indigenistas' perception of female virginity as cultural purity in chapter 4). Inca theater was an efficient tool for demonstrating the elite's cultural purity and their self-perception as morally (racially) superior cuzqueños, the gente decente.

The instrument upon which the performance of cultural purity rested was the Quechua language. "Nothing connects us affectively to the dead more than language," Benedict Anderson wrote, and cuzqueño elites proved him right (1993:145). Elite appropriation of Quechua to represent themselves as Inca heirs and legitimately subordinate commoners was an important component of cuzqueño elite colonial life (Mannheim, 1991:71–74). During this modern period, indigenistas used the Quechua language in their dramatic interpretations of Inca history to represent the essence of *their* race. Quechua was the exemplary and tangible element that historically and culturally distinguished them from commoners, whether mestizos or Indians.[43] Since most native cuzqueños spoke Quechua, they built distance from the lower classes resorting to the same subterfuge that colonial elites had used: the elites claimed they spoke Capac Simi, the putative language of Inca rulers, not the plebeian version of Quechua, which was identified as Runa Simi.[44] The following quotation by Valcárcel, during the inauguration of the Instituto Histórico del Cuzco, eloquently illustrates this position: "We still possess the marvelous tongue of Great Empire's founders, . . . the harmonious language of the *harawes,* the epic language that produced Ollanta's haughty speech before Cuzco; but the victors' destructive labor continues to wear it away to the point of reducing its vocabulary to perhaps only a thousand words, making it more mestizo every day, making it lose its philological individuality. The institute plans to cultivate the pure Quechua that is still preserved in certain places and cultivated by many illustrious people."[45]

By this logic, the Quechua language, in its alleged aristocratic version, was essential to the historically inherited culture of the elites. The people to whom Valcárcel referred were all elite men (and included no women, at least not prominently) like Santiago Astete Chocano, considered a "distinguished gentleman, descendant of one of the principal families of the ancient society" and a distinguished Capac Simi scholar, whose pamphlet "Quechua Alphabet" was widely known.[46] To represent Incas and to write Inca dramas, one had to be recognized as a *quechuista,* a role only granted to the elite. Their erudition and their sheltered leisure time permitted them to preserve Quechua free from contact with the plebeians and thus from miscegenation. Playwrights and actors proliferated only among the cuzqueño elite.[47] Contrary to the general canons of modernism — which associated the theater with alternative lifestyles and irreverence toward society — in Cuzco, writing or acting in Inca dramas was a way of affirming a place among the elite — or even constructing one.

By placing the emphasis on Capac Simi, the physical similarities between elites and plebeians were downplayed, as language became the conduit for constructing an idealist symbiosis between culture, nature, and race. In this way cuzqueño elites claimed their historically preserved cultural purity. Furthermore, personifying Inca nobility and being a Quechua specialist was a means for acquiring quasi-aristocratic rank. To preserve the purity of Capac Simi, and to keep theatrical canons in accordance with Inca history and prevailing norms of decency, the elite lambasted plebeians who ventured into Inca drama. When Nemesio Zúñiga Cazorla, a non-elite priest from the province of Urubamba, presented *Huillca Cori,* he was "punished by the audience with whistling" for having presented a spectacle "appropriate for hamlets of the lowest class," "mixing the Quechua with Spanish," and "having presented on stage dogs, pigs and chickens."[48] The opposite happened to Luis Ochoa Guevara, who was one of the most versatile cuzqueño theater enthusiasts, a performer and writer of dramatic works, famous for "his impeccable Quechua." In 1921, Ochoa opened "his beautiful *revista* [pageant] of Incaic customs, *Huarakko,* with select music, special decoration and elegant costumes" to benefit the General Hospital.[49] Newspaper critics praised the show even before its first performance. Luis Velasco Aragón, commented months in advance that the play was a "drama of great Inca value . . . a revue of customs of life during the epoch of Tawantinsuyu."[50] Another theatrical troupe, Compañía Incaica Huáscar, "directed by the distinguished gentleman Nicanor M. Jara," also met with critical praise when it returned from a tour of the northern Andean countries.[51]

Teatro incaico of course did not aspire to purely artistic ends. Nor was the construction of gentlemen's identity an explicit item in the elites' dramaturgical agenda. One of its overt functions had always been collecting funds destined for public works.[52] Albert Giesecke, the rector of the university, actively used Inca theater for fund-raising purposes, particularly when he was a member of the city council of Cuzco. He remembered: "During my twelve years as a member of the city council, my more interesting duties were to control municipal finances . . . [O]ur city treasury did not have funds for public works. Hence it was necessary to seek public cooperation by means of theatrical performances . . . I was invariably a member or the initiator of these public works. In this manner the Municipal Theater was built. It was productive. With the revenues from these sources, and other financial aid, the central market was built. Money generated by Inca theater functions, for example, was used to build the new marketplace."[53] Not surprisingly, given the allure Inca theater had among the elite, this local dramatic genre became in the 1920s integral to the regional nationalist discourses. Intellectuals conceived of it as a political activity, an instrument to promote Cuzco-centered national feelings, essentially embedded in cuzqueño history. Staging pure Capac Simi and accurate Inca history, Inca theater set itself up to contrast with the impurity of *criollismo*, the artistic genres identified with Lima, a symbol of hybridity. "Teatro incaico represents today our only nationalism; this theater has to spring forth pure, without race mixtures," declared Luis Velasco Aragón. Some months later he wrote, "If Peru has been criollo, this does not represent even the tenth part of its history. . . . [C]riollismo is racial hybridism . . .[,] the return to our radical *I* of *Incanos* is artistic sincerity," which to him meant cultural purity.[54] The culturalist indigenistas certainly led the quest for cuzqueño nationalism, but they were eagerly joined by organicist positivists — like Lorena and Giesecke. Regionalist political accords were stronger than conceptual and philosophical disputes and — undergirded by decency — produced the discourse that unified local elite politicians. Inca theater ratified indigenismo as the intellectual and political ideology of elite cuzqueños. It also promoted the glorification of their city as the capital of the Inca Empire and as the material complement to their dramaturgical cuzqueñismo.

Indigenistas and Hacendados versus Gamonales
A Racial Consensus

Paralleling their crusade to moralize the city, scientific politics launched a liberal crusade to modernize the countryside. Rural modernization entailed uprooting abuses against Indians. If the urban modernization had targeted mestizo working women as the embodiment of filth, immorality, and misdirected enrichment, in the countryside liberal gentlemen of the indigenista era aimed at eradicating a specific male rural type, which they defined as the *gamonal*. Like the urban mestiza, this character invoked for the dominant groups images of ill-achieved wealth (Luna, 1919:34; Aguilar, 1922; Valcárcel, 1925). According to historian Pablo Macera, the term "gamonal" was first used in the mid-nineteenth century, when "Peruvians began to call hacendados 'gamonales' " (1977:283). According to Deborah Poole, the word derived from the "name of a virtually indestructible perennial plant of the lily family, the *gamón* [which] grows on even the harshest of soils and is sometimes classified as a parasitic plant, whose flowering and propagation occurs to the detriment of its less aggressive neighbors" (1988:372). Writing in the late nineteenth century, Manuel Gonzáles Prada, a limeño resident and an influential iconoclastic writer, used the term *gamonalismo* to identify what he called "the numbing trilogy" (*trinidad embrutecedora*) formed by the priest, the landowner, and the lawyer, which deterred the development of a national state. Years late, José Carlos Mariátegui, defined gamonalismo as a pervasive system of local control imposed by large estate owners (1968:159–160). Specifically, gamonalismo was the concept Peruvians used to refer to *caudillismo,* the political system that early twentieth-century Latin American intellectuals identified as inherent in the racial make-up of their region, and which allegedly had prevented the development of democracy as a form of government (Hale, 1986; Lynch, 1992).

As a political phenomenon gamonalismo weighed heavily in the debate between serrano regionalists and limeño centralists. At the turn of the century, Manuel Gonzáles Prada had written, "If the serrano gamonal serves as the political agent of the Lima *señorón* (power hungry gentlemen), the Lima señorón defends the serrano gamonal when he barbarously abuses the Indian" (Gonzáles Prada, 1982:175). In a similar vein, Mariátegui demanded: "Which caste, which category of persons, which class, opposes the Indian's redemption? The answer is only one: gamonalismo, feudalism, and *caciquismo*. Therefore, how can we doubt that a regional administration of *caciques* and gamonales, the more autonomous it be-

comes, the more it would sabotage and reject any effective indigenous revindication?" (1968:159–160). Although both authors were
critical of limeño centralism, they also thought that serrano gamonales jeopardized regionalism or the autonomy of highland provinces vis-à-vis Lima. The political rhetorical act of acquitting hacendados of abuses — by separating them from what was identified as
gamonalismo — therefore became crucial, as many landowners were
also enthusiastic regionalist politicians. Because of their prestige as
pro-Indian champions and their supposed knowledge of rural reality, liberal indigenistas — had the elite's public endorsement to distinguish hacendados from gamonales within the large category of
landowners. To do so, most indigenistas concurred in stressing the
indecency of gamonalismo. As Valcárcel's brother-in-law stated:
"Ordinarily, all hacendados are lumped under the denomination of
gamonales, but this is a mistake and an injustice. Gamonalismo is
not grounded in plain landholding, but rather and more so in the
moral aspects of the individual, in his tendencies, in his way of life, in
his psychology" (Aguilar, 1922:116). During the indigenista era, the
cuzqueño modernizing elite concurred in a moral definition of the
gamonal as a spurious landowner who, being himself a hack lawyer
(*tinterillo*) or with the assistance of one, had "acquire[d] indigenous
lands through fraud or brute force" (Mariscal, 1918; Aguilar, 1922;
Luna, 1919). Always a male figure, raised without the family values
of decency and lacking the spiritual refinement proper of the cultivated intelligence of gentlemen, the gamonal was the antithesis of a
righteous patriarch: "Generally, the gamonal is not a cultivated, let
alone an enlightened man. He has the pragmatic education and the
ungainly flashy deportment facilitated by money, but he does not
care at all about either cultivating his intelligence and elevating his
ideas or ennobling his feelings and moralizing his conduct" (Aguilar,
1922:111). The lack of refinement and the ignorance characteristic
of gamonales were expressed in their physiognomic attributes: a
combination of African phenotype, culturally disgusting bodily attributes, uneasy speech, and tacky wardrobe. An article in a Cuzco
newspaper written in 1922 describes one gamonal in graphic terms
as "scarred by smallpox, of small sunken eyes, with curly hair and
almost bald, his skin almost black, with a flat nose and thick lips,

"Autoridades: Varayoq and gamonales," Sicuani, ca. 1933. Photograph by
Abelino Ochoa. From the collection Grandes Maestros de la Fotografía Cuzqueña. The collection was put together by contemporary local cuzqueño
intellectuals, under the lead of Adelma Benavente, who employed the elite
cultural definition of *gamonales* in their caption, " 'Autoridades' Varayoq
y gamonales." Notice the phenotypic similarities between the gamonales
(sitting down) and the indigenous authorities (back row).

heavy mustaches, beardless, of cannibalistic look, . . . stuttering and
mumbling instead of speaking, always wearing a black suit and a red
or green tie . . .[,] given to stealing the lands of the defenseless Indians," and so on.[55]

   Considering that the original term dangerously and erroneously
included *caballeros decentes,* Cuzco intellectuals and politicians narrowed the concept of gamonalismo to distinguish themselves from
disreputable inferiors. The definition that became consensual among
cuzqueño elite politicians was proposed in the following terms: "A
landowner is [not] always a gamonal. Gamonales, in my opinion, are
people who have nothing and earn a living by exploiting the Indians.
Gamonales are . . . those who stand only to obtain gains from the

Indigenista intellectual and Indian. Personal archive of Mariano Turpo.
Courtesy of Aroma de la Cadena and Eloy Neira. Cuzco ca. 1925.

Indians, [like] the provincial and district authorities, the priests, the
hack lawyers, the propertyless villagers, all those who need to live by
violently expropriating harvests from the Indian, by subordinating
the Indian into his service without pay. The legitimate landlord, who
has inherited his estate from his elders and has many indigenous
families working the land as *colonos* and living in the hacienda as if
they were the landlords in a hacienda that has not been expanded by
the hacendado who has owned the same land for three or four generations, . . . is *never* a gamonal" (Escalante, 1922:230, my emphasis).

The moral contrast between the hacendado and the gamonal was
related to the origin and status of their land possession: ancestral
property was perceived as legitimate and the defining feature of hacendados. "Newly" acquired estates were considered illegitimate
properties obtained through exploitation. The gamonales' "illegitimacy" at birth paralleled their illegitimate possession of property.
Using as a background the indisputable virtues of decency, the dominant cuzqueño construct of the gamonal allowed the elites to acquit

themselves of abusive behavior and espouse liberal pro-Indian politics. The obstacles for hacendado identification with indigenismo were thus removed, and the broad doctrine of indigenismo took the lead in proregionalist elite politics. Yet since the distinction between hacendado and gamonal was a top-down racialized invention grounded in the racial-moral discourse of decency, it was not necessarily shared by cuzqueño gente del pueblo. Abuses and violence against Indians were not mere mirages. They were social facts performed by landowners regardless of racial status, as any so-called Indian or mestizo worker of hacienda would attest. As I will present in the next chapter, gente del pueblo did not distinguish between the behavior of caballeros and mestizos, and, when necessary, called all of them abusive gamonales. Yet the dominant distinction became state policy. The defense by cuzqueño representatives in the Cámara de Diputados (one of the two chambers in the national Congress of Peru) of Ezequiel Luna, a member of one of the wealthiest cuzqueño families and a congressman himself, illustrates how the cuzqueño elite's moral-cum-racial distinctions coincided with official state designs for rural modernization and development. An indigenous political leader had accused Luna of murdering several peons on his hacienda, which was one of the largest in Cuzco. Confronted with this accusation Congress representatives argued: "[Luna has] legitimately inherited the property of the hacienda, he maintains a school for the Indians of Compone, grants them a higher salary than what is customarily paid ... [G]iving them treatment that is both humane as well as worthy of imitation, he has defended them from the abuses of *tinterillos,* and from district authorities. . . . He has made of Sucllupucquio [the hacienda] a model livestock hacienda."[56]

Decency, the attribute of gentlemen, was incompatible with gamonalismo. Calling someone a gamonal became a gendered insult that emphasized the lack of valor constitutive of masculine decency. It meant a "sucker of Indian blood" and a coward, "who, using his economic and social position, appropriates for himself large extensions of land, even villages."[57] A caballero decente would not behave as a gamonal; his education instructed him about the proper use of his authority and social position. The category was thus reserved for immoral mestizos, the inhabitants of rural towns, that Luis E. Valcárcel labeled *poblachos mestizos*. By acquitting hacendados of guilt, this racial definition of the political phenomena of gamonalismo removed any obstacles that could cause unnecessary ruptures between pro-Indian lawyers and "decent" landowners, the rightful masters of Indians. Instead, the definition of gamonales as mestizos complemented the dominant racial definition of Indians, and eventually prevented indigenous self-representation, as I explain in chapter 2.

Conclusions

It is flattering for the University of Cuzco, that fifty percent of its academic production is devoted to study the indigenous problem in all its phases. All academic works that treat the subject suggest measures to supplement juridically [the Indian's] deficient personality, to cancel the negative factors that contribute to his degeneration, and to facilitate his leveling from the stage they have been left, to that of contemporary civilization. — FÉLIX COSIO, 1921

Indigenismo broadly inspired the study of "the indigenous problem in all its phases." But, as I have proposed in this chapter, it was also a political, academic, and daily life discourse through which the cuzqueño leading class forged a series of internal agreements that enabled them, as a heterogeneous group, to dispute limeño supremacy and acquire nationwide academic status and political influence. United in the feeling of cuzqueñismo, which they enlivened through their practice of Incaism, they modernized previous indigenismos and launched a new one as a scientific doctrine that loomed large in the debates between regionalists and centralists. In the 1920s, cuzqueño indigenismo became a national project that represented the provincial alternative to limeños' modernizing mestizaje proposal.

Indigenismo deployed the elite folk ideology of decency and selectively borrowed from foreign thinkers about race the ideas that accommodated dominant personal and regional political needs. The lingering colonial notions of "purity of blood," combined with the liberal beliefs in the "equalizing" powers of education that undergirded folk decency, instructed them that, as cultivated elites, they were not mestizos. This perception that Cuzco's regional politicians had of themselves enabled them to reject the promestizo position of limeño intellectuals, which was interpreted as anti-Indian, anti-Inca, and pro-Hispanic from the indigenista perspective. As in the limeños' project, however, race was central to the ideology of indigenismo. Hazily defined, race implied moral and cultural inheritance, also susceptible of being molded by the environment. In the 1920s, the indigenistas' concept of race and their project for a (morally) pure racial/cultural nation was informed also by the notion of decency, built upon Inca memories and protective of inferior Indians. Likewise, by defining themselves as the morally and intellectually superior cuzqueños, indigenistas assumed the authority to clean the city and countryside from racially suspect characters, namely mestizas and gamonales.

Defining indigenistas as racists would be simplistic and anachronistic. The intellectual vanguard of their times, culturalist indigenistas posed that culture was more powerful than biology in defining race and thus could modify it. Even organicist indigenistas believed that environmental conditions could modify races. Peruvian indigenistas do not conform to definitions of racism in a period when intellectuals from countries like Brazil and Argentina favored biological eugenics (Stepan 1991:136). Their pro-Indian position signified a rejection of what they called "Indian-phobia" or the inclination to "destroy the Indian"[58] and which they considered the result of academic ignorance. But I certainly do not mean to acquit them.

In the next chapter I present how indigenismo, guided by ideals of decency (a local version of *noblèsse oblige*) ironically became a pillar of the defense of cuzqueño gentlemen. Rather than protecting the Indians, it protected the hacendados against whom the Indians struggled. This resulted in a distorted representation of the Indians' quest (a quest that ignored elites' racial-moral distinctions) and provoked the eventual disagreement between Indians and their troubled advocates.

2

Liberal Indigenistas versus Tawantinsuyu

The Making of the Indian

In addition to having been the capital of the Inca Empire, Cuzco has become famous in the regional and national political tradition since the 1960s as the scene of indigenous rebellions that allegedly took place from approximately 1921 to 1926.[1] However, during the 1920s, regional groups disputed the meaning of the same events. On one hand, landowners (in some cases backed by subprefects) denounced the events as rebellions; on the other hand, the Indian "rebels" accused landowners of inventing rebellions, disclosed their abuses, and framed their political activities within the new state policy that, they stated, favored Indians' claims. To everybody's surprise the prefect, the regional representative of the president, backed the Indians' version. Whatever the events were, the disorders occurred in the initial years of the second term (1919–1930) of a modernizing president, Augusto B. Leguía. Thus the contention about the meaning of the rural events also signified a political struggle among the various groups to situate themselves in a favorable position vis-à-vis the new regime.

Between 1920 and 1923 political actors were negotiating alliances with the new president. In 1919 when Leguía assumed the presidency for the second time, he baptized his new government *Patria Nueva* (New Fatherland) and professed his determination to modernize Peru by replacing the country's old political and economic structures. During the initial years of the New Fatherland the president reached out to emerging political groups and introduced an unprecedented degree of populism into the government. The period was particularly favorable to the struggle for indigenous rights and organizations. Leguía himself had adopted a liberal version of indigenismo, which he inaugurated by issuing in 1921 a new constitu-

✗ Self-ident.

tion that proclaimed that the state would protect the "Indian race" and officially recognize "indigenous communities," the collective property of agricultural and pastoral lands held by self-identified Indians.[2] Indeed, the president managed to reconcile his liberal indigenismo with his modernizing capitalist agenda. For example, the Ley de Conscripción Vial, which he authored in 1920, was a coercive labor system that forced men between eighteen and sixty years old to build the roads required for national progress. Needless to say, the conscription mainly affected the poorest individuals and greatly affected so-called Indians.

Defining who the Indians were from the dominant viewpoint was neither a political nor an academic debate in the 1920s. Regional racial/cultural identity politics allowed an economically privileged cluster of individuals (male or female, literate or illiterate, but usually rural) to self-identify alternatively as mestizos or Indians, depending on the specific circumstances of their interactions. Yet the dominant intellectual and political definition of Indianness overrode this dynamic and rigidly defined Indians as illiterate agriculturalists who lived communally in highland *ayllus,* the lands of which they possessed collectively. This simplification required therefore that literate Indians become non-Indian, that is, mestizos.

Following those authors who assert that race — and in this particular case, racial labels — are defined through struggle (Gilroy, 1987; Omi and Winant, 1986), I contend that the so-called rebellions of the 1920s were part of a harsh political dialogue among several groups of the regional society, which implied a dispute about the racial definition of Indianness and gamonalismo. In Cuzco, the actors that participated in the struggle to define "Indian" and "gamonal" were a group of local landowners, the official state representatives, liberal indigenistas, and the so-called Indians, some of whom integrated a pro-Indian rights organization, the *Comité Pro-Derecho Indígena Tawantinsuyu.* The landowners asserted that the Indians had unleashed a racial war against anything non-Indian, aimed at reinstating the Inca Empire. Liberal indigenistas denied this version of the story. Instead, they explained, the Indians were agitated because gamonales — abusive mestizos — had provoked their anger, and because a radical group of politicians from outside the region, organized in the Comité Pro-Derecho Indígena Tawantinsuyu, was instigating Indians to attack landowners indiscriminately, including righteous hacendados. The committee certainly did participate in the organization of the disturbances, and its stated goals were to empower Indians through literacy campaigns and to assist in the granting of official titles to the indigenous communities. Included in this agenda was the repossession of the ayllu lands that had been usurped by landowners. Crucial in the committee's political project was an alternative definition of Indianness: the radical indigenismo represented by Tawantinsuyu Committee countered the dominant vision of Indianness as equated with illiteracy and instead envisioned Indian citizens empowered by literacy. From this viewpoint then, Indians did not become mestizos when they learned to read. Perhaps some liberal cuzqueño indigenistas might have agreed with this idea. Yet a significant disagreement persisted over the committee's definition of "gamonales," which for them included hacendados, the decent gentlemen that liberals excluded from their definition of the word. Consequently, liberal indigenistas opposed the committee's political project. Several liberal champions of Indians delegitimized Tawantinsuyu indigenous leaders on the grounds that they were literate and some relatively well-off, framing them as ex-Indians, opportunistic mestizo exploiters, who were misleading real Indians with the false idea that they would be allowed to even possess hacendados' properties.

Although not everybody agreed with it, the landowners' version prevailed, and many of the indigenous leaders were imprisoned and charged of rebellion. In the courts, liberal indigenista lawyers defended them. But this defense did not consider self-identified Indian politicians as conscious subjects of their own struggle (Guha, 1983:4). Instead it brandished an image of "Indians" as irrational, primitive beings either instigated by abusive mestizos or manipulated by fake Indians, the radical Tawantinsuyu advisers. Ultimately, this defense by the cuzqueño liberal indigenistas led to the defeat of the committee's project for indigenous citizenship and of its alternative racial quest for literate Indianness. The political disturbances of the 1920s, rather than being a racial war between Indians and non-Indians, implied, instead, a confrontation between radical and liberal indigenistas over the racial definition of Indianness and of gamonalismo. Yet, if the defeat of the radical project meant that Indians were defined as illiterate agriculturalists (later called peasants), liberal indigenistas were not successful at shielding hacendados from gamonalismo. Fifty years later, in the 1970s, a progressive propeasant military junta sympathized with the peasants' denunciations of gamonalismo and expropriated hacienda lands. I will refer more fully to this event in chapter 4. Meanwhile, let me return to the 1920s, to the saga of how indigenous politicians became "rebellious and irrational Indians," a label they retained for posterity. These individuals were trapped in a historical conceptual impasse as dominant racial theories blocked their political project: Indians were racially defined as irrational, politicians were not. Each group, therefore, belonged to a different stock. Indians did not have room to be politicians in the liberal racial/cultural definition of race in spite of its optimism about Indian redemption.

The Comité Pro-Derecho Indígena Tawantinsuyu
A Radical Indigenista National Project

In July 1921 President Leguía celebrated the second anniversary of the Patria Nueva. Still in his populist stage, and in need to fight his conservative foes—the oligarch civilistas whom he had defeated in 1919—he was looking for allies everywhere, even among liberal and radical indigenista ideologues. As a part of this search for supporters, in 1920 the Ministry of Development had officially endorsed the Comité Pro-Derecho Indígena Tawantinsuyu. It was an association of Lima-based pro-Indian ideologues, radical provincial indigenistas, and self-identified indigenous leaders of diverse tendencies.[3] Conspicuously absent were the radical cuzqueños who rejected indigenismo in its radical and liberal version and who were at the time actively organizing a local branch of the Communist Party in Cuzco (Gutiérrez, 1986).

July 1921 also commemorated the first centennial of the Peruvian Declaration of Independence and, not coincidentally, assorted political groups promoted their specific national projects. Among them was the Tawantinsuyu Committee, who, stimulated by Leguía's populist ambitions, approached him to request support for their First National Indigenous Congress.[4] He granted the petition, sent a presidential representative to inaugurate the congress, and provided lodging and food for the Indian representatives.[5] The Tawantinsuyu Committee celebrated the independence centennial by inaugurating what they called the First Indigenous Congress, held from June 24 to July 1, 1921. Their ending communiqué read:

> [We consider] the 28th of July of 1921 as the point of departure of a new era, when we should learn . . . to protest and rebel against the oppressive hand. . . . *But before being bold it is necessary to be literate.* Even if the government has the best intentions, if we [the Indians] do not impel those intentions, we will never ever be able to do anything that will really favor us. *An educated Indian is an inconvenience for gamonalismo;* gamonales know that their regime will end the day the Indian knows how to read and write, and that is why they prevent the functioning of schools. *But now the Indians are ready to do by themselves what the Supreme Government would not be able to . . . [T]he organized community should support the school they already have or build another one, at their own expense. . . .* If ten years from now each community has its own school, the fate of the Indian will change. . . . *Respected for his knowledge, the Indian will have strong fists to defend his rights.* (My emphasis)[6]

This statement more than likely refers back to 1896 when illiterates were officially denied suffrage (Mallon, 1995). Memories of the Indians' efforts at electoral participation might have been hovering in the atmosphere of this first congress. Tawantinsuyu's national project heralded a new political era, which was inaugurated with literacy campaigns designed to create room for indigenous citizenship and to turn Indians into modern, literate individuals.

In contrast to the dominant racial politics of the period (which assumed that literacy transformed Indians into mestizos), the committee's literacy campaign implied that literate Indians would remain Indians, with all the rights and duties of Peruvian citizens. This was even stated in the organization's Declaration of Principles.[7] Additionally, in a letter to President Leguía, Ezequiel Urviola, a radical,

[handwritten marginal note: literacy → racial transformation]

Indigenous conference organized by the Tawantinsuyu Committee, Lima, 1922. Photographer unknown. Photograph from the Lima magazine *Mundial,* August 1922. The original caption reads: "Pro-Indigenous Congress. The closing of the pro-indigenous congress was held in the Student Federation. Some of the attending delegates were wearing typical dresses from the regions they represented."

Puno-born lawyer who self-identified as Indian, expressed his yearning for the day when, empowered by literacy, Indians became "citizens and conscientious workers, valuable for the progress of the fatherland."[8] Moreover, he felt that educators should belong to "the Indian race." In another letter he petitioned the president: "I appeal to your spirit of patriotism and progress, begging you to [officially allow us] to establish schools on our own in the entire department of Puno; we also earnestly beg you to favor us with the foundation of a school of arts and trades [*escuela de artes y oficios*] for the indigenous race and preparation of pure-blooded Indian teachers in the city of Cuzco." Dora Mayer, a Lima-based radical indigenista and cofounder of Tawantinsuyu, published Urviola's letter (Mayer, 1921:108). In keeping with the tenants of the Tawantinsuyu literacy campaign, Urviola himself had rejected the mestizo garb and had dressed "in humble Indian attire, [and] replaced shoes with *ojotas* [Indian sandals], and his felt hat for a *chullo*" (Kapsoli and Reátegui, 1972:196). Thus he asserted educated Indianness. Another *puneño* who was actively involved in Tawantinsuyu was Pedro Chiquiwanka Ayulo, an intellectual who, like Urviola followed the same inverse "racial" trajectory, resigning his mestizo identity and asserting Indianness instead (Kapsoli and Reátegui, 1972:196).

The Tawantinsuyu Committee represented an assortment of socialists, anarchists, and indigenistas who used the modern language of progress and literacy to empower Indianness and in so doing rejected the assimilationist ideology that characterized some prevalent viewpoints of the time, for example, Mexican indigenismo. For Tawantinsuyu, equality was political, and did not require racial/cultural homogeneity. However, their project also drew from culturalist definitions of race, which they imagined (as did liberal indigenistas) as a historically inherited tradition in the form of customs, symbols, memories, and remains, some of which the Tawantinsuyu Committee used to launch its campaign for Indian citizenship. The name "Tawantinsuyu" (the Quechua name of the Inca Empire), linked the committee's project to the pre-Hispanic past. Likewise, the committee's official documentation bore a logo depicting a chain of mountains and a rising sun, symbolizing the Andes and the Inti, the sun god of the Incas, as an "emblem of the restoration of liberty."[9] Similarly, members of Tawantinsuyu commemorated symbolic Inca figures and dates with indigenous historic significance in the three congresses they celebrated in Lima between 1921 and 1924.[10] Moreover, the congresses themselves were stages where Indian identity was dignified and literacy was stressed. Proudly displaying their racial/cultural specificity, representatives to the congressional sessions spoke in Quechua, and their speeches were translated to Spanish for official authorities. According to a witness, the congress attendants were "very well prepared; they discussed their problems thoroughly. . . . Very few of them appeared surprised or afraid to speak."[11]

Since these political actions on the part of Tawantinsuyu took place in the early 1920s when there was a transition from conservative *civilismo* to the modernizing and populist, pro-Indian Patria

Nueva, the committee leadership rallied for its insertion in *leguiísta* politics. After the closing of the First Indigenous Congress, for example, members of Tawantinsuyu approached the president; "Delegates from Puno, Cuzco, Apurímac, Huánuco, Ayacucho and other places visited President Leguía to explain to him their problems. The commission was led by Víctor Tapia. Leguía offered them all the *garantías* as well as solving their problems. More schools, the distribution and restitution of their lands. . . . The indígenas publicly expressed their admiration and gratitude to Leguía and later approached the newspapers to inform the public about it."[12] Víctor Tapia is a name that the reader should bear in mind. He was an organizer of the committee's activities in Cuzco who, intriguingly, became an ally of the prefect of Cuzco, Belisario Godoy.

Early in 1921, the civilista congress representatives had blamed President Leguía for the social unrest that had occurred in the southern department of Puno at that time. Their specific complaint against the president was that he had appointed to governmental positions radical politicians such as Puno-born lawyer José Antonio Encinas (who was also a member of Tawantinsuyu), whom the parliament blamed of organizing the upheavals in his place of origin.[13] The news media emphatically linked the events in Puno to "antinational" and pro-Bolivian attempts at resurrecting the Inca Empire.[14] Accusations of antinationalism of this kind were not unusual, nor were they totally unfounded. A few years earlier, Puno had been the stage of an attempt at organizing an alternative nation formed by indigenous groups of Bolivia and Puno. Although they were not pro-Bolivian, there were rumors that its organizer, Teodomiro Gutiérrez Cuevas, had political connections in the neighboring country (Rengifo, 1977; Flores Galindo, 1986). In the early 1920s these conjectures touched a particularly sensitive nationalist nerve, as the accusations were almost simultaneous with a plebiscite to discuss the fate of several southern provinces lost to Chile in the late nineteenth century. In this juncture, the presence in Lima of hundreds of delegates to the First Indigenous Congress, asserting their Indianness by parading through main streets dressed in ceremonial garments, led to interpretations of a racially inspired war. The Indians were accused of trying to destabilize the entire country. According to an article in a Cuzco paper in

1922, "They attempt to divide Peru into races; they want to re-establish the Tawantinsuyu, the commune, and bring chaos to Peru. The very stability of the government is in danger, because we have to be aware that there are more than three million Indians, and if they are going to assume a bellicose attitude, it is going to be very hard to stop them."[15]

Members of the National Congress in Lima (composed mostly of hacendados) issued their condemnation of Tawantinsuyu, and demanded the committee's suppression early in 1921. However, given Leguía's need of allies among the popular classes, the Tawantinsuyu leadership was able to weather accusations for several years. Responding to the congressional charges, they in turn denounced the antipatriotic attitude of their accusers and underscored their own resolution to adhere to national laws. In one rebuttal they stated emphatically, "We do not want to crush the national institutions, but to stop the abuses and the vicious obstacles to their enhancement."[16]

Tawantinsuyu's leadership went beyond Lima-based intellectuals. The countrywide organizational structure branched into subcommittees located in the departmental capitals, with representatives in the provinces, districts, and ayllus. As much as possible, the representatives, called messengers, were literate.[17] Chosen at public assemblies in their places of origin, they received written identification credentials, which included their photographs.[18] The departmental branch of the Tawantinsuyu Committee in Cuzco was organized in October 1921. Local leaders were not "official" intellectuals but literate men (I have found no mentions of women among them) who lived in the countryside and traveled long distances to market their products in the neighboring departments of Arequipa and Puno. As one contemporary put it: "The best men among the Indians are organizing and leading Indigenous societies (*Sociedades Indígenas*) in spite of their relative lack of literacy" (Almanza, 1930:72). And nascent or not, literacy was in fact actively used to propagate Tawantinsuyu's goals. Concerned about the written propaganda, Luis Felipe Aguilar, a lawyer with whom the reader will be soon more familiar, lamented that the committee's *delegados* had sold "thousands of their printed sheet in the Canas, Canchis, Espinar and Chumbivilcas" (Aguilar, 1922:62). Those places were known in Cuzco as the Provincias Altas, the High Provinces. There, Tawantinsuyu delegates were usually *estancieros,* relatively wealthy ayllu members who owned large herds of sheep and alpacas. Since many of them were literate and because commerce was an activity associated with mestizos, away from their place of residence, they could identify themselves as mestizos. In their villages, because of their ayllu membership, they could define themselves, and were defined by the authorities, as Indians. It was precisely an estanciero from the highland province of Espinar, Nazario Zaico, who was appointed the secretary general of Tawantinsuyu in Cuzco.[19]

In Cuzco the committee framed its activities as lawful attempts to support the Patria Nueva and to foster the implementation of the presidential pro-Indian legislation, even against its opponents, specifically the subprefects of the High Provinces. In November 1921, Antonio Mamani from the ayllu of Huarca, in the province of Canchis, addressed a communication to Nazario Zaico, the departmental secretary of the Tawantinsuyu Committee. In it he accused a group of local landowners of ransacking the Indians' properties. Following this letter, the committee sent another one to the provincial subprefect of Canchis, urging him to behave as a "true representative of the government" and to follow the dictates of President Leguía, "an illustrious man who fulfills his obligations with the sacred pro-Indian crusade" (hombre ilustre y cumplidor de sus deberes de la sagrada causa pro-indígena).[20] In 1922, the committee organized two public demonstrations that were high points of their pro-leguiísta activity in Cuzco. The first commemorated the third anniversary of the Fourth of July, the day Leguía was sworn in for the second time as president in 1919. During the gathering, Miguel Quispe, a famous Indian leader whom anti-leguiístas abhorred, delivered the central speech demanding security for their properties and lives. It was addressed to the prefect, Belisario Godoy, who answered with "courteous words."[21] The second demonstration coincided with the national holidays celebrated on July 28. On both occasions the demonstrators displayed banners in open support of "our protector Mr. Augusto B. Leguía and his mighty minister Germán Leguía y Martínez," whose pictures they carried.[22] Such a juncture, with harmonious and close relations between state representatives and pro-Indian political leaders was unprecedented in Cuzco. Making the agreement even more obvious, the committee organized a homage to the prefect, the "representative of the paternal government whom we have the fortune to have ruling over the destinies of the country" (que en buena hora rige los destinos de la patria).[23]

This juncture came to an end when Leguía removed Belisario Godoy from the prefecture in 1923.[24] As Leguía solidified his power among liberal modernizers, he dismissed the more radical officials, and Godoy, who backed Tawantinsuyu, might have been among them. Allies such as Tawantinsuyu remained allies insofar as they supported Leguía's goals. An important test case among these was the Ley de Conscripción Vial, a forced-labor system to build roads. The law was Leguía's most visible weak spot in his efforts to appear as a champion of Indians, since the opposition felt that the roads would favor hacendados at the expense of Indian laborers. A heated debate about this controversial law sharpened the fissures within Tawantinsuyu in 1923, during the meeting of the Third Indigenous Congress (Kapsoli, 1984:222–225). As a result, radical leaders (among them the cuzqueño Víctor F. Tapia) gave up their positions as directors of the committee and the positions were taken over by conservative leguiístas. The new leadership named Augusto B. Leguía as the committee's honorary president, and the minister of government, Manchego Muñoz—a modernizing landowner from Huancavelica, in the central Andean region—as its vice president (Kapsoli and Reátegui, 1972:188). These events (including Godoy's removal and Tapia's resignation) were closely linked to others in the highest spheres of the government: in the early months of 1923, Germán Leguía y Martínez had resigned his position as minister of government and was replaced by Manchego Muñoz. The reason for Leguía y Martínez's resignation was his disapproval of the president's intentions to reform the Constitution in order to allow for his reelection. José Antonio Encinas, the indigenista advisor of Tawantinsuyu and a congressman, was imprisoned for having defended Leguía y Martínez (Basadre, 1961:chaps. 171, 180). The indigenous congress held in 1926 was the last of the congresses. In 1927 President Leguía had solidified his position enough to outlaw the committee and ordered: "Indians should make any claim they have directly to the government or to the juntas that represent the Patronato de la Raza Indígena."[25] The Patronato was established in 1922, and represented the government's official indigenista arm (Kapsoli and Reátegui, 1972).

In 1927 the president did not need Tawantinsuyu anymore. What he needed was the support of the local landowners whom the committee had repeatedly denounced as gamonales, and which the Patronato would treat as lawful hacendados. The president shifted his alliances and concurred with the liberal indigenista distinction between hacendado and gamonal. Combining the prevalent beliefs about racialized morality with his modernizing thrust, he asserted: "[The gamonal is] diseased in his moral and civic responsibilities and retarded in his business . . . for his failure to realize that the toll he forcibly extracts from the Indians would multiply a hundredfold if he worked to keep them well paid, well fed, and content instead of squeezing out their very last energies. The gamonal seems to have a head of stone for the Indian's tribulation because he has a head of cement for the most elementary principles of modern economics."[26]

In the 1970s, a progressive military junta dismissed this distinction, and forced by the peasants — who were massively seizing hacienda lands — expropriated large agrarian properties, regardless of whether they belonged to modernizing hacendados or regressive gamonales.[27] Back in the 1920s, however, gamonales won the round; their accusations against Indian rebels — and the definition of their political activities as rebellions — became historical facts, even against the many written denials that indigenous leaders published in the regional press.

Production and Denial of Indian Rebellions

During the initial years of the 1920s, the Tawantinsuyu Committee's activity altered the political life of the cuzqueño countryside, particularly in the High Provinces, where the confrontations between ayllu estancieros and private landowners intensified and became more frequent. Virtually a frontier zone, land titles were scarce, even nonexistent; "justice" and "law" were euphemistic terms, and power depended on private armed forces (Poole, 1988). Local authorities (specifically the subprefects) were tacitly independent from the central government and hence virtually omnipotent. The boom in wool production and the subsequent price crisis had provoked serious land and market conflicts among local landowners, estanciero and peasant ayllu members, and merchants (Piel, 1967; Orlove, 1977; Burga and Reátegui, 1981; Jacobsen, 1993). In such a context, the presidential indigenista rhetoric, and its early endorsement of the Tawantinsuyu Committee, implied a critique of the regional dominance of traditional authorities. Likewise, it implied support for the estancieros' attempt to obtain legal land titles for their ayllus. Undoubtedly, the presence of the committee in the High Provinces shook the foundations of traditional authorities. Accusations of antileguiísmo against those authorities were effective weapons: in 1921 the government removed the subprefects of Canas as a consequence of complaints from indigenous delegates (Burga, 1986:480).

Maybe reacting against this governmental decision, on April 4, 1921, a few months before the First Indigenous Congress met in Lima, the subprefects of Chumbivilcas, Espinar, Canchis, and Canas sent a series of telegrams reporting upheavals. From Livitaca (Chumbivilcas), the authorities reported that Indians had occupied the Plaza de Armas, and distributed fliers containing *principios proindígenas* ("pro-indigenous principles," probably a reference to the committee's Declaración de Principios). After listening to "Indians who [had] arrived from Lima," the meeting had "quietly disbanded," the telegram reported. In Espinar, a confused subprefect, after witnessing the same type of gathering, claimed that the Indians were "instigated by hundreds of gamonales who intend to subvert order." Señor Villa, the Canchis subprefect reported that he had already imprisoned four Indians and was organizing parties to capture others who were burning haciendas.[28] This clique of subprefects, who were the authorities of the High Provinces, would become in the next few months the target of Tawantinsuyu regional leadership. Their mutual animosity derived from their competition for grazing lands and for control of the regional wool and livestock market and shaped their political desire to attract Leguía's support.

On June 25, 1921, the same subprefects denounced the presence of

Tawantinsuyu in their four provinces, and claimed that the Indians were organizing a generalized indigenous upheaval. The newspaper headline read: "Indigenous uprising in the Province of Canas. Five hundred Indians under the command of the aborigine supreme chief, Valentín Choqueneyra. He orders the Indians to obtain the newspaper *Tawantinsuyu* [since it] contains information about indigenous rights. [The situation] means the restoration of the Empire through blood and fire."[29]

The article denounced the appointment of an indigenous subprefect (whom they identified as Lucas Huaraya) and narrated a scene in which "the supreme aborigine chief Valentín Choqueneyra" had directed a meeting of "one thousand five hundred Indians from different provinces." At the gathering, the reporter observed the presence of "more than three hundred women cooking food for the Indians who [had] declared the war." He implied that the radical congressman José Antonio Encinas had attended the meeting. Two days later, another newspaper article reported how the subprefect had discovered a plot to burn the village of Checca, in Canas, and kill all its white inhabitants.[30] To prevent a racial confrontation, the article said, the subprefect had captured twenty-five Indians "who had been gathered in Checca" and took them to Yanaoca, the capital of the Canas. He suggested that the Indians' meetings were part of a general upheaval involving the provinces of Chumbivilcas, Espinar, and Canas.

From my viewpoint the subprefects were trying to stop the incipient organization of the local branch of Tawantinsuyu, as it would mean an effective challenge to their power. The meetings that the local authorities were reporting as "prerebellions" might very well have been local gatherings sponsored by Tawantinsuyu to celebrate the inauguration of the First Indigenous Congress in Lima, which started on June 24, the same day that the "rebellious Indians" gathered for the first time in Checca. It was not a coincidence, then, that the judge found a Tawantinsuyu newspaper among the prisoners.[31] To outlaw the committee and legitimize the persecution of its leaders, authorities presented the meeting as part of a conspiracy "to reinstate the Empire," starting with the Indians' appointing their own authorities. Once the subprefects and their group had situated themselves defensively, they were in a position to capture the insubordinates, imprison them, and demand the presence of troops to sustain their control of the region. Drawing from G. Joseph's comments about how notions of banditry could have aided authorities to suppress political movements, I argue that using accusations of antinationalism, racialized as antiwhite, local authorities criminalized Tawantinsuyu organizers to nullify their political claims (1990:26).

Rather than ending with the imprisonment of the conspirers, the conflict actually heightened at that point. A few days after the "rebels" had been jailed, a local landowner, Leopoldo Alencastre, died. A document prepared by the judge remarked that the same Indian faction gathered in Checca since June 24, had killed the landowner on the 30th of the same month.[32] Presenting the death as a result of a violent Indian riot, the ensuing description of the murder could not have been bloodier. It was initiated by Esteban Alencastre, nephew of the deceased. In a telegram to the newspapers he said: "Insurgent Indians attacked the estate of my uncle, Sr. Leopoldo Alencastre, barbarously assassinating him, mutilating his cadaver. They burned down the house, stole money, clothing. Burial took place yesterday. If a permanent garrison with ten men is not established in each district, other killings are feared."[33] The previous day, the same newspaper had published an even more terrifying and bloodier version of the episode: "At dusk [July 1] . . . more than five hundred Indians burst into town in the most devastating fashion. . . . [The cadaver of Alencastre], according to reliable information I have obtained, was mutilated member by member and thrown off a cliff. . . . I have information that the Indian cannibals [*antropofagos*] remain in hiding in the mountains, with their desire to satiate their bloodthirsty ferocity unabated."[34] The inconsistency between both versions is obvious. Suffice to ask how they could bury a corpse, as the nephew of the deceased claimed they had done, if according to the correspondent, the Indians had eaten it, or in the best of cases, "thrown it off a cliff"? But the early days of July 1921 were not a time for coherence. The celebration of the Independence Centennial approached, and Tawantinsuyu leaders were visiting with the president with apparent success: he demanded the resignation of the subprefect of Canchis (where Alencastre died).[35] But faced by the threat of indigenous actions, provincial authorities confronted it decidedly. Backing their subprefect, the "Vecinos de Canchis" produced an impressive communiqué, where they acquitted themselves of gamonalismo, using liberal indigenista terms to delegitimize the Indians' actions and reinforce their story of an indigenous uprising. Indians were organized in an "exterminationist avalanche . . . insatiable hordes of cannibals [*antropofagia*] amongst which there has been discovered various outbreaks of sedition instigated by notoriously dangerous political agents."[36]

Echoing these rumors, Cuzco representatives in the Congress reported that the region was being invaded by political instigators who incited the Indians to rebel.[37] In the midst of the convulsion, another dead person was identified. This time the victim was an Indian called Domingo Huarca, who had died earlier, in May that same year. He was an estanciero leader from Espinar, who had visited Lima along with a delegation of Indians from Canas, Espinar, and Chumbivilcas, and had contacted the Tawantinsuyu Committee in March 1921.[38] The death of Alencastre, the "white [*misti*] landowner," and of Domingo Huarca, "the Indian *comunero*," became integral to a contemporary oral and written historiographic tradition about "Indian rebellions" in Cuzco. Initially aided by the prevalence of a particular concept of race (and later, ethnicity), this tradition was built upon the presupposition of rigid essential cleavages between Indians and whites. (Many years later, in the 1960s and 1970s, academic "peasant studies" and political Marxist-Leninist analysis represented this period as an example of millenarianism, characteristic of both the revolutionary potential and political limits of "the Andean peasantry." I will elaborate this point later; meanwhile I return to 1921.)

To explain Huarca's death the Espinar authorities sent an avalanche of information to the local press in the same turbulent month of July 1921.[39] They described an Indian riot "against all the powers of the republic," targeted not only against gamonales (whom they defined in elite cuzqueño terms as illegitimate land owners and abusers of the Indian) but also against *haciendas inmemoriales* (timeless haciendas), that is, legitimate landholdings possessed by honorable owners. To counteract the assault, and "legitimately" defend what was honestly theirs, the authorities and hacendados had sent their own armed troops to capture the Indian leaders. Domingo Huarca, they said, died in this confrontation, "shot by one of his partners." Following the pattern established by authorities from Checca—the place where Alencastre died—the article continued, saying that the Indians had held a meeting where they proclaimed their own authorities, in hope of reinstating the Inca Empire. At the meeting they had been able to identify "an instigator from Lima, a man called Andrés Vicaña" (a founder of Tawantinsuyu in Cuzco). He was allegedly inciting the Indians to rebel, collecting money for the Tawantinsuyu Committee, and "teaching the Indians to exterminate the white inhabitants." The article also disclosed the presence of another local leader of Tawantinsuyu, Nazario Zaico, who, "appointing himself secretary general of some organization [Tawantinsuyu] had led the attacks on the haciendas and the public forces."[40] The last report from the Espinar authorities that I was able to locate, appeared in August 1921. It conveyed desperation over this antinational and antiwhite Indian movement, which allegedly menaced the department's capital and indeed the nation: "This indigenous movement, if it is not contained opportunely, will increase greatly. The very imperial capital will be besieged next. Only God knows what scenes of savagery await the Fatherland!"[41]

The accusations of upheavals did not deter Tawantinsuyu leaders but, on the contrary, gave them a better target. They responded to the last message from the authorities of Espinar, and all the previous ones, with written refutations of the versions that presented the Indians as cannibals ready to invade the civilized sectors of Peruvian society. In their refutations Indians presented themselves as Peruvians striving for their civil rights, and for the country's progress. The nationalist arguments of these refutations confirm that Tawantinsuyu had imagined an alternative nation, one that included Indians. Crucially, the active use of the local and national press confirmed that the committee agenda conceived of literate Indians as citizens. To anti-indigenista government officials and to most of the press, this was a subversive ploy. From their viewpoint "the indigenous race" was unprepared for national feelings, just as literacy was extraneous to "Indians," as such. Nation-builders of the dominant groups simply ignored the many written denials of "rebellions" that the Tawantinsuyu local leaders produced.

In July 1921, at the peak of the accusations of widespread indigenous conspiracy, Indian delegates from Livitaca also denied the existence of such plots. They wrote: "It is completely false that we want to organize any kind of upheaval; we only pursue justice and *garantías* from the prefecture."[42] Espinar representatives followed Livitaqueños and addressed a public communication to the "Peruvian Nation." In it, they disclosed "the stupid inventions of our torturers [*verdugos*], who, in order to hide their despicable crimes have malevolently invented the farce . . . that we [the Indians] . . . have rebelled against the white inhabitants." The message further explained that the local authorities had devised a plan to kill indigenous leaders because they had "demanded justice from the president and other higher authorities." The local authorities had partially accomplished their goal by killing "compatriots such as Domingo Huarca, Juan de Dios Charca, Pedro Huamán, and more than thirty other Indians." To intimidate any possible followers, the bodies of the dead Indians had been hung in the Plaza de Armas of Yauri. In order to present their version to the prefect and send the communiqué to the newspaper, self-identified indigenous delegates had fled Yauri, just as their foes besieged the area. Once in Cuzco, in the prefect's office, they had confronted the subprefect, who they called "our terrible enemy, gamonal of the province, and unfortunately an authority." In front of his superior, the provincial official had acquiesced and supported the Indians as the prefect ordered him. But this, they said was only a momentary pose. Nazario Zaico, the departmental secretary of the Tawantinsuyu Committee, signed the document.[43] Surprisingly, one month later, in October 1921, the subprefect resigned his position, "because the president credited the Indians more than himself."[44] This was the third subprefect resignation that had been induced by Tawantinsuyu activism in 1921. These victories were accompanied by the intensification of the committee's activities in the region of Cuzco, including rebuttals of accusations of antinationalism.

From Canas, Francisco Pauccara, also a committee delegate, wrote a long article explaining the circumstances of Leopoldo Alencastre's death and denouncing the retaliation of the authorities, who had killed several Indians. According to Pauccara's version, Alencastre was killed by his own partners, who either did it knowingly or were confused by the darkness.[45] He also denied that the events leading to Alencastre's death were part of any preconceived upheaval. On the contrary, he explained that in the month of June, they were preparing a military demonstration for the celebration of the Independence Centennial, meant to show the country that they — the Indians from Checca — were also capable of understanding the needs of the Patria. The military exercises that they were performing were absolutely legal, as they had obtained authorization from the prefect, he affirmed. Moreover, Pauccara added, to avoid a clash with district and provincial authorities, they had retreated to the estancias to organize their military display. There, under the orders of an army sergeant, they started their exercises on June 22. On June 30, while they were awaiting the prefect, who had announced his arrival, they were attacked at midnight by the landowners and merchants of Layo who brandished rifles and guns. There had been no provocation from their side.

Pauccara's narration also demanded the removal of the authorities from Canas and highlighted the contradictions between the prefect and the local subprefect. District delegates of Tawantinsuyu supported Pauccara's version and identified the Canas subprefect and his subordinates as antileguiístas. Mariano Sullcarana, for example, addressed a letter to President Leguía in November 1921, in which he directly accused the authorities of being

addicted to the previous regime of President Pardo, when [the subprefect] was a secretary of this province, and ever since he has abused us. Now that he is the subprefect he wants to ignore your government. After our interview with you, Sr. President, we went back to our homes because you had given us your word that our constitutional rights [nuestras garantías] would be respected, but we could not reach our houses because he is chasing all of us who went to complain to you. This is why we denounce this subprefect who is celebrating in the province, saying that your government has ceased and that you are not president of the Republic anymore and that you have been replaced by Sr. Pardo.[46]

The same letter requested the president to appoint a man called Víctor Tapia to be subprefect of Canas. "He was the same man that accompanied us in our visit to you," Mariano Sulcarani mentioned. Tapia, who was a member of Tawantinsuyu in Cuzco had accompanied the delegation that visited Leguía when the First Indigenous Congress ended in July 1921. Hipólito Pévez, a founder of the committee, recalled Tapia in his memoirs as "a fervent defender of the indigenous race" (1983:141). Tapia was not appointed subprefect of Canas, but the following year when Belisario Godoy was prefect, he was a scribe in the prefecture of Cuzco.[47] Such a close interaction between a high state official and the leader of an indigenous organization was new, and certainly unexpected. In the latter months of 1922, the interaction between the prefect and the power clique of the High Provinces was, at least, uneasy, and this favored Tawantinsuyu. In December 1922, the Alencastres, the landowning family that had lost Leopoldo, saw his local power weakened. One of its members, a man called Agustín, complained that the military governor, Comisario Gonzáles, had not protected his lands from Indian invasions. Outraged, he also asked for his replacement and accused him of being an agent of the Tawantinsuyu Committee.[48] Unfortunately for the Indians, the combination of forces that favored them did not last long. The shifts in Leguía's politics after his reelection as president in 1923 gradually led to the banning in 1926 of Tawantinsuyu.

At the time, accusations of rebellion were frequently against political foes and even involved leading cuzqueños.[49] A newspaper commented: "It is becoming a comfortable system to attribute any common crime . . . to politics or to Indian uprisings, so that impunity covers with its protective cloak delinquent acts that demand the severest sanction."[50] Given this context, the charges against Tawantinsuyu were not surprising. More than likely, the credit that provincial subprefects gave to accusations of "Indian rebellions" depended — partially at least — on the political inclination of these provincial authorities and their liaisons with the local power cliques. Usually, antileguiísta subprefects supported denunciations of rebellions. The opposite would occur where the authorities were sympathizers of the New Fatherland, as happened in the province of Paucartambo. There, in November 1922, landowners accused Miguel Quispe, a leguiísta Tawantinsuyu leader, of organizing an up-heaval. Alarm spread when it was rumored that the leader "appoint-ing himself an Inca, [had] occupied Paucartambo with his troops."[51] Instead of requesting troops to crush the rebels, the subprefect of Paucartambo, recently appointed by Godoy, denied the validity of the rumor. He sent a telegram to his superior in Cuzco, the prefect, that read: "Miguel Quispe and others, bringing music and flowers, presented himself in a respectful way to salute [my] office, mani-festing [that he] had attended [the] Indigenous Congress held in Lima. . . . [He also] presented official communications from the Development Ministry ratified by you to concede them guarantees whenever necessary."[52]

Miguel Quispe denied the alleged uprising, confirming the sub-prefect's information. He explained that his enemies — rather than he himself — had labeled him "Inca."[53] Instead, he stressed his political identity as a leguiísta. When interviewed by two prominent indi-genistas, he denied insurgent activities. He said: "I went to Paucar-tambo . . . carrying a decree from Prefect Godoy in which he ordered the subprefect of that province to give us guarantees . . . [against the landowners from Saillapata]. I did not go with a warlike attitude. . . . [T]he proof is that I brought the subprefect flowers and we went about hoisting the flags that the president gave me. The residents [vecinos] became alarmed because the consciousness of their respon-sibilities makes them tremble."[54]

Certainly the agreement between dominant and subordinate poli-ticians in Paucartambo was exceptional by regional standards. Yet it suggests that a correlation between uprisings and local antileguiísmo might have undergirded the accusations of upheavals in the High Provinces, the stronghold of antileguiísta subprefects, and the region from where relatively prosperous estancieros were actively building linkages with the Tawantinsuyu Committee.

Indigenistas' Reactions to the Tawantinsuyu Committee

Liberal indigenistas doubted the certainty of "uprisings." Early in 1922, the local newspaper El Sol — where they were influential — published the pro-Indian liberal evaluation of Leopoldo Alencastre's death (in Canas) and Huarca's rebellion in Tocroyoc (Espinar). In it the authorities of the High Provinces were referred to as criminals and the validity of their reports was questioned: "We only learned of the bloody events of Canas and Espinar from the biased reports published by some of the very criminals involved [referring to the provincial authorities], and of course they presented the facts to us completely inverted and adulterated. There is no one, not even one among the partners or brothers of the deceased [Alencastre] who participated with him in the struggle, who can certify that the Indians killed him."[55]

By dismissing the subprefects' version of events, liberal indigenistas implicitly acquitted the Indians of rebellion. Yet they blamed the Tawantinsuyu Committee for inciting Indians and fostering turmoil in the countryside. In 1921, Félix Cosio, a well-known lawyer, had warned the local intellectual community about the activities of the committee, telling them that "indigenous leagues have come forth in most of Cuzco's regions, and they have a propaganda committee in Lima" (Cosio, 1921). The following year, Luis Felipe Aguilar, an ardent Indian champion and a trendsetter among indigenista lawyers, blamed the committee for the regional turmoil. He wrote: "The so-called indigenous conflict has been provoked by that infamous committee, which has stolen and continues to steal from the Indians as not even all the gamonales have ever done."[56] Curiously, he concurred with another lawyer, Dr. Casanova, who was not considered an indigenista. Months earlier Casanova had remarked: "That committee has sole responsibility for the difficult situation all property owners are going through and is responsible for the massacres as well."[57]

The agreement between cuzqueño liberal indigenistas and nonindigenista lawyers and landowners should not be surprising. It was based on notions of legitimacy and property, which, as Deborah Poole (1990) has suggested, were then central to legal practice in Peru. In Cuzco, "legitimate property" (embedded in the racial ideology of decency) represented the crux of the indigenista distinctions between gamonal and hacendado, whereby the former was a fraudulent (mestizo) landowner, while the latter (a caballero decente) righteously owned ancestral properties. Likewise, legitimate collective property of ayllu lands defined Indians. The distinctions are conspicuous in Aguilar's writing. For example, he evaluated Tawantinsuyu's activities in accordance with the tenets of decency: "The claims against landowners include many of the real exploitative gamonales, but they also ominously include other men, who are not only innocent of the charges made against them, but who are honorable gentlemen, real benefactors of the indígenas."[58] Accordingly, Aguilar assessed the indigenous congresses of the committee as "absolutely futile masquerades," useful only to "tell the story of the gamonal to some apostolic and compassionate [limeño] journalists," who lacked basic knowledge about the nature of Indians and the Cuzco region.[59]

In 1922, in the midst of the regional agitation, Aguilar published a book titled *Cuestiones Indígenas*. The press considered it "a work of enormous relevance and contemporary importance, 'must' reading for authorities, hacendados, owners, and professionals, and all those interested in solving this extremely important [indigenous] problem, and concerned by the enhancement of our nation."[60] Although intended as a legal treatise, it went beyond lawyers and attracted a wide audience because of the solutions it proposed to the "Indian problem." Like many of his indigenista colleagues, Aguilar believed that the social danger Indians represented (their *peligrosidad*) was the result of the tyranny of the regimes that had subdued them, and had thereby hindered the education of the indigenous race, and promoted their primitive ferocity. Thus, although the region was agitated, Indians were not the only ones to blame. Their criminal instincts and ferociousness had been provoked by external circumstances, more specifically, by the gamonales, the worst oppressors of the Indians (Aguilar, 1922:63). Protecting the region from violence entailed preventing gamonales from unleashing the Indians' ferocity. Likewise, for Aguilar, it entailed revealing the fraud represented by the Tawantinsuyu Committee, which was "telling the insignificant and stupid Indians that . . . they will recover all the haciendas and lands that whites and mestizos currently possess" (Aguilar, 1922:101). The solution Aguilar proposed was to respect both Indian *and hacendado* legitimate properties. The latter was something Tawantinsuyu was not doing, he said. Aguilar identified Tawantinsuyu local leaders as *cabecillas*, the worst exploiters of Indians, yet another type of gamonales, and even a more dangerous one (101–107).

It should come as no surprise that when the League of Southern Hacienda Owners (Liga de Hacendados del Sur) organized in 1923, its founders used indigenista language to free themselves from any responsibility of being anti-Indian in their attitudes or actions (Collins and Painter, 1990). Likewise, they identified gamonalismo as the source of the regional social tension. Clearly, "legitimate" landowners could join the wide legal doctrine of liberal indigenismo, despite their anti-Indian persuasions. The dominant liberal version of cuzqueño indigenismo that Aguilar represented had more in common with the hacendados than with the Tawantinsuyu radical advisors, in spite of sharing with them the title of indigenistas. Illustrative of the discrepancy is the debate Aguilar held with Dora Mayer, a limeña intellectual and a non-Indian founder of the Tawantinsuyu Committee.[61] Raising one of the first Marxist arguments in Peruvian indigenista debates, she disagreed about the cuzqueño distinction between gamonales and hacendados. While acknowledging her "brilliant masculine thought, exquisite sensibility, and noble sentiments," Aguilar wrote extensive critiques of Mayer's arguments. First, he delegitimized her interpretations of the reasons for the Indians' misfortune, which Mayer had attributed to landowners' exploitation of Indians. Aguilar invalidated these points by arguing they represented an "exclusively theoretical point of view," and lacked "the knowledge provided by direct experience with the indigenous population." Moreover, Mayer was not a credible source, since she had received the information from Indians, who Aguilar considered to be insincere by (racial) nature and thought to harbor such antiwhite racial hatred that they could not distinguish friends from enemies, much less gamonales from hacendados.[62] Thus, Aguilar warned Mayer, "If the Indians of Peru triumph, the writer would then see, if either one of us, she or I, would escape their vengeance, or all the indigenistas who have sacrificed and continue to sacrifice for the sake of their redemption much of our own lives."[63] The conclusion of Aguilar was that the committee had erroneously empowered Indians: they were racially treacherous. Indian leadership and their engagement in politics were racial absurdities. Being a politician required loyalty and reason, and Indians instead had instincts that showed an "invincible aversion toward the white man" and "ungratefulness toward their benefactor."[64] Clearly, from Aguilar's viewpoint Tawantinsuyu was an unviable project, given the absurdity of indigenous leadership: "Fortunately for the white citizens, the Indians lack intelligent and prestigious leaders who can focus and shape their aspirations and who can unite their dispersed forces to resist or attack, and thus avoid those partial and ineffective upheavals, by organizing instead a real political campaign of social and economic defense" (Aguilar, 1922:105). To avoid the "illegal" representation of Indians by the Tawantinsuyu Committee, liberal indigenistas recommended that gamonales' abuses should be reported to the Patronato de la Raza Indígena. Created by Leguía in 1922 as part of his official indigenismo, cuzqueño elites used the Patronato to counter gamonales' power and to curtail Tawantinsuyu's leverage. Composed of lawyers and other distinguished cuzqueños who were either hacendados themselves or personally acquainted with them, the Patronato was legally and socially equipped to identify what they themselves had defined as gamonales. In sharp contrast to Tawantinsuyu, their defense of Indians distinguished good landowners from abusive ones.

Backed by liberal benevolence, the Patronato mounted a crusade to prevent the abuses perpetrated by "the improvised hacendado," "the lustful priest," "the dishonest judge," "the astute and social-climbing hack lawyer" and "by all the other species of mestizos." Similar ideas supported the arguments of the lawyers who defended the "Indian rebels" in the courts. This defense, parts of which I describe below, confirmed that integral to indigenista politics was a racialized legal campaign against illegitimacy of property and blood, elements that caballeros conceived of as the intertwined racial-moral causes of regional violence and Indian criminality. To protect society, Indians needed to be protected from gamonalismo: this was an important indigenista goal.

The Liberal Indigenista Defense of the Indian
The Defeat of Tawantinsuyu Radical Indigenistas

Indigenous denial of rebellions did not mean that there were no conflicts between private landowners (gamonales or hacendados) and the users of collective land, the Indians. On the contrary, confrontations between both groups were constant and particularly intense during the initial years of the Patria Nueva. The deaths of Domingo Huarca and Leopoldo Alencastre, as well as the subsequent murders of several Indians in Espinar and Canas, were bloody consequences of these conflicts. Another was the death of Carlos Vidal Berveño, a landowner from Quiñota (in the province of Chumbivilcas), who died at the hands of a group of his enemies. Liberal indigenista lawyers interpreted the struggle as a confrontation between Indians and mestizo gamonales provoked by the abuses of the latter. In response to Berveño's death, Luis Felipe Aguilar published a trenchant article in which Berveño is portrayed as an archetypal gamonal:

> Sr. Berveño was like all the gamonales. All are *born and live* with the conviction that the Indian is a means of enrichment . . . [,] a being destined for iniquitous and merciless exploitation. . . . [T]here are already many cases in which the *Indians have committed true atrocities* horrifying everyone by the *refined cruelty* with which they proceed. [Public opinion] has not found words sufficient to anathematize them. But no one has ever bothered to inquire into the motives for such ferocity and savagery. . . . It is necessary to know that *the Indian never rebels unless he is harassed.* (My emphasis)[65]

This interpretation coincided with the liberal indigenista racial-moral taxonomy. As a gamonal, Berveño was immoral by birth; incited by his abuses, the Indians — primitive and innately harmless, but ferocious if provoked — killed him. But they were not responsible for their behavior. This portrayal of Berveño countered the Tawantinsuyu Committee's political definition of gamonales and simplified the political dynamic that led to Berveño's death. Probably Indians did assassinate Berveño, but this was the result of a complex power struggle in which the killers and the dead man had, for a long time, keenly disputed pasture land and control of the regional cattle and wool market. At that moment in the 1920s, Berveño's foes, the estanciero (Indians) were in league with the Tawantinsuyu Committee.[66] In what follows I outline the complexities of the power struggle that resulted in Berveño's and several other deaths. Then I examine the indigenista defense of the alleged Indian murderers, which was guided by ideals of liberal (and racialized) views of justice and informed by academic notions of positive criminology (Poole, 1990).

During his lifetime, Carlos Vidal Berveño had made a long list of enemies and allies in his hometown, Quiñota, and in the neighboring district of Haquira. His foes and friends were from assorted occupational backgrounds: estancieros, ayllu members, hacendados, wool merchants, cattle rustlers, and some outlaws who used the region as hideout. Racially, they were Indian or mestizo, some were *medio Indio* (half-Indian), and others were Indian on some occasions, and mestizo on others. Berveño's most important allies were the Arredondo extended family, which identified itself as hacendados, and which lived in Haquira (Valderrama and Escalante, 1981).

During the period between 1921 and 1923, the estancieros' quest to obtain from the state legal titles for their ayllus sparked their confrontation with Berveño and his allies. Legalizing the collective pasture land owned by an ayllu by naming it an indigenous community was an option offered by the 1919 Constitution of the Patria Nueva. Thus legalized, collectively owned pastures could be protected from private owners like Berveño, who customarily usurped ayllu possessions. At the time, pastures — the grazing area for sheep and alpacas — were highly disputed lands, as wool was the most significant source of cash income in the High Provinces. This region became extremely volatile when wool prices plummeted as a result of the international trade crisis provoked by World War I (Orlove, 1977; Jacobsen 1993). But the indigenous struggle was not only about lands. While they strove for legal titles, estancieros also conducted literacy campaigns that even led to the imprisonment of a teacher, who identified as an Indian and worked in the local school built by the ayllu members (Valderrama and Escalante, 1981:15).

Indeed, the principal indigenous leaders were literate, and, like Huarca, Zaico, and some others already mentioned, they were relatively well-off owners of large wool herds. At least two of them (Fortunato Mendoza and Crisóstomo Molina) had traveled to Lima, where they held interviews with central authorities denouncing land invasions. Crisóstomo Molina had even financed his trip by selling one of his bulls.[67] The third leader was Esteban Huillcapacco, about whom the local oral tradition had it that, as a child, he had been given as a servant to the family of a hack lawyer, who raised him and taught him to read and write. Back in Haquira, he had worked his way up to become a prosperous estanciero. The estancieros were backed by a group of *kuraqkuna,* traditional Quechua authorities, two of whom held the ranks of lieutenant governor and municipal agent and as such were local state representatives at the time of the confrontation (Valderrama and Escalante, 1981:14).

As part of their struggle, estanciero ayllu leaders communicated constantly with central authorities in urban Cuzco. In 1922, Molina and eight other ayllu members sent a letter to the Patronato de la Raza Indígena and another to the prefect of Cuzco, Belisario Godoy. The communications denounced the local authorities, who, the letters said, ignored their "concrete claims" and supported the hacendados, and most specifically Berveño.[68] Responding to the claims, the Patronato summoned Berveño and censured his abusive conduct. On learning this, the Haquira hacendados proceeded to intimidate the *indiada* (Indian crowd) and killed Esteban Huillcapacco, one of the estanciero leaders of Haquira.[69] Following this, another leader, Fortunato Mendoza, published (and signed) an accusation against the Haquira hacendados in the local press. He closed the article by addressing central state authorities: hopefully, he said, the advent of the Patria Nueva would mean the end of gamonales' era.[70]

In 1923 the conflict intensified in both districts. In Haquira, the estancieros' forces occupied the district's Plaza de Armas in July, in what hacendados interpreted as a declaration of interracial war. Indians were "appointing their own officials" and "hailing Tawantinsuyu, calling for death to the whites," the landowners claimed.[71] At the same time, Molina and Mendoza actively organized meetings and collected fees to pay the expenses to obtain legal titles for their indigenous communities.[72] In Quiñota, the neighboring district, the year of 1923 began with disputes for agricultural lands between the Berveño and Quiñoteño estancieros. An armed confrontation between both groups followed the incident.[73] On September 13, Berveño imprisoned a man called Huamaní and accused him of usurping the state representation and appointing himself a local authority.[74] Berveño was killed eleven days later.[75] Local authorities captured Molina and other Quiñota leaders, but Mendoza, who was from Haquira, managed to escape and hide. His family was tortured, raped, and killed.[76] From his hiding place, he wrote three letters in December 1923, one month after the massacre of his relatives and friends. He sent one of the communications to the local press; the other two were *oficios* (official communications) to the authorities in Cuzco (Valderrama and Escalante 1981:43).

In his public letter, Mendoza denied the participation of Haquireños in the assassination of Carlos Vidal Berveño, and openly accused the subprefect and the mayor of murdering Haquireños in retaliation for Berveño's murder. He asked the attorney in Cuzco to whom he addressed the letter why, if they had indeed killed Berveño, were they not judged and punished legally. "Are we not considered Peruvians by the laws of the nation anymore?" he inquired of the magistrate, pointing out that instead of being judged, authorities physically punished and killed them.[77] In concluding, Mendoza joined the other cuzqueño Indian leaders in their refutation of the indigenous upheavals: "We also know that people are talking about supposed revolts and dangerous Indians, which is false, a complete falsity invented by the gamonales . . . with the exclusive aim of . . . seeking pardon for their abuses for their exploitation, for their crimes. . . . [I challenge them] to demonstrate to us a single concrete case of revolt or even of individual or collective threat; they won't be able to do so ever because we have never attempted any of this, despite how much we are frequently slandered and accused of hairraising uprisings."[78] Mendoza's communication was not by any means an Inca-revivalist manifesto. Instead it was a strong denunciation of the crimes committed by provincial authorities and a claim that his adversaries' testimonies about Indian rebellions were false. In December 1923, the month when Mendoza's letter was made public, a trial to judge the assassins of Carlos Vidal Berveño began. It went on until 1928.

The atmosphere in cuzqueño elite circles must have been contradictorily suffused with antigamonal feelings and anti-Indian terror. In this environment, indigenista champions asserted their antigamonal doctrine and implicitly justified Indians' actions and absolved them from guilt. Many months before Berveño's death, Luis Felipe had peremptorily acquitted Indians: "Although I admit they have racial defects, I justify their actions in terms of their being individual acts of defense against the current enemies."[79] Liberal indigenistas did not see the regional turbulence as a confrontation between politically organized Indians and provincial authorities, where the former questioned the legitimacy of the latter to represent the state. Instead, indigenistas argued, the regional violence was produced by the natural antagonism between two racially opposed types, gamonales and Indians.

The indigenistas' implicit interpretation of Berveño's death was that the gamonal had provoked the Indians' ferocity. From this viewpoint the political dimension of the conflict disappeared, as did the self-identified indigenous politicians who had repeatedly sent the newspapers and the Patronato communiqués explaining that they were not rebelling. Indigenous politicians were reduced to ferocious beings, moved by their instincts for self-defense. Modern liberal indigenistas were not historically equipped — intellectually or emotionally — to understand a political program that included articulate indigenous leaders. On the contrary, their conceptual baggage blinded them to the fact that insurgent indigenous leaders might be what Guha would call, "subjects of their own struggle" (Guha, 1983:4). From their perspective, a "civilized" Indian, using modern political reasoning to claim national citizenship was an impossibility. Guided by that image and by their desire to protect Indians, liberal indigenistas launched a pro-Indian campaign and even paid with their own money to bail out the innocent prisoners.[80] Félix Cosio led the legal defense of Indian defendants in the court. He proclaimed that he did so "more than as a professional duty, out of a feeling of merciful humanity, to help them as much as possible and within licit means so that they may recuperate their lost liberty."[81] Cosio, like Aguilar and many other indigenistas, was guided by his yearning for social justice and by his knowledge of positive criminology, which taught that crime could be effectively repressed and society protected by controlling the environment and the social factors that induced the deviant conduct (Poole, 1990:352). From their viewpoint, Berveño's crime had been provoked by his own actions; in killing him, Indians were only taking justice into their own hands.[82] Granted they did so ferociously, but were not responsible for this behavior. Ignoring their racial lack of responsibility was a tremendous error of the national legal systems, which treated Indians as civilized individuals, which they were obviously not. To protect society Indians had to be civilized — not punished — and gamonales were to be controlled.

But the district attorney did not accept this interpretation. In September 1927, he sentenced all the culprits of Berveño's death to six years in prison.[83] Félix Cosio protested the sentence. His argument was that the Indians had attacked Berveño under the influences of the "unconscious influence of an agitated crowd." This limited the Indians' responsibility and was legally considered a "mitigating circumstance." The lawyer presented the Indians as irrational human beings, guided by animal-like instincts who were defending themselves in an extremely abusive situation. During the following days, other defense lawyers argued against the sentence, contending that as a result of Berveño's abuses, "in all indigenous families . . . a violent emotion of terror was born [which exploded] in a sudden and irrational defensive reaction. . . . [T]he Indians got drunk and attacked, expressing feelings of fury [against their exploiter] who endangered the life of the poor Indians."[84] Summarizing his strategy Cosio published an article entitled "Una fórmula legal conveniente," (An Acceptable Legal Formula):

> Those tumultuous tendencies are naturally more likely to exist . . . in the less cultivated masses, in those who are closer to their gregarious customs, in the rustic sites where solidarity manifests itself as the primordial sentiment of common defense against the harshness of nature and the ferocity of those who suppress their most precious rights. The Indians of our highlands will be the groups most susceptible to these collective deliria, unwrought by the brutality of their exploiters and aroused by any agitator who provokes the gruesome explosion of their rage.[85]

This interpretation is highly racist from a late twentieth-century viewpoint. However, in the 1920s, it represented an alternative to conservative criminologists of the classical school who considered that all men were equal before the law. Denying "mitigating circumstances," classical criminologists argued that punishment had to be apportioned strictly to the nature of the crime (Gould, 1996:170). Instead, Cosio and his aids emphasized the social and environmental causes of the crime, rather than evaluating the punishment in terms of the crime; his defense might have been inspired by the teachings of Enrico Ferri. Highly influential among Peruvian criminologists (Poole, 1990), Ferri had argued that the primary principle of penal justice was to consider the personality of the criminal, "in place of the objective gravity of the crime," and thus, "penal sanctions had to be adapted to the personality of the individual" (Ferri, 1911, quoted in Gould, 1996:171). Taking into account social causes instead of the crime itself was a well-intended liberal position, which, to no-body's surprise, wanted the racial status of the individual to be taken into account, and in this specific case, the inferiority of Indians.

Cosio's defense suggested that any legal sanctions for the culprits had to be based on "the specific circumstances" of the Indian crimi-nals. Eventually, the "pro-Indian" indigenista criminologists inter-preted what could have been a social movement led by literate indig-enous leaders under the banner of Tawantinsuyu as a desperate and irrational action of pathologically abused masses, led by instinct and not by a political rationale. Crisóstomo Molina, Esteban Huillca-pacco, and Fortunato Mendoza were totally ignored as politicians; instead, they were presented as victims of the gamonal Berveño and his allies. In prison, they had no alternative but to acquiesce to this portrayal. A document signed by Molina read: "The sentence is igno-minious [infamante] for all of us unfortunate beings who, with the denomination 'indigenous race,' form the majority of the region . . . since in the Quiñota events we have done nothing but unleash [our] ferocious social instincts."[86]

The legal documentation for this case is incomplete, and I could not find the final outcome of the trial. Probably the Indians' sentences were reduced, judging from the new Penal Code issued in 1924, which shows signs of some indigenista influence. Using the notion of mitigating circumstances this new code qualified Indians as "semi-civilized, degraded by servitude and alcoholism." It recommended that judges take into account their "degree of mental development, their degree of culture and their customs." Then, they should proceed to punish the Indians "cautiously" (prudencialmente).[87] This argument was central to the defense of the culprits in Berveño's death. Although it may have reduced their individual sentence, it also altered the course of their social struggle for complete citizenship as Indians. Contrasting with the early 1920s when declaring Indianness publicly could be empowering and even defiant, in the decades to come Indianness lost this potential. "Indian" was reduced to an insult, and the courts became almost the only public space where an indigenous cuzqueño would claim being one. There, they would assert being Indian to deny full responsibility of their actions (and thus mitigate their penalty), resorting to legal claims of lacking the essential liberty proper of civilized persons, known in legal lexicon as *libre albedrío* (Poole, 1990). The indigenista-inspired Penal Code enjoyed a long life. A group of limeño judges still used it in the 1980s, to "help" a young man who had migrated from a "peasant community" to Lima. Minimizing his guilt, the judges "considered him a semi-civilized Indian and reduced his sentence to eighteen months."[88]

The Historiographic Production of Indigenous Messianic Rebellions

In 1967 Jean Piel, a French historian, published an analysis of what he considered "one of the first turbulences among the vast agrarian tempest that swept the Andes during this period" (1967:395). The theme of the study was the events surrounding the death of Domingo Huarca in Tocroyoc, Espinar. Piel deemed his work "the beginning of the contributions to the historical analysis of one of those upheavals which occurred in the southern highlands of Peru, in Cuzco and Puno, between 1920 and 1930."[89] His analysis linked Leguía's Incanist discourse to the revival among peasants of latent Andean mythic ideologies:

> Among the Andean peasantry, the Incaic themes thoughtlessly exalted by the government and by the opposition [the radical indigenistas] communicated a hope: that of the *mythic rebirth* of the Andean "nation." This *messianic thrust* can be perceived in every indigenous rebellion from the 16th and 18th centuries (particularly

in that of Tupac Amaru) and *seems to survive* even at present. It is *grounded in . . . myths* such as those of Inkarri. . . . [I]t is not coincidental that, on showing their anger on one particular day of 1921, the demonstrators (in Tocroyoc) shouted "Long live Tawantinsuyu!" . . . This was not only the result of an artful indigenous appropriation of a theme used by the government in its official propaganda, but, *above all a wail in which a despised culture, a culture which was systematically persecuted since colonial times, recognized itself. . . . It represented the promise, beyond the punas of Tocroyoc that the rebellion would extend to other punas, and other highlands of the ancient Inca Empire. That Empire that would return in effect in the following years.* (1967:396–397, my emphasis)

My italics highlight Piel's emphasis on the idea that a timeless Andean culture lay behind the "Indian rebellion" in Tocroyoc. In the previous section I argued that the racial concepts of the indigenistas kept them from seeing Indians as political leaders. In a similar fashion, although carrying different conceptual baggage, an essentialist notion of culture obscures the indigenous display of modern political tactics in Piel's analysis. He described Huarca's personality as a modern Andean leader, mentioning that Huarca had served in the army, that he was literate (as he had attended school to "an advanced degree"), that he had traveled to Lima, and that he was in contact with other regional indigenous politicians. Yet Piel's view of Andean peasants as victims and of their culture as messianic — and therefore, according to his view, outside modernity — colored his final interpretation of what happened in Tocroyoc:

In 1921, the community of Tocroyoc is a victim of the administrative authorities, a victim of the large landowners, a victim of the intermediaries of Yauri and Ocoruro. . . . Additionally, the community is a victim of an unfavorable economic situation. They need nothing more before they mobilize behind the program of their spokesman Domingo Huarca. To this we may add a colonial situation which in fact relegates everything Indian to the inferior world of the despised caste, and which in response provokes a will to violence, buried but latent, *only waiting to manifest in any more or less messianic form. Everything is in place for a rebellion.* (1967:400–401, my emphasis)

Piel introduced his study with a description of the economic situation and of the Patria Nueva policies, yet when he shifted to Tocroyoc his analytical lens is mostly local. Therefore, the political historical impasses involved in the triangular negotiation among local Tawantinsuyu leaders, the subprefects, and Prefect Bernardino Godoy—which were, I believe, linked to presidential policies—are absent from his analysis. The local leader Nazario Zaico, who was also the secretary general of the Cuzco branch of the Tawantinsuyu Committee, is absent from Piel's rendition. Domingo Huarca, rather than being an active member of Tawantinsuyu, was in the French historian's words "a *prototypical case* of those Indian caciques who had *survived* the colonial and independent period in Peru." Similarly, unaware of the local political activities of the Tawantinsuyu Committee, Piel interpreted the indigenous hailing of Tawantinsuyu as being a millenarian (and in his view prepolitical) call for rebellion. The "Tocroyoc rebellion"—which he reduced to "Huarca's attempt"—failed, he concluded, because, "in spite of its contacts with the exterior, the Tocroyoc movement remained essentially local in its objectives. These pitted ayllu members only against neighbors and immediate exploiters. Beyond that [Huarca's followers], invocations of the Tawantinsuyu meant that [the movement] was doomed to envision their bigger, long-term objectives in a mythic form" (1967:403). Visions of "local peasants" involved in a mythic way of thinking—crucially incompatible with modern politics—plague this study, which appeared shortly after another historian, Eric Hobsbawm, had published *Primitive Rebels* in 1959. In that study, Hobsbawm represented peasants as prepolitical, where Piel saw them as messianic. Both saw them as "local."

After Piel's brief study, the "Tocroyoc events" and Domingo Huarca became a recurrent reference in regional historical analyses of Cuzco. These later analyses do mention the political rivalries between some provincial subprefects and the state representatives, either the prefect of Cuzco or the Patronato de la Raza Indígena (Burga, 1986; Rénique, 1991; Glave 1992). Yet by this time, scholars had already defined the 1920s events in Cuzco as "rebellions," and in some cases even "messianic" ones. The historiographic tradition following Piel connected with the version of events promoted by the High Provinces subprefects and neglected the Indians' denials of the rebellious character of their strife. Consequently, it did not see the events as part of an alternative proindigenous quest, which entailed forcing the president to implement his declared pro-Indian rhetoric and to gradually actualize an alternative image of the nation in which Indians could become citizens, qua Indians. Rather, the events were presented as rebellions, and antistate ones at that. Ironically, the authors of the 1960s–1970s academic version that denied modern political status to the 1920s indigenous efforts were radical propeasant activists. I do not mean to exclude myself from the group: I too contributed to reproduce this allegedly propeasant view of Andean culture, explicitly or implicitly, as a student in anthropology classes or as an activist in political events.

Wilfredo Kapsoli, a historian and professor at San Marcos University in Lima, was among the first in the Peruvian academia to argue the messianic character of the 1920s alleged rebellions. In 1967, Kapsoli and others published a political-academic journal titled *Campesino* (Peasant), which was politically linked to the Confederación Campesina del Perú (Peruvian Peasant Confederation). As I elaborate in chapter 4, the sixties were years of intense leftist organization in the countryside. According to Peruvian historian Luis Miguel Glave, *Campesino* provided an academic platform for historians to write "primarily about peasant movements, the topic that legitimized history as a politically useful discipline, to be practiced by militants striving to revolutionize the countryside" (1996:17). *Campesino* lasted until 1975, and in 1977 Kapsoli published *Los movimientos campesinos en el Perú, 1879–1965*. This book was the first comprehensive presentation of peasant movements in Peru. Significantly, its analysis included the year of 1965, a climactic one for peasant political mobilization. Following Piel's line of reasoning, Kapsoli believed that "millenarianism" had informed the Tocroyoc struggle and the political strife of the *colonos* (sharecroppers) of the hacienda Lauramarca. In his words: "Peasant consciousness flourished displaying its own ideology: the Apus, the Auquis, Tawantinsuyu, Inti, the Inkas. In sum, Andean cosmogony was the subjective movement that impelled the peasant movements. . . . Precisely where the productive forces maintained their archaic and primitive forms, this millenarian ideology demonstrated the greatest strength and projection" (1977:63). Inspired by Marxism, authors like Kapsoli considered the "productive forces" of peasant economy as precapitalist and therefore insufficient to produce a "peasant consciousness." Yet Andean peasants could still be rebels: their consciousness stemmed from their own millenarian ideology. At the time, this was a daring reformulation of orthodox Marxism, which reduced ideology to false consciousness. Yet in this interpretation "messianism" — which I do not aim to dismiss — eclipsed abundant information indicating that the Andean peasants had very pragmatic goals as well, particularly so in the case of Lauramarca. Intriguingly, Kapsoli himself presents the following information, which he however neglected to analyze. Led by Francisco Chillihuani, "active delegate to the indigenous congresses of the Tawantinsuyu Committee," the "millenarian peasants" of Lauramarca had petitioned for an eight-hour workday, for wages (instead of free labor), and for the revision of hacienda property titles (Kapsoli, 1977:70). They even organized an innovative form of strike. They refused to sell their wool to the hacendado and transacted directly with the representative of what we would now call a transnational company: "The Saldívar were powerless to stop the Indians from taking all the wool in Lauramarca to sell in Checacupe and Sicuani" (Kapsoli, 1977:70). There, they sold their wool to representatives of English wool-trading firms.

Several years later, another Lima resident and historian, Manuel Burga, presented additional documentation confirming the success of Lauramarca leaders at connecting directly with the wool merchants, thus skirting the hacendado's brokerage: "The indígenas conquest was concrete: it was a very original way to break with precapitalist constraints imposed by the hacienda systems in southern Peru" (Burga, 1986:501). Subordinating this aspect of the struggle, Burga produced one of the most elaborated interpretations of the "rebellions" as "a utopian project that emerged from the popular indigenous imagination." He dismissed the restoration of the Inca Empire as an invention of landowners:

Reality and imagination combined in the minds of the landowners, in an effort to give coherence to a fiction that they wanted to convert

into the political program of the Indians: the restoration of Tawantinsuyu. . . . The nativist restoration was a product of the imagination: the landowners were well aware of it, *but how could peasants
make the same distinctions with similar precision?* For a peasant,
marginalized from the rights of citizens, attached to his customs,
traditions, and language, hearing the rumors [about the restoration
of Tawantinsuyu], the landowners' fiction could seem logical, necessary, even a nice proposition. (1986:477)

Amazingly, Burga believed that peasants were unable to distinguish their reality from the invented version of landowners. Unable
to reconcile modernization with utopia, Burga continued his interpretation of the events: the indigenous peasants followed the landowners' invention and developed it into a vision of utopia, the millenarian restoration of Tawantinsuyu. This project, Burga remarked,
was *different* from that of the Tawantinsuyu Committee, which he
considered a modern political proposal elaborated by nonindigenous leaders (1986:497).

The 1920s indigenista essentialist definition of Indians survived in
the 1980s under another essentialist notion, that of "peasant culture," which held it useless to think of Andean individuals as being
simultaneously modern politicians and local ritual specialists using
Andean cultural symbols in their mobilizations to action. These two
possibilities excluded each other; messianic Indians were not theoretically viable as modern leaders.[90] Although it was popular among
intellectuals and nonindigenous activists, the way that the indigenous leaders conducted their political activities denied the conceptual opposition between "Andean ideology" and modern politics. In
Lauramarca, for example, important local leaders were also Andean
ritual specialists, and, far from being contradictory, their dual activity was compatible and even necessary (Eloy Neira, personal communication; Gow, 1981). Likewise, in the political struggle that resulted in the death of Berveño, at least two Andean ritual specialists
participated: the lieutenant governor and the municipal agent, that
is, two individuals who were thus also state representatives (Valderrama and Escalante, 1981:14).

Armed with an ahistorical concept of Andean culture (defined as

"peasant" culture) and a rigid Marxist account of class consciousness, the 1960s propeasant intellectuals refurbished the anti-Indian
authorities' 1920s story, presenting the rural political situation of the
time as one of *peasant* rebellions. Certainly, the new radical interpretation introduced changes. On analyzing Domingo Huarca's and
Leopoldo Alencastre's deaths, leftists intellectuals did not speak of
the "Indians' ferocity" but of their "cultural millenarianism," a form
of peasant class-consciousness and "resistance." However, within
this new interpretation, the Indians' written denials of rebellion disappeared. Even historians who questioned the factuality of the rebellions, like Flores Galindo, dismissed the written repudiations as
anti-Indian forgeries. To me this is consequential, as it reveals at least
partial adherence (in the 1960s) to the essentialist racial/cultural
definition of Indians as illiterate — and therefore irrational — which
was a central argument in the indigenista dismissal of the Tawantinsuyu Committee in the 1920s.

Considering that testimonies "in which the peasants express themselves directly" were lacking in the historical record, Flores Galindo
turned instead to "look . . . in the silence that cloaked peasant life
during the whole republican period: a defensive culture that protected itself in lies or in muteness" (1986:281). This assertion echoed
indigenista representations of Indians, and particularly those of
Luis F. Aguilar and Luis E. Valcárcel. From their viewpoint, Indians
resorted to lies or silence to defend themselves from their oppressors.
Early in 1923 Aguilar had described the typical Indian as someone
who "lies, steals, and kills, to defend himself from the social conspiracy that overwhelms, oppresses and annihilates him" (1922:59).
And a few years later Luis E. Valcárcel followed with: "When the
Indian understood that the white man was simply an insatiable ex-
ploiter, he withdrew into himself. He remained silent, hieratic, like a
sphinx" (1937:38).

Immersed in the academic culture of his time, Flores Galindo had
inherited the indigenistas' legacy and had shaped his definition of
"Andean peasant" accordingly; therefore, he used prevailing images
of the unspeaking silence and illiteracy of the indigenous people and
implicitly equated both with written silence. Based on this, he denied
credibility to the communiqués that literate Indians wrote denying

the "rebellions." It is problematic, of course, as Joanne Rappaport has indicated, to privilege orality over written communication, "even among those who are not generally characterized as participants in the world of literary production" (Rappaport, 1994:177). Like Flores Galindo, many other analysts of the period dismissed the written disclaimers signed by numerous self-identified indigenous leaders that were published in cuzqueño newspapers. The general impression of intellectuals was that Indians had not produced the communiqués. "They were always mediated by the landowner, the journalist, the judge, or any other authority," Flores Galindo remarked (1986:281). Ironically, during the period of the so-called rebellions, dismissing this kind of written denials "because Indians are illiterate" was a common practice precisely among those individuals that indigenous leaders had accused of inventing rebellions. Enticed by images of Indians as illiterate, silent beings, the 1960s historiography suppressed the written information local leaders produced.

Conclusions

In spite of their efforts, indigenous political leaders were prevented from representing themselves. In a situation similar to the one Gayatri Spivak (1988a) presents in her analysis of subaltern representation in India, indigenista intellectuals eventually spoke for indigenous leaders in 1920, as Marxists did in 1960, and in so doing expressed their own political agendas. Yet, unlike the situation in Spivak's analysis, in which the subalterns *acted* but did not speak, self-identified indigenous leaders from Cuzco both acted *and* spoke about their actions. Their written and physical struggle communicated an alternative racial and class path for themselves. The Tawantinsuyu Committee project saw literacy as the means that would allow Indian citizens to participate in national political life as peasants, merchants, estancieros, or professionals, without becoming mestizos. From this viewpoint literate Indians were officially entitled to preserve an indigenous identity. In the 1920s this proposal contradicted dominant national projects and their prevalent racial politics about Indianness, which assumed that literate Indians were destined to become mestizos. Although liberal indigenistas might have supported some of Tawantinsuyu's proposals, the committee's disregard of the distinction between gamonal and hacendado was an important reason for the liberal animosity toward radical indigenistas. The consensus among the liberals was that Tawantinsuyu Committee radicals incited Indians. Hence they ignored the Indians' political claims. In the 1960s, from the viewpoint of leftist politicians, the "subalterns' " written declarations of political agreements with Leguía, the developer of Peruvian capitalism, contradicted the Marxist intellectual images of peasants as a class opposed to the state. Similarly leftist intellectuals could not see the 1920s indigenous leaders' assertion of Indianness and their use of Andean culture as a modern political strategy. Instead it entered the new historiography as an unconscious revival of Andean myths. In a significant historical irony, the 1960s radical class analysis ignored the other radical project of the 1920s, which was to create Indian citizens.

What then were the alleged "rebellions"? From my perspective they were what the cuzqueño insurgents declared they were: a plot against the local authorities of the High Provinces, yet not against Leguía or the state. Aware of an unforeseen favorable political situation, indigenous local leaders intensified their activities in the High Provinces to remove the political clique that had supported Leguía's predecessors in the government. Additionally, these leaders were organized at the regional and national levels in the Tawantinsuyu Committee, whose central radical indigenista leadership had adopted a national literacy project to strengthen indigenous identity.

Aguilar and Valcárcel would have dismissed my interpretation of Indians as intelligent, modern political actors, who were not irrationally reacting against gamonales' torments nor stupidly following Tawantinsuyu indoctrination, but were, instead, organizing against their foes and implementing an alternative regional (and maybe even national) project. However, the two indigenistas would have agreed with me that the "rebellions" were not rebellions in the sense that local authorities cast them. Aguilar said: "Most of time the uprisings [*las sublevaciones*] are deliberative gatherings, where [the Indians] discuss some aspects of their situation and deliver their ideas, without practicing any act of hostility, free from the pressure and immediate presence of the white man. Mestizos regard those meetings as a menace, and before anything happens they rush to prevent their imagined effects, producing a wholesale Indian manslaughter" (1922:28). Valcárcel, in turn produced his interpretation of the "rebellions" in a short story:

> The Indians had risen up. Their rebellion was simply a refusal to work for the landlord. The news reached Cuzco, greatly exaggerated, and the alarmed prefect sent fifty policemen to suppress the uprising. The Indians had gathered one Sunday in the town square. They ate and drank together, recalling times past when their open-air feasts were presided over by the Inka or the Kuraka. They were all assembled together! They were conspiring! Without further ado, the leader of the soldiers gave the order to shoot. The Indians did not flee. Nor did they defend themselves, since they were unarmed. Bullets were everywhere and the first victims began to fall. (1978: 60–61)

The two most vocal indigenistas denied the authenticity of rebellions. In most cases they were a forgery produced by the gamonales, they said. In other cases, they were wrathful explosions provoked by the same abusive landowners. These doubts filtered into the writings of the two most prominent Peruvian historians: Jorge Basadre and Alberto Flores Galindo. In a critique of Jean Piel's interpretation, Basadre (1971:20) argued that the events called rebellions might have lacked the dimension the new historiography attributed. At the time, local historians had ignored them, he said. Years later, discussing the historical accuracy of the alleged rebellions and commenting on Basadre's remark that "the most important event in 20th century Peruvian culture was the increasing awareness [*toma de conciencia*] among writers, artists, men of science, and politicians about the existence of the Indian" (Basadre, 1978:326), Flores Galindo asked: "Without rebellions — real or imaginary — would this [awareness] have been possible?" (1986:308).

In Flores Galindo's view, whether rebellions were real or invented was irrelevant to the more important issue as to what the indigenous rebellions produced: they made Indians visible in the political and academic discourse. While I certainly agree that the rebellions brought Indians to the political fore, I would modify Flores Galindo's assertion: what the rebellions did was to reinforce the specific, dominant image of Indians as illiterate and prerational. Moreover, in the courts, indigenistas certified the idea of Indians as irrational rebels, unprepared for citizenship, and thus defeated the project that the Tawantinsuyu Committee shared with self-identified cuzqueño indigenous leaders.

One final caveat: I do not mean to imply that local committee leaders were unanimously setting in motion a solidly shared political project. Rather, I suspect their projects were heterogeneous and possibly, at a point, conflicting. Additionally these projects, whether conflicting or not, might have been utopian or even messianic, but historically so, and therefore they were politically modern too. Yet the dominant image of rebellions reproduced in the 1960s, by stuffing "Andean culture" with atemporality, obscured the political engagement of local leaders and made them exclusively "messianic messengers" moved by myths and utopias. Thus interpreted, rebellions provided the historical grounds to stimulate the leftist imagination to envisage a potentially revolutionary peasantry, possessing a millenarian culture, and directed by competent leaders: they had to be urban and literate, hence non-Indians. Thus in the 1960s, the "Andean peasantry" emerged as a group that was the natural (and subordinate) ally of the urban proletariat.

On their part, local rural leaders pragmatically looked for new political allies to connect their local struggles to the regional and national spheres of power. The 1930s marked a new political era in Peru, inaugurated with the creation of two populist political organizations, the Peruvian Communist Party and the Apra Party. The same year a military man, Luis Miguel Sánchez Cerro ousted Augusto B. Leguía from the presidency and was fraudulently elected the following year. His opponents were the Apra leader (Haya de la Torre), and Eduardo Quispe Quispe, a "puneño indígena" from the Communist Party (Basadre, 1964). During the electoral campaign, communists emphasized the indigenous identity of their candidate while subordinating race to economic factors. In this they followed the teachings of José Carlos Mariátegui who had pronounced: "The problem is not racial, it is social and economic; but race has its role in the problem and in the means to address it" (1981:44–46).

Cuzqueño communists joined their comrades' rhetoric and coupled revolutionary rhetoric with references to "exploited Indians."[91] At the dawn of Sánchez Cerro's rule, their program attacked the Ley de Conscripción Vial (which had survived Leguía's ousting) and supported the repossession of lands by ayllus. One of its fliers read: "Let us appeal to our soldier brothers who are workers and Indians like us: Do not fire against the ayllus, but instead help them to recover their lands!"[92] Some indigenista leaders who had been active in Tawantinsuyu allied with the Communist Party. Obviously, new ones joined in the new political period. Indigenous leaders adopted class vocabulary and activities in their political work: they self-identified as *campesinos* (peasants) and *compañeros* (companions) and organized *sindicatos rurales* (rural unions) as part of their struggle. From this position, they toppled the distinction between hacendado and gamonal coined by the indigenistas. In 1933, Mariano Turpo, a campesino from the hacienda Lauramarca was imprisoned on the charge of "communist" activities, as he had helped organize one of the first peasant unions. While in jail, he addressed a letter to his "compañeros del Sindicato de Campesinos de Lauramarca" (companions of the Lauramarca Peasant Union). In it he asked them "to insist . . . on our need for literacy as not knowing how to read makes us *more Indian [más Indios,* my emphasis], easy victims of the gamonales and their lackeys."[93] In this version, "gamonal" retained the negative implications with which indigenistas suffused it; the innovation was that, if needed, indigenous leaders could use the label to accuse gentlemen of abuses. Illustrating this, the gamonales Turpo mentioned, the official owners of Lauramarca, belonged to one of the most powerful elite cliques, the Saldívar family. They were respected gentlemen and ladies, the elite of cuzqueño society, who, during indigenista years, would have been sheltered by their decency from accusations of gamonalismo. Turpo (who in the 1920s was an aide to Chillihuani, an elder Tawantinsuyu leader) was a literate estanciero who had committed himself to build schools in Lauramarca (Eloy Neira, personal communication). In his letter he identified illiteracy with Indianness, considered an adverse social condition. Implicit was the message that literacy canceled Indianness, thus departing from the view of Tawantinsuyu's project, which was to use literacy in order to *assert* an empowered Indianness. Years later, in the 1960s, rural leaders who had called themselves Indians self-identified solely as peasants or compañeros. The label "Indian" was silenced and receded to the domain of injuries. I will return to this in chapter 4, where I also explain that this process, which I label "de-Indianization," did not mean shedding indigenous culture, as class analysts presumed.

3

Class, Masculinity, and Mestizaje

New Incas and Old Indians

I will tell you that the time has come for us to recognize that in
ourselves there is only fifty percent of Gutiérrez, and that the other
fifty percent is authoctonous blood. . . . We are descendants of the
Indians, the Kana runa [people from Canas] . . . we are mestizos
by blood and neoindios by spirit. — ANDRÉS ALENCASTRE
El Challakuy, ca. 1940

Under the influence of local and international political changes, discussions about race among the cuzqueño elite intellectuals changed
significantly in focus in the 1930s from the purist indigenista ideology to one that welcomed mestizaje as the project for national and
regional identities. This shift occurred amidst other regional and
country-wide political transformations. In the late 1920s, at the end
of the Patria Nueva, Cuzco became an important bastion of antileguiísmo in the southern Andes. Augusto B. Leguía's main opponents in Cuzco were the locally famous indigenista scholar Luis E.
Valcárcel and Víctor Guevara, a lawyer who was reputed as a conservative in Indian matters. They disagreed over Indians, but this difference was insignificant compared to the force of their shared antileguiísta commitment. When a military coup obliged the president to
leave the country, both politicians left Cuzco for Lima. Luis E. Valcárcel was certainly more prominent than Guevara, and Luis Miguel
Sánchez Cerro, the general who ousted Leguía, appointed him director of the important Museo Nacional, where he remained until 1964
(Osterling and Martínez, 1983).
   During the same decade, other prominent indigenistas also left
Cuzco to fill official positions in different parts of the country.

Among them were Luis Felipe Aguilar and Félix Cosio, who had actively defended Indians from charges of rebellion, as seen in the last chapter. Their absence, coupled with the dominant populist trend propelled by the central government, expedited the change in the cuzqueño intellectual leadership, which was replaced by a group that identified itself as opposed to liberal indigenismo, which they found conservative and even obsolete. The new group was significantly matched by the establishment at the national and local levels of two new political parties: the Apra Party and the Communist Party.

As in the rest of Latin America, the period between the 1930s and the late 1950s was marked in Cuzco by the sway of populism (Rama, 1996), and by the worldwide impact of World War II. In Peru, the initial years of the period were colored by an intense nationalist debate on two broad trends: indigenismo and hispanismo. Not surprisingly, Valcárcel was one of the important national spokespersons for indigenismo. Although his antimestizo feelings had not mellowed, his purist proposals included the idea that Indians could be gradually incorporated into the nation as agriculturalists, thus preserving their racial/cultural essence (Valcárcel, 1945). At the other extreme of the debate was the proponent of *hispanismo*, Víctor Andrés Belaúnde, a Lima resident and aristocrat, born in the southern department of Arequipa. He advocated an "integral Peruvianness," which he discussed in a book entitled *Peruanidad* (Peruvianness).[1] Although his hispanismo eventually projected a mestizo identity, this was a culturally "whitened" one, framed within the spiritual teachings of the Catholic religion and on respectable family values, both of which (he underscored) were legacies of the Spanish colonization (Belaúnde, 1965). In an era when Spain was swept by the fascist ideology of General Francisco Franco, hispanismo did not gain official support from the Peruvian state, which was moving in a populist direction. Instead, a mellowed indigenismo began shaping state educational policies from 1945, when Valcárcel became minister of education. From approximately the late 1950s until the early 1970s, in both the academic and political spheres, indigenismo competed with an insurgent leftist rhetoric of class. Official indigenismo engaged in rural development projects, ranging from the construction of irrigation channels to literacy campaigns in the countryside. Promoters of class rhetoric organized peasant unions and the seizure of hacienda lands. During the same time period (1930–1950), a new intellectual movement replaced former indigenistas in Cuzco. Valcárcel's absence, and the affiliation of his purist indigenismo with the national government, motivated an important shift in cuzqueño manifestations of indigenismo. Opposing purist indigenismo, local intellectuals hailed the mestizo identity of cuzqueños of all social backgrounds and brandished a new ideology which they called *neoindianismo*. Opposing hispanismo, neoindianismo was anticlerical, artistically inclined, and rejected all things foreign while claiming authenticity through spiritual mestizaje. As indigenismo had previously done, the neoindianistas defined race as culture, as illustrated by Alencastre's linking of blood and neo-Indian spirit in the epigraph to this chapter. The novelty was that at the heyday of this new period (1930–1945) the notion conveyed an enthusiasm for mixture and common vernacular art that was absent from previous indigenista manifestos. Likewise, in this new period, the accent on culture was intended to express a rejection of race, which cuzqueños, at this point, had begun to limit to biological aspects.

Rejecting biological notions of race was relevant internationally as a consequence of World War II. In Cuzco however, it represented a rhetorical shift. During the high period of racial thought (1900–1930), notwithstanding existing disagreements, dominant indigenismo had opposed racial biological determinisms by defining race as inheritable culture, soul, or spirit. When race was internationally questioned, neoindianistas preserved beliefs in the force of culture (soul or spirit) to shape identities, while dropping from their rhetoric references to race. This, however, did not eliminate the cultural determinism that had characterized racial thought during the preceding period and, consequently, cloaked in culturalist rhetoric race silently lingered. Yet this did not preclude some innovation. Neoindianismo inaugurated a new cuzqueñismo by including commoners and vernacular art in their projects. The 1934 celebration of the four-hundredth anniversary of the Spanish founding of Cuzco was an opportunity for the public presentation of neoindianismo. On this occasion, cultural authorities from the city council invited commoners to impersonate the Incas on official stages, thus transgressing some cherished indigenista "purist" canons. Nemecio Zúñiga Cazorla, a provincial priest whose Quechua dramas the preceding intellectual elite had censored, staged the central performance of the celebration, *Cuzco y los XIV Emperadores* (Cuzco and the Fourteen Emperors), performed by his Compañia Dramática Urubamba, which was made up of schoolteachers and informally educated actors from ordinary social circles.[2] Likewise, a provincial group of indigenous musicians led by a neo-Indian cultural authority presented an "Inca opera" called *Tito Kkosnipa,* in which the Inca was impersonated by "an Indian dancer, specially chosen because of his agility in performing the difficult *Danza Guerrera de los Pomacanchis.*"[3] Some actors and playwrights active in the indigenista years were swayed by the new trend and shifted from Inca theater to the writing and representation of village life and rituals. Luis Ochoa, who came from a prominent family, was versed in Capac Simi and had acted the part of Incas onstage in the 1920s, was among the playwrights who yielded to this trend; he staged in the 1930s a piece he had written, *Qosqo Qawarina* (Looking at Cuzco). In it, rather than presenting Incas, he depicted the confrontation between a brave Indian called Chapaco and his master.[4] These dramas called *costumbristas,* which had preexisted neoindianismo as a scorned dramatic genre, competed in this era with the representation of Incas and contributed to the exaltation of the common mestizo, the *cholo.*[5]

The populist promestizo rhetoric was complemented by an emphasis on masculinity that served to justify belittling the discriminatory attitudes of the elite and thus to reject purist indigenista canons. A contemporary critic (a neoindianista) illustrates this attitude: "Undoubtedly, the select audience of sissies and gente decente will find *El Santo del Patrón* [The Patron Saint's Day, the title of the drama] shocking, vulgar, and immoral because it is about 'cholo stuff.' Yet, this is exactly why this and other works that speak about the people and for the people ought to be presented and should become well known."[6]

The year of 1944 marked the climax of this overtly gendered populist ideology. Its highest achievement was the creation of Cuzco Day, along with its central staging of the Inca ritual of Inti Raymi. Specifically in this period, "culture" was the key semantic terrain in intellectual discussions about cuzqueñismo and national singularities, and thus it was a declared arena where cuzqueños of assorted backgrounds struggled to define the meanings of regional racial/cultural identities.

Cuzco
A Populist City

Cuzqueños received Leguía's fall with demonstrations of joy in the Plaza de Armas of Cuzco. They interpreted the ousting of the president of the Patria Nueva as the victory of regionalists over centralists, not just as an expression of support for the new president, Luis Miguel Sánchez Cerro. Starting in the 1930s, and through the following decades, local expressions of regionalism amalgamated with populism to become the dominant national political ideology in the country during that period.

Under the leadership of the two new parties, the Apra and the Communist Party, the combination of regionalism and populism soon became *anti-imperialismo,* which implied the assertion of strong, uncompromised *nacionalismo.* Antileguiísmo suited the manifestation of antiimperialist and nationalist ideologies, since the ousted president had granted concessions to several North American enterprises. Under the banner of nationalism, individuals of diverse political persuasions, from leaders of the burgeoning Communist Party to representatives of the governing military junta, attended the initial populist *mítines anti-imperialistas* (anti-imperialist political rallies). Speakers in the demonstrations included well-known ardent radicals as well as representatives of the status quo, such as the decano del Colegio de Abogados (dean of the bar association) or the mayor. For example, in October 1930, the Communist Party organized a political demonstration against the North American Peruvian Corporation, which administered the railroad system. The prefect of the city, Alberto Delgado, a well-known antileguiísta, declared that as a representative of the military junta, he would see to the people's demands because "he felt proud that the cuzqueño people had recovered their legitimate possessions."[7]

However, the populist honeymoon ended quickly. Sánchez Cerro was assassinated in 1933 (allegedly by an Aprista activist) and was succeeded by another general, Oscar R. Benavides, who governed until 1939 and banned the Apra and the Communist Party. He was replaced by Manuel Prado, a civilian, who governed until 1945, when José Luis Bustamante y Rivero assumed the presidency. That year the proscribed Apra party came out of its clandestine existence, only to be outlawed again in 1948 following another military coup, this one led by Manuel A. Odría, who governed until 1956 (Kapsoli, 1977). Periods of political persecutions (ordered by both the military and civil governments) against Aprista and communist politicians and intermittent truces characterized the period. The two parties used the periods of truce to express their populism by calling diverse social sectors to coalesce in their political programs. The political force of these groups was a result of both the political persecutions they endured and the active organization of workers unions throughout the whole country. As will be discussed in the next chapter, unionization (*sindicalización*) was particularly intense in the cuzqueño countryside during this period. Rumors about *sindicatos campesinos* (peasant unions) and "Communist Indians" may have begun to circulate in the 1940s. In 1946, for example, Julia Espinoza de Teves, one of the largest landowners in the province of Canchis, denounced the emergence of a "sindicato campesino among the communist indígenas of Lahua-Lahua," which, she stated, was promoted by the "Unión Provincial Comunista de Canchis."[8] As illustrated in this instance, the conventionally racialized social landscape of Cuzco, was becoming tinged with an emerging class rhetoric linked to notions of Indians as "peasants." Populism, however, colored this class rhetoric and served assorted social groups. Demands for better salaries and for lowering the cost of living by controlling the prices of food and transportation merged as central points in the regionalist rhetoric. According to the Peruvian historian José Luis Rénique, in those years "workers' demands for salary increases and for the improvement of living conditions became entwined with the repudiation of centralismo" (1991:186). Rulers responded favorably to these requests. In a visit to Cuzco, President Manuel Prado (1939–1945) and the local congressmen (who represented the cuzqueño landed oligarchy) donated a locale for the newly inaugurated Federación de Trabajadores del Cuzco, which, in the sixties, became the bastion of demonstrations against landowners and their political representatives (Rénique, 1991:175). On this occasion, however, Prado received homage from several of Cuzco's popular organizations, as well as from well-known communist leaders.[9] At the end of his government's term, the president responded to this favorable relationship with a salary hike for workers. The pattern was repeated during the government of José Luis Bustamante y Rivero, who officially recognized the Communist Party. This group had a wide scope at this time, as they focused on "forging a movement of popular unity, so vast that it should include conservatives and communists, independents and apristas" (Rénique, 1991:175). Because of the gains made by leftist class rhetoric, communists narrowed their view and gradually distinguished "antagonistic forces" where they had previously seen "popular unity." However, Marxist-Leninist rhetoric would survive for another decade before their activities reached a climax in the 1960s, a period I describe in the next chapter.

Undoubtedly, from the 1930s to the late 1950s, cuzqueños lived an intense political period. Yet, the city continued to be a small town. Despite its demographic expansion (from something over 12,000 to nearly 40,000 inhabitants), the urban areas had not stretched into the agricultural land that surrounded the city. In 1991, the director of archives for Cuzco, Bernardino Cecenarro, told me that "the first blocks of Avenida de la Cultura [four blocks away from the archive], where the public high schools are now located were still *chacras* [fields] when I first came to Cuzco in 1947." "This Avenida Tullumayo [where the archive was located] was an open, filthy channel where the river crossed, and openly ran to the station of the Peruvian Corporation, which then administered the railroads," he added. And he was not wrong. In May 1945, after visiting Cuzco, British envoy to Bolivia, wrote a note. In it he praised the Inca and Spanish architecture and lamented the physical aspect of the city, noting that, "in principal streets there are emanations from sewers and drains. . . . This reveals defects in the city's sanitary system."[10]

Coinciding with the dilapidated infrastructure was the city's relatively backward industrial development. In 1937 the generalized opinion among the highest cuzqueño authorities was that "with the exception of textiles, the state of the industries in the department of Cuzco is ripe for development."[11] The "working classes" that protested in anti-imperialist rallies were artisans either employed at or owners of workshops. The "proletariats" of cuzqueño industry were workers in a brewery or in the city's three textile factories. The *Guía General del Cuzco,* a commercial guide, described Cuzco as "a city of artisans. The most widespread workshops [are dedicated to] carpentry, shoemaking, smithing and tailoring."[12] Technology in workshops was limited, as was their capacity to employ labor, since these workshops were generally family enterprises in which the trade passed from fathers to sons, or where labor relations were immersed in ties of spiritual kinship (*compadrazgo*).[13]

Indeed not all artisans were poor, and probably not all of them were considered gente del pueblo, or working class. The most successful ones were beginning to transform their workshops into manufacturing enterprises. Among the most successful were those in the garment industry, headed by two tailors, the brothers Luis and Francisco Hermoza, graduates of U.S. and European institutes. In recognition of their contribution to Cuzco's development, the municipal council had honored them in 1928 and 1934. They owned "spacious workshops in the Plaza de Armas, with a large staff that fluctuates between twenty-five and thirty expert workers." The Maison Aguilar, owned by Señorita María E. Aguilar, was another successful enterprise. "Elegantly established in Espinar Street," it was a firm that produced "exquisite wedding gowns, sumptuous overcoats, and magnificent evening dresses." Señorita Aguilar employed "seven dressmakers and two competent tailors." Besides these two factory-workshops, which produced goods for elite consumption, there was a plant that manufactured "shirts, overalls, and handkerchiefs." It was owned by a *turco* (that is, a Lebanese or a Syrian) who had arrived in Cuzco a decade earlier, and it employed twenty female workers, "all of them young, all of them good-looking." A friend of mine who was born in the late twenties recalled her job in this "shirts and overalls" factory. "In the Fábrica Volcán I sewed shirts when I was twelve years old. . . . I started out sweeping the floor and I learned by watching. One day the ironsmith got sick and I replaced him. They paid me *a destajo* [on a piecework basis], just like the *maestros* of that time." As this vignette illustrates, in spite of their relatively large size, these factories were modeled on artisanal workshops. Other relatively "large" production plants included one chocolate factory, one ceramic works, two leather factories, a factory producing cookies, and two flour mills.[14]

The rhythm of industrial growth was slow; the urban infrastructure was stagnant. Apparently, life continued as it had always done in this provincial city. Yet, during this period, the inhabitants of Cuzco did see cultural innovations. The introduction of the radio was a technological change that suited the populist ideology and stimulated the new cultural politics. The first station, Radio Cuzco, was inaugurated in April 1936. Local civilian, military, and ecclesiastic authorities, and indeed members of populist parties, were all present to celebrate this important civic event. Since radios were not commonly owned by cuzqueños, to effectively reach the population the authorities ordered the installation of loudspeakers in the Plaza de Armas. The result could not have been more successful: "The popular classes have become the owners of the loudspeakers and of the Plaza de Armas."[15] In 1948, a second station was inaugurated, designated Radio Rural, which was later changed to Radio Tawantinsuyu.[16]

Another important change was the surge of tourism as an economic and cultural activity. In the 1920s, inspired by the frequent visits of foreigners (mostly archaeologists, novelists, or members of official diplomatic delegations), government officials, hoping to develop Cuzco's tourist potential, organized a branch of the National Tourism Corporation to be set up in Cuzco.[17] This institution was replaced in 1940 by the Touring Automóvil Club del Perú, an organization specially created to promote tourism in the country; it opened a branch in Cuzco "to attend to the tourists who visit this capital and its provinces." The representative of this agency in Cuzco was José Gabriel Cosio, a prominent indigenista, who had written one of the first tourist guides for visitors to the city of Cuzco.[18] When commercial flights became regular in 1948, tourism began a definite upsurge. It was clearly linked to the promotion of cuzqueñismo, and intellectuals wrote pamphlets legitimizing this venture by comparing Cuzco to other historical cities ("*la Atenas de Sud-América,*" the Athens of South America) and to familiar contemporary tourist attractions such as Toledo in Spain and Tasco in Mexico.[19] These efforts yielded positive results, and by 1959 Cuzco newspapers could report that more than 23,000 tourists had visited Cuzco that year.[20] In the 1970s cuzqueños experienced even higher economic benefits from tourism, but they had started the development of this industry in the 1930s.

Mestizaje
Neoindianistas against Indigenistas

The rejection of biological notions of race was an international progressive tendency that followed from the events of World War II (Barkan, 1992:271–341; Skidmore, 1993:205–207). As noted, since the turn of the century Peruvian intellectuals had been among the first to dismiss racial biological determinism and had instead equated race with inherited culture, conceived as the "soul" or "spirit" of a people. During this specific period cuzqueño indigenistas, renamed neoindianistas, removed the historical and cultural contents ascribed to race and rewrote the concept to connote phenotype and biology. Racism (then an emerging notion) became associated with biological determinism and official segregationist policies. With "race" thus defined, leftist members of the Communist Party discredited it as false consciousness and resorted to Marxist class rhetoric to distinguish social differences, previously attributed to (historically and culturally defined) race: "We do not have to go beyond the door of our houses to observe the parade of our diverse people: gentleman, lady, cholo or mozo, chola or mestiza, male and female Indians. These are our social classes, defined by their economy and not by their blood as believed by some naïve people — those who think their blood is blue and contact with the air turns it red."[21] The leftist position had to wait until the 1960s to gain regional (and national) significance. Until then, from the 1930s to the 1950s, the tendency was to use references to culture rather than class to naturalize social differences. Already present in earlier definitions of race, "culture" during this period continued to refer to the allegedly inheritable spiritual peculiarities of Peruvian social groups, which resulted from an assortment of historical legacies anchored in the diverse landscape of the country. Naturalized by history and inscribed in the geography, race was still silently invoked, as immanent cultural tradition, along with its dismissal as a biological concept. The rhetorical shift to culture did not cancel the racialized structure of feelings (Williams, 1977) underpinning cuzqueño society and continued to permeate practices of social discrimination as well as academic and political thought. "Racism without [biological] race" (Gilroy, 1990; Balibar, 1988) openly prevailed in Peruvian thought from the 1930s onward and continued to be articulated by racialized notions of culture used in Peru since earlier years.

Crucially, populist intellectuals associated the rejection of race with the rejection of notions of purity endorsed by old indigenistas. This suited Aprista politics, which, drawing direct inspiration from the Mexican postrevolutionary national experience, influenced the cuzqueño cultural movement from the 1930s to the late 1950s, when communists assumed the leadership. In this initial period, the Mexican indigenista José Vasconcelos influenced cuzqueños via aprista politicians. Their leader, Víctor Raúl Haya de la Torre, had worked with Vasconcelos during his exile in Mexico, where he had also founded the Apra party in the 1920s. Specifically, Mexican indigenismo influenced apristas' endorsement of mestizaje. They were joined by socialists and communists who identified this endorsement with a nationalist pro–working class position. Within this context, indigenista "purist" propositions lost their previous oppositional thrust and gradually entered the realm of official state legislation.

José Vasconcelos's denial of the existence of pure races and his support for racial-cum-cultural miscegenation expressed a rejection of theories that attributed the alleged degeneration of Latin Americans to racial hybridity. Aimed against European and North American thinkers, in this populist period the Mexican theorist's proposal had an aura of anti-imperialism that attracted Peruvian nationalist communists and apristas.[22] In his famous book *The Cosmic Race* (1925) Vasconcelos wrote: "The central thesis of this book is that the different world races tend to mix more and more, until they form a new human type formed by a selection of each of the existing races." In the chapter entitled "El Mestizaje," he proposed that if the racial mixture was in accordance with social laws of harmony, sympathy, and beauty, the new racial product would be superior to the original ones.[23] Vasconcelos's bid for mestizaje credited "the spirit" as the highest, invincible force that shaped mixed unions and that could improve even the most incongruous of them. This consideration of "the spirit" and "culture" in the shaping of social types allowed the Mexican indigenista nation-building project, and their celebration of mestizaje, to coincide with the explanations prevalent in Peru about social difference and the means to surmount its problematic aspects.

Cuzqueño aprista intellectuals embraced Vasconcelos's idea of mestizaje as the future vehicle for a continental identity whose unique combination of pre-Hispanic and colonial Spanish legacies traversed national frontiers and had the power to counter U.S. "imperialist" influence.[24] For example, Atilio Sivirichi, another Lima resident from Cuzco and a respected aprista intellectual, stated that "mestizaje [is] a universal law from which only small minorities that can be said to be 'racially pure' escape. It is a transitional state in America's spiritual process toward a new cultural formation."[25] If during the previous period "race" had a strong spiritual component, during this second one "the spirit" became the agreed reference for talking about the nation and national identity.[26] Mestizaje was (in the words of Sivirichi) the "spiritual, artistic, economic, and sociological issue" central to any nation-building project. Defined as spiritual essence, mestizaje blurred references to phenotype and conveyed instead intertwined allusions to virility, class, and culture, geographically tied to the highlands.

Among the main contributors to this notion of mestizaje was a group of iconoclast cuzqueño intellectuals who had been active since the early 1920s (when, coincidentally, Haya de la Torre spent several years in Cuzco, although he had yet not formulated his doctrine). This intellectual circle included artists, poets, and writers who belonged either to Apra or to the Communist Party and who were united by their common interests in culture, their opposition to the old indigenista canon, and their public irreverence toward (selected) elite social conventions.[27] Thus, for example, they rejected formal academic titles as paths to social ascent, and many of them were consciously "degreeless" intellectuals. They organized a cultural group called El Ande, invented an "oral periodical," and published several oppositional pamphlets.[28] Although they were as fond of cuzqueño culture as purist indigenistas, they rejected the indigenistas' liberal conservatism and instead styled themselves as a bohemian intelligentsia with a penchant for political innovation and the talent to join ordinary people's culture and merriment. They considered themselves the "dissident generation of 1927," and they named their ideology neoindianismo. They thus distinguished themselves from previous intellectuals known as the "escuela cuzqueña" (Cuzco school), the generation that had transformed the university in 1909 and produced modern indigenismo.

Despite severe discrepancies and animosities between the Apra and the Communist Party, neoindianismo represented the new regional-cum-nationalist project that cuzqueño aprista and communist intellectuals sponsored.[29] A foundational piece was a treatise, first published in 1930, titled *El nuevo indio*.[30] Its author, Uriel García, "was one of the oldest members of the dissident generation of 1927" (Gutiérrez, 1986:31). García, politically a populist, was supported by the aprista Drivers Union during his candidacy as congressman in 1939. Once elected as such, he helped legalize the Communist Textile Union of Workers in 1943 (Aranda and Escalante, 1978:40). Adhering to the international tendency to reject "race," he began his prologue to *El nuevo indio* with the following statement: "Our era cannot be one of the resurgence of the 'races' that created the original cultures of antiquity, nor can it be one of deterministic prevalence of blood over the intellectual process, and therefore over history. Instead, I think we have reached the predominance of the 'spirit' over 'race' and over blood" (1937:5).

Shaped by the spirit, "the New Indian" was not molded in terms of phenotype but styled on the invisible, moral excellencies inspired by the American nature: "The Indian is not only that bronze-colored man, with slit eyes, with thick, lanky hair, but also [any person] who grows internally upon contact with the incentives that this great American nature offers him, and who feels that his soul is rooted in the land. . . . The neo-Indian is not . . . properly an ethnic group but a moral entity. . . . Non-Indians are the guides of our peoples who give the continent its personality" (García, 1937:6).

Brandishing geographically bounded notions of cultural heritage and, by their own declarations, inspired by Henri Bergson's identification of art as the utmost spiritual manifestation, cuzqueño populists held that the indigenous culture had survived in serrano vernacular art, thus making the mestizo soul possible (Sivirichi, 1937:5). Significantly, they replaced the earlier, indigenista concept of racial/cultural purity with one of "geographically ascribed authenticity" as the proof of legitimate nationalism. Curiously, although neoindianistas countered indigenista canons by means of their appreciation of all things mestizo, they did not alter the class contents of the category: "the mestizo soul" referred to the moral essences of commoners and working-class people as it had in previous years. Consequently, gente decente continued unmarked as mestizo although they were granted the possibility of joining in the mestizo (plebeian) spirit.

Opposing the upper-class mestizaje projects elaborated in Lima (which they deemed antinational and hispanicizing), the regionalist nationalism of the neoindianistas hoped to *peruanizar* the country by using Cuzco as the original geographical source of their prospective *indolatina* (Indolatin) nation. This they saw as a means to build an "autochthonous" Peru. Anchoring their reasoning in geography, they argued that "the customs, the traditions, the ways in which Peruvian life is expressed and that form the substantive elements of Peruvian nationality have been preserved in the sierra, while the coast has lost them."[31] For Stuart Hall (1993), the new British racism has recoded race through references to cultural belonging. Notwithstanding obvious differences, new indianistas also recoded race, but they did so as environmentally instilled cultural authenticity and, indeed, belonging.

Using the sierra as their stage and serrano art as their expression, neoindianistas prevailed among cuzqueño intellectuals. In 1937, searching for national recognition of their preeminence the new dominant group created an organization that brought together "renowned intellectuals, representatives of every aspect of culture" and that they called the Instituto Americano de Arte (IAA), the American Art Institute. It was the Peruvian branch of a continent-wide institution that had representatives in Mexico and Argentina and other Latin American countries. The cuzqueño group was formed by historians, linguists, a folklore professor, lawyers, musicians, and painters. They did not hail from Cuzco's economic upper echelons: only two belonged to the landed oligarchy; the rest were middle-class urbanites, some of whom owned small rural properties. Yet the members of the assembly that created the institute were conscious of their position as the intellectual elite of Cuzco, and they attempted to keep membership "limited" to the founding members.[32]

Supported by a few United States academics who, during this period made frequent research visits to Cuzco, neoindianistas defined vernacular art as folklore and granted it academic status by inaugurating the teaching of folklore at the local university in 1943. Following a classic definition, cuzqueños defined folklore as "associated with songs, stories, customs, rituals and proverbs which shaped the collective spirit of a particular people" (Rowe and Schelling, 1991). While the study of folklore was a science, the practice of folklore itself existed in any society where an educated group (who did not necessarily practice it) coexisted alongside those who practiced it, the social stratum that lacked formal education.[33] Because of its all-encompassing definition and its inchoate quality, folklore did not exclude anybody. Thus it was the perfect arena for the encounter between academics (gente decente) and lay folklorists (gente del pueblo). Folklore as an academic discipline, and as a vehicle of expression of the mestizo soul, fit like a glove the populist political emotions of this period. Eventually, the promotion of folklore opened the way for the advancement of provincial intellectuals. Likewise (as I will show in chapter 6), it allowed for the mushrooming of nonacademic folklorists, who used their dances and music to express their alternative views about their region and their identities.

Cultural Authenticity and Masculinity
Neo-Indian Cholos

Neoindianistas' proposal of mestizaje was a regionalist public project aimed at forging the seamless (male) comradeship (Anderson, 1983) that cuzqueñismo allegedly required to coalesce as a political feeling of national scope. This project, as one of its partisans put it, rather than preserving pure Indian race/culture, aimed at "merging the two nationalities, to make one nation for all Peruvians, to erase the deep differences, so that all of us Peruvians can march together with one and only one national feeling" (Vidal Unda, 1938:53). But neoindianistas had a personal agenda as well. In the words of one of them, they expressed the desire to eradicate the "inferiority complex" that being serranos produced in (elite) cuzqueños.[34] Neoindianismo, as much as cuzqueñismo in general, was based on what Herzfeld (1997) has called "cultural intimacy," or the cultural awareness of social flaws, which in turn are also culturally constructed. In the case of Cuzco, the "flaw" resulted from the lingering nineteenth-century environmental determinism, according to which the mountainous Andean geography implanted in serranos regressive racial/cultural features. To counter their geographically determined inferiority, instead of discrediting environmental determinism, earlier indigenistas accepted it and claimed that the Andean landscape had in fact preserved the superior values of the racial/cultural "purity" instilled in Indians.

The neoindianistas shift from "racial purity" to "mestizaje" did not dismiss the effect of environmental factors. Indeed, they enlarged on it, with a gendered interpretation of the effect of Andean geography and the vernacular art it inspired. They elaborated a gendered interpretation of the behavior of their purist indigenista predecessors and linked it to indigenista intellectual and political ideas: cuzqueño gentlemen, including indigenista intellectuals, the neoindianistas claimed, were effeminate imitators of limeño aristocrats. Their lack of masculinity, interpreted as lack of valor, had prevented them from identifying with the regional unrefined culture and limited their performances to tame representations of Incas.[35] They had denied their folklore, which they only dared practice in the isolation of their rural haciendas or in the intimacy of kitchens, always excluding it from elegant *salones*.[36] Therefore, the neoindianistas argued indigenistas had belittled Cuzco instead of promoting its authentic culture. In a radio program broadcast in 1936, a passionate writer of the times, using the Quechua pseudonym Eustaquio K'allata, referred to former indigenistas as follows: "The uprooted ones, the small group of affected upper-class parasitic *señoritos* [ladylike men] and fake virgins . . . feel an ancestral hatred toward indigenous music, just as their slave-trading great-grandfathers must have felt toward the belligerent sounds of the *pututo* of Manco Segundo's and Tupac Amaru's armies, but these pretty children yield sheepishly . . . at the sight of imported useless rubbish."[37] Neoindianistas instead promoted "cultural sincerity."[38] They were going to represent what really belonged to cuzqueños. Unlike those effeminate gentlemen, mestizos could be authentic by valiantly feeling, sharing, producing, and performing serrano art. This was rough and unsophisticated, yet masculine like the surrounding landscape. To incarnate the neo-Indian authentic masculinity they chose the cholo as the prototype. In the 1940s, "the word 'cholo' acquired connotation of pride, of distinction, of authentic cuzqueñismo," wrote a cuzqueño historian recalling the neo-Indian years (Aparicio Vega, 1994:52).

To construct the cholo, the new elite was vague about his physical appearance and phenotype, thus allegedly dismissing race. The neo-Indian was "más bajo que alto, más obscuro que claro, más cholo que indio, más indio que mestizo, más mestizo que blanco" (shorter rather than taller, darker rather than lighter, more cholo than Indian, more Indian than mestizo, more mestizo than white).[39] The cholo, hence, incarnated a resolute denial of whiteness. Significantly, while defining the cholo neoindianistas repudiated race by repudiating whiteness. Yet, given the implicit association of whiteness with femaleness, they challenged male effeminacy, rather than "race," and certainly subordinated femaleness to "masculinity," glossed as the boldness to be unrefined yet "authentic."

The ideal neo-Indian was an essentially virile entity harboring a class component in his unrefined and putatively plebeian sensuality. In this interpretation, however, "plebeianness" did not belong exclusively to commoners. Rather, it was attached to the geography of the highlands, which irradiated roughness onto all those serrano males who, regardless of their background, yielded to the influence of their environment and dared to be unrefined and thus "authentic" Peruvians. From the neoindianista viewpoint, plebeianness defined national belonging and was not determined by race (which these intellectuals supposedly rejected) or by class origin. Instead, plebeianness was a spiritual leaning that was born out of highland-shaped "masculinity." Thus as race was rhetorically dismissed, gender became the conceptual sphere that aided intellectual efforts to essentialize culture and thus produce the authenticity that their regionalist-cum-nationalist ideologies required. Anchored in the highlands, the "masculine cholo" construct alluded to a particular artistic "breed," and thus silently reproduced racialized academic and social beliefs and their associated hierarchies.

The prototypical cholo was incarnated regionally by the *ccorilazo*, described as a familyless, disinherited, and possibly illegitimate serrano cowboy (Poole, 1994). He combined the attributes of brave, undomesticated virility with artistic talent, which subdued the women surrounding him and the audiences for whom he performed. In Cuzco the paradigm came alive in the figure of a guitar player and signer named Francisco Gómez Negrón. Born in Chumbivilcas — the land of ccorilazos, also known as legendary Bold Lands (tierras bravas), because of its geographic and social ruggedness — Negrón allegedly drew his inspiration from this landscape. He was a successful artist who played the guitar and the Andean mandolin (the *charango*), who shared humble, non-Indian rural origins with the despised gamonal. Yet if non-Indian rurality had meant illegitimacy to the 1920s intellectual elite, to neoindianistas it was a marker of authenticity: this ccorilazo artist was considered the "genuine representative of the *arte serrano*." He earned his living playing *música neo-Indiana*, and traveled the country winning every national contest where the definition of "authentic Peruvian art" was at stake.[40] His unquestioned authenticity, exemplified in his extraordinary talent and virility, accounted for his great success, which was recognized throughout all of South America, where he traveled promoting Indo-Americanismo. The Chilean poet Gabriela Mistral — the 1945 Nobel laureate in literature — had endorsed his art, and Argentineans had shed nostalgic tears when they remembered their *gauchos*, whom Francisco Gómez Negrón resembled. In spite of his success, plebeianness persisted as the characteristic of this man's life: he was so poor that, on one occasion when he was sick, the dwellers of Colquemarca, the district where he had been born, organized a charity event to pay for his medicine.[41]

The populist sharing of folklore and the definition of masculinity as essentially plebeian called for a reformulation of earlier paradigms of elite male sexuality and sensuality built upon racial/cultural purity and therefore challenged earlier norms of race/class endogamy. As neoindianistas distinguished their "proper homosociality" (Parker et al., 1992) from that of the indigenistas, elite *caballerosidad* underwent changes in some respects. As I explain in chapter 4, neoindianistas' perception of plebeian women also reflected new rules of gentlemanly behavior. Additionally, a new elite perception of "masculine art" influenced their cultural activities and productions.

Contrasting with what was deemed effeminate intellectual segregation, neo-Indian *caballeros* mingled with the populace and even drew inspiration from this experience. Their art expressed the virile sensuality of the plebeian soul. Men like Andrés Alencastre, a poet, playwright, and musician who used the pseudonym K'illko Waraka, represented the prototype of new caballeros. Although he was not born there, he was associated with the rough region of Chumbivilcas, given the boldness of his art, and known as "the bard of the ccorilazos pampas, creator of powerful songs, [and] a rough member of his race."[42] Andrés, ironically, was also the son of Leopoldo Alencastre, the landowner from the High Provinces who died allegedly at the hands of "savage Indians" in the 1920s, an event discussed in the previous chapter. The son wrote poems and dramas in Quechua, as did his predecessors, the indigenistas. Yet, he reversed the latters' cherished belief in the purity of Capac Simi, which was one of the bases of their nonmestizo identity. Indigenistas, as indicated in the first chapter, differentiated common Quechua, or Runa Simi (which they claimed was bastardized by Spanish) from pure Quechua, or Capac Simi, which they claimed their erudition and social refinement had preserved from contamination. While mestizo and Indian plebeians spoke Runa Simi, indigenistas used Capac Simi in their public presentations, and they thus enacted their social distinction. Andrés Alencastre was instead a champion of *quechua mestizo,* who proposed that the same "common" Quechua language the people deployed in their daily lives should be used in academic performances (Itier, 1995). Also contradicting his predecessors, Andrés's prize-winning Quechua-language productions depicted the village life that indigenistas abhorred as barbaric. "I adore these customs," Alencastre wrote in the prologue to one of his books (ca. 1940). To neoindianistas, men like Alencastre, who exalted regional rural culture and challenged prevailing canons, provided examples of brave manliness and were the vanguard of the new mestizo soul.

To promote "authentic Peruvian art" the self-proclaimed cholo intellectuals used the radio. A radio program called *La hora del charango* (The Charango Hour), which aimed at spreading these ideas, was first broadcast in 1937, one year after radio made its debut in Cuzco.[43] The charango is a musical instrument, best described as an Andean mandolin, and played exclusively by men. The creator of *The Charango Hour* was Humberto Vidal Unda, a man who, like Andrés Alencastre, professed rural origins and who, years later, would promote the inauguration of Cuzco Day, a celebration that became central to the city's identity.[44] The editorial read by Vidal of the first program said: "The charango is modest and it's cholo, the producers of this program *identify ourselves* with that enormous mass, the indigenous and cholo classes who are the national majority and who pour out their feelings following the rhythm of *huaynos*" (my emphasis).[45] Implicit in their identifying themselves with the cholos was the assertion that the neo-Indians were not *really* cholos; thus, notwithstanding their declarations, the populist exaltation of plebeian mestizaje was not meant to eradicate social hierarchies. Built upon an "intimate" knowledge of their culture (that included knowing its alleged flaws, and hiding them from the view of strangers) the neoindianista promotion of authentic serrano art implied a Janus-faced cultural policy. One side proudly displayed local folklore; the other strove to hide or soothe the social flaws that they had identified in the regional culture. Hiding or soothing such "cultural intimacies," the new intellectual elites implemented a hierarchical representation of regional identity, which, to a large extent, continued to reproduce the earlier social canons of decency I described in chapter 1. During the indigenista era, university degrees were indicators of social status. Neo-Indian hierarchies abided by similar norms. Granted, as iconoclast populists they promoted unschooled bohemians like Negrón, but they also recognized that Alencastre's educated talent had a higher status. Their measure of masculine talent connected the proclivity to artistic ruggedness with the ability to present their plebeian-inspired art with refinement. Neither virile authenticity nor folklore had canceled the social ranks fostered by decencia, nor had they supplanted formal education as a marker of social differences.

Previous social beliefs were also present in the art that neoindianistas produced. Alencastre wrote a drama entitled *El Challakuy,* which described gamonales' hunting of "ferocious Indians" who, instigated by a landowner's abuses, had killed him.[46] Obviously, the drama duplicated many indigenista beliefs concerning Indians as victims of gamonales' violence, thus revealing that the significant difference between neoindianistas and indigenistas was that the new intellectual leaders (driven by their virile boldness, I repeat) were not embarrassed to present "Indians" on public stages. *Indios netos* (genuine Indians) were part of the neoindianista promotion of mestizaje. Although their authenticity, as shown by the inherent ruggedness of their art went unquestioned, to present their "primitive art" to "civilized audiences" their performances had to be "polished." Then, they could be presented to the public and adequately represent and even promote regional identity.

The flipside of the image of "the coarse Indian artist" was the neo-Indian intelligentsia's self-representation as artistic "tamers" of the countryside. Like their Mexican counterparts in the same period, these intellectuals imagined music and art as means to penetrate the Indian spirit in order to transform it (Knight, 1994; Becker, 1995). A common feature used to control and yet present Indian artists publicly was to form *conjuntos musicales,* ensembles led by well-reputed neo-Indian directors and made up of "genuine Indians." For example, Andrés Alencastre, the poet and playwright, led a group from Canas, known as Kana Llactayoc, or Canas Villagers, a name which connoted a flavor of legitimate autochthony.[47] Using this method, neoindianista tradition opened the theatrical stages to cuzqueño commoners and endorsed their use of mestizo Quechua in official performances. Contradicting their declared goals to homogenize the region, this project fostered the emergence of a renewed intellectual elite consecrated to the study of regional cuzqueño culture that now included vernacular art (folklore) and not only Incaism. Central to this focus on regional culture was Cuzco Day, an invented holiday that bolstered cuzqueñismo while opening to commoners the feeling of regional pride.

The Populist Reinvention of Cuzco

The neoindianistas' highest achievement was the creation of Cuzco Day, a day to celebrate their city. Celebrating Cuzco was not a new idea, as it had been part of elite cuzqueñismo since its inception. The novelty was that, in accord with the populist political environment, this specific celebration would be opened to "the masses" to share what had previously been an exclusive elite feeling of cuzqueñismo. The events leading up to the invention of Cuzco Day unfolded spontaneously. As the originator of the idea tells it, it all started in one of the frequent celebrations promoted by the neoindianista intellectuals:

> It all happened in an *almuerzo* [lunch] to celebrate Journalist's Day [Día del Periodista]. . . . As is customary, the oratorical contest began, exalting the date being celebrated. Each orator had to strive to be inventive to say something new because the first ones to speak had already said everything. When my turn came, the topic was almost exhausted. I heard, "Let Vidal speak . . . , it's Vidal's turn . . ." and suddenly, it came to me: just as the Journalist's Day, had been established, the Teacher's Day, Mother's Day . . . Cuzco's Day [el Día del Cuzco] should be established. And I continued, saying, "Cuzco is, gentlemen, the symbol of the essence of Peru, the source from which one of the most admirable cultures radiates. . . . There are the ruins, the temples." . . . I was so emotional in the speech that the attendants at the meeting were swayed by it and ended up acclaiming the initiative to such an extent that everyone, standing up, made a promise to carry it out.[48]

The orator was Humberto Vidal Unda, who in 1939 founded "La Sociedad de los Cholos" in homage to the neo-Indian ideal type (Aparicio Vega, 1994). He was a middle-class intellectual who taught metaphysics at the local university and Spanish grammar at a boys' public high school. Like a good neo-Indian, he played the charango and the *quena* as well as the zithern, violin, and mandolin. He also enjoyed theater and had performed several times the role of Piqui-chaqui (Flee Foot), a buffoon in *Ollantay*, the favorite dramatic piece of cuzqueños.[49]

When local authorities approved of Vidal's idea, the Cuzco Day Committee was formed, headed by the prefect, and comprising the local cultural experts: the university rector, the president of the American Institute of Art, the director of the Archaeological Institute, and the president of the Touring Automobile Club, a private countrywide institution committed to the promotion of tourism. Vidal Unda was appointed secretary of the committee, the most important post after that of the prefect.[50] The day chosen to celebrate Cuzco Day was June 24, already known as the Día del Indio. Vidal explained that the date coincided with the pre-Hispanic celebration of Inti Raymi, the Incaic solstice ritual, and it was close to the religious festival of Corpus Christi, a popular festival that neoin-dianistas were seeking to promote.[51] The festival was billed as a celebration of regional identity, featuring folklore and art, and also aimed at achieving political gains and at promoting tourism for which purpose June was an appropriate month.

Although he expected a negative reply, Vidal Unda invited Manuel Prado, then president of the country, "to preside over the events that will tribute to this Cradle of Peruvianness."[52] To everybody's surprise, the president accepted the invitation. To him, it might well have been part of his presidential reelection campaign for the following year. Yet from the committee's viewpoint, it was a political success: the president's attendance to the celebration of the Cuzco Day would satisfy the regional elite's yearnings for greater cultural and political recognition. The visit provided the occasion to prove that Cuzco deserved the longed-for title "Cradle of Peruvianness" and to transform it from being the symbolic center of low-status Indianness into a source of national pride.

For the town to merit its title as the Cradle of Peruvianness, Cuzco Day needed to convey paramount self-esteem. Therefore, the occasion required an efficient management of the cuzqueñista cultural scene and its intimately perceived flaws. Following classic nationalist scripts, in a way that Benedict Anderson (1983) and Eric Hobsbawm (1990) would have savored, the inventors of the Day of Cuzco created symbols that projected a faultless representation of their society. Plans for the celebration included the creation of a Cuzco anthem "that everyone can sing" (para que todos puedan cantarlo), and a central parade in the Plaza de Armas "without class distinctions" (sin distinción de clases). The new additions were geared to representing the shared glory of all cuzqueños and demonstrating their local pride. Yet Prado's unexpected visit, which catapulted Cuzco to the fore as the potential center of Peruvian identity, convinced the organizers that presenting indigenous folklore was not enough to stimulate the idea of Cuzco as the Cradle of Peruvianness. Neo-Indian promotion of indigenous folklore was a good regional agenda for promoting cuzqueño self-esteem and stimulating camaraderie among regional elites and plebs. But the national magnetism of Cuzco had to come from the Inca past, already canonically established as an icon of regional identity and source of nationalism. Moreover, actual Indians were not refurbished enough to be the source of national pride. The sessions held by the Cuzco Day Committee celebration were plagued by statements that alluded to a lamentable Indian present, such as "The pain of your subjugated and sad race, that abandoning its wooden club, has in its hands only the plaintive *quena* [wooden flute] to bemoan its past." These stood in sharp contrast to references made to the glorious Inca days that were to be used to invigorate the future: "Making ourselves aware that we were great in the *past* will make us understand that we can be so in the *future*."[53]

Unlike folklore, which might carry an association of shame, Cuzco's urban monuments of huge Inca stones and colonial sculpted walls provided a superb, substantive source of pride. The enduring archaeological remains (rather than the people) represented the historical guarantee of an immensely promising Peruvian future. The archaeological assets of Cuzco gave the city precedence over any other Peruvian city, including Lima. As demonstrated in the following remarks, cuzqueñistas equated pre-Hispanic monuments with history and took them to represent "national essence" or Peruvianness: "Only peoples that have a history can be sure to have a future, and Cuzco has its foundations firmly grounded in the hard rock of a past that mocks the centuries; it is a city, the intimate beating of whose venerable heart offers us the possibility of seeking in our own selves the permanent consciousness of Peruvianness" (Yépez Miranda, 1945:27).

June 24, 1944, the first official Cuzco Day, was a joyous, glorious day. Huge public events and private political ones were held, at which politicians of all leanings delivered speeches. The celebration of their city meant the virtual reification of "Cuzco" as an evocative symbol of the past, the source of history, and the origin of timeless nationality. For example, in a speech that was similar to many presented that day, the aprista Guillermo Guevara, said that Cuzco was not only a city but "a possibility, an ideal on which to ground the Peruvian soul. Within its territory all of our cultures merge and cohabit [and] in the silent majesty of its old stones the glory of our history breathes." José Gabriel Cosio, a historian and probably the most traditional of the group, ended his message in the following way: "I salute you, and upon reverently kissing your sacred ground, formed of everyone of the different soils of the Inca Empire, I wish your future days will live up to your millenary grandeur. Sacred Cuzco, Hail!" Julio Gutiérrez, a journalist and communist politician, wrote: "Center and heart of America, vital knot, goal, compass and center of gravity of a whole continent, we are proud to have been molded out of your clay like the stone men of your mythology."[54]

As politicians of diverse political persuasions rejoiced in the consensual glorification of their city as the cradle of nationality, they also revealed that neoindianista dismissal of race was only rhetorical. Their exaltations of the city continued to articulate cuzqueñismo by means of racialized notions of cultural heritage embedded in memory and history (rather than in biology), just as indigenistas had previously done when race was not a discredited notion. Like their predecessors, they saw their legacy as imprinted in the urban remains that inspired cuzqueñista emotion and potential source of "national essence." To counter the inferior status assigned to them by environmental racial theories, on the occasion of Cuzco Day, elite cuzqueño intellectuals articulated an archaeologically rich version of geographic determinism. Using it, they placed their city high enough on the pedestal of "history" to be able to infuse its "spirit" onto the nation, thus obliterating extraneous "cultural essences" and creating authentic Peruvians. The racial undertones of this regional-cum-national, incommensurable yet geographically bounded feeling were evident, although overt mentions to race were absent from their speeches.

The populist reinvention of Cuzco as the cradle of nationality was also the occasion to declare partisan allegiances and obtain tangible political advantages. Humberto Vidal Unda presented an important speech with this in mind. After thanking the president for his respect toward "the millenary city, cradle of *Peruanidad,*" he expressed his personal admiration for the president's "diplomatic tact, which had for the first time in our history" successfully put an end to an old border conflict with "the northern republic of Ecuador."[55] The first celebration of Cuzco Day was also an occasion to acclaim the Peruvian victory in the recent war against Ecuador and to relate it to the newly reborn Inca nationalism.

Cuzco had been the capital of Tawantinsuyu, the Inca Empire. Inca domains had encompassed the territories Peru lost in the nineteenth-century war against Chile and in skirmishes with Colombia. It also encompassed a stretch of land that had been definitively recovered from Ecuador through a fresh treaty arranged by President Prado.[56] Vidal implied that if Cuzco's Inca leaders had been able to consolidate that vast territory in the past, the peruanidad that emanated from Cuzco had similar potential in contemporary times. The enduring Inca monuments demonstrated that the city of Cuzco persisted as the center of the Tawantinsuyu (the Inca territory), the territorial defense of which was the proof of peruanidad that the president had given.[57] Manuel Prado could have hardly imagined a better stage to celebrate "his" triumph against Ecuador and therefore to intensify his bid for reelection. When it was his turn to respond to the speeches he concurred with Cuzco orators, using the same rhetoric: "Upon finding myself for the second time in this legendary site, I offer as worthy homage to its grandeur the work of five years of government consecrated to the maximum exaltation of the values of peruanidad."[58]

Prado's presence legitimized cuzqueños as politicians, and reciprocally Cuzco, the Inca dynasty's dwelling place, endowed him with the wisdom of "a contemporary Inca."[59] Having been equated with the Inca and in touch with the highest values of peruanidad, the president occupied the center of the ritual celebration and was incorporated, if momentarily, into the evocation of the Inca Inti Raymi. The actor performing the Inca addressed an improvised speech to him "from statesman to statesman," recognizing his task of guarding the territory of Tawantinsuyu, and urging him to continue to do so.[60] The main performance was witnessed, of course, by thousands of people, who had climbed to nearby Sacsayhuaman, an Inca fortress two miles from central Cuzco, on top of one of the hills surrounding the city.

Lastly, Cuzco Day had an economic function, designed to make Cuzco "one of the most important tourist centers in the world." At the end of his visit, Manuel Prado inaugurated a modern hotel and ordered further construction of the public sewage system. These ceremonies were all included in the celebration of the sacred day. The following year, when he was nominated as mayor, Vidal Unda traveled to Lima. There, along with Cuzco's representatives to Congress, he lobbied for and obtained congressional legislation creating the Semana del Cuzco, Cuzco Week.[61] In the years to follow, June 24 became an important central date, on the occasion of which national authorities visited the Sacred City, inaugurated *obras públicas* (public works), and sealed political pacts.

Inti Raymi
Dominant Inca Tradition and Subordinate Folklore

The central act of Cuzco Day featured the first official production of the Inti Raymi (Festival of the Sun), a commemoration of Inca culture that belongs to what Eric Hobsbawm and Terence Ranger (1983) have called invented traditions. Like other invented traditions, this production implied a conscious process of using the past to create a public ritual for political ends. The apparent paradox of this invented Inca tradition is that it was accomplished by a political group that had dismissed previous representations of the Inca past and favored instead performances of plebeian folklore. The same

man who launched the initiative for Inti Raymi in 1944, Humberto
Vidal Unda, had declared in *La hora del charango,* the radio program he directed, "We cannot continue to use the Inca past; we have
to use our present glories."[62] However, intellectual history is not at
all tidy, and individuals can hold different and often contradictory
ideas in their minds, which they rally for different purposes. And
thus, when the moment arrived to feature cuzqueño culture nationwide, the Inca past occupied the center stage and subordinated the
indigenous dancers who danced in the periphery, representing the
folkloric present for the consumption of tourists.

Three weeks before the commemoration of the first Cuzco Day, the
committee approved the staging of a *fiesta evocativa* in Sacsayhuaman. The program included "the Inti Raymi, authored by Roberto
Ojeda"; one scene of the Argentinean Ricardo Rojas's *Ollantay,*
which Rojas had written in Spanish; and another scene taken from
the cuzqueño *Ollantay,* originally written in Quechua. Presenting a
scene of each, the Spanish and Quechua versions, was congruent
with the neo-Indian ideology of mestizaje. In the same tenor, the
performance was to finish with "a symbolic and evocative parade, *a
manera de ballet incaico* [in the style of an Inca ballet]."[63] The "evocative parade" was to feature the "best folkloric ensembles," the win-
ners of a contest specifically organized for the occasion. The state,
through the Ministry of Education, supported the commemoration
economically.

As indicated in chapter 1, cuzqueños were well acquainted with
theatrical stagings of Inca dramas. Scripts, clothing, and actors who
could impersonate Incas already existed. The idea of using Sacsayhuaman, a nearby Inca fortress, as a natural amphitheater was
not new either. At least since the 1920s the cuzqueño intellectual elite
had performed dramas that needed open spaces in Sacsayhuaman.
They were also used for staging the Quechua version of the colonial
drama *Ollantay* in closed theaters. A semiestablished cast of actors
had performed it several times before and could do it once more, as
well as rehearse a Spanish version. Not even the staging of Inti
Raymi was a novelty, as several Inca dramas, dating from the 1920s
and earlier, included a sketch of the ritual. The neoindianistas' challenge was to introduce in Inti Raymi their populist political creed,

without altering the "historical authenticity" of the presentation, as it was the latter that guaranteed Cuzco's national potential.

The script used in the 1944 representation of Inti Raymi closely followed the description of Garcilaso de la Vega as interpreted by Luis A. Pardo, an archaeologist who was then the president of the Instituto Arqueológico del Cuzco and a member of the Instituto Americano de Arte and the Cuzco Day Committee. He was the cultural authority to whom local politicians had entrusted the task of protecting the authenticity of cuzqueño history. To inform the literate public about what would be presented in Sacsayhuaman, Pardo published a summary of Garcilaso's account in the newspaper. Adhering to the emotional and political needs of cuzqueñismo, Pardo related the magnificence of the ritual to the spiritual significance of the city of Cuzco, where the Incas enacted it yearly. He explained that Cuzco, as the center of the pre-Hispanic world, was endowed with a powerful sacred relevance that illuminated the whole continent. Drawing a parallel between neoindianista nationalist mestizaje and Inca time, Pardo argued that the ritual meant the culmination of a pilgrimage joined by a large and multiethnic constituency from every corner of the empire to worship the Inca god, through its highest representative, the Inca, in the most sacred and powerful place of his territory. To convey his idea of pilgrimage and sacredness, and to number Cuzco among the internationally renowned sanctuaries, Pardo compared the Andean city to the Muslim Kaaba. He thus emphasized the exemplary specialness of this city, which during pre-Columbian times, attracted authorities from every corner of the empire, thus from virtually the entire South American continent.[64]

Cuzco's unique ability to unify the national territory, together with the aristocratic quality and hierarchical organization of the festival as transmitted by Garcilaso, was also salient in Pardo's description. The Inca's military potential—an obvious reference to Peru's victory in the recent border confrontations—was emphasized in the commemoration as well. A parade of might and wealth opened the festival:

Here comes the Sapan Inca, the Ccapac, powerful lord of one hundred nations, seated with solemn and hieratic gesture in his *tiana* or litter covered with gold plate. They carry him on their athletic shoulders, the valiant *rukkanas*. . . . The sovereign looks magnificent with the finest *unccu* woven by the Virgins of the Sun. . . . On his forehead the scarlet tassel of the maskaipacha shines like a symbol of his divine descent. . . . The *Koya* or royal consort, his brother the *Huillac Uma*, the *Huaminkkas*, generals of the empire, the princesses of royal blood, form his royal entourage. A multitude of *huallahuisas* [soldiers], servants of the cult and peoples of the empire, march behind the royal retinue. . . . The bellicose shells, the trumpets, the flutes, the *pinkuillos* of the *kkanas* and the *zampoñas* of the *sicuris* who have come from the legendary lake of the cosmogony, resound.[65]

In addition to the military parade, the first Inti Raymi of the neo-Indian era featured the presentation of gifts to the Inca by actors playing the inhabitants of the empire, the sacrifice of a llama and its offering to the sun, the prognostication of the future by reading the entrails of the animal, and a final libation with sacred corn beer. Finally, to communicate Cuzco's "historic" power to unify a large territory (including neighboring countries) the 1944 version of Inti Raymi presented a visual image of the *cuatro suyus,* the four territorial divisions of Inca administration.

In spite of the obvious rivalry between Luis E. Valcárcel, the ardent proponent of racial/cultural purism, and neo-Indian cultural promoters of mestizaje, the reinvention of Inti Raymi had followed Valcárcel's interpretation of Inca government, as presented in his book *De la vida inkaika* (1925). In agreement with Valcárcel, the 1944 Inti Raymi portrayed the Inca as the "master of an empire, appearing before his beloved people, majestic like a god and splendid like the sun."[66] Abiding by the hierarchies, when the ritual stretched beyond the performing stage to include President Prado as the Tawantinsuyu ruler, it was significantly the Inca who addressed him and advise him to be "as wise as the Inca had been to procure the happiness of his people as the Inca had done."[67] In the 1944 representation, the polar figures of the Inca and the people were central to the whole act. While the Inca figure represented the sacred and aristocratic aspects of the empire, the people denoted reverent obedience and subservience: "The Inca appeared on a litter carried by many vassals. Thou-

Faustino Espinoza Navarro's first performance as Inca, Inti Raymi, Cuzco, 1944. (Below) The Inca, carried by his vassals, making his entrance to the fortress of Sacsayhuaman, the scenario of the Inti Raymi. Cuzco, 1944. Both photos: photographer unknown. Courtesy Faustino Espinoza Navarro.

sands of Indians wearing special costumes descended the nearby mountain, others brandished their arrows and greeted the Inca monarch. Thousands of *pututos* resounded in the air. . . . Then began the presentations of the innumerable bands, arriving as in former times from all the *suyus* of the empire, that is, the thirteen provinces."[68]

The celebration was egalitarian inasmuch as it allowed every social sector to participate. Yet Inti Raymi was not intended to cancel the racial hierarchies embedded in cultural intimacies that the neoindianistas shared with the preceding purist indigenista project. A salient conviction both groups shared was that Indians were inferior and did not belong to the city but to the mountainous countryside. Representing this belief, contemporary "Indians" (whom the Cuzco Day Committee officially compelled to participate) were assigned their "proper place" during the celebrations: they either "descended from the mountains" or came from the jungle as suggested by the image of men "waving bows and arrows," a cultural convention relating those implements to the inhabitants of the easternmost slopes of the Andes.

Language and Race
Pure Quechua Preserving the Inca Past in the Mestizo Present

But even respecting the hierarchies dictated by cuzqueñista historical wisdom, this Inti Raymi could still be neo-Indian and populist. As indicated in chapter 1, before 1930, to guarantee "accurate" knowledge of both the pre-Hispanic historical past and the language of the Incas, only members of the elite could write, direct, or perform in these dramas. Likewise, through the performances the local gentry styled themselves as the only heirs of Inca culture, nobility, and glory, thus excluding commoners—mestizos and Indians—from it. Breaking this social convention, the 1944 staging of Inti Raymi included nonelite actors in the roles of the Inca and his noble retinue. This inclusiveness aimed to show the horizontal community that their mestizaje project had been promoting and indeed transgressed indigenista Inca theatrical canons.

It was not a complete break, as it included a compromise on historical accuracy. The compromise centered on language and required that the acting be in Quechua. Because every cuzqueño has mastered the indigenous language, using daily-life Quechua in the ritual could have been an inclusionary move toward a homogeneous regional identity, thus blurring the distances between the populace and the nobility that indigenistas maintained. But neoindianistas did not use common Quechua in their Inti Raymi. Instead they yielded to the academic canons set by their indigenista predecessors, by requiring that the Inca and his escort be versed in Capac Simi. Hence they included selected nonelite actors who allegedly mastered that sociolect. As I mentioned in the first chapter, the linguistic canons of Capac Simi were first invented in colonial times and were constantly renewed by elite self-declared Quechua specialists. Starting in the neoindianista era, representing Incas was no longer exclusively an elite privilege, but it was still a privilege, extended to selected commoners, specifically those with the talent to reinvent Capac Simi.

To impersonate the role of the Inca, the cultural authorities found a man called Faustino Espinoza Navarro. The son of a small landowner who lived in a nearby pueblo, he belonged to a theatrical troupe that indigenistas had repeatedly scorned in public. He was tall and handsome, and most important of all, he claimed to speak Capac Simi, a language that he declared he had learned from his father and his own research.[69] The actual Inca role had no text, with the exception of a Quechua prayer, the elaboration of which required a specialist. Espinoza wrote the prayer and eventually the short dialogues for the rest of the cast (Espinoza Navarro, 1977:6). Controlling the Quechua speeches of the actors in successive performances of Inti Raymi allowed this man, who had no academic degree, to become officially an intellectual and a public cultural authority.

Benedict Anderson (1983:145) has stated that by means of language "one could be invited into the imagined community" that the nation represented. Cuzco would have proved Anderson right, if his intention had not been to show that this was an inclusive process, unconnected to such social discrimination practices as those associated with race. Indigenistas and neoindianistas imagined their community in Quechua, but in the dynastic and exclusive Capac Simi. Thus in Cuzco, language was also about race. Since Capac Simi had been considered to be a property of gente decente, and therefore not of mestizos or Indians, the old intellectual elite would certainly have excluded the neo-Indian Inca Espinoza from their community because of his mestizo (not *decente*) social background. Conversely, neoindianistas invited him into their community precisely because of their appreciation of the cholo identity that Espinoza embodied. Yet, the role of Inca required that Espinoza observed the aristocratic precepts of Capac Simi. Initially this meant Espinoza's rubbing elbows with the elite. Ultimately it granted him status as a *quechuólogo,* and thus an intellectual. In the 1920s, as mentioned in the first chapter, brown-skinned, serrano intellectuals had countered the mestizo identity imputed to them by limeños by flaunting their academic status as indigenista ideologues. In 1944, the enduring social image of intellectuals as nonmestizos and the fact that he impersonated "the Inca" eclipsed Espinoza's cholo identity. Through the years, his continuous performance in Inti Raymi and his intellectualized mastery of Quechua gradually endowed Espinoza with the status of an academic and gente decente, a notion that connoted the same type of cultural superiority that existed in the high period of cuzqueño racial thought (1900–1930). The political and academic rhetoric that dismissed race had not canceled the racialized, discriminatory underpinnings of the everyday category that "decency" represented and which continued to organized social interactions in Cuzco during this era when antiracism was declared part of the intellectual ideology of the time.[70] Similarly, as in the 1920s, being a self-taught quechuólogo continued to indicate status as intellectual and connoted a lofty position.

Notwithstanding their iconoclastic rhetoric neoindianistas were respectful of historical "truths." They rejected purity and proclaimed mestizaje as a regional project. But those ideas were used to imagine the present and the future. The Incas were the past, and the accuracy of their representation had to be above reproach. Endowing the past and its specialists with absolute authority was a cultural compromise that cuzqueñismo demanded. By resorting to primordial Capac Simi as the required language in the performances, as well as highlighting the authority of "Inca culture specialists," the neoindianistas recreated a new intellectual elite. Many among them had working-

The Inca and his retinue salute President Manuel Prado, Cuzco, 1944.
Photographer unknown. According to Espinoza, the Inca advised the
president to be as wise as Pachacutec, the ruler under whose command the
Tawantinsuyu allegedly reached its largest expansion. Courtesy Faustino
Espinoza Navarro.

class origins, yet the fact that they were intellectuals entitled them to
be included among the regional elites and thus raised their status in a
manner that echoed former times. Mid-century populism was therefore about redefining elite membership requirements rather than
about leveling hierarchies.

State Indigenismo and the Official Script of Inti Raymi

During the years that followed the first official presentation of Inti
Raymi, the rivalries between old indigenistas and neoindianistas increased. At times it paralleled the conflict between the state (represented by indigenistas) and its political opponents, the Apra and the
Communist Party (represented by neoindianistas). Manuel Prado's
administration ended in 1945 when, in spite of his efforts to be

reelected — including his visit to Cuzco in 1944 — he was defeated by José Bustamante y Rivero, who governed from 1945 to 1948. During this administration Luis E. Valcárcel served as minister of education. This fact may account for the central government's lack of interest in the cuzqueño production of Inti Raymi during those years. Valcárcel, who was Cuzco's highest and most politically successful academic authority, despised neoindianista thought. In 1944, the year of the first staging of Inti Raymi he wrote:

> Cuzco's life should be intense and brilliant in its secular style, at the same high level, in the same noble lineage of its rank. Cuzqueños should make themselves worthy of Cuzco. Not to compromise in their pride as Incas, not to descend to the puerile condescension of *cholismo*, of *criollismo*, merely transitory phases, ashamed of the culture of great style that existed in ancient Peru and that will be the future America. . . . [C]holismo and criollismo are embryonic states of evident inferiority, incipience, and barbarism; let's not convert them into ideals. . . . Atop the granite pedestal the creation of the new culture will be raised, not the hybrid mixture in which only the accelerated disintegration of the colonial is perceived clearly.[71]

Although this eminent indigenista might have agreed with neoindianistas' promotion of folklore, the problem was Luis E. Valcárcel's professed abhorrence of hybridity. "I don't like the mestizo," he unabashedly declared in an interview in 1947. "He represents only an undefined middle-class element. He suffers the double tragedy of his two irreconcilable souls and the double slight from above and from below." He added, "We should learn from the United States where, despite the *razzias* applied to the Redskins during the course of the three centuries, they have for the last ten years put into effect a New Deal for the 400,000 natives that live there. In the United States, spiritual authority has been restored to the Indian. The Indian chooses what he can adopt from the white man's civilization and the latter no longer tries to force happiness on him" (Tealdo, 1947:268). Neoindianistas, apristas, and communists might well have labeled these thoughts by Valcárcel "proimperialist."[72] Yet, rather than imperialism, the internal threat his opinions represented was that he implicitly associated ethnic autonomy with racial/cultural viability (Balibar, 1988), an academic belief that later shaped the thought of Peruvian politicians as divergent as Mario Vargas Llosa, the conservative writer, or Antonio Díaz Martínez, the Shining Path ideologue.[73]

During the 1940s indigenismo à la Valcárcel dropped its oppositional thrust. It became official state rhetoric, antagonistic to the promestizo project which, thus, became emblematic of Apra (although this was not the only group to sponsor it). It should come as no surprise that in spite of his ex officio role as the adviser in the re-creation of Incaism, Valcárcel was completely absent from the enactment of Inti Raymi and probably expected the spectacle to fade gradually.[74] Contradicting his hopes, Inti Raymi did not languish. Instead the popularity of the invented ritual grew and drew the attention of official cultural authorities just as internal and foreign tourism was peaking.

In 1952, the state intervened to oversee the ceremony. The reason given was that if the ritual was to present the Inca past to the largest national and international audience in the country, it had to present an "accurate" representation of history. However, "correcting" the version of Inti Raymi that had been staged for so many years was a very delicate task, as the festival had been assembled by cuzqueño cultural authorities and was allegedly based on irrefutable chroniclers' historical information. A very respected and fondly appreciated cultural authority was chosen to supervise the rendering of the Inca past. His name was José María Arguedas. The son of a provincial lawyer, born in the sierra province of Andahuaylas and bilingual in Quechua and Spanish, he could not be accused of imperialism, communism, or aprismo. Additionally, he was acquainted with cuzqueño provincial life, since he had worked for several years as a primary school teacher in the cuzqueño province of Sicuani. In 1941 he had published *Agua*, one of his most acclaimed writings. He was also very active in the preservation and diffusion of Andean folklore. In 1944, in a newspaper article entitled "En defensa del folklore musical andino," he had declared: "The folkloric songs of the absolutely original peoples, of those who have no other music than folklore, cannot be interpreted by outsiders. Only the artist born in the community, who has inherited the genius of folklore, can interpret it and transmit to the rest."[75] Echoes of the indigenista notions of "purism" and of proper places for the races resonated in the writings of Arguedas, who unlike Valcárcel did not scorn mestizos. However, Arguedas did agree with Valcárcel that the cultural differences between Andeans and non-Andeans were incommensurable. His style was close to what Taguieff (1990) has called "differentialist racism," the doctrine that does not make the "other" inferior but exalts irreducible differences among groups of people. Calling Arguedas racist would be simplistic, but clearly a kind of cultural determinism molded his depiction of differences between Andeans and non-Andeans, images themselves interlocked with notions of racially defined proper places. Like Luis E. Valcárcel, Arguedas believed that Indians had to be educated in Quechua, an idea that had been implemented by the Ministry of Education since 1945 (Contreras, 1996:23), when the indigenista Valcárcel was its highest authority. As education minister, Valcárcel had appointed Arguedas (who had been Valcárcel's student in 1946 at the newly created Instituto de Etnología de San Marcos) as folklore curator of the Ministry of Education. In 1952, a year of military rule under the populist leadership of General Manuel A. Odría, Arguedas, by now a respected ethnologist and poet-novelist, was still an adviser at the Ministry of Education (Valcárcel, 1972; Murra and López-Baralt, 1996:351). He was a unique figure in that he bridged the gap between the older generation of indigenistas and the younger neoindianistas, who, given Arguedas's penchant for folklore, might even have regarded him a promoter of "national culture."

As a representative of the Ministry of Education, Arguedas addressed a letter to the Cuzco Week Committee in which he criticized previous Inti Raymi performances. He stated that "from the photographs that have been sent to the Ministry of Education, I noted certain mistakes and anachronisms that are unworthy of the solemnity which should cloak this act."[76] To "safeguard the dignity of Inti Raymi," he made two crucial suggestions: first, the Inca's escort should not be formed by high school students but by soldiers from the Peruvian army. Second, the clothing for the Inca warriors needed improvement, as did the litter on which the Inca was carried. If the ceremony was to represent the national past, it had to convey an image of the empire as overflowing with military power and material wealth. The Cuzco Week Committee agreed with Arguedas's suggestion. Since the first staging, they said, the representations had been "completely improvised" and the ritual needed "improvement" bringing it more in line with "history." Moreover, they had already begun doing so, by appointing a commission of several cuzqueño archaeologists and historians.[77]

The 1952 performance marked the beginning of the direct and constant state intervention to raise Inti Raymi's standard to that of a national symbol of Inca history. The Ministry of Education financed the production, and the military official in charge of the army headquarters in Cuzco, General Indacochea (who was also a member of the Cuzco Week Committee) gladly approved the participation of a battalion of soldiers. Their presence would enhance the show by adding the realism that their discipline and racial aspect implied, said the rector at the local University, Luis Felipe Paredes.[78] The decisive economic support of the state, and the national success of the celebration marked the beginning of the end of the discrepancies between Cuzco-resident purist indigenistas and promestizo neoindianistas. Sustained by elite Incaism and complemented by the presentation of folklore for "the people," Inti Raymi became in the late 1950s the pillar of cuzqueñista emotion.

Confirming the vulnerability (and probably the intellectual inferiority) of the oral tradition that had sustained the ceremony since 1944, orders were that an "official script" of Inti Raymi needed to be written. Traditional intellectuals including archaeologists, ethnologists, ethnomusicologists, and artists were commissioned to do it.[79] While all of them were cuzqueños, some were indigenistas, others were neoindianistas, and still others represented a mixture of both ideologies. United by their cuzqueñismo, none of them declined the state-sponsored opportunity to devise "the official version of Inti Raymi," which would last through the years. Not only would a written script enhance the accountability of the ceremony, it would heighten the intellectual status of their authors, projecting them as guardians of national history. When the specialists finished their task, they sent the official version of Inti Raymi to Arguedas in Lima, and he approved it. Since then, many cuzqueño directors have staged

Inti Raymi and have always been compelled to follow the "official script," as the 1952 version is known. The word "oficial" undoubtedly emphasizes the fact that the enacted version was approved by the state, and indeed, connotes a certain historical realism.

According to its authors the official script was "as close as possible to historic truth," the only significant changes being the place and time for the presentation, "since it is not possible to do it at dawn or in the Plaza de Armas." The authors had relied on three chroniclers, and all of them had claimed to have witnessed the ceremony. They were Garcilaso de la Vega, Cristóbal de Molina "el Cuzqueño," and Cieza de León. Their main reference was Garcilaso, from whom they appropriated the ritual's main plot. Cristóbal de Molina provided the commission members with Christian liturgical references. In addition to the Inca's central prayer, which has continued to be said throughout the years, they followed Molina's text to introduce a "communion," which obviously resembles Catholic liturgy. According to the 1952 script, during that communion, which is placed at the end of the ritual, as in the Catholic mass, the Inca was supposed to drink corn beer along with *çancu,* a special kind of bread. Finally, Cieza de León provided the contemporary official authors of Inti Raymi with the titles of some of the Inca nobility who participated in the ceremony.

The authors of this official script received "special congratulations from the Ministry of Education" for their work.[80] A journalist who had been specially sent to Cuzco to report on the event wrote the following in an article entitled "Inti Raymi, reminiscencias de un pasado esplendoroso" (Inti Raymi, reminiscences of a splendorous past):

> Maybe this year "Inti Raymi" . . . has emphasized most conspicuous details and characteristics because the ceremony has been restricted to what the historical documents of well-known investigators indicate. . . . After nine years of representations this festival has restricted itself in the most loyal way to historical truth. . . . The minister of education of the Republic, General Juan Mendoza Rodríguez, witnessed the festival accompanied by his official retinue and by the principal authorities of the department, such as the prefecto,

the mayor of Cuzco, the president of the Supreme Court, and civil and military authorities . . . [A]lso witness[ing] Inti Raymi [was] the ambassador of Italy, who is currently visiting the city.[81]

The script was accurate enough for the central state to endorse it. The presence of the minister of education and the civil and military authorities from Cuzco ultimately sanctioned the script as official history. Given its antecedents as exclusive Inca theater, Inti Raymi had become a passageway to intellectual recognition of the actors and writers involved in its production. However, the "official script" marked a turning point in the way the invented ritual had been until then used by "unofficial" intellectuals to acquire academic recognition. The "written version" eliminated their improvisations and thus curtailed their self-styling as intellectuals. Conversely, it endowed the official script authors with absolute intellectual authority as "specialists" in Inca culture. They realized that the actor who played such a role could acquire excessive and undeserved recognition, as illustrated by Faustino Espinoza Navarro's career as Inca. Measures were taken to control the intellectual sway of these actors, as is suggested in the following commentary from a well-known Lima-based critic, full of racial sarcasm:

Faustino Espinoza is what we can call a professional Inca, as he has represented the lord of the Empire in the successive performances of Inti Raymi in Cuzco. This picturesque personage, who has even occupied many pages in popular international magazines is identified in Cuzco more as the "Inca" than as the owner of a small restaurant in a village near the archaeological capital. He knows by heart everything that has to be said in Inti Raymi and he takes his role very seriously. He speaks parsimoniously and smiles diplomatically, showing his gold teeth. He gets irritated when asked how much he makes as an Inca and declares that he does everything for free. Indeed, this mestizo is not indifferent to the flattery of being famous and greets his subjects with a carefully studied dignity.[82]

The written script favored the confiscation of the Inti Raymi by representatives of the state and subordinated self-taught intellectuals like Espinoza to traditional academics. As a result, after years of success, when Faustino Espinoza presented the Inti Raymi in Lima allegedly without consulting the intellectual authorities responsible for the spectacle, he was "dethroned." Enraged with Espinoza's transgression, limeño cultural authorities criticized the "historical inadequacy" and "lack of respect" with which the Inti Raymi had been staged: "The fiesta of Inti Raymi was . . . a pantomime in which disorder, adulteration, and chaos coalesced. . . . Espinoza's presentation lacked conformity to historical truth — it did not even approach it. . . . Historical truth and the living manifestations of popular art are a national patrimony upon which surveillance has to be exerted."[83] The local press in Cuzco joined these accusations, and in 1958 academic cultural authorities replaced him in his role of the Inca in the Cuzco production by Ricardo Castro Pinto, an informally educated musician who had participated in the Inti Raymi since it was staged in 1944, playing Willac Uma, the second most important character in the drama.[84] Appallingly for Espinoza, the press said that the 1958 Inti Raymi in Cuzco had been "much better than those of the previous years, especially because Ricardo Castro Pinto showed much better interpretive qualities than his predecessor and even brandished a purer Quechua."[85] Crowned as the new Inca by the local academia, Castro Pinto also had the opportunity to write his own dialogues and those of his escorts, following of course the official script.[86] Outclassing Espinoza's Capac Simi proficiency granted him entrance in the local intellectual sphere.

Conclusions

A few months after the first official staging of Inti Raymi in 1944, Humberto Vidal Unda, its principal promoter, had fervently declared: "Next year, Cuzco Week will serve to attract world-wide tourism so that all Peruvians will arrange to meet in this land to receive our baptism of Peruvianness. Along with the world-class festivals of Seville's Holy Week, Venice's Carnival, Leipzig's Fair, etc., we will establish another world-class festival: Cuzco's Inti Raymi, in our magnificent setting, Sacsayhuaman."[87]

His words were prophetic, at least partially. Probably because of its weak infrastructure and low budget, Inti Raymi has never achieved a status like the First World tourist festivals. However, in 1947 Cuzco was proclaimed Tourist Capital of Peru, and along with the ruins, indigenous folklore, and villages, the Inti Raymi was its most important marketable image.[88] Since 1944, Cuzco has annually hosted the celebration of the Inca ritual of Inti Raymi on June 24. The date and the ritual currently conjure up what Benedict Anderson has termed an "imagined community" of cuzqueños who gather yearly in the fortress of Sacsayhuaman. Along with them, the audience includes foreign and Peruvian tourists, local authorities, and at times official visitors from Lima or foreign countries.

The eventual achievement of neoindianismo was to produce an image of Cuzco that had room for the past, represented by archaeological remains and Inca rituals, as well as for the present, represented by indigenous folklore. This representation did not cancel regional hierarchies as neoindianists had initially declared. On the contrary, one aspect of the dominant modes of cultural intimacy, specifically the elites' feelings of racial inferiority vis-à-vis limeños, required the representation of an Inca past as glorious and superior, so gentlemen could use it to identify themselves while at the same time providing a possible source of national essence. Yet, the gendered aspect of the same cultural intimacy compelled neo-Indians to be "real men" and "bravely" accept their regional culture and thus moved them to present Indians on the stage, and, likewise, to open up the roles of Inca nobility to be represented by nonelite actors. Even if hierarchized, these inclusions aided the construction of cuzqueñismo as a hegemonic feeling potentially shared (albeit differently) by cuzqueños of all social backgrounds. Although this important achievement of the neo-Indian did not cancel race, nor racial feelings, it marked a turning point in cuzqueño intellectual history.

The new cuzqueñismo intertwined with prevailing racialized images of the lofty social status of intellectuals and stimulated their proliferation. As the regional festival culture became important, both as a region-making device (in the 1940s) and as the basis of a successful tourist industry (in the 1960s), the image of Cuzco as a unique cultural site acquired the potential to generate intellectuals. Established intellectuals enhanced their names by producing books that were a combination of tourist guides, historical information, and ethnographic folklore with titles that invoked both their academic quality and the cuzqueñista mystique that had inspired the scholarly publication.[89] Self-taught quechuólogos were also successful in using cuzqueñismo to style themselves as intellectuals. As indigenistas and others had done previously, they deployed their intellectual identity to counteract the racialized hierarchies that could hinder their access to influential positions as guardians of cuzqueñismo, which they eventually attained.

Faustino Espinoza is a good example, although he is certainly not the only one. When he was removed from the Inti Raymi cast, he had already founded the Academia de la Lengua Quechua, which approved its statutes in January 1954. The academy was one of the places where unofficial intellectuals could gain status as proper intellectuals. To certify their scholarly rank they elaborated a peculiar opinion about Quechua according to which "Qhapaj [Capac] Simi was a type of evolved Quechua taught in special schools or *jashaiwasi* that existed in this city [Cuzco] and were attended by members of the Inca nobility."[90] Envisioning that Capac Simi was taught in "special schools" may have been intended to grant intellectual status to Inca teachers of Quechua and, conceivably, by extension to its contemporary guardians, the members of the Quechua Language Academy. True or not, this institution, since its inception, has represented a permanent obstacle to any attempt from the state to officially determine Quechua spelling or syntax (Godenzzi, 1992; Niño Murcia, 1997).

In addition to the specific case of Quechua and its self-taught intellectuals, the success of cuzqueño "popular culture" also promoted the proliferation of more traditional intellectuals, such as anthropologists and historians. These intellectuals, by establishing their profession in cuzqueñismo, scaled the local social ladder in spite of the insignificance of their careers as income-generating professions. Being an intellectual in Cuzco, and contributing to the glorification of the city, was one of the social tools that nonelite cuzqueños deployed to overcome potential working-class origins and to achieve entrance into the local elite.

As the feeling and performance of cuzqueñismo was officially

The Inca, Cuzco, 1991.
(Below) The Inca being
interviewed for local radio
inside the Coricancha, before
the representation begins.
Cuzco, 1991. Like Espinoza
in 1944, the 1991 Inca
addressed the president of the
Republic, Alberto Fujimori,
saying, "*Ama sua, ama llulla,
ama keya*" (Do not steal, do
not lie, and do not be lazy) —
the three precepts that guided
Inca rule, according to
national tradition. Both
photographs by author.

opened to commoners, representations of regional culture, whether of Incas or of folklore, also provided a space for the emergence of cultural producers who were not interested in rising as official intellectuals. These were the performers and creators of folklore, who celebrated Cuzco from a subordinate indigenous position, but who through their performances established an implicit dialogue with official intellectuals. Obviously, "cuzqueño culture," and most specifically "indigenous culture," was and continues to be among the central themes in this conversation which unfolded (and continues to unfold) in almost as many directions as there were folklorists. In chapters 5 and 6 I describe the implicit dialogues between elite intellectuals and common interpreters of cuzqueño culture. I contend, simply, that folklore provides an important arena where its cuzqueño producers discuss and constantly reformulate their views about local race and culture in ways that intersect with their own identities.

In this chapter I have proposed that the neoindianista elite articulated its project through a racialized notion of culture as a heritage bounded to a masculinized construction of the Andean landscape. The ideal type that the project produced was the cholo, the conqueror of the *chola* (female) and master of Indians. In the next chapter I present the response of the cholas to neoindianista project. Through their response these women stressed their self-identity as mestizas and proposed an alternative understanding of culture as a social position that is not necessarily inherited, but that can also be achieved through education and hard work.

4

Insolent Mestizas and Respeto

The Redefinition of Mestizaje

Considering:

That Cuzco Week (June 24–30) has been created to evoke the past grandeur of the capital of Tawantinsuyu and to render homage to the purest that remains of its race;

That the peoples of the sierra preserve up to our times the racial purity of those who forged a culture that awes the world;

That it is equitable to exalt this ethnic group, the root and nerve of our Peruvianness, in one of its most salient aspects, which is the beauty of the Andean woman;

The Centro Qosqo de Arte Nativo RESOLVES:

To convoke an "Autochthonous Beauty Contest" among the representatives of each province of the Department of Cuzco.

The epigraph comes from the opening paragraph of a document entitled "Bases para el concurso de belleza autóctona departmental"[1] and refers to the beauty contests for indigenous women that took place in Cuzco for several years starting in 1957.[2] Early that same year a limeña, a member of a leading family, had won the title of Miss Universe in an international beauty competition. This must have stimulated the cuzqueñista feeling that propelled elite Neo-Indian male cholos to organize the beauty contests for Indian women. According to Juan Bravo, its inventor and organizer, the event sought to convince the dominant sectors that these women "could be beautiful, with a different beauty than the one to which we [the elites] were accustomed." His persuasive official argument was that the contest was meant "to serve as the basis for an ethnological study of bio-typological character, of the inhabitant of the southern Peruvian sierra; to serve as a folkloric study of typical attire; to be another tourist attraction during Cuzco's evocative week."[3] In the previous chapter I presented neoindianista expressions in favor of art and the spirit and against race. I also explained how these declarations had continued earlier racialized thought, which was refurbished in the forties by means of neoindianista emphasis on a (masculinized) notion of culture geographically bounded to the highlands. Yet on that occasion, race was conspicuously silenced by the spirit and mestizaje prevailed over purity. Thirteen years later, earlier notions of racial purity again surfaced. This time they wore the attire and bore the image of Indian women, as part of the neoindianista project to promote ideas of indigenous female beauty. As the rules for the Indigenous Women's Beauty Contest indicates, race intertwined with references to "ethnic groups," a concept coined by academics in the late fifties and aimed at eliminating race as a category to mark differences (Stolcke, 1993; Montagu, 1962). The racial feelings of the organizers shaped the rules of the contest: to be accepted as candidates women applicants had to prove their "racial purity" and "verify their indigenous lineage" by showing either a birth or baptismal certificate. Reproducing notions of geographically bounded race and culture, the contest organizers required the participants to "present themselves with the typical festival outfit *characteristic of the place* to which they belong" (my emphasis). Finally, in keeping with dominant ideas about the intertwinement of race and sexuality, the all-male, "decent" jury determined that the candidates' racial purity had to be embodied by physical symbols emblematic of their peculiar sexuality. Accordingly, the candidates had to have non-protruding breasts, short legs, and scant pubic hair; these implied the "passionless" eroticism that, according to organizers, characterized pure Indian women.

Noticeably, the *bases para el concurso* were embedded in gendered racial beliefs, the most obvious of which was the idea that Indian women were frigid and therefore "morally pure." Mestizas, working-class urban indigenous women, represented quintessential female immorality and thus were the paradigmatic counterpart of Indian women. In this chapter, which covers the period from 1950s to the early 1970s, I analyze how gendered racial beliefs about mes-

tizas' essential immorality influenced urban politics. Shaped by a
relative growth in the urban economy (resulting from the surge of
tourism and commerce) and the economic and political decline of the
traditional hacienda system in the late sixties, historians consider the
period from the 1950s to the early 1970s the most politically intense
in Cuzco (Tamayo H., 1981; Rénique, 1991). The indigenous beauty
pageants were certainly not at the center of the political dynamics.
However, these celebrations of Indian women stood in stark contrast
with the official policing and harassment of mestizas in the marketplace. During this period, the antiplebeian "moral panic" (Hall et
al., 1978), always latent in the ideology of decency, influenced the
municipal control of the marketplace. Probably a consequence of
produce shortages resulting from a long drought that affected the
region in the fifties, the municipal surveillance of market vendors,
the mestizas, became stricter. From chapter 1 we know that in the
dominant imagination gamonales occupied an intersection of race
and gender that defined them as immoral rural patriarchs and hence
illegitimate landowners. During the moral panic of the 1950s, mestizas became the female urban counterpart of male rural gamonales:
the women's economic gains were seen as the product of dishonest
manipulation of prices, "typical of their immoral breed." Years later,
when Marxist rhetoric pervaded the political environment, the unclear position of the mestizas in the Marxist class taxonomy (they
were neither peasants nor proletarians) obscured their active participation in demonstrations, strikes, and other forms of leftist protests. Scorned by conservative elites and ignored by the left, these
women were the main target of the urban official control inspired by
the combination of populism and decency that characterized regional politics during the period.

Obviously, market vendors were not passive victims of male disin-
terest, obliviousness, or aggression.[4] During the period when dramatic economic and political changes were taking place in Cuzco, the
marketplace became a site of major confrontations between the authorities and mestizas. Mikhail Bakhtin thought of marketplace
speech and gesture as "frank and free, permitting no distance between those who came in contact with each other and liberating
them from norms of etiquette and decency imposed at other times"

Participants at an indigenous beauty pageant, Cuzco, date unknown. Photograph by anonymous local photographer. The photographer, who did not want his name published, found it strange that I was willing to pay for pictures of an event that nobody remembers. He did not recall the year of this contest but said, "It could have been the first one."

(1984:10). The mestizas, who shared many of the features described by Bakhtin, defended their interests and contested their alleged immorality by using physical and verbal aggression against city rulers and its representatives. In so doing, they canceled the distance between themselves and the authorities, and they also transgressed norms of decency. But, working-class marketplace behavior in Cuzco was not as free as Bakhtin had envisioned. Mestizas' marketplace behavior followed (and continues to follow) an alternative moral code (they call it *respeto*), which contests the dominant image of female decencia as sheltered domesticity and sexual virtue. During my fieldwork period I learned that hard work and achievements in everyday life form the basis of marketplace mestizas' morality, which also dismisses the elite's obsession with sexual propriety as the basis of hierarchies. However, their alternative morality of respect ac-

Participant at an indigenous beauty pageant, Cuzco. Date and photographer unknown. Juan Bravo, a neoindianista and one of the organizers of the beauty pageants, reports that participants had to prove their indigenous "racial" authenticity. The judges required that the participants in the beauty contest pose nude; short legs, small breasts, and scant pubic hair were the physical characteristics that the gentlemen organizers chose as markers of the bodies of *real* Indian women. Courtesy of Juan Bravo.

Isabel Mamani, from Tinta, winner of the first beauty pageant being interviewed by Juan Bravo for the national television, Cuzco, ca. 1960. Photographer unknown. Courtesy of Juan Bravo.

quiesces to social hierarchies based on education and urbanity. These indicate relatively successful hard-working lives and identify distinctions among cuzqueño commoners that potentially coincide with elites' categories of difference and exclusion. Decency and respect are hence, simultaneously, discordant and mutually sustaining discourses. This parallel, however, does not cancel the fact that respect represents an alternative, working-class moral code. Mestizas assign value to past or present rural experience in their urban-based codes of morality, and thus they reformulate the dominant regional intellectual definition of indigenous culture that ties it to the countryside. However, rules of respect fit hegemonic forms of discrimination when the mestizas divide indigenous identity into mestizo and Indian experiences. According to the definitions they formulate, mestizas (and their partners) are those individuals who live in the city but whose commercial activities imply constant commuting between city and countryside. They are mostly urban, but they are also rural. Indians are those individuals whose experience is predominantly rural and agricultural. Urban Indians are unsuccessful immigrants from the countryside. Although at first glance this is similar to the taxonomy of the elites, it is not the same. In the marketplace the women vendors taught me that being mestiza does not connote a process in which the nonindigenous aspects of the identity gradually replace the indigenous ones. Since according to marketplace rules of respect, mestizas are successful indigenous women, their being mestizas does not imply the decay but the buttressing of indigenous culture. The market women also taught me that being mestiza or Indian is a social condition, and both fall within the scope of indigenous culture. The bitter side of my newly acquired knowledge is that even though the mestiza identity represents an alternative category of self-definition for subordinate indigenous sectors of the city, these women represent a bastion for the enforcement of cuzqueño racism, elite and plebeian.

Commercial Development in Mid-Century Cuzco

The 1950s began with a powerful earthquake, which some historians consider decisive in the configuring of contemporary Cuzco

(Tamayo Herrera, 1992; Rénique, 1991). The quake destroyed the walls of colonial mansions and accelerated the transformations that were already taking place in the city, namely the surging immigration from the countryside of people who, decades earlier, had been seasonal commuters from the provinces to the capital city. The emergency made the national government pay attention to the former capital of the Inca Empire and resulted in a greater presence of state agencies in Cuzco. Ten days after the earthquake, a law was passed that authorized the interior minister to create an "account for the reconstruction of the City of Cuzco," by utilizing that decade's profits from guano sales. At the end of 1950, another law took effect that increased the cigarette tax; the earnings would be used for public housing projects, for the development of cuzqueño industry, and for loans for private property reconstruction.[5] Hence while new buildings were constructed, and old ones were renovated, the construction industry generated an important increase in the demand for urban workers. In addition to new edifices, the number of brick factories skyrocketed.[6] The demographic growth of the city was also the result of another natural "accident": the countryside was devastated by one of the hardest droughts in regional history. Consequently, the already increasing population increased even more, and as newcomers settled, they created new neighborhoods in the hills that surrounded the city. Official statistics record that the urban area of the city grew from 311 hectares in 1950 to 1,312 hectares in 1972 (Ruiz Bravo and Monge, 1983). The pace of growth was so rapid after the quake and the drought that new settlements were established in hills formerly used as grazing pastures that surrounded the city.[7]

Luckily for cuzqueños from all walks of life, the city was favored by the growth of tourism, which began its surge by the end of the fifties and reached a peak in the seventies. An important (and persistent) characteristic of tourism as a commercial activity is that cuzqueños of all social groups participate. At the beginning of the boom, owners of old colonial houses that had survived the quake took advantage of the construction upsurge and transformed the mansions into hotels. Likewise, owners of some *chicherías* and *picanterías* (working-class restaurants) washed their walls and committed themselves to operating to the standards of their new clientele. Re-

Table 1. Municipal Income in the City of Cuzco (in thousands of soles)

Source	1934	1942	1953	1956	1960
Industry taxes	3.0	22.1	295.3	380.0	480.0
Licenses[a]	8.0	8.0	55.1	100.0	108.0[b]
Slaughterhouse tax	19.2	21.0	150.0	103.0	195.0
Marketplaces tax[c]	29.7	23.2	134.2	250.9	285.4
Fines	1.0	1.0	67.7	120.0	135.0
Health certificates	—	0.2	14.6	50.0	140.0
Barracas[d] tax	—	—	106.5	—	—
Public spectacles	—	—	111.0	130.0	283.0
Landed properties tax	—	—	—	—	2,000.0
Subtotal	55.9	76.6	9,343.7	1,133.9	3,392.0[e]
Total (includes "other income")	440.4	312.4	1,924.3	1,916.2	6,394.1

Source: Archivo Historico Municipal del Cuzco, Legajo 178 (1907–1968); Legajo 157 (1953); Legajo 166 (1956).
[a] Licenses and patents include all types of establishments from chicherías and teterías to large hotels and restaurants.
[b] Sixty-eight thousand soles derive from licenses for marketplaces stalls.
[c] Marketplaces tax includes vendors in kiosks and small stores as well as peddlers.
[d] *Barracas* are makeshift kiosks that served as housing for those cuzqueños who were left homeless after the 1950 earthquake. Many used them as shops where they sold everything from groceries to shoes and office supplies.
[e] The municipal income did not include landed properties until after 1956. In this table only the column for the year 1960 reflects this income (which is equivalent to real estate tax and included urban and nearby rural properties).

cently arrived immigrants created *artesanía turística* (handicrafts for tourists), adapting local items of attire to tourist needs and tastes. Last but not least, travel agencies — with English names such as Inca Land Tours — became part of the urban landscape.[8]

Thus, even as the rural economy declined as a result of the drought, urban commerce, big and small, grew at an unprecedented rate and developed into the most important venture in the economy and a source of income that included even the poorest sectors of the city. In 1952 a municipal census of the street vendors located in the Plaza San Francisco, registered seven hundred peddlers of every type of product. For a plaza that measures less than one thousand square meters, that is an astonishing number of vendors.[9] Certainly, in mid-century Cuzco, commerce had displaced manufacturing as the main economic activity. The money that the central government pumped into Cuzco after the earthquake was used to augment the flow of commerce, which was already on the rise before the natural catastrophe.[10] Former prosperous artisans forgot their own attempts to modernize their production and shifted to commerce, becoming store owners. Tailors marketed "imported cashmere," ironsmiths retailed beds and scales they bought in Lima, shoemakers sold footwear imported from Arequipa.[11]

Table 1 — displaying the municipal income of the city of Cuzco between the years of 1934 and 1960[12] — shows the general growth of commerce during the period, and most specifically in the marketplace, the infrastructure of which municipal authorities expanded three times during the fifties: in 1953, 1957, and 1959.[13] Two figures stand out in the table: tax proceeds from the marketplace and the slaughterhouse and income from *multas* (fines) and certificates of health inspection were among the highest revenue producers. Vendors at the marketplace, who benefitted from the increase in commercial activities provoked by the growth of tourism, were targets of municipal control throughout the period. Women vendors resisted paying fines or demanded the improvement of facilities in exchange for their contributions, thus politicizing their relationship with city authorities. I will return to this topic later.

Populism and the Unionization of Cuzqueño Workers

The reader may have the impression that social unrest in Cuzco was limited to the countryside. However, such was not the case: urban riots were also frequent. One particular disorder vividly retained in the popular memory is the assault against Casa Calvo in 1918. It was provoked by a severe scarcity of coins, which especially affected the economy of Cuzco's working classes (Kruggeler, 1993:221). Another urban demonstration of social unrest, also well remembered, was the stoning of the mayor's house in 1923, when he was accused of implementing the controversial law of Conscripción Vial.[14] This riot happened on Holy Monday, after the traditional procession of the "Lord of earthquakes," when the people—who had convened for pious purposes—shifted their focus from sacred to political and demonstrated their anger.

Urban riots consisted of looting and stoning, which was specifically known by its Quechua name *ch'akeichis,* literally, "to stone." An important cuzqueño historian describes these events as "carried out by the masses of artisans and plebes, the famous *weratakas,* called this because of their *wiswi* [greasy] clothing, . . . in which the lapels of the jackets, and the necks, preserved the signs of not having ever stumbled upon soap or water." The same historian also recalled a famous leader of ch'akeichis known as Qatamayo ("turbid river," in Quechua), "who, wearing hat and poncho, devoted himself entirely to organizing the disorders, preferably on Holy Monday" (Tamayo Herrera, 1992:821–828). Qatamayo died in 1930, at the dawn of a new political period in Cuzco.

The new era started with the political modernization that followed Leguía's fall in 1930 and was launched following the organization of the first two populist political parties, the Apra and the Communist Party.[15] Partha Chattarjee (1986:150–153), on analyzing the process of political modernization in India, proposed that the change in politics in that nation marked a split between a "domain of rationality and a domain of unreason, from a domain of organization and a domain of spontaneity." The same split can be discerned in Cuzco, when modern populist cuzqueño politicians condemned spontaneous riots and distinguished them from organized party-led activities, perceived as legitimate political actions. For example, when the Communist Party was accused of organizing looting in Cuzco, Casiano Rado, one of its leaders responded, "We communists have a science and a faith. Our labor is limited to a simple indoctrination and the organization of the workers in order to teach them to have class consciousness; but we always display our activities within legal [limits] and order."[16] The new professional politicians defined the urban tumults, which had been integral to cuzqueño political culture, as social disorder. Likewise, nonpartisan leaders of *el pueblo* like Qatamayo were considered prepolitical as they were "still igno-

rant and uncultivated" and therefore, did not have political compe-
tence.[17] Qatamayo would not live long enough to witness how professional politicians replaced ch'akeichis with the organized strikes,
negotiations, rallies, and unions promoted by Cuzco's Communist
Party, the most important political group in Cuzco from the mid
1940s until the late 1960s. Ideologically, it was a very peculiar
group. By the end of the 1950s, a U.S. anthropologist who visited
Cuzco was informed by the local prefect that "75 per cent of cuzqueños are communists, but a peculiar breed of communists who
talk of Lenin today and tomorrow may support a right-wing military
coup'" (Patch, 1958:7). The same anthropologist noted that the
party was formed by "all brands of communists, from intellectuals
who have spent years in Russia, to illiterate workmen who at different times have been apristas, or followers of Odría" (a populist
general and former president in the 1950s) (1958:6).

In a trend integral to the nationwide modernization of politics,
guilds were replaced by workers unions. Although in the 1920s there
were many artisanal guilds, by 1950 only the barbers guild and the
butchers guild remained. The Apra and the Communist Party organized the unionization of workers in Cuzco until the 1950s, when the
Communist Party became the sole leader in the process (Portocarrero, 1990). The organization of workers was particularly important in the countryside, where hacienda workers formed *sindicatos*.
Communist-led rural political activities had begun in the 1930s,
when indigenous leaders organized one of the first peasant unions
in the Lauramarca hacienda (in the province of Quispicanchis). In
the following decade, sindicatos — coordinated by the Federación
de Trabajadores del Cuzco (the Federation of Cuzco Workers) —
became an uncomfortable yet familiar presence in the countryside.
Two of these, which were to become famous years later, organized in
the 1940s: one in Maranura, at a hacienda in the lowland province
of La Convención, and a second one in Chhuro, at a hacienda in the
highlands of the province of Paucartambo (Aranda and Escalante,
1978:65).

Employing class rhetoric, rural unions discarded the label "indigenous," and chose instead "peasants." The reader may recall from
chapter 2 that in the 1920s, the rural social movement inspired by

the Tawantinsuyu Committee aimed at empowering its activists' identities as Indians. The new communist-led unions departed from Tawantinsuyu's emphasis on indigenous education, citizenship, and Indian cultural revitalization. The racial era had been ideologically superseded, the new political activists claimed. Instead they defined their actions within the framework of class struggle, and they issued economic demands. No free labor, better salaries, and eight-hour workdays were among the salient requests (Aranda and Escalante, 1978:65). Granted, members of the sindicatos rurales were Indians, but for the communist leaders their class identity as peasants was more important in their struggle. Likewise, because class was considered to be definitive, landowners, whether gentlemen or not, were all "owners of means of production" and hence all gamonales. For example, in 1933, Mariano Turpo, a leader of Lauramarca, while in jail, addressed a letter to his "compañeros del Sindicato de Campesinos de Lauramarca" (companions of the Lauramarca Peasant Union), in which he called the owners of Lauramarca gamonales.[18] The men that Turpo accused of gamonalismo belonged to one of the most powerful elite cliques, the Saldívar family, whose members were reputable cuzqueño elite gentlemen and ladies. During the indigenista years, decency had sheltered them from the accusation of gamonalismo. Initially only a rhetorical expression, this language shift was going to prove crucial in cuzqueño politics as the unionization escalated.

Coinciding with the insurgence of the populist parties in Cuzco, indigenista ideologues moved to Lima, where they joined official institutions. As mentioned in chapter 3, when the state-sponsored Instituto Indigenista Peruano was established in 1946, Luis E. Valcárcel, the early champion of purist indigenismo, became its first president. The institute (promoted by the U.S.-sponsored Pan American Union) aimed at implementing rural development projects, sometimes jointly with U.S. universities.[19] The same indigenistas and a party of North American Andeanists (initially grouped to collaborate on *The Handbook of South American Indians*) promoted the organization of the Instituto de Etnología y Arqueología (at the University of San Marcos in Lima), and of the archaeology and anthropology section of Cuzco University. Drawing on U.S. anthropological theories, cuzqueño intellectuals (indigenistas and neoindianistas alike) equipped themselves with "culturalist" viewpoints and joined the international rejection of racial rhetorics. Following this rejection, they used "ethnic groups" to refer to Indians and mestizos, the chosen target population of Peruvian anthropological studies since its inception.[20]

Not surprisingly, union leaders dismissed indigenismo as a "engañosa retórica liberal, filoindígena de ayuda cultural y jurídica de parte de los blancos y mestizos civilizados a los bárbaros indios" (deceptive pro-Indian rhetoric that was promoted by 'civilized' white and mestizo liberals who claimed to help the 'barbaric' Indians culturally and legally).[21] Instead of "development projects" during the Primer Congreso Obrero Departamental in April 1950, leftist leaders demanded that the uncultivated latifundia to be distributed among peasant workers. Likewise, the leadership of the Federación de Trabajadores del Cuzco announced at the same convention the prevalence of the "working class" and proposed the "unification of all workers without racial, sexual, or ideological distinctions."[22] In the late fifties, studies of culture (and of ethnic groups) belonged either to official state discourse or to what leftists perceived as "apolitical" academic research. The oppositional forces instead were replete with class rhetoric. Yet, neither arguments canceled preexisting racialized feelings, which declared the inferiority of Indians and the superiority of intellectuals. This status quo was legitimized by attitudes of paternal benevolence influenced by populism, in which superior intellectuals were to provide for the well-being of Indians, labeled an "ethnic group" by conservatives or "peasants" by leftists leaders.

Union politics escalated in the last years of the 1950s as hacendados gradually lost regional power in a process that was to be irreversible. In 1961, a new organization, the Federación Departamental de Campesinos del Cuzco, emerged to consolidate all rural unions. It had become evident by then that peasants represented the strongest opposition to state institutions in Cuzco. However, the Peasant federation, abiding by Marxist-Leninist principles and asserting the subordination of (Indian) peasants to the city (mestizo) proletariat, followed orders from the urban-based Cuzco Workers

Federation. The argument was that "given their insufficient education [*preparación*] the peasants would not be able to make their
institution work" (Aranda and Escalante, 1978:84). Contradicting
this evaluation, peasant leaders during the 1960s organized the rural
sindicates in the haciendas and surpassed the urban-based leftist
leadership. Under peasant leadership, union agendas in the 1960s
went beyond the moderate reforms requested in previous decades
and produced an avalanche of successful land seizures. In November
1962, as Manuel Prado's second government was coming to an end,
the peasants, dressed in Indian garb, invaded the Plaza de Armas to
demand agrarian reform in one of the largest official demonstrations
ever seen. The demonstrators obliged the prefect to negotiate with an
official commission, which later announced the agreements in a public speech, amplified with loudspeakers.[23] Significantly, it was delivered in Quechua, demonstrating that this language was no longer
only for festivals; it was now overtly associated with political demands and even "revolution." Peasants wielding Quechua, and fill-
ing the Plaza de Armas in their wool ponchos and chullos (caps)
made it clear that the uprising had a cultural identity, even if the
leadership subordinated it to class rhetoric.

Massive incursions by peasants were frequent events in the urban
panorama of Cuzco in the 1960s. One occasion was Emiliano Huamantica's funeral. A prominent leader of the Cuzco Federation of
Workers, his memorial service was attended by hundreds of his followers. The elite must have shivered at the sight of the funeral and at
the irreversibility of the social changes that the region had under-
gone. Contrasting with funerals in the 1920s (which I described in
the first chapter) in which elite gentlemen delivered moral lessons to
the populace, union leaders used Huamantica's burial to defy dominant hacendado society.

Saturnino Huillca, an indigenous peasant leader active since the
1920s, dressed in his ceremonial poncho and chullo, made a public
speech "en la esquina de la calle del Marquez" (on the corner of
Marquez Street). In the speech, delivered in Quechua, he urged his
compañeros to continue in their struggle against the landowners.
Police detectives, who had recorded his speech, later interrogated
him about its contents. Significantly, the interrogation—held in

the Cuzco jail—began with the following words: "Indio, por qué hablaste así? A ver ahora habla" (Indian, why did you talk like that? Let's see if you'll talk now) (Neira, 1975:59–61). In the 1960s the word "indio" no longer played an empowering note in political campaigns; instead, it was used when Indians were tortured or as a means to humiliate indigenous leaders. Ex-Indians identified themselves as peasants and referred to each other as "compañero," an identity that empowered them and represented their challenge to the dominant taxonomies that had made them inferior. The practice of calling each other "compañero" might have been introduced by leftist politicians but may have been adopted because it helped obliterate the enunciation of insulting social distinctions and thus soothed some wounds. The usage of the term "compañero" became part of everyday language, and it continues to be used nowadays, even in religious rituals. However, silencing of the term "Indian" implied consensual acceptance of the inferior social condition of those meriting that name.

In the late 1960s indigenous Cuzqueños joined their worker leaders in using class struggle as an empowering banner. Even if the Marxist political ideas that replaced former notions of racial-cultural differences did not explicitly proclaim the inferiority of indigenous culture, they did privilege class over all other forms of identity. Hugo Blanco, a famous cuzqueño union organizer, was unique in identifying himself and his fellow leaders as "revolutionary Indians." Similarly, he was one of the few vocal Marxists—if not the only one—who overtly declared that indigenous oppression was "not simply economic." But even Blanco subordinated cultural domination to "the land problem." "The Indian struggle," he wrote, "with all its richness, is only one part of the entire Peruvian revolution. It exists, but there is no reason to exaggerate its importance; it is less important than the Afro-American problem in the United States" (Blanco, 1972:133–134). Even though he only acknowledged that culture had ancillary importance, Blanco was an isolated voice among the opposition.

In general, the leftist intelligentsia opined that class was the crucial category in political and social analyses. Illustrative of this tendency were the historians that interpreted the 1920s rural disturbances as "messianic rebellions." As I noted in chapter 2, these intellectuals were persuaded that the insignificant "development of the productive forces of the Andean peasant economy" could not instill "class consciousness" in so-called Indians. Hence, intellectuals thought, the driving force of rebellious Indian peasants derived from Andean culture, conceived as millenarian and premodern. In addition to this (a)historical interpretation of indigenous agency, the sociological diagnosis of "rural reality" denied Indians the capacity of political leadership: "[They] are unable to create leadership, because they are emotionally dependent on the norms of the old order" (Quijano, 1978:148). "The Indian leader is himself going through a process of *cholificación*," the sociologist Aníbal Quijano would also assert in a famous intellectual meeting in 1965 (Arguedas et al., 1985). The definition of Indians as illiterate, rural simpletons who needed guidance from more educated classes to survive in a national society dominated by the written word was the dominant academic position. It swayed intellectuals who considered themselves as "organic" to the "proletariat cause." Implicit in their view of Indians was the idea that to empower themselves Indians had to be literate. Yet, once literate they would become mestizos or cholos, and step into a new stage in their working-class evolution, yet still subordinate to cultured intellectuals. The turn-of-the-century intellectual belief in the power of education to transform the racial configuration of the country continued to shape mid-century political imagination in spite of overt rejections to the notion of race itself.

Individuals like Mariano Turpo from Lauramarca, and Saturnino Huillca, who had been political leaders since the early 1930s and were still active in the 1970s, conceded that literacy was a path to empowerment. The reader may remember that in 1933 (when the Communist Party was in the early stage of the process), Turpo addressed his fellow unionists as compañeros and recommended that they should "insist on our need for literacy, as not knowing how to read makes us more Indian" (más Indios). Like elite intellectuals, this politician believed that literacy removed the social condition of Indianness. Yet, to him, this did not require shedding indigenous culture, as dominant intellectuals thought. Leaders of Lauramarca were among the most astute and successful cuzqueño sindicalistas of the century, and they sustained a struggle for over seventy years. Throughout this period they were able to negotiate with conservative and progressive official politicians.[24] Their political practice, however, included participating in indigenous religious duties. In the 1970s, when they were most successful, at least fifteen of the leaders were specialists in Andean rituals (Gow, 1982:201).[25] This did not mean, however, that they embraced Indianness as their social identity.

In the 1970s, indigenous peasants tended to remove themselves from Indianness, which they deemed a pathetic social condition. Marxists considered Indianness a form of "false consciousness" and inferior to "peasant" class identity, and conservative intellectuals defined Indians as an unprogressive ethnic group. Indicative of the consensual belief both in the inferiority of Indians and in the need to redeem them, in the 1970s political rhetoric the term "peasant" replaced the previous "Indian" category. The military government that issued the agrarian reform — the most drastic reform implemented by a non-Marxist Latin American government — complemented the policy by erasing the term "Indian" from official vocabulary. Implicitly agreeing with the measure, from the opposite side of the spectrum, the leader of a Maoist party stated that "if there is any differentiation [among peasants] it is not as Indian peasants, mestizo peasants, and white peasants but rather among poor peasants, middle peasants, and rich peasants" (Paredes, 1976:31).

Along with this deracialization of labels, the subordination of "peasants" to "urbanites" (proletarians or intellectuals) also went unquestioned. Marxist and culturalist rhetoric alike assumed the superiority of the urban intellectual knowledge of leaders. Neither the insurgent rhetoric that had successfully empowered unionists nor the cultural rhetoric (in its indigenista or neoindianista version) objected to the dominance of the city over the countryside. But neither did it object to the subordination of women to men. The participation of women in politics was simply discounted and hence, market women (the protagonists of this chapter) occupied one of the blind spots of class rhetoric.

Yet the peasant leaders, who did not confine their activities to the countryside but also demonstrated in the Plaza de Armas, did so frequently in conjunction with urban *huelgas generales* (general strikes). And there was no successful strike without the participation of market vendors, who helped to paralyze the city by closing the marketplace. Newspaper articles describing the success of strikes organized by workers unions, specified that "marketplaces did not open their doors, thus contributing to the success of the strike."[26] These vendors were mestizas, women who during the "premodern" phase of Cuzco politics had joined the ch'akeichis organized by leaders such as Qatamayo. Likewise, they had participated in the unionization process since 1944, when the Sindicato de Mercados Unidos was inaugurated (Aranda and Escalante, 1978:49). However, amid the political modernization of mid-century Cuzco, market vendors had a controversial role. On one hand, the political leadership identified them as an important oppositional force, in as much as they were gente del pueblo. On the other hand, the same leadership saw them as potentially guilty of raising the prices of meat and produce, and thus being contrary to the "intereses del pueblo" (working-classes' interests). During the 1950s and 1960s, the Communist Party did not drop its populist rhetoric; rather, making subsistence foods cheaper, struggling against price speculation, and lowering the prices of primary-need items" continued to be central themes in their political agenda.[27] In the years when populism, combined with class politics, prevailed among the leftist opposition, market women had an unclear "class identity." Perhaps their ambiguous class status (along with their gender identity) shielded them from the irresistible political tendency to erase racialized categories from the official rhetoric. Unlike the Indians who became peasants, market women remained mestizas. However, as I will demonstrate, the identity they maintained was different from dominant racial meanings ascribed to mestizaje.

Intellectual Images of the Indian Woman and the Mestiza

The first impression that an Indian woman produces is a profound disgust and even repugnance. Savagery is found written in her physiognomy, in her distrustful and shy attitude. She does not reveal intelligence nor imagination, nor reason, nor even common sense; only stupidity, stubbornness. In her moral personality meekness and lewdness are quickly discovered. Meekness is her natural state, distrust her weapon of defense, gossip and lies the instruments she uses to win sympathy and to plant misunderstandings that bring her profit. . . . [Nevertheless] the ignorant, uncultured, miserable Indian woman is still a good mother, a good wife, a good daughter and, above all, she does not stifle the voice of nature, she does not oppose its wise mandates even when she has motives to hide a fault. (Del Pino, 1909:345)

Although it may seem unlikely, the above statement was intended to defend Indians against the opinions of some limeños who found no virtues at all in Indians. Despite the pejorative tone of the initial section, in the last portion its author claimed for Indian women a commendable female nature, which made them good mothers, daughters, and sexually acquiescing wives. Cuzqueños (who as we already know from previous chapters, belittled limeños' contempt toward everything Indian) celebrated the Indian woman's fidelity to "her man," which they explained in terms of her peculiar sexuality. Dominant among intellectuals was the impression that female Indians' sexuality was noticeable by its natural rejection of "foreignness," a feature that had contributed to the preservation of the "purity of the Indian race." In her recent analysis of European contemporary discriminatory behavior, which she calls "cultural fundamentalism," Verena Stolcke (1995) concluded that it is legitimized by xenophobia defined as the cultural instinct to reject strangers. Like contemporary European policy makers, cuzqueño intellectuals imagined that female Indians possessed a xenophobic sexual reaction against foreign men. Unlike current European cultural fundamentalists, who distance themselves from explicit racial discourses, early twentieth-century cuzqueño writers considered that such reaction was inherent to female Indians' sexual racial make-up. They enthusiastically asserted that "the Indian woman is never an adulteress and prefers to die before being unfaithful. Unmarried women cohabit with their fellow villagers, rarely with the *misti* and never with the white man" (Flores Ayala, 1913:14).

The female Inca pantheon that cuzqueño thinkers identified consisted of four powerful women: Mama Huaco, Chañan Cori-Coca, Cori Ocllo, and Isabel Chimpu Ocllo. The first two were warriors. Mama Huaco had saved her lineage in mythic times, and Chañan Cori-Coca fought the Inca's enemies, the Chancas, in historic Inca times (Cornejo Bouroncle, 1949:7–9). The last two were Inca noblewomen who witnessed the Conquest. Isabel Chimpu Ocllo was the mother of the famous chronicler Garcilaso de la Vega, and the prototype of the indigenous princess who surrendered to the conqueror and was subsequently abandoned by her Spanish lover. She represented the colonial origins of mestizaje. Cori Ocllo instead represented the preservation of indigenous racial purity: she was the Inca noblewoman who preferred to die rather than surrender to the conqueror.

Cori Ocllo's figure perfectly suited the 1920s indigenistas' drive for a racially pure self-identity. Luis E. Valcárcel wrote down Cori Ocllo's story, and her statue presided over his office at the Instituto Histórico del Cuzco. He translated the name Cori Ocllo as Golden Breast (Seno de Oro):

> Golden Breast, the most beautiful wife of Manko, was a heroine. The well-established Don Gonzalo wanted her for himself, but she was faithful to her race. How could she offer her body to the impure assassin of her gods and of her kings? Death first. So she lay tranquilly, without further vexation; the white beast would not dare come close to her cold flesh. . . . Kori Ojllo (*sic*), in order to frighten away from her the Spanish gallant, had covered her perfect torso with something repugnant, capable of driving away Don Juan himself. But still more virulent was the hatred that her eyes distilled. . . . Kori Ojllo has revived in the Andes, there where the Indian returns to his pre-Columbian purity, there where they shook free from the filth of the invader. Kori Ojllo lives, a fierce female, whom the whites can no longer conquer. The hatred, stronger than ever, inhibits her latent sexuality, conquers her temptations, and the Indian woman of the hostile clans prefers to die than to surrender herself. What disgust there would be if she gives up. She would be exiled from the ayllu. She would return no more to her adored native region. Even the dogs will come out to bite her. *The impure Indian woman finds*

refuge in the city. Flesh of the whorehouse, one day she will die in the hospital. (Valcárcel, 1978:78, my emphasis)

Evidently Valcárcel was not the only one to propagate this myth.[28] During a period when debates about the pros and cons of mestizaje were intense, the image of Cori Ocllo fit the purist racial projects. Insurmountable differences between the sexuality of "more developed" races and that of Indians (they believed) made hybridity impossible. Sexuality, some of them proposed, was dependent on the cultural capacities of any given race. Because of the undeveloped intellectual abilities of the Indians, their sexuality was instinctive, devoid of "the feeling of love," and driven exclusively by primitive procreative desires and needs (Flores Ayala, 1913:27–28; Escalante, 1910; Aguilar, 1922).[29] The newspapers reported this colorfully: "The Indian man joins with the female as flowers do, by the law of the attraction of pollen"; and sexual encounters were "real fights that lasted hours" in which the pair exchanged "pinches, even removing pieces of flesh from the arms."[30]

Notwithstanding their supposed primeval state, Indian women, intellectuals thought, were crucial for the prevention of promiscuity within and outside indigenous society because "sexual fury [was] stronger in the male Indian than in the Indian woman" (Flores Ayala, 1913:28; Delgado, 1909:21). Like Cori Ocllo, Indian women would allegedly reject men that were not Indian. Illustrative of this idea, a news item published in 1926 narrated the punishment received by a university student when he attempted to seduce an Indian woman. Pretending to consent to his pleas, she had led him to a trap formed by "a strong chain of a hundred men" who after beating him turned him in at the house of the town's priest.[31] However, to those of her own breed she presented no objection, patiently bearing all the primitivism of the Indian man. The process was in fact described in a contemporary newspaper article, also published in 1926: "When the *maccta* [young single man] is about twenty or twenty-five years old he seeks the *pasña* [young single woman] who does not withdraw her favors from the male's attacks."[32] This racially selective nature of Indian women's sexuality (which also neutralized them as targets of non-Indian male's sexual desire) inspired poems to the "Indian virgins, pure and strong of soul" (Masís, 1927:12). The priest Jorge A. Lira, who was a well-known Quechua specialist, believed to have found the image of the Indian woman in the canticles of King Solomon (Lira, 1960).

To spark this kind of intellectual admiration, the Indian woman had to remain rural. In the countryside, although she suffered her husband's primitivism, the ayllu could shelter her from sexual assaults of mestizo gamonales. In the city, where she was unprotected by the ayllu, underclass men victimized her. Thus, indigenistas believed, the migrant Indian woman was condemned to poverty, violence, and illness. She could only inspire pity. The "impure Indian woman" — as Valcárcel called those who did not follow the example of Cori Ocllo — ended up as a prostitute or was jailed as a thief. Nancy Leys Stepan noted that freed blacks in the United States were also considered the "most corrupt, depraved and abandoned element in the population" (Stepan, 1985:101). For indigenistas, mestizas were their Andean equivalent. Mirroring notions of "racial proper places" and "degeneration" described by Stepan (1985), the cuzqueño proponents of purist theories of race thought that Indians were negatively affected by the city. Migration to the city marred the Indian women's virtue by deforming the moral basis of their racial-cultural xenophobic sexuality, the cornerstone of the male indigenista purist project. Cori Ocllo's image was emblematic of indigenistas' repudiation of mestizaje; it signified the immoralization of mestizas, who were thus the female urban equivalent of gamonales in the countryside.

Not surprisingly, Cori Ocllo lost ground in the promestizo neo-indianista period. Uriel García, the champion of the *nuevo indio* wrote, "Kori Okllo (*sic*) is that Indian woman who smeared her body with manure and mud and allowed herself to be killed with arrows, tethered to a tree, instead of surrendering to the sensual passion of the invader and conceiving maternally the other America, [in an] infertile defense of the autochthonous tradition. She is the Indian woman who preserves her quaternary purity, that purity whose touch returns everything to the primitive" (1937:142). Both indigenismo and neo-indianismo were gendered projects that viewed female sexual racial/cultural virginity as the pillar of racial purity. Theories of hybridity were covert theories of desire according to Young (1995:9), and indeed they represented such for cuzqueño elite intellectuals. While indigenistas repressed their lust for indigenous women, neoindianistas exalted desire in promoting mestizaje and calling for interracial/ cultural sexual mingling and its resulting motherhood. Cori Ocllo the Indian virgin was eventually surpassed by Isabel Chimpu Ocllo, the Indian mother of the first mestizo (male) intellectual according to official history. This woman represented "the docile woman who served as amiable solace when the conquistador was an orphan of love. . . . [S]he was fertile earth for all seeds. She was history peacefully accepting destiny . . . [and] America overcoming its tragedy. Isabel is the American cave that indigenous mythologies call *pakarinas* [places of accession], from where the makers of the new culture arise again. From her belly, as from these marvelous grottos from which the Incas demiurges emerged, the undomesticated mestizo is born, who will give a renovated vigor to the continent" (García, 1937:142).

During the neoindianista era, mestizaje ceased to signify female racial treason and the origins of degeneration. Indian women who accepted foreign men's sexual demands were not perceived as immoral women, possessors of a promiscuous sexuality that deviated from the racial norm. Instead, since they were required to reproduce the "new Indian" (male) culture (García, 1948:212), the virile neoindianista fraternity idealized cholas' motherhood (cf. Parker, et al. 1992:6). García deemed these women "the rejuvenated organic force that advances impudently and without fear toward the city and toward the present, nurturing with her abundant and maternal breasts the maternal energy of the race, like a mother or a wet nurse, smelling of *chicha*, and with a *huayno* [a serrano melody] in her throat" (García, 1937:182). The preeminent characteristic of these cholas was their expressive eroticism, which allowed for the procreation of cholos. This was a spiritual manifestation of a normal female sexuality, a "symptom of the organic youth, and of the spiritual health of a complete woman in whose blood the hormones of femininity function normally" (García, 1937:184). Their "proper places" were deemed to be markets and chicherías — "the sacred marriage beds of their social maternity" (García, 1937:183) — where they displayed their coarseness and obscenity, expressions of their "frank," racially unobstructed sexuality, which when privately expressed, produced mestizaje.

Neoindianista preaching about the chola had international and national reverberations. Uriel García's ideas were echoed by the Mexican indigenista Moisés Saenz, who was seduced by the role of cholas in the national mestizaje project. He wrote about the chola, "She is the literal symbol of the nationalism. . . . She represents the organic force of the rejuvenated race. . . . The superiority of the chola over the Indian woman seems indisputable. . . . She is more agile of spirit, more active, marches erect along the roads, . . . speaks in a loud voice, a little vulgarly. . . . The chola travels all the roads of the highlands singing half in Spanish, half in Quechua, adorned with a tight bodice and her fluffy petticoats of boiling colors" (1933:275).

In Peru, the chola figure even functioned as a catalyst to express the political friction between indigenistas and neoindianistas, represented by Valcárcel and García respectively. José Varallanos, an author born in the department of Huánuco, was one of the most fervent promoters of Uriel García and a critic of indigenismo "à la Valcarcel." He also championed the chola, about whom he wrote:

> Generally the chola does not marry, she is a concubine and a partisan of free love. . . . She does not have same concept of virginal love that the Indian woman does. She gives herself to the man for love, because of the free expression of her feelings and her will. . . . At home the chola exercises a kind of matriarchy. Different from the Spanish woman [who acts as] a decorative figure [and from] the Indian woman who is the submissive servant of the husband . . . the chola is the boss of the house whose moral and economic responsibility she assumes. . . . She is involved in all of the businesses of the village and of the city, and in the small industry, woman of energy and masculine will, she is the social revolutionary of her environment and of her time. (Varallanos, 1962:65)

In Cuzco the alleged sensuality of cholas inspired poems that were very different from those inspired by the alleged virtue of Indian women. Luis Nieto, a locally famous poet who in 1944 wrote the lyrics to the "Hymn to Cuzco," also dedicated a poem to the cholas of Cuzco. He entitled it "Romance de la Barbaracha" (1942), and some of its lines say, in praise of the chola:

Chola, I love you as chola,
fresher than an apple
with your round skirts
and your blouse of percale.
Your smile shines clean
as the crystal of the hoarfrost.
Your eyes shine mischievously,
the sun frisks on your lips,
the moon envies your face.
Your two braids to me seem
two vipers along your back.
It is so pleasant to look at you,
walking towards the plaza
arousing at your step
the jealousy of the *cholada.*
I wish I were a hawk
to seize you with my claw
and to behead in your bosom
your two slave doves.
Nobody loves you as I do,
bold and fleshy chola,
with your fourteen skirts
and your pure wool shawl.
Little chola, very pretty chola,
lift your skirt a little.
They have told me that your thighs
are rosier than the dawn.
It must be seen how you like
to furiously move your buttocks
They make me want to loot it
with my pirate hands!

Luis Nieto was the best known versifier of the cholas' physical attractions, but not the only one.[33] Unlike the Hottentot woman, whose genitalia and buttocks were publicly displayed to exhibit her uncontrolled sexuality (Callaway, 1993; Gould, 1985), neoindianista male writers only made poetic allusions to them. Yet like the Hottentot woman, in the eyes of these cuzqueño men, what distinguished cholas was their unfettered sexuality and its external physical manifestations: big breasts, ample thighs, and prominent lips. Additionally, they firmly believed that Indian women became mestizas (cholas) just by transforming their racially conditioned sexual xenophobic deportment. Notwithstanding their rejection of race, neoindianismo was deeply rooted in the conception of sexuality as a racial and gendered feature that, if properly managed, could open the gates to national mestizaje.

In this stratified, populist, *and* masculine racial project, cholas were the sexual ideal of neoindianista men, who styled themselves as conquerors of the cholas, as expressed in Nieto's poem. But the project was not necessarily meant to uplift plebeian cholos. Although neoindianista intellectuals had boldly challenged the norms that prescribed male elite sexual endogamy, they maintained many other masculine norms of decencia. Cherished among them was their patriarchal responsibility to shelter women from the hardships of wage earning, an attribute that they considered missing among cuzqueño male commoners. Notwithstanding neoindianista admiration of male cholos' joy, strength, and artistic inclinations, even García, a model neoindianista, accused them of being lazy and of abusing cholas (García, 1937:118). Like their intellectual predecessors, neoindianistas believed that plebeian cholos were not good patriarchs because of their lack of education. In spite of the unquestioned masculine sexuality of working-class men, their negligence as fathers and husbands compromised their virility and subordinated them to neoindianista cultural leaders. Nevertheless, being neither effeminate aristocrats, like their predecessors nor irresponsible mestizos, like their working-class peers, this cholo elite placed itself at the summit of regional masculinity. The reproduction of cholo culture by promoting folklore (as explained in chapter 3) went hand in hand with conquering cholas and ultimately granted them a lofty placement among regional males as reproducers of mestizaje, almost in a literal sense.

Although they also criticized the lack of patriarchal responsibility of cholos, the "decent" groups of society rejected neoindianistas' populist preaching. Their mestizaje project, they contended, had an indecent underpinning: the intellectuals' own public testimony about their sexual attraction toward cholas. This attitude, judged impudent by the upper classes, only increased their deeply ingrained scorn of mestizas, whose image as unsheltered working women was already at odds with the canons of female decency. Cuzqueño ladies in particular resented the intellectuals' attitude, and although the most progressive elite women participated in the cultural revival that neoindianismo represented, they repudiated the sexualized aspects of mestizaje.[34]

Cori Ocllo's image continued to thrive among the regional elites. At the height of neoindianismo in 1944, when Carlota Oliart de Ocampo, a lady from Cuzco, gave a speech in honor of the first Cuzco Day, she praised Cori Ocllo as "the pure and strong woman who preferred to die to save her honor and that of her race. She constitutes the most beautiful example of what the Cuzco woman is worth morally in any time."[35] Similar images must have stimulated the imagination of the organizers of the Autochthonous Beauty Contest. Thus, despite the relative popularity of the cultural-historical aspects of neoindianismo, the grotesque figure of the *mujeres del pueblo* or the *chola vulgar* as described by the sexually conservative elite was the image that survived within cuzqueño society and was never replaced by the sensual and bold chola that neoindianistas praised. The chola was neither Cori Ocllo, the virgin, nor the decent lady sheltered from the hardships of work. Her working conditions — inappropriate for a woman — placed her in the realm of transgression. Helen Callaway has suggested that in the nineteenth century images of the exoticized, colonized woman emerged as a nexus of erotica, fantasy, desire, and pleasure and was always shadowed by the fear of unknown risks, pollution, disruption, degeneration, and destruction (1993:34). Although some dominant mid-century cuzqueño image-makers had overcome these fears, for those who abided by the sexual morality of decencia the neoindianistas' emphasis on the cholas allegedly free eroticism only increased beliefs in their supposed sexual immorality and degeneration. This, they thought, spread into other forms of delinquency, and was particularly obvious in the marketplace, which was thought to be the cholas' proper place.

Race, Delinquency, and Sexuality
Decent Populism and Mestizas

Early in the twentieth century some cuzqueño criminologists, following international assumptions about laws of racial inheritance, believed that the hardships of coping with poverty and a lack of education, damaged the poor and caused hereditary deficiencies. Limited access to education among the lower classes resulted in their having an undeveloped cerebral capacity and a natural inclination toward crime (Luna, 1919:18–19). In keeping with the tenets of decencia, this belief assumed the power of education to shape individuals' lives. The lack of education of the poor led to violence because "the more ignorant the man is, the more he approximates the animal, in that the savage instincts manifest themselves immediately through violent and bloody acts" (Luna, 1919:20). Even in the mid-twentieth century, the pages of the newspapers continued to relate poverty to ignorance, laziness, and delinquency. References to "families of thieves" (with their implicit notions of racial atavism) were common.[36] In the midst of populist and neoindianist renewal, dominant beliefs about the working classes' lack of education continued to legitimize differences between gente decente and gente del pueblo, the commoners. Allegedly ignorant and hence unrefined, they were inevitably inclined to crime in the mind of the elite. The formal dismissal of race and the reevaluation of mestizaje had not removed the pillar of cuzqueño racial thought: the belief that education distinguished the elite from the rest. In this supposedly raceless era, it became a more important class marker than the economic achievements of some working-class groups, whose jobs, albeit menial, yielded relatively high profits. Cattle dealers, butchers, and an array of produce intermediaries, were among this group of well-off commoners, whom the elites continued to group with the poor. Using moral ideas similar to those that distinguished gamonales from hacendados, which portrayed gamonales as illegitimate landowners,

economically successful urban commoners were deemed ostenta-
tious speculators and immoral. Sustained by racialized beliefs in the
innate differences imprinted by (class) education, gente decente separated themselves from gente del pueblo and shaped discriminatory
urban routines in Cuzco.

Male and female butchers — mestizos — were in the 1950s among
the better-off among the gente del pueblo. As table 1 indicates, revenues from taxation in the marketplace and in the slaughterhouse
increased approximately tenfold between 1942 and 1960. Not coincidentally, *carniceras* (female meat vendors) and *camaleros* (cattle
butchers who worked at the slaughterhouse) were seen as examples
of the working classes' latent violence and ignorance derived from
their immoral use of wealth. When the butcher Cornelio Velásquez
killed his concubine's father, a newspaper narrated the bloody deeds
with a wealth of detail. According to the author of the article, Velásquez's "lucrative business had allowed [him] to live comfortably and
to drink abundant amounts of chicha with great frequency." Drunk
and furious, "seizing a pig-decapitating knife" he had stabbed his
father-in-law to death.[37] If they had continued to be poor and Cornelio had not been able to drink so much, the tragedy would not have
occurred, in the opinion of the journalist. "The gente del pueblo will
always be ignorant in spite of having the means to stop being so" is
another moral that could have been drawn from this episode.

The counterpart of this belief was that "decent people" were not
delinquents. On August 31, 1942, Cuzco's deputy, Roberto F. Garmendia proposed a law against livestock rustling. As part of his
proposal he defined cattle rustlers as "persons of notorious social
condition, who do not work. They are lazy, alcoholics, and degenerate. . . . They fluctuate between the Indian and the mestizo. They are
individuals who have developed the instinct of living off strangers."
He thought the hacendados, in contrast, "because of their social and
economic situation [, were] not liable to commit this class of crime;
the prosecution of a hacendado would be a very unexpected case"
(Garmendia [1940]: 91). Notwithstanding political modernization,
and although class rhetoric exposed hacendados to accusations of
gamonalismo, decencia protected them from accusations of cattle
rustling, just as it had earlier protected them from gamonalismo. Ro-

berto Garmendia, himself an hacendado, exonerated his peers and instead incriminated mestizos in *abigeato* (cattle rustling). Garmendia encouraged "social improvements," the most important of which he saw as a law against livestock theft ([1940]:79–92). It was geared at a tighter control of cattle rustling, which was deemed the worst of the rural scourges during the long drought of the 1950s. Garmendia's argument was that by controlling theft, the law would lower the price of meat, a crucial item in the diet of urban cuzqueños.

The exculpation of hacendados from wrongful participation in increasing meat prices, paired with dominant images about the gente del pueblo's innate propensity to delinquency, tightened surveillance of the other groups involved in meat commerce: female meat vendors and cattle slaughterers. These were mostly mestizas and their spouses. In the 1950s, a period of drought and populism, racial beliefs in the common people's immorality merged with populist calls for price controls to further stigmatize market vendors with the additional charge of illegal price gouging. Racialized moral panic (Hall et al., 1978:16) spread across the city, as mestizas and their spouses emerged as an economic and political threat to regional well-being.

To provide the city with adequately priced foodstuffs, several "subsistence commissions" (comités pro-abaratamiento de subsistencias) were established in Cuzco throughout the forties and sixties. In addition to preventing market women from raising their prices, and to collect fines more efficiently, the city council hired a larger number of market guards — known as municipal police — and stationed them primarily in the market of San Pedro.

The image of mestiza market women as transgressors was not new. The reader may recall from the first chapter that "immoral" market women were also targets of earlier cleansing campaigns. At that time, these women were certainly not passive victims of those campaigns as the following news item from the 1920s makes evident:

> Yesterday a woman called Rosa Pumayalli, a meat seller, set off a serious disturbance in the marketplace when the guard . . . informed her that she had to wear her apron and clean her belongings in conformity with the orders from the mayor's office. That was enough for Pumayalli, whose Quechua name means vanquisher of tigers.

She tried to attack the guard and chased him brandishing a knife and showering him with insults from her well-supplied repertoire. . . . This was enough to encourage the rest of the sellers to rebel against the municipal decree concerning tidiness and cleanliness. . . . It would not be surprising if one day we had an armed strike in the Mercado Oriental, where there is an abundance of dirty and indecent Pumas who do not want to remove their impious crust of filth.[38]

During the populist 1950s and 1960s accusations of price hikes further damaged the longstanding image of the coarse and filthy mestiza. The neoindianistas celebration of mestizas' sexual eroticism only ignited the antimestiza moral panic, as it heightened the interpretation that these women were a threat to society. The authorities had to persecute "and clean the environment from such a lack of morality," which was the result of "an absence of self-control common among mestizas and sapped the most vital collective interests."[39] Populism thus combined with gendered rules of decency to cast an image of mestizas and some of their suppliers — the mestizo merchants and cattle slaughterers — as adversaries of the people's well-being and as a menace to the economic interests of cuzqueños of all social classes.

If in previous decades controlling the vendors was a serious task, it became even more so by mid-century when, because of regional economic transformations, the marketplace came to be considered the "stomach of the city" and, as such, the first priority.[40] How would food reach Cuzco's homes if mestizas refused to sell it? The relationship between the municipal government and market women was marked by constant conflict and negotiation. Although mestizas had some leverage, in order to sell, they needed a municipal license, which was renewed annually. If they had many fines, or did not pay them, the all-important license would not be renewed. To this end, they negotiated with the council, which, in turn, chose to obtain income by fining mestizas rather than confronting them when they protested the council's denial of their licenses.[41]

Resolutions like "The [municipality] is committed to correcting outrages and abuses . . . for this reason it resolved to fine the unscrupulous owner [so-and-so]" occur frequently in municipal records.[42] The "certificate of conduct" granted by the marketplace supervisor was a very effective means of control, and it was crucial to the politico-moral policing of the placeras.⁴³ City rulers used the certificate in their distribution of rewards and punishments. A "good behavior" rating gave women vendors access to additional stalls within the marketplace and also to loans for housing, or to pardons for slight acts of misconduct.⁴⁴ On the other hand, if they "misbehaved," the vendors faced strict enforcement of the city's regulations.

In keeping with the elite's belief that immoral behavior and lack of education went hand in hand, the fines that the municipal council applied to market women had an "educational" purpose. When Lola Díaz refused to sell meat to "a lady," she was fined "so that she would observe the most correct conduct in the exercise of her business." Benedicta Alvarez, "who sold chicha at a prohibitive price," was fined because "it was necessary to enforce morality with sanctions." Twenty soles were levied against a woman who sold bread "for using dishonest words to the detriment of the neighborhood." Similar treatment was meted out to a woman who sold trout "so that she will learn to not offend the municipal police, the buyers, and the neighborhood."⁴⁵

Male vendors were fined as well, but the purpose of their punishment was different. A drunken seller of spring water was fined for "having violently and disrespectfully insulted the slaughterhouse veterinarian." Ernesto Calderón suffered a similar fate because "in a drunken state he hurled insults and damaging words" at a municipal policeman.⁴⁶ The fines levied on the men served to restore the authority that their insults had damaged. Mestizas' insults were considered to be only expressions of the women's essential vulgarity; consequently they did not threaten the authority of the men against whom the insults were directed.

Mestizas Atrevidas
The Political Use of Insolence

During this period the marketplace was the scene of many political riots. However, the particular way in which prevailing cultural beliefs cast mestizas as potential criminals shifted the focus away from their political struggle. This made it possible for their persecution to be condoned, and it also trivialized mestizas' arguments against municipal policies. Market women's aggressive demands and their self-defense were depoliticized as "typical" and vulgar marketplace incidents. Control of mestizas was perceived as preserving the general well-being and containing the "immoralities" of these *mujeres del pueblo* (women of the people).

Mestizas were not unaware of the rights that they had under populist rule. They knew that positioning themselves as women of the people entitled them to confront and negotiate with city authorities and to shield themselves from the image of vulgarity and transgression that cuzqueño society had forced on them. In negotiations, mestizas presented themselves as morally trustworthy women, mothers, and workers, who demanded benevolent behavior from the authorities. María Centeno Paucar used such an argument when she was found selling llama meat instead of beef. The authorities judged María's crime "a breach of public health" and canceled her license. She pointed out that she was a first-time offender and cried that "since [they suspended my license] I have been without work; my seven younger children are suffering the consequences of this erroneous decision." She asked that her license be returned so she could continue working. She regained her license.[47] Playing on fears of impoverished families teetering on the brink of delinquency and earnestly insisting that they were "respectful workers" generally yielded positive results for mestizas in their negotiations with the municipal authorities.

Another strategy was to exact from the municipality the same conditions that the authorities demanded from them. In 1952 a group of flour sellers complained to the prefect and to the government minister that the mayor wanted to change the location of their market stalls and raise the price for rentals. To prevent the relocation, the vendors employed the very concept of hygiene that was continually used against them. They argued, "The items that we sell are of primary necessity; consequently we need a properly clean and hygienic locale. [T]he smell of flour is harmless and contributes to beautification of the marketplace." In rejecting the higher rates they argued, "We are women of humble backgrounds . . . dedicated to the daily sale of flour, we are workers, mothers, and widows who count only on our humble and honest work to support our children. We need protection and consideration from the municipal authorities."[48]

By stating that they were hard-working women, market vendors aimed to reverse the image of filth, delinquency, and vulgarity that cuzqueño society had forced on them. But along with such peaceable negotiations, market women also quarreled daily with municipal guards and participated in political struggles. This shaped their image as unremittingly bold. "Female leaders of fanatic crowds," "initiators of stonings," "accomplices of thieves and bandits" were phrases Uriel García used to describe them (1937:185). The municipal police records are filled with sentences like "these women do not heed warnings" and "their frequent fines are repeats."[49] *Esas no tienen miedo a nada ni a nadie*" (Those [women] are not scared of anything or anybody) was (and still is) the elite's negative appraisal of mestizas' temerity.

The vendors displayed most vividly their controversial boldness in their public confrontations with the authorities. In several of my innumerable incursions to the marketplace (and also in many elite houses), I heard a story that has become part of the legendary imagery of the market mestizas in present-day Cuzco. It also coincided extraordinarily with images of "the grotesque" described by Bakhtin, in which plebeians use tripe and its scatological connotations to affront the representatives of order. As Bakhtin explains, "[Tripe comes from] the center of bodily topography in which the upper and lower stratum penetrate each other" (1984:162). This interrelationship between the upper and lower social echelons is also part of the Cuzco legendary tale. The story tells about a prefect whom meat sellers forced to wear a necklace made of tripe because his wife wanted to buy a piece of meat at a lower price than that asked for by a meat vendor. First there was a verbal quarrel between both women, and when the prefect's wife returned with the prefect to punish the insolent butcher, the other meat sellers backed their colleague and attacked the man, draping tripes around his neck. I heard the story from persons belonging to assorted social classes and political persuasions: a university professor, an elite woman, a university student, a union leader, and various market women. Market women, and many of their sympathizers, tell the story with pride. Elite people tell it with horror. Interestingly enough, no one remembers the name of the humiliated prefect. Although the story might have been made up by quite diverse social sectors, including the vendors themselves, those who told it to me think it "really happened." Depending on who tells it, putting a tripe necklace around the prefect's neck was either a "grotesque" affront or a political act of boldness.

In the municipal archives, I have found descriptions of events in which market women display boldness equivalent to that described in the "prefect's tripe necklace" story. Manuela Díaz de Salas, a meat vendor was the protagonist of a striking confrontation. One October morning in 1953, she was in her stall selling meat as usual, when none other than the lieutenant mayor of Cuzco, the mayor's second in command, appeared. According to Manuela, he chose three good pieces of meat, "and recognizing the quality of the meat offered to pay higher than the regular price, over my opposition and insisting that there was nothing to fear because he was a municipal authority." Manuela accepted the inflated price and was later blamed for speculating with meat prices. In court, she accused the gentleman of tricking her and not keeping his word.[50] Certainly, confronting one of the city's highest authorities in this way was not a wise strategy; Manuela had to pay the fine.

Together with verbal and physical violence against the authorities and the market guards, mestizas fought for their right to respect using sober written demands for a proper marketplace infrastructure, fair commercial procedures, and political justice from the authorities. Immediately after the fall of President Leguía in 1930 and prompted by his gradual retreat from his original populism, a group of market women circulated a flier directed to the "People of Cuzco" criticizing the presidential policies and the market administrator. Their flier captured the generalized antileguiísta populism of the time while denying their alleged impropriety. It read, "There is no human power that will oblige us to harm the interests of Cuzco; we will pay the quotas to the council with great pleasure. . . . Be alert women and men food sellers! The period of exploitation of the fatal Leguía is over. Unite all! *Viva la justicia! Viva Cuzco!*"

Protected by this unthreatening preamble, they went on to denounce the market administrator—a leguiísta—who "treated us with no consideration for our sex or our condition, shouting at us and tiring us with insults for no good reason."[51] Thirty years later, unionized mestizas led the way in the generalized political transformation of the region. They continued to play the role of women of the people, and they even engaged class rhetoric. In a 1961 press release from the strike committee of the Sindicato de Mercados Unidos (United Markets Union), the vendors first presented themselves as "impoverished workers, small-scale merchants . . . who live from hand to mouth in the worst possible conditions." Using class vocabulary, they then proceeded to reject the price speculation charges lodged against them, arguing that the only speculators were the "big capitalists, the big merchants, the big landowners and merchants."[52]

As mentioned, the creation of the United Markets Union in 1944 was part of the process of political modernization in Cuzco. Ever since then, Apra and the Communist Party had competed for the leadership of the union, given the crucial importance of the marketplace for the success of urban general strikes. If the mestizas joined in the paralyzation of the city by closing the market building and picketing around it, the strikers' chances to prevail increased. In the oral political tradition there is one particular general strike that took place in April 1958 that working-class cuzqueños still consider one of the most glorious moments of the Federation of Cuzco Workers. The strike, called in response to a rise in the price of gasoline, was of particular importance to market women because fuel was part of the costs of transporting harvests and cattle from the countryside to their market stall. Several witnesses of the event recall the important part mestiza vendors played in it. One of them narrated: "The repressive brutality climaxed in the Central Market, where [the army] attempted to silence the vendors who were demonstrating. The police entered the marketplace violently, and the vendors reacted, repelling the aggression. . . . [S]ome moments later the women captured General Daniel Vargas Dávila. . . . [S]ix female market vendors participated in his kidnapping; they grabbed him by the neck and pulled off his military jacket and his hat, which they urinated in" (Aranda and Escalante, 1978:61). Agustín Mamani, then secretary general of the United Markets Union and a member of the Communist Party, remembered mestizas as the protagonists of the event. In a conversation, he told me that the strikers prevailed when he kidnapped General Vargas Dávila (the local commander of the army) with the help of several market women. They took him to the Drivers Union, where they forced him to negotiate an end to the strike.[53] Although Mamani did not mention that the women had urinated in the general's hat, he did recall their participation contributed to the workers' victory.

Not surprisingly, official historians of Cuzco ignore the mestizas' participation and only narrate how the army officer "was captured by an angry crowd and dragged to the Plaza de Armas, where had it not been for the incredible oratorical powers of Huamantica [the most senior Communist leader] the general would have been lynched" (Tamayo Herrera, 1992:211). Obscuring the mestizas' decisive role is not something that only conservative historians did. In mid-century Cuzco, the oppositional, mostly leftist political leadership was unclear about the political identity of these women. On the one hand, they saw market women as an important force among the "popular classes." On the other hand, the same leadership joined the elite in believing that market women could raise the prices of meat and produce and thus be in opposition to the people's interests. The market women's gender and unclear class identity (neither workers nor peasants) blurred the obvious political character of their struggle and helped shift the focus to their scandalous immorality.

Whether self-identified mestizas confronted the authorities "insolently" in face-to-face confrontations or whether they channeled their claims through their unions, the authorities interpreted their political activities as "scandals," or the actions of improper women. The women accepted this characterization; however, for them, "scandal" did not connote immorality. To make a scandal was, for them, to use every possible weapon in confrontations. It could include closing the marketplace and convening en masse in the Plaza de Armas, from which they paraded through the streets of the city, shouting defiant slogans at the buildings where the antagonistic authorities worked. It could also include scatological acts like urinating in an army general's hat or draping a prefect with tripe. These actions were, indeed, scandalous reversals of dominant moral norms and very effective political weapons.

For mestizas the "moral defects" attributed to them, such as insolence (*atrevimiento*) expressed the courage (*valentía*) to defend their interests as respectful members of the working class, as women of the people. Through their boldness and a broad array of formal negotiation tactics they changed the connotation of "scandal" from one of immorality to "civic virtue" (Longsdale, 1989) and their identities from "indecent" to "respectful." Wielding insolence as civic virtue they forged a counterimage of mestizas as *mujeres que se hacen respetar* (women who make themselves respected), thus re-creating their mestiza identity as "a site of strategic contestation" (cf. Hall, 1995) and redefining the dominant notion of mestizaje.

Indecent versus Respectful
Mestizas Struggle for Their Families

The political might and fearlessness of market women did not produce a tranquil working environment. Differentiation in the marketplace and divergent economic interests among mestizas provoked day-to-day quarrels, *odiosidades* (hatefulness), and *envidia* (envy) among vendors. Generally, vendors and buyers viewed the women butchers, *vendedoras del más noble artículo de consumo* (vendors of the most essential foodstuffs), as the most problematic group. Among meat vendors, those whose husbands bought and slaughtered livestock were certainly powerful, and they kept at a disadvantage meat vendors who were single or whose partners were not in the same business and had difficulties acquiring the product. On one occasion Pilar Huamán had to leave the general slaughterhouse without meat, because the slaughterer Mateo Alarcón did not want to sell her the product. When she attempted to buy from another woman "who had more meat than she could sell," this vendor wanted to charge an "exorbitantly high price for her product." Confronted by the impossibility of acquiring meat, Huamán denounced the cattle slaughterer and the meat vendor before the municipality.[54]

Quarrels among privileged and unfortunate female meat vendors were frequent and sometimes, as in the above case, produced alliances between the municipal authorities and the institutions that represented the less privileged market workers. Not infrequently, the

United Markets Union, which allegedly represented all the vendors, was embroiled in internal marketplace conflicts as a representative of the less privileged vendors.

In 1959 the United Markets Union, still led by Agustín Mamani, and the Meat Section Defense Committee, led by Luisa Inga Flower, presented a petition to the council. They requested that "the price of meat in the slaughterhouse and in the market be fixed." The petition produced an alliance between the municipal authorities and the market union. Both agreed that "the prices of meat for the population's consumption are altered arbitrarily by the slaughterers . . . who impose prohibitive prices on the market vendors. . . . [T]hese price increases originate in the *Camal General* [the city's slaughterhouse]. . . . The cattle slaughterers monopolize the meat, and give it all over to a single person, generally their wife, daughter, or associate who increases the price at their will."[55] The slaughterers in turn petitioned the municipality to allow their wives and daughters to continue selling meat. "We sell through our wives in the central market to earn five cents more," they argued.[56] But more important than obtaining a higher income was the political leverage that butcher couples obtained. Controlling the business from diverse positions (the women as retail marketplace vendors, the husbands as wholesale buyers) placed these couples in an advantageous position to force the municipality to negotiate the price of meat. Authorities met with the President of the Market Meatsellers Society and the cattle slaughterers at least three times a year to discuss meat prices.

These powerful couples contradicted the image of cholos that the neoindianistas had depicted. They had praised the self-sacrificing and lonely *chola,* devoid of patriarchal protection either because her partner had abandoned her or because he was a drunk who did not work. But in 1940, when neoindianismo surged, sixteen female meat vendors (out of a total of twenty-five in the central market) were married to or living with cattle slaughterers.[57] The neoindianista writers' lust for cholas — or the fact that the women were living in "immoral concubinage" — probably blinded them to the evidence that market women did have domestic and not only sexual partners. Usually when market vendors applied for a license to sell meat, they justified their petition by arguing for the conjugal character of their income. Rudecinda Porres, for example, revealed that she earned her living selling "beef and wool from the slaughterhouse in the company of my husband. Consequently I wish to rent a stall to work personally."[58] Similar petitions were frequent and certainly not restricted to carniceras. The common-law partner of Raimunda Cusi was a fruit wholesaler and she was a fruit retailer.[59] Indeed, women meat vendors, *fruteras* (fruit sellers), and *paperas* (potato vendors) had male partners, and although they were not officially married, they were productive workers. Unlike gente decente, successful plebeian couples operated as economic units, not simply as conjugal pairs. Unlike decent women who earned incomes only when confronted with the lack of "a good patriarch," plebeian women worked with their spouses to increase their family's income. Working as couples in different niches of the same business was the basis of both their ability to control the food supply in the marketplace and their political leverage.

In some cases, the same strategy was useful to organize political leadership. Sixty-two-year-old Lucrecia Carmandona, a manioc and potato vendor, is the wife of union leader Agustín Mamami. She arrived in Cuzco (from the nearby town of Urubamba) in the 1950s, when the Communist Party was organizing important rural and urban unions. The Cuzco Workers' Federation owned a locale where political leaders and future unionists met. This was one of Lucrecia's favorite places to sell her fruit because while doing so she could listen to political discussions. "They said that they worked on behalf of the poor, and I was poor: I had nothing, not even a family. There, at the Federation I met my husband, Agustín Mamani. My husband's father was an Indian, who wore poncho and *ojotas* [sandals] and worked as a peon in a hacienda in San Jerónimo."

Agustín became one of Cuzco's most active union leaders, and he and Lucrecia had ten children. "All because I wanted them, not one by accident," Lucrecia proudly recalled, assertive about the way she had controlled her sexuality during her reproductive years. "I hadn't had a family, and I wanted to have a big one," she told me. Lucrecia, like her partner, became an important union leader organizing the women vendors of the central market. She described herself this way to me:

I am a mestiza fighter, I have always worked along with my husband so that my children would never want for anything. I have stood up to anyone who disrespected me. . . . I have insulted them and chased them out with knife in hand. I learned to talk to defend myself, and I have done it. . . . I do not belong to the high society of Cuzco, those who despise us. They call us 'those *cholas*,' they insult us; they think we are thieves and whores. . . . I am only a worker and I have helped my husband all my life. . . . [I]f I have defended myself and insulted them, it is for my children. Because of that all my sons have been educated and now all of them, every one is a professional . . . but my struggle continues because now I still have grandchildren who have to grow up.

In the seventies, when General Juan Velasco Alvarado governed Peru, she was appointed the city's "revolutionary mother." Although (as she admits) ladies have insulted her more than once as "vulgar chola" and "indecent, Indian whore" as a consequence of her feistiness, she knows that it is precisely this attribute that earned her the regional recognition of the military government that also decreed the agrarian reform. Although (congruent with the gendered vision of politics) she was not recognized as a politician, she was conferred the honor by virtue of being a "mother," an occasion that she proudly remembers. When I asked her how she felt about this she said, "My struggles have been political. I have always been an organizer. But people do not need to be organizers to fight for their children, or for their families, and that is what we all do here in the marketplace." Being a mestiza mother is to be a political fighter.

Women like Lucrecia Carmandona and the fearless meat, vegetable, and fruit sellers have produced an identity that the plebeian sectors of Cuzco have chosen for themselves. Rejecting categorically the label of "cholas," which is tainted with allusions to an uncontrollable female sexuality, they have developed their own interpretation of moral behavior. They build it on values both of honorable work (*trabajo honrado*) and boldness (*atrevimiento*) in protecting their families. They describe their behavior as seeking *respeto*, which includes promoting their children's formal education. The powerful mestiza, usually a mother and wife, who proudly rebukes the moral

Lucrecia Carmandona, doing the workers' salute
as she leads the Sindicato de Mercados Unidos,
Cuzco, early 1970s. Photographer unknown.
Gift of Lucrecia Carmandona.

codes of female decency both as women who work and fight in the
marketplace, is the figure with whom men and women of Cuzco's
working classes identify today. In her self-description as a new (Chi-
cana) mestiza, writer Gloria Anzaldúa declared, *"En mí está la re-
beldía encimita de la carne"* (Anzaldúa, 1987:15) and cuzqueño
mestizas appear to echo her. Like Anzaldúa, they situate themselves
in a borderland that is crossed by intertwined gendered class and
cultural lines. From that borderland, by wielding fearlessness and
relentless energy to cope with harsh conditions, the self-identified
mestizas of Cuzco have overturned the dominant image of the shel-

tered and sexually virtuous woman. Additionally, by dismissing the elite's obsession with "proper sexual deportment" mestizas have produced an alternative moral code that makes them irreconcilable with prevalent images of decent women. At the heart of their moral code is *respeto,* which consists of the urge to fight and work against all odds for their family's well being. From the gendered class lens of decency, this deportment is inappropriate of women. Hence, although respect dignifies mestizas to their own eyes, it maintains the culturally conceived cleavage dividing elites and commoners. The prevalence of decency over respect explains why in spite of the economic success of some common women and men, they continue to be scorned by Cuzco's elite. Illustrative of this scorn (all the stronger because it is directed against a female) is the nickname that the elite has given to one of the most successful mestiza entrepreneurs, a tomato wholesaler. They refer to her as *la reina del tomate* (the tomato queen) and in indignant tones tell the story (which I was unable to confirm) that this mestiza has "even bought a colonial residence that belonged to a Cuzco aristocrat" who had fallen on hard times.

Mestizas as Successful Indigenous Women

During my fieldwork season I spent hours in Doña Lucrecia's market stall. Sitting on sacks of produce and helping her to peel yuccas, I listened to her stories about police incursions in the marketplace. But she also told me about her life as a child and how she had met Agustín Mamami. Lucrecia Carmandona was one of the first persons to call my attention to the meaning of "mestiza" in cuzqueño working-class identity lexicon. "I am an indigenous woman," she said to my surprise, as I thought that being mestiza replaced being indigenous. "My mother was a market vendor as well. My aunts called her a *chola placera,*" she continued her explanation.

Lucrecia's father was a relatively well-off hatmaker who lived in the city and had rural properties in the nearby town of Urubamba. "My aunts considered themselves *damas* and my father a gentleman. That is why my father never married my mother; she was just a chola, an Indian, to them. But he loved her very much, that is what my mother used to tell me. But his sisters never let him marry her." So Señor Carmandona, the hatmaker, never married Lucrecia's mother because of family pressure. To hide the shame that the relationship with a chola mestiza would bring to their family, the Carmandona sisters took Lucrecia to Urubamba, where the sisters administered the hatmaker's property. There they raised Lucrecia as a servant. "They made me a servant because of my father's crime of loving a chola placera as they called my mother, my crime was being the daughter of the placera." As a servant she walked barefoot, or "with rubber sandals. My hands and face were always dirty, but they did send me to school. . . . Perhaps that was because my father obliged them to do so. . . . I was not raised as a mestiza because my aunts were not mestizas, they pretended to be ladies [se las daban de damas] that was why they did not let me see my mother, and they raised me as an Indian servant. I became a mestiza by myself."

When she was still a girl her aunts sent her to a weekly market in nearby Calca to sell basketfuls of produce from her relatives' plots. Little by little, as she learned to sell, Lucrecia told me, she became a mestiza. She bought a license that allowed her to sell in the streets around the marketplace in Calca. To protect her head and face from the sun she wore a white hat that she bought "in the market of Calca, I used it only when I sold. . . . In my aunt's house they did not allow me to wear the hat." She also bought an apron to keep clean as the produce she sold was dirty with earth from the fields. Her hat and apron were the first tokens of her mestiza identity. When Lucrecia was fifteen she escaped from her relatives' house. She went to the city. In Cuzco she bought a basket and a few bananas, and she started off by selling "walking up and down the streets."

Cuzqueños in general consider clothing as a salient feature of mestizas' identity, insofar as it distinguishes them from "the Indian woman."[60] Uriel García defined the mestiza working woman as "the peasant who stays in the city and changes her peasant's dress for that of the cook, servant, seamstress, artisan, or merchant in the market" (1949:139). Comparing the process of changing clothes to a natural metamorphosis, he thought that the female skirts were the "chrysalis of the Indian woman who becomes mestiza" (1949:139). Lucrecia also emphasized the symbolism of her clothes as markers of her identity as mestiza. However, what clothes symbolize is different in each case. Neoindianistas imagined mestizas' sexuality as a racial feature that had changed from the xenophobic frigidity characteristic of Indian women to the erotic passion that inclined mestizas to yield to the requirements of non-Indian men. From this perspective, the clothes were external symbols of specific sexual behaviors, and changing attire from that of an Indian woman to those that represented mestizas went hand in hand with acquiring a different sexuality. It meant (sexually) "passing" from one racial/cultural group to another and implied discarding those cultural behaviors considered developmentally previous and inferior. Instead, from the mestizas' viewpoint, as illustrated by Lucrecia's narration, being Indian or mestiza is not about racial/cultural sexual differences but about a social condition. Changing clothes in Lucrecia's case (from being an Indian servant to being a mestiza) meant passing from one social condition to another, but this did not imply cutting ties with the regional indigenous community but enhancing or, even maybe bringing about for the first time, her own links with it. To illustrate this let me quote Lucrecia Carmandona once more. "When I was a servant, I knew about Coyllur Rit'i, but I could never go. It was too expensive for me," she remembered. Coyllur Rit'i is a pilgrimage, and an occasion when so-called indigenous Cuzqueños convene to pay ritual homage to one of the sacred landmarks of the region. Although tourists and anthropologists have become a growing presence in Coyllur Rit'i, nonindigenous cuzqueños do not participate (or they do so only as observers), as the festival is emblematic of indigenous culture. Lucrecia participated in the festival once she became a mestiza market vendor who could afford to attend the Andean ritual; as she told me, "I went several times when my children were growing, when I was selling in this stall."

Besides their distinctive attire, mestizas stand out among indigenous working classes because they earn relatively high incomes. They are literate and speak Spanish, but they also share the indigenous legacy of the Andes. Although as ethnocategories "Indian" and "mestiza" do connote certain cultural differences (mainly achieved education and urban manners), these do not imply the type of evolu-

tionary hybridity suggested by the dominant notion of mestizaje.
Neither do these categories denote the existence of cultural boundaries separating Indians from mestizos. Rather, this alternative mestiza identity and the notion of mestizaje in which it is embedded
suggest that the existing differences between Indians and (indigenous) mestizos define a relational hierarchy inscribed in historically
and culturally defined power relations. Mestizas command authority
vis-à-vis Indians because *unlike the latter,* they earn a decorous income, they are not servants, and they have acquired cultural skills to
survive in the city. Most important, with these achievements, they
have "lost their fear" (*hemos perdido el miedo,* they say), and this
implies that they have learned to defend themselves. Situated at the
margins of gendered hegemonic racism, mestizas represent an alternative femaleness that informs the construction of working-class hierarchies and identities. Although this cultural and class alternative
way of being a woman continues to occupy a subordinate position, it
affects subjective levels and self-representations and thus influences
the micropolitical practices of daily life that may become sources of
power or of empowering investments (cf. de Lauretis, 1987:25).

Unlike Esperanza Hernández, a Mexican marketwoman, who told
Ruth Behar (1993) that suffering had redeemed her, Lucrecia Carmandona (and many other market women I befriended) told me of
having stubbornly and vibrantly rebelled against suffering and of
the feeling they have of having permanently defeated it in order to
achieve respect. "Suffering is for Indians," Lucrecia once said; "I
never accepted it, always defeated it." This self-perception that mestizas are different from Indians is not racial. Rather, it approaches a
conceptual understanding of ethnicity as cultural attributes that can
be acquired and disacquired, and that distinguishes fluidly among
individuals rather than rigidly among groups. The salient feature of
ethnicity as enacted by mestiza cuzqueñas is its inherent relationality.
Mestizas are high-ranking indigenous women vis-à-vis others they
consider Indians. Located at the edge of racist hegemony, mestizas
indeed contest certain aspects of it while enforcing others and even
resorting to violence to do so. Thus they are new empowered subjects who, however, carry vestiges of the discourses against which
they struggled. I illustrate this in the following section.

Boundaryless and Hierarchy-Laden Indigenous Ethnicity

Focusing on mestizas, and particularly on their clothing, the working classes have constructed a gendered taxonomy, where male subordinate identities are less overtly marked, and plebeian men — also called *weratakas* by the elites "because of their greasy clothing" — are more easily called *caballeros* by marketplace people. Scrutinizing differences in the quality of the fabric, the type of shirt, the way of wearing the shawl, the material of the hat, and their cleanliness, indigenous cuzqueños "rank" women within an ethnic continuum, in which the "Indian women" and the *casi dama* ("almost a lady," like the successful tomato wholesaler) occupy the inferior and superior ends, respectively.

In addition to their attire, the produce they sell aids female vendors in their mutual classification. Indigenous female buyers and sellers are classified as Indians or *mujercitas* (small women), *mestizas simples* (simple mestizas), *buenas mestizas* (good mestizas), *casi damas* (almost ladies), and (rarely) *damas* (ladies). This ranking allows for the relational interpretation of interactions.[61] Teófila, for example, is a fruit seller who identifies her mother as a simple mestiza while identifying herself as almost a lady. From such a position, and using food as an additional signal of social identity, she explained: "Mujercitas never eat chicken; on special occasions they buy menudo (beef parts) for their parties. In February, when their own harvest runs out, they buy handfuls of potatoes. They do not buy anything else in the market. Mestizas buy second- or third-grade beef, maize, wheat, *chuño* [freeze-dried potatoes], potatoes, onions. Damas buy chicken, first-rate meat, potatoes, and fruit of the valley. Gringos buy lots of fruit, vegetables, and chicken."[62]

The distinctive character of this classification (one that is not apparent from the above quote, though it derives from the inherent relationality of the alternative ethnic taxonomy) is that indigenous cuzqueños do not have an individual fixed identity but identities that are relative to others and contingent on the status of the persons in the interaction. This is not a recent feature. In the early decades of the century, for example, Polonia Arnao, a woman from the nearby town of Yucay, insulted her brother calling him "Indio hereje ladrón de la casa de tu padre" (heretical Indian, a robber of your own father's house) after a domestic quarrel over their father's property. At the same time she self-identified as mestiza. The same Polonia, in the larger stage of her trial in urban courts of Cuzco, called herself an Indian probably to claim the favors granted by the law to "semi-civilized" Peruvians, but also because the judges would willingly classify Polonia as such.[63]

The above is another example of the inadequacy of the intellectual account of cultural "passage" from Indian woman to mestiza, based as it is on rigid evolutionary taxonomies. The inherently relational quality of cuzqueño indigenous ethnicity questions evolutionary racial/cultural taxonomies and cancels the notion of fixed identities while maintaining the lexical classification. As in Polonia's case, it is not infrequent for indigenous cuzqueños to self-identify as Indians or as mestizos depending on the relationships involved in a particular social situation. Likewise, symbolic actions can alter identities in a single interaction. For example, when the municipal police wanted to offend market women, the officers pulled their hats or shawls off, as both articles identified them as mestizas. By removing these markers the police implied that they had the power of recasting them as Indian women.[64]

The dynamic relational of ethnicity operates in spite of — and together with — the appearance of solid univocal identities implied in the taxonomies. This corresponds with the analytical observation of Jean and John Comaroff, who propose that "most people live in worlds in which many signs, and often the ones that count most, *look* as though they are eternally fixed, although the same signs are in constant flux and subject to contestation" (1991:17, my emphasis). Adding to the complexities, the relative identities recognized in the continuum constantly change, as identity categories appear and disappear. The category "Indian market woman" or "urban Indian woman" that people identified in the forties and fifties has become in the nineties the *mestiza campesina*. The *buena mestiza* is another fading ethnic category.[65] Until the mid-sixties, this label included the powerful working-class women, currently classified in the marketplace as *señoras*. These are today's wholesale intermediaries and truck owners, who subordinate small-scale market vendors using monetary credit relations. In Cuzco's central market "*señora*" may be subdivided into *señora de verdad, señoras,* and *señoras simples.* Señoras are considered such because they use "the clothing of the damas" and "have gone to school." They are relatively well off, and educated; yet they are not considered damas because they work in the marketplace, where *el trato* (how people deal with each other) is considered to be crass.

Trato as Dangerous Social Proximities
Discrimination and Respeto

There is a popular maxim in Spanish (it may even date from colonial times) that says "*Dime con quién andas y te diré quién eres*" (Tell me who you deal with and I'll tell you who you are). This saying aptly describes "el trato," the patterns of interaction in the marketplace and on other cuzqueño stages. Closely associated with an individual's job, el trato is a subtle marker of individual identities and implies a classification of jobs on a scale of prestige that may be a modified cultural residue of colonial times, when certain manual occupations were considered dishonorable. Shared by elites and the working class in Cuzco, norms of trato may signal the culturally defined class boundaries between indecent and decent cuzqueños and can prevent economically successful working-class individuals from including themselves in the elite, even if they have the economic capacity to buy former aristocrats' houses, as in the case of the despised tomato queen. She is the most famous successful market woman but not the only one. Like her, many relatively wealthy market women have seen their social ascent limited as a result of their interaction with Cuzco's indecent sectors. Dionicia, who I also met in the marketplace, represents one of these cases. She is fifty-nine, is married, and completed high school when she was nineteen. Her mother was a *buena mestiza* (good mestiza) who sold vegetables. Dionicia inherited from her mother the occupation of vegetable seller, her stall in the marketplace, and her clientele. Dionicia and her husband expanded her mother's business and became intermediaries, owning a truck. Dionicia believes that "she is more than a mestiza" and that she is a "señora de verdad" or "casi dama." Nevertheless Dionicia says she is not "a real dama, because I deal with mestizas and other market people." Although other people in the marketplace may consider her relatively a lady, neither she nor the elite would venture to call her such.

Beliefs in el trato as signifier and marker of status and social identities contribute to the hegemony of cuzqueño categories of difference, exclusion, and discrimination, and thus pose a limit to the challenge to decency that respect represents. Just as el trato limits their social ascent, by controlling it mestizas can prevent their descent and defend their higher status in the marketplace. Since el trato includes the people from and to whom the market women buy and sell, to preserve their social position — that is, their respeto — mestizas choose their clientele. Frequently when doing so, they display crudely discriminatory behavior. On one occasion a woman accused a meat vendor of not wanting to sell her a piece of meat. "That meat is not for mujercitas like you," the potential buyer reported the meat vendor had told her. When the alleged mujercita complained to the municipal guard and went with him to the stall, the seller continued to refuse to sell "with the pretext that she did not have change."[66] The apparent irrational behavior of this woman and many other carniceras who choose their clientele in ways that hinder their economic profit is shaped by the rules of el trato. Who has sold the food and who will buy it indicate who the market vendor deals with, thus revealing to others the seller's status, which, evidently, outlasts the minor economic gains involved in one transaction. Consequently, price negotiations and the resulting marketplace quarrels, more than using a logic of profit, are colored by considerations about the status of the parties involved in the relationship. All of this is part of el trato and integral to market women's struggle for respect.

The interpersonal behavior resulting from "el trato" is nuanced in such a way that it implies an opinion about where a person and his or her interlocutors belong in the regional social scale. Following the fluidity of marketplace identities, the trato between the same two persons is not fixed and can change from disrespectful to respectful depending on the circumstances. To demand respect means demanding the trato that corresponds to one's place on the ethnic-social scale. Conversely, "to disrespect someone" (faltar el respeto) means to diminish his or her social place, thus lowering that person's ethnic position. Disrespectful trato consists of verbal and body language that code-switches the interlocutor "down." Addressing a person in Quechua instead of Spanish in public situations, giving him or her a plate of food that does not have a piece of meat in it, sitting down, wearing a hat while addressing an individual, or imposing a price without negotiating it, are either disrespectful manners with superiors, or those that "lower people" deserve. It is in this intimacy of everyday relations (in streets or marketplaces) that decisions are made about who is the superior or inferior in the relationship. Once a person's status is agreed on as relatively inferior, he or she cannot demand respect, but can complain of mistreatment (*maltrato*). Depending on who inflicts it and the circumstances in which it occurs, maltrato can be perceived as abusive.

José, a monolingual and illiterate Quechua-speaking porter (*cargador*) in the central market, recalled the abusive behavior of a "hacendado gentleman" who accused José of being a thief. To recuperate what José had allegedly stolen, the hacendado shook him so hard he lost consciousness. José remembers that before passing out he heard the market women saying "look at that gentleman abusing that *hombrecito* [little man, or Indian]." As this example shows, abuse is evaluated on a scale of power, which sometimes, as in this case, is constructed on alleged differences in masculinity.[67]

Reprimands, however, are not always considered abusive. Sometimes it is not even considered mistreatment but the trato a person merits depending on his/her behavior, as seen through the lens of his/her ethnic status. On one occasion I witnessed how a vegetable seller scolded a porter in the marketplace. She told him, "*Cuchi indio ocioso apaway caran* [Dirty, lazy Indian, you should have carried] the basket like I told you to, it was your obligation to do so." When I asked the other witnesses — mostly market women — about their colleague's behavior, they told me that since the porter had refused to work for the vendor and to carry her basket to a hotel, it was the woman's right to scold him. "That señora is nice. When they do what she commands, she even gives the porters lunch," some women agreed. They thought the porter was receiving the trato his Indian "insolence" deserved. To imply the insubordination of the socially inferior and vindicate the damage to her superior status, the vendor's reprimand was in Quechua and accompanied by an insulting ethnic designation.

In the marketplace — and in socially equivalent places — working-class cuzqueños use accusations of insolence to demand respect from the socially inferior, usually identified, if contingently, as Indians. Thus, although demanding respect is a weapon market women use in their confrontations with municipal authorities it is also integral to the mestizas' discriminatory practices. Built on different moral codes, respect and decency are nevertheless mutually sustaining discourses. Both share beliefs in the legitimacy of hierarchies that result from urbanity and education. Through this coincidental conviction dominant racism leaks in and colors mestizas' ethnic taxonomies and discriminatory practices. Mestizas expect from porters and walking vendors a behavior as subservient as the one the elites expect from them.

Given this dynamic, it is not surprising that marketplace interactions erupt in conflict. Every interaction is a potential site of insolence, of an attempt to subvert the immediately superior order. Incessant quarreling between superiors (whether gentlemen, ladies, or mestizas) and inferiors (whether mestizas or Indians) has yielded a social dynamic of permanent tension between the mercurial, inherently relative identities and the fixed taxonomy that, notwithstanding the conflict, continues to prevail both among the elites as within working classes. People from outside the marketplace comment that mestizas are at present "más alzadas que nunca" (more uppity than ever). Mestiza vendors say about porters that "cada día son más vivos [they get smarter every day]" and don't work as they used to do anymore.

Conclusions

In the first chapter, I explained how the cuzqueño elite's version of the scientific definition of race dodged external phenotype and resorted to a class version of innate cultural morality to draw racial differences. From this perspective, although cuzqueño mestizos could share phenotype with gente decente and with Indians, they were mestizos because they were neither as educated as the first nor as miserable as the second. The two images of mestizaje that the Cuzco elites created were the gamonal and the mestiza. The defining element of both these figures was their immorality, which bordered on delinquency, and was defined by academics as being integral to race. However, while the gamonal was abhorred by elites and commoners alike, mestiza market women became esteemed personalities in the working-class lore.

To common cuzqueños the "moral defects" that the elites attributed to mestizas, such as insolence, are expressions of the courage (valentía) with which market women defend their rights as members of the working class, as mujeres del pueblo. Rejecting categorically the label "cholas," which tainted their identity with allusions to alleged uncontrollable female sexuality, they developed their own interpretation of moral behavior and forged a counterimage of themselves as *mujeres respetables*, women who seek respect. They build respect on values of honorable work *and* boldness in protecting their families, and promoting their children's formal education. Through the figure of the mestiza, and their struggle for respect, working-class cuzqueños have redefined the indigenista and neoindianista elites' notion of mestizaje, both of which stressed racial/cultural mixture. Popular sectors overtly dismiss this construction and instead assert respect (achieved through hard work and education) as the underpinnings of their alternative taxonomy, in which mestizas are high-ranking indigenous women.

In spite of their relative economic success, mestizas are still rejected by Cuzco's elite. Their dealings with male truck owners and wholesale vendors, along with their fearless, incessant confrontation with authorities, contribute to an image that is at odds with rules of patriarchal decency. Hence, while representing the accomplishments of working classes, market women also occupy the particular social space where gender influences the inner workings of cuzqueño identities and limits the mercurial quality of indigenous identities otherwise present in their everyday interactions. Gender places mestizas behind their male partners in their quest for ascent in the regional social ladder, as they are farther from becoming ladies than their husbands are from becoming gentlemen.

The analysis of the gendered belief that limited successful mestizas' sociocultural ascent (and thus prevented their assimilation into a homogeneous regional mestizo identity) allowed me to learn that when indigenous Cuzqueños use the ethnocategories of Indian and mestizo, rather than reflecting cultural differences, they indicate social conditions. From this perspective, Cuzqueño mestizas are successful indigenous women, equivalent to the Aymara women of La Paz, who straddle city and country (Gill, 1993). They erase the dominant rural-urban dichotomy that confined indigenous culture to the countryside and thus implied that urban migration meant de-Indianization, or the rejection of indigenous ways. Canceling this dichotomy makes urban indigenous culture possible and recasts the meaning of the changing of clothes that takes a woman from Indian to mestiza. Changing of clothes *does* convey de-Indianization, yet this process is limited to signaling a change in social conditions and does not suggest "cultural passage" or the rejection of indigenous ways. The differences between mestizas' and Indian women's clothing, whether striking or subtle, convey power differences, generally accompanied by economic differences, always present among indigenous sectors. "De-Indianization" eloquently illustrated in changing clothes, is not a matter of shedding indigenous culture but — as shown by mestizas' behavior — acquiring the markers of respeto.

While this redefinition of social categories explodes any possible fixed dichotomy between indio and mestizo and represents an empowering social strategy, de-Indianization has a discordant dynamism. Respect, fundamental to de-Indianization, requires a pattern of behavior that — through trato — acknowledges superiors and inferiors in a relationship. Although superiority and inferiority are defined situationally and decided in face-to-face relations, once the parties involved reach an agreement about who is who in the interaction, de-Indianization allows for discriminatory practices within indigenous working classes. Thus, mestizas live themselves in the grip of cuzqueño racism. Respect means observing the social hierarchies that market women and men recognize, and although they abide by alternative working-class moral codes, working-class hierarchies do not alter the dominant social status quo. The next two chapters explain this in more detail.

5

Cuzqueñismo, Respeto, and Discrimination

The Mayordomías of Almudena

Mikhail Bakhtin (1984:229) observed that throughout the history of Corpus Christi festivals in France and Spain, "the grotesque body prevailed in the popular marketplace aspect of this celebration and created its specific atmosphere." The same can be said about the annual commemoration of Corpus Christi in Cuzco. There, the marketplace establishes the atmosphere of the festival, as "insolent" market place mestizas preside over an immense crowd of commoners that invade the Plaza de Armas and subvert the symbolism of this place as the icon of elite decencia.

The *día central* (main day) of Corpus Christi (a feast that takes place over several days)[1] features a main procession that displays the social order of the city. The *Santísimo* (holy body of Christ) — borne by the archbishop — is at the head of the procession, which includes in hierarchical order the military, the city authorities, and the religious congregations. The images of patron saints follow, surrounded by marketplace mestizas, who clearly dominate the smaller parades honoring specific saints.[2] This privileged ritual location is granted to them as *mayordomas*, the sponsors of *mayordomías*. These are ritual institutions charged with many activities that culminate with the weeklong celebration of Corpus Christi and require the money and labor of mayordomas and their families throughout the year. Plebeian mayordomas are directly responsible for the magnificence of the Corpus Christi procession, one of the central features of contemporary cuzqueñismo and, indeed, an attraction featured in glossy tourist magazines. Once the procession is over, social hierarchies become diffuse as commoners and elites mingle in make-shift restaurants and kiosks, where they all relish buying the best selection of fruit from the valley and eating *chiri uchu* (literally "cold peppers"), the central dish of the fiesta, consisting of a spiced combination of a fish-egg omelette, roasted chicken, beef, potatoes, and cheese. Apparently indifferent to social hierarchies, cuzqueños also mingle in the cathedral, where the "ladies" and "gentlemen" visit the saints' images, which the low-class mayordomos have accompanied inside.[3]

However, as soon as the main celebration of mayordomías begins, this apparent indifference vanishes. The cuzqueño mayordomía is, briefly, a ritual through which a kinship-related male and female couple (spouses, siblings, or parent and offspring) sponsor the celebration of a fiesta in honor of a patron saint, a cross, or an image. The central event is the celebration of ritual banquets, which take place in the atrium of Cuzco's cathedral during Corpus Christi. The sight, odor, and noises of these parties provoke the elites' contempt. On one occasion, as I was walking with an elite acquaintance of mine through the cathedral atrium where one of these banquets was taking place, she unabashedly told me, "Me dan nausea" (They make me sick). However, the elite do tolerate mayordomías and their banquets, attributing this tolerance to their cuzqueñismo, the veneration they profess to cuzqueño culture, especially if it derives from what they define as Inca tradition.

The cuzqueño celebration of Corpus Christi has roots in the colonial period. According to a cuzqueño historian, "The sixteenth-century cuzqueño Corpus Christi was a direct transplant of the Sevillian Corpus, since most of the conquistadors living in Cuzco were of Andalusian origin, mostly Sevillian" (Aparicio Vega: 1970:43). Colonial chroniclers mention that, intriguingly, this Catholic ritual coincided with Inca solstice rituals and already then debated its syncretic character. Following the chroniclers, Luis E. Valcárcel, the most reputed cuzqueñista intellectual of all time wrote, "Corpus was celebrated around the same days as the ancient Feast of the Sun [Inti Raymi]. . . . [O]ften, parish priests and missionaries discovered Indian symbols hidden in the altars, old *huacas* with signs of recent worship" (1945: 45). During the years of populist cuzqueñista fervor, the local elite intellectuals esteemed Corpus Christi because they

Buenas mestizas wearing their festive garb during the celebration of the
Corpus Christi mayordomía, Cuzco, ca. 1992. Their straw hats, woolen
shawls, embroidered shirts, and shoes (instead of rubber sandals) mark
them as well-off market women.
(Below) Mestizas and their families celebrate during a mayordomía ritual
banquet in the atrium of the cathedral, June 1992. Both photographs by
author.

thought that its celebration *was* a continuation of the precolonial
Inti Raymi, which they had officially revived and enacted annually
since the popular inauguration of Inti Raymi in 1944. Although it
might have been a coincidence, Valcárcel's book was published a
year later, in 1945, and maybe in spite of himself—given his disdain
of neoindianistas' invented ritual—his remark supported the syncretism between Inca and Christian traditions. Repeated annually in
newspapers from 1945,[4] it gradually became an academic belief. In
1957 students at the University of Cuzco were taught that Corpus
Christi was a continuation of the Inca Inti Raymi. In 1982 the idea
had made its way to the *Calendario Turístico del Departamento del
Cuzco* (Tourist Calendar of Cuzco Department), which explained
that the procession of the saints during Corpus Christi constituted
"remembrances of the Parade of Panakas from the Incaic epoch."[5]
Panaka is a Quechua word meaning Inca royal descent group. The
idea that for "the Indians" the images of the saints were like Inca
mummies was following a clear path of intellectually produced syncretism: from the chroniclers to Luis E. Valcárcel's academic speculations. These speculations reached the newspapers and university
students as a fact, and were reproduced in the *Calendario Turístico*
as local folklore. In 1990 the "Incaization" of Corpus Christi had
reached such a point that a cuzqueño intellectual remarked, "Corpus
remains without alteration in its structure. The eight traditional
sixteenth-century Indian parishes, whose roots are in the pre-Hispanic neighborhoods of Qosqo, continue to participate in it" (Flores
Ochoa, 1990:132). Earnestly clinging to this cuzqueñista historical and theoretical framework, local intellectuals annually submerge
in their cherished Inca past and overlook the participation of cuzqueño commoners, who, year after year, reproduce and transform
the festival.

   This chapter narrates a different story. Rather than presenting a
historical interpretation of Corpus Christi, I present the history of
the institutions that make it possible; specifically I describe the mayordomías of a neighborhood (*barrio*) of Cuzco called Almudena,
based on the accounts I heard from market women and their relatives. From these people I learned that—unlike Inti Raymi, which
continues to be controlled by elite intellectuals—Corpus Christi is a

cultural event that grassroots intellectuals produce via the mayordomías. Its protagonists are the market women and their male partners who are the mayordomos or together, *carguyoq*.[6] I also learned
that, notwithstanding the differences, producers of the Inca festival
and of the mayordomías conceive their tasks similarly, inasmuch as
they aim at replicating images of the regional social order through
their celebrations. However, the celebrants of the Inca festival think
of their performances as copies of the Inca past or of an Indian
present that is not their domain but that of regional subordinate
mestizos and Indians. Instead, for the self-identified mestizo mayordomos, mayordomías are analogous to what Stuart Hall calls "a
theater of popular desires," a stage where mayordomos (and mayordomas) imagine and represent their identities not only to the audiences, but to themselves (1995). Hence, rather than rigid performances where everyone had a preassigned role, during mayordomías
identities are defined interactively. Not surprisingly, the rituals present many situations when an individual is mestizo in one interaction
and Indian in another. Moreover, because mayordomías are also
stages where the participants can socially ascend or descend, they
also function as public arenas where individuals officiously negotiate their urban mestizo identities by distancing themselves from
Indianness.

I have limited my analysis to the neighborhood of Almudena, the
home of gente del pueblo, traditional Cuzco urbanites (marketplace
mestizas, chicheras, cattle slaughterers, and artisans), as well as recent immigrants. I chose this barrio partly because of the conspicuous place that the celebration of its patron saint (the *Virgen de
Natividad,* or the Virgin of the Nativity) occupies in current official
cuzqueñismo, but mostly because in the early months of my fieldwork I befriended Timotea Gamarra, a seller of handicraft in the
marketplace. She promised to tell me the story of how she had created the Hermandad de la Virgen Natividad, an association of men
and women who carry the image of the patron saint of the Church of
Almudena in ritual processions. Timotea took me to the meetings of
the association, where I met the rest of the members and confirmed
Timotea's past and present important role. Timotea, a bilingual
Quechua and Spanish speaker, who is in her fifties and considers

herself a mestiza (although does not dress herself as such), introduced me to every living mayordoma she had ever met. To my surprise, most of them were vendors at the central market, those who
day after day boldly confronted the municipal authorities. Having
met them also in the marketplace led me to analyze mayordomías as
part of the mestizas' quest for respeto. From their viewpoint mayordomías are rituals in which, by means of a display of a combination
of material largess and religious piety, mestizas refute their image as
dissolute merchants and immoral women, and instead confirm their
economic and political feats as marketplace workers. In so doing
they discriminate against those they deem to be Indians, such as new
urbanites, former countryside dwellers. In turn, they are also subject
to the contempt of another group of mayordomos, who consider
mestizas Indians because they wear *polleras* (ample woolen skirts)
and speak Quechua.

Anthropologists have studied Andean and Mesoamerican mayordomías almost as fervently as mayordomos enact their celebrations.
As I already mentioned, cuzqueños think of mayordomías as institutions in which precolonial elements exist under the guise of Catholicism (Flores Ochoa, 1990; Roca Walparimachi, 1992). Several other
Andeanists and Mesoamericanists make similar arguments and refer
to mayordomías as expressions of hybridity or syncretism (García
Canclini, 1995; Bonfil Batalla, 1996; Friedlander, 1975; Meyers and
Hopkins, 1988; Rasnake, 1988; Chance and Taylor, 1985). They
argue either that unconscious cultural principles preserved these precolonial elements, or that the Indian elements found in Catholic garb
constitute acts of defiance against colonial domination. Another
common trend is the interpretation of mayordomías as economic
institutions. From this perspective there are those who have seen
them as "redistributive mechanisms," or as rituals for obtaining
prestige, or both (Cancian, 1965; Warren, 1989). Class analysts have
seen mayordomías as either impoverishing mechanisms manipulated
by hacendados or priests or strategies that "rich peasants" used to
subordinate the less privileged (Brass, 1986). More recent studies
have presented mayordomías as political institutions and, using
a broader framework that includes gender analysis, have linked
this institution to regional and even national contemporary politics

(Mathews, 1985; Stephen and Dow, 1990; Stephen, 1991; Crandon-Malamud, 1993; Frye, 1996). Drawing inspiration from many of these writers, using Pierre Bourdieu's notion of symbolic capital (1993), and building on Gramscian studies of hegemony (Hall, 1986; Laclau and Mouffe, 1985; R. Williams, 1977) I analyze mayordomías as charters of respect, which I interpret as the culturally shaped working-class symbolic capital that challenges elite decency yet requires the enactment of consensual cuzqueño categories of difference and exclusion. Mayordomías are thus crucial pieces of hegemonic cuzqueñismo and of the social discrimination couched in it.

Clearly, while being economic institutions is not their main feature, mayordomías are rituals that allow prosperous gente del pueblo, the mayordomos, to ritually secure and even accumulate respect among their peers and subordinates. As symbolic capital respect functions in two interrelated ways. On the one hand, it facilitates access to components of the mayordomos' businesses: labor, credit, transportation, storage. On the other hand, it confirms or transforms old social hierarchies and creates new ones among commoners. Whether old or new, commoners evaluate hierarchies through the achieved qualities of respeto and thus are a far cry from racial/cultural classifications that highlight innate traits. Yet inasmuch as respeto allows for discrimination, dominant racial categories seep through its discursive practices, rendering racism hegemonic.

In the cuzqueño definition of categories of difference and exclusion, an individual's place of origin is as important a component of his or her identity as gender or economic factors, such as income or occupation. Following beliefs that privilege the city over the country—which are not exclusively Andean (cf. Williams, 1977; Rama, 1996)—gente del pueblo as much as gente decente assess identities according to a geographical scale, where people coming from lower valleys and towns, or people with a longer period of urban residence, are considered to be socially superior to those from higher villages or to recent migrations to the city. Place of origin and of residence (the most common marker of which is the attire) may define the status of individuals and their "culture" and may even be the source of social hierarchies among people who otherwise share similar traits.[7]

This cultural perception of geography, activating as it does social differences and exclusions among cuzqueño working classes, limits the challenge against decency that the commoners' struggle for respeto represents. Geography, however, is accepted as an instrument of differentiation because it leaves a margin for individual negotiation: no geographical spaces, or the identities they assign, are in themselves superior or inferior; rather, they become such relative to one another. Moreover, the determinacy of an individual's place of origin in his or her identity may be altered by other qualifiers, above all by formal education. The constellation of mayordomías that exist in Almudena and their multiple points of Indianness and mestizoness provide the social stage for the ritual enactment of hierarchies that, albeit relational, continue to draw from the same politics of place and social differentiation (cf. Gupta and Ferguson, 1992) that backed modern definitions of race at the turn of the century and which still organizes daily life in the Almudena neighborhood and the city of Cuzco as a whole.

Mayordomías
Elite Folklore and Working-Class Symbolic Capital

The central act of the mayordomías is a public ritual banquet, which takes place in the atrium of the cathedral and is marked by the abundance of beer, chicha, roasted pork, guinea pigs, potatoes, and Andean legumes. During the banquet mayordomos and mayordomas display the lavishness that earns them the respect of their peers and subordinates. The central figure in the distribution of food and chicha or beer is the mayordoma, the mestiza wife (or mother) aided by her female relatives, *comadres,* and female neighbors. The male mayordomo sits surrounded by peers, his task being to drink with them. Although both members of the couple are present, the women have a protagonistic role in the ritual protocol that, to the elites, would be conspicuously transgressive of what is expected of a decent woman. Like elite women in an analogous situation, mestizas control the food. Unlike "ladies," they eat and drink as much, or more, as their male counterparts and they shout and quarrel if there is a need to. To the elites this behavior duplicates mestizas' crass behavior in the marketplace, where they handle businesses and mingle with a swarm of coarse men: truck drivers, package carriers, and municipal guards.

In the previous chapter I showed how at the height of neoindianismo several male intellectuals, in a gesture meant to be favorable to mestizas, portrayed them as strong, hard-working matriarchs. Uriel García (1937:185), for example, wrote: "The chola works harder than the man [the cholo], and her desire for economic gain is higher." Years later, newspapers reported that mujeres del pueblo "contribute to the household economy more than their men," and that the "lack of a good patriarch compels women to make the crucial household decisions."⁸ The portrayal of mestizas as "matriarchs by default" allowed these women to enter the pantheon of cuzqueñismo as a "typical folkloric" attraction of Corpus Christi. In 1988 a cuzqueño anthropologist (who on several occasions also played the role of the Inca in Inti Raymi) described the procession in an earnest cuzqueñista style: "Mamacha Belén and Taytacha Temblores are the images toward which *el pueblo cuzqueño* [Cuzqueño commoners] profess special veneration and for whom they have the greatest fanaticism. [Mamacha Belén is] the preferred image of the market women . . . who have economic preeminence over their men and impose the image of their devotion as a symbol of their matriarchal longings" (Huayhuaca, 1988:142).

The mestizas with whom I talked ignored or dismissed the "matriarch" label given them by the elite while proudly accepting their central role in the festival as divine in origin. For example, Belén Ramírez, a prosperous mestiza who worked as a juice seller when she did her mayordomía, remembered, "When one dreams of the Virgin, she is mestiza, one doesn't dream of her as a dama. . . . She wears a hat and her apron. When one dreams of her, she comes and says: Go and put on this apron and go sell. . . . [T]he Virgin of the Nativity is a mestiza, all Virgins are mestizas like us." Rather than explaining their role in terms of "typical folklore," she explained that mestizas were more prominent than men in mayordomías because "it's a woman's way [*es propio de mujeres*] to be more pious, we women go the Novena for the Virgin all eight days, we work more for the *mamita* [little mother, referring to the Virgin] because we as women and as mothers venerate her more." Above all else, market women perceive that their identity as mestizas glows at the heart of the Corpus Christi festival and infuses their patron saints, the images of the Virgins that participate in the celebration.

Countering the image of mestizas as forsaken matriarchs (the neo-indianista, view) these women believe that their womanly religious devotion adds to their respect, as does having a male partner. Belén explained to me: "My husband was an *enfermero* [health worker]; he gave injections. But we began to work together in my *picantería* [working-class restaurant] because the presence of a man in his woman's business imparts respect and attracts good clientele, not just *borrachos y pobretones* [drunkards and penniless people]. Together we have had a chichería and a *pollería* [chicken restaurant], buena gente [good people] always came."

Not surprisingly, individuals without partners are mayordomos or mayordomas only on rare occasions, as "working by yourself it is impossible to do everything that mayordomías require, and besides people do not respect you if you are *sola* [single or without a partner]." Belén went on to tell me that mayordomos consider themselves "well-known and respected people." She added, "We also have to respect others and give respect for the very reason that we take on the mayordomía; we always have to live as a family in an organized life." This is important since to live an "organized family life" is a fundamental rule of respect for commoners. Yet, unlike family life among the elite, to be respectful their family life does not need to conform to official marriage institutions. Hence the elite sees women like Belén as immoral because she is not officially married, which makes her children illegitimate. This consideration is irrelevant among mestizas, for whom respect is earned by striving not to be poor, and morality presupposes a hard-work ethic. Although sexual monogamy is important once a heterosexual couple is established, female chastity is not a precondition of respect, nor is "divorce" considered a blemish. Consider Belén's response when I asked her about respect: "Respeto doesn't have to do with being a virgin before you find a definite partner. You can have many *compromisos malos* [bad engagements], if you aren't lucky. It's not your fault, so it's better to get a separation. The important thing always, even if you don't have a partner, is to go around well fed and well dressed, not to steal, or to beg for food. Your children have to go to school, not go around collecting charity. Then you have to send them to the university. Then they will help you in your old days, and you won't have to beg like those poor *viejitos mendigos* [old beggars], the beggars who did not know how to educate their children."[9] If families earn respect by feeding and educating their children, so mayordomos earn respect when they provide the food that is the central aspect of the ritual banquets. They use the products of their year-long work as a couple to lavishly feed their guests, and spend money on an exuberant display of mayordomía paraphernalia, such as music, fireworks, and flowers. The payback is the accumulation of symbolic capital that they will use to strengthen their household, in the same way that they will use their offsprings' labor to help them get by in their old age.

The elite interpret mayordomías otherwise. The exuberance is, from their point of view, unnecessary expenditure. Moreover, anticlerical cuzqueñistas envision religious "cargos" (the mayordomías) as obligations imposed by the Catholic Church on the gente del pueblo, forcing an unnecessary "poverty trap" upon the cuzqueño working classes. On commenting about a play featuring an artisan couple during a mayordomía celebration, Vidal Unda the inspirer of Cuzco Day, and certainly a champion of working-class art, considered the drama excellent because "of its great sense of capturing a raw and painfully tragic reality such as the life of a poor cobbler artisan who sees himself hurled into an even crueler misery, if that is possible, by fulfilling one of those social imperatives that . . . constitute a veritable impediment to the worker's progress, that is, the so-called cargo."[10]

Sol Tax, a U.S. anthropologist concerned with development issues in Guatemala in the 1950s considered rural mayordomías wasteful spending (1953). During the same period, cuzqueño intellectuals considered mayordomías irrational acts, product of the ignorance of the populace and a financial burden that hindered the progress of the working-class economy. The Latin Americanist intellectual consensus about the absurdity of cargos led the academics and politicians who participated in the *Congreso Indigenista Interamericano* that met in Cuzco in 1949 to advise the Peruvian government on "the necessity of doing away with the cargos and mayordomías." Like Humberto Vidal Unda, they considered that cargos constituted "true sentences of misery for the Indians and their families" (Cornejo Bouroncle, 1949:156). Years later in the 1970s, I was a witness of how the progressive military junta that ruled Peru saw it as their obligation to ban cargos, most specifically, the rural ones.

The mayordomos I conversed with agreed that they spent a considerable amount of money and time on their celebration. Like Carlos, a prosperous arts and crafts merchant, most of them acknowledged that to sponsor a mayordomía "you have to work harder . . . to wake up earlier, to go to bed later, to travel carrying the merchandise you want to sell, to make contacts for your business." Yet they unanimously rejected the idea that these stewardships condemned them to misery. For example, according to Juan, who was mayordomo in 1983, through the mayordomías individuals may "make more and better connections in every way, you acquire more friends and better commercial relations." Additionally, they forcefully denied that mayordomías are an ecclesiastical "imposition." One mayordomo emphatically told me "no matter how drunk you are when you accept the cargo, you only accept it if you think you can afford it; then accepting the mayordomía is a pleasure." Mayordomías are ritual mechanisms that relatively well-off commoners (not poor artisans as in the play Vidal Unda criticized) use to improve their social status and accumulate symbolic capital. Yet, the manners cuzqueño commoners display in fulfilling them do not follow norms of decency. Thus they are classified as gente del pueblo even if the level of income of many mayordomos surpasses that of some individuals reputed as gente decente. However, they are not allowed to join the company of the elite, because decency (another form of symbolic capital) is more than the amount of income. For an individual to be considered decent, his or her income has to be properly acquired and properly disbursed. The rules of propriety are set by the elites, of course, and commoners who earn their living in the marketplace through the joint work of men (and women) and spend it publicly (displaying "bad manners") do not fulfill them.

The Inclusive and Discriminatory Inner Workings of Mayordomías

The ritual sphere of mayordomías is a social space reserved for cuzqueño commoners, where they can accumulate respect. I could interpret this arrangement as an accomplishment of the gente del pueblo, who, by displaying their coarseness, scare gente decente away from mayordomías and monopolize the most important Catholic ritual sphere of cuzqueñismo and the symbolic capital derived from it. To the extent that this is so, mayordomías represent an unquestionable working-class feat. But the flip side of this feat reveals hegemony at work: the commoners' monopoly of mayordomías certifies those rituals as "folklore" and publicly stigmatizes its participants as gente del pueblo, thus limiting their social accomplishments precisely to the common sphere. These institutions are arenas where the cultural limits of class are actuated because participation in them sharply distinguishes elites from commoners. Moreover, mayordomías selectively include individuals in some aspects of the celebration while excluding them from others, thus creating and reaffirming social differences among commoners (see Crandon-Malamud, 1993). Because the selection of who participates (and how) and who does not is influenced by discrimination against Indianness, the enactment of mayordomías opens the door to the reproduction of hegemonic racism.

A mayordomía demands expensive paraphernalia: a musical group, clothes and jewelry for the saint's image, decorations and repairs for the church to which the image belongs, and fireworks. Also important are less expensive objects such as *detentes* (lapel pins framing the image of patron saints), candles of all sizes and prices, flowers, vases, and printed programs. Last but not least, they require food and beverages. In order to acquire all these goods mayordomías rely on a system of mutual help called the *jurka,* a culturally formalized invitation with which the carguyoq couple — the couple that has the cargo — requests the presence of friends and relatives to celebrate the mayordomía, and, simultaneously, solicits contributions from them. These ritually invited persons receive the name of *jurkados* and live in the city, in the countryside, or in both. The wealthier guests are expected to contribute for the musical group, for clothing or jewelry for the saint's image, or for the fireworks. The poorer urban guests help with the corn beer, while the poorer rural residents contribute guinea pigs, potatoes, and corn. Guillermo, one of the most esteemed Corpus Christi mayordomos, boasting about the success of his celebration remembered: "I can't complain. . . . My cargo has been one of the best because I have had what none of the other mayordomos has had. . . . We put seven fireworks in place, seventy-seven triumphal arches. The food also went very well. It's enough to tell you that we had roast pork, guinea pigs, and lamb for two months after our cargo, that much was left over. We gave a lot of food to the people."

He continued: "According to one's category [social condition] one invites friends, engineers, lawyers. . . . Not all the cargos are the same because it goes according to the mayordomo. If you are mayordoma and have good friendships, you have good jurkados. If you are not a professional, your friends correspond to your category. In my case, the majority of my jurkados are merchants. . . . [T]he majority of people who have more faith are not well-educated; they are poor people, [so] you have to invite them also." Guillermo's opinions aptly describe the social dynamic underlying the celebration of the mayordomías. The festival's magnificence speaks of the mayordomo's *categoría,* the local term for social standing or status. The idea is that the higher a person's social rank, the higher the social condition of jurkados, and the more numerous they will be; therefore the better, and more abundant, the contributions. The numerous fireworks and arches that Guillermo mentioned were offered to him by his merchant friends. But the success in terms of food resulted from the couple's myriad of peasant godchildren, who contributed roasted guinea pigs, fava beans, potatoes, chicha, and pork and lamb, without which no mayordomía can be considered good.

The jurka is the mechanism that sets in motion the symbolic capital that the mayordomía requires and reproduces. Presented as invitations by mayordomos, jurkas are an imposition on people to be guests; thus they actually imply gentle forms of violence (though they are not recognized as such by the participants) that appeal to the personal loyalty of guests and oblige them to donate produce, time, or even money (Bourdieu, 1993:192). As a form of symbolic violence jurkas are distinctive because they constitute both inclusive and differentiating invitations. Mayordomos request the presence of acquaintances regardless of their social status. Yet they require contributions according to the standing of the guests, which assigns them their social place in the celebration. Also, residents of the *barrio* are included in or excluded from a pool of future mayordomos according to their achievements as jurkados in mayordomías. They are ranked socially in agreement with the "quality" of the celebration, which is evaluated according to the display of paraphernalia. Salvador Serrano, president of the Hermandad de Cargadores de la Virgen de Natividad told me: "In the assembly we discuss about who does bad cargos, who does the good ones, who has responded well. . . . We make an assessment and we give diplomas to those who have done the best cargos."

The fame — good or bad — acquired by the cargo-holder after the celebration spreads rapidly in the neighborhood and the city. A diploma confirming the high quality of the celebration is conspicuously displayed in every successful Mayordomo's house. The working classes in Cuzco still live in multiple-family dwellings in which individual household units have rented rooms and where the residents share patios, bathrooms, and clothes-washing facilities. In these shared areas they comment on the incidents in the cargo's celebration, and assess the quality of food, music, and drink. Chicherías, the marketplace, streets, and churches are also public spaces where former mayordomos (*mayordomos pasados*) are praised or condemned. By chatting and meddling, the mayordomos and their guests assess the cargos and use them to define social differences among the popular classes.

In spite of their inclusive quality mayordomías do not erase social differences among guests. On the contrary, as reproducers of symbolic capital expressed as respect, mayordomías require the assertion of social differences. In order to safeguard their respect, people who belong to social circles considered superior may deny access to the central domain of their mayordomía to individuals they consider "inferior." Frequently, these attitudes provoke conflicts that originate new mayordomías, which excluded "inferiors" invent in order to create a social space from which to acquire respect and establish the network that will secure them symbolic capital. Social identity is central to this network. This dynamic undergirded the creation of the Corpus Christi mayordomía of the Virgen de la Natividad, and the ensuing production of numerous less prestigious neighborhood mayordomías in Almudena. As I will explain in some detail later in this chapter, neoindianismo, which was at its peak in the late fifties, stimulated the proliferation of these rituals, thus actually bringing about a grassroots cultural revival that reinterpreted elite rhetoric and adapted it to their social needs and beliefs.

Until 1956 the barrio of Almudena honored its patron saint, the Virgin of the Nativity, with a neighborhood mayordomía commemorated every September 8. In that year the image of the Virgin of the Nativity of Almudena joined the Corpus Christi procession and paraded for the first time in the Plaza de Armas in the month of June. A family named Velasco Quintanilla, created a specific mayordomía for this ritual in order to distinguish themselves from those who had recently settled in the hills surrounding Almudena, whom the barrio urbanites deemed "recently arrived from the rural highlands" (recién bajados). Since then, religious cargos in honor of the Virgin of the Nativity have mushroomed. Excluded from the two central mayordomías — the old September 8 one and the new for Corpus Christi — the newcomers, former comuneros (dwellers of the rural villages officially called indigenous communities until 1969 and peasant communities thereafter) were first invited as members of dance troupes (comparsas). While at first they joined the celebration peripherally, the newcomers later created their own mayordomías to secure the participation of their dance groups. Led by Timotea Gamarra (a woman whom I befriended and who helped me understand mayordomías), a group of old-timers in Almudena unable to afford either the central Corpus Christi or the September cargos but willing to assert their identity as long-time urbanites, created the Asociación de Cargadores de la Virgen Natividad (Association of Porters of the Virgin of the Nativity). Years later, several urban healers created the Brotherhood of the Virgin and Her Holy Angels (La Hermandad de la Virgen y Sus Santos Angeles). Prompted by their belief that "the Virgin is a doctor," they wanted the Nativity

Virgin to authenticate their reputation in the city. In the 1960s, a group of former immigrants from the neighboring department of Puno also created their own celebration in honor of the Virgin. Finally, a new wave of immigrants from Cuzco's lowland provinces, mostly shoemakers or mechanics (who did not identify with the dance troupe mayordomías because the dances represent highlanders), created the Mayordomía de Comadres. New mayordomías are peripheral to and less prestigious than the old September 8 celebration (the "Cargo Grande") and to the Corpus Christi Cargo begun in 1956, which rivals it in prestige. Mayordomos for each are chosen carefully among two socially differentiated working-class groups. I will examine the way these choices reproduce consensual beliefs about cultural/racial identities and status, after the brief description of Almudena that follows.

The Barrio Setting

The paint on the walls is peeling off through the whole church [of Almudena], deadened by the dust of years and of the dead. Nothing seems to remind [us] that there was life. Now, one only hears the creak of the doors and a silence that comes and goes like the howl of the dogs. . . . Nonetheless, every September 7, the Hermandad de Esclavos de Nuestra Señora de Almudena [Brotherhood of Slaves of Our Lady of Almudena] dances with scant energy but stimulated by large quantities of liquor and the wind that blows up the stench of cadavers. — ANGEL AVENDAÑO, 1980

The Almudena neighborhood, located in the district of Santiago, is a ten-minute walk from Cuzco's Plaza de Armas. Cuzqueño intellectuals such as Avendaño depict the decay of the neighborhood, which they consider the social and cultural periphery of Cuzco, characterized by the barrio's main buildings: the jail, and the cemetery.[11] For the neighborhood residents, its symbolic center is the Church of Almudena, founded in the seventeenth century by a Spanish bishop, who entrusted it to the Bethlehemite order so that they would administer an Indian hospital. In 1689, the nephew of the founding bishop, a Spaniard known as Antonio de Mollinedo, founded the Hermandad de Esclavitud de Nuestra Señora de Almudena, a brotherhood charged with "the worship and care of the church" (Villanueva, 1948:58). This responsibility included celebrating the festival of the Virgin annually on May 1, the date when, according to legend, the image of the Virgin of Almudena was placed on the church's altar. The oral tradition has it that the festival lost its colonial luster in the nineteenth century, and it did not recover it until its successful revival in 1956 under the lead of the Velasco Quintanilla family. At present the neighborhood celebration is one of the most famous in the city and rivals the oldest mayordomías in the city.

At the turn of the century, Almudena was a working-class, but not poor, neighborhood, a home to merchants, principally male cattle dealers and their wives, who sold meat.[12] There were also some mid-level landowners of rural properties located in the hills surrounding the neighborhood or in rich lowland valleys.[13] Because of its proximity to the slaughterhouse, cattle dealers on their way to the marketplace had to cross the Almudena bridge, thus lending commercial dynamism to the neighborhood and allowing the chicheras' and shopkeepers' businesses to flourish.[14] Its proximity to the central market — when it was inaugurated in the 1920s — increased the population of merchants in the neighborhood. Its present-day inhabitants are these old-time urban merchants, and their offspring, as well as new residents originally from the countryside.

The neighborhood's appearance in 1992 reminded me of the city's history. After crossing a bridge, reconstructed in the 1920s by the modernizing programs of President Leguía, there is a central cobblestone street — Hospital Street — which ends up at the church of Almudena, in the plaza of the same name. Until the sixties, muleteers arrived by way of this cobblestone street with their llama trains, along with the merchants who brought cattle to the slaughterhouse.[15] Now a few cars and many pedestrians circulate there on their way to the city's center. Perpendicular to Hospital Street and across from the plaza runs an asphalt highway, the road that currently bears most of the commercial traffic, trucks and buses, that merge together from the Chumbivilcas and Anta routes. Behind the church rise the hills, which became densely populated when waves of migrants arrived between the 1950s and 1970s and organized new urban settlements (with the names of Dolorespata, Coripata Sur, Zarzuela, Viva el Perú, General Ollanta, and Manco Capac) in former grazing pastures (Porcel et al., 1992:18–20). Because of this dramatic surge in population, Almudena became a parish (*parroquia*) in 1972.

The inhabitants of the hills and their houses contrast with those on Hospital Street. The hills are dotted by many one-family, newly self-built houses owned by artisans, university students, street vendors, hotel workers, public high school teachers, mechanics, and owners of public transport vehicles. The houses in the "lower" streets, such as Hospital Street, date from the end of the nineteenth century, although some were reconstructed after the 1950 earthquake. Traditional urban inhabitants of Cuzco rent rooms in multiple-family houses owned by impoverished landlords. Both tenants and owners are artisans, chicheras, market sellers, owners of grocery stores or of small rural properties. Generally, those who live "down below" (*en las calles de abajo*) descend from urban mestizas, either a grandmother or mother, while, usually, those from "above, from the hills" (*los de arriba, los de los cerros*) are at most second-generation migrants from the countryside. Replicating the traditional geographical politics of identity, traditional urbanites tend to identify the latter as recently arrived from the highlands (*recién bajados*), meaning that they are less urban or "closer to Indian," and scorn them as such. The "newcomers" (many of whom are not new anymore) must display a recently acquired profession, urban employment, or the ownership of a truck or taxi to receive better treatment from traditionally urban Cuzco. In the previous chapter, I explained that working in the marketplace reduces the social value of the mestizas' relatively high monetary income and marks them as gente del pueblo, socially inferior to gente decente. Similarly, the evident rural origins of the new urbanites tends to make them inferior relative to the traditional mestizo working-class inhabitants of Almudena, even if occasionally the income of the newcomers is higher. During mayordomías, the role recent migrants play in the rituals indicates their status as '*recién bajados*' inferior to urban old-timers, thus enacting hegemonic perceptions of social hierarchies as influenced by the regional geography.

The Revival of the Mayordomía de la Virgen Natividad
Grassroots Neoindianismo and Cuzqueñismo

According to a contemporary cuzqueño anthropologist, the muleteers from Chumbivilcas—a well-known cattle-raising province—who settled in Almudena in the early decades of the century played decisive roles in the creation of the Virgin's feast in its current form, since *Mamita Natividad* (little mother of the Nativity) is Chumbivilcas's patron saint as well (Flores Ochoa, 1992:282–283). The same anthropologist argues that when muleteering declined from the second half of this century on, mestiza merchants from the central market, who were then thriving commercially, inherited the organization of the festival (1992:300–301). Evidently the growth of mestizas' businesses (resulting from the urban demographic increase and from the tourism boom, as explained in chapter 4) contributed to boost the Natividad festival. However, neoindianismo in its nonelite version was just as important in the revival of the celebration.

When I observed the Almudena festival for the first time on September 8, 1991, an old cuzqueño and his son approached me. The old man asked me immediately what I was doing at the festival. Since anthropologists frequently observe the festival, my fieldwork tools—notebook, pencil, camera, tape recorder—had attracted his attention, and he asked me if I was an anthropologist. When I answered affirmatively, he was very enthusiastic and invited me to come to his house the next day. "Bring your tape recorder because this story is long, very long," he told me. I went several times because, just as he had warned me, the story he had to tell was long.

Manuel Velasco Quintanilla wanted to tell me that he and his brother Isaac, old neighbors of Almudena, were the originators of the Festival of the Virgen Natividad as it presently exists. Current residents of the neighborhood also identify them as such. Although the crucial date is the 1956 cargo, Don Manuel, who could remember everything but his age, began his account in 1914:

In midst of the [First World] War my mother carried out the mayor-domía of the Virgin. She had to repeat it in 1915 since, because of the famine unleashed by the war, no one wanted to take on [the cargo]. My mother didn't have anything, not even a potato for the party and said, "And now what do I do for those who are getting the Virgin ready?" At ten in the morning, an Indian [*un indiecito*] with a bundle of potatoes and *lisas* [another tuber] shows up at the door of the picantería that my mother had. He says, "Do you want to buy some potatoes?" "Come in, son," my mother says to him. "You're going to eat breakfast." My mother asks the Indian to bring more, and there were enough potatoes, in the middle of a time of hunger. . . . Who could that Indian have been? Maybe the Virgin sent him as a miracle.

Don Manuel was one of the few cuzqueños I heard refer to Indians without excusing himself for doing so and even expressed com-miseration as well as superiority in relation to them. Born in the late nineteenth century, Don Manuel—who was almost one hundred years old—was still using in 1992 the categories he had learned in his youth, a time when cuzqueños felt at ease using "Indian," "mes-tizo," and "gente decente" to speak about the city's social hier-archies. Manuel and his brother Isaac also used these categories to describe their family's place in Cuzco. They were the sons of a "good mestiza," the brothers told me, whose name was Doña Fortunata Quintanilla de Velasco, and according to her son Manuel "she used very fine shawls and had a lot of jewelry, a lot of gold and silver." The matron of this working-class family, she had two occupations: she worked as a midwife in the Almudena Hospital and she ran a picantería in their own house. Her husband (Manuel and Isaac's father) worked in the cemetery "as administrator and builder of niches." He was also a musician, a profession he taught his children. In 1907 they bought a house on Hospital Street—Almudena's most important—where they rented out some rooms. They also owned plots in the countryside, and the family spent the agricultural sea-sons there. Immersed in patronage networks (their father might even have corresponded to the type the elite indigenistas labeled "gamo-nal"), Isaac and Manuel's parents acted as godparents of the "In-dians" who worked on their properties, while Manuel and Isaac were godchildren of the gentlemen of the cuzqueño elite. At the turn of the century, the Velasco Quintanillas were thus a relatively well-off working-class family who straddled the city and the countryside and continuously strove to improve the urban standing of their family within the gente del pueblo. Their mayordomías were an important tool in such an endeavor. As a good mestiza (*una buena mestiza*) and member of a respectful family (*una familia de respeto*) Fortunata Quintanilla de Velasco was always active in the neighborhood's religious festivities. In 1922, along with her husband she carried out the mayordomía of San Juan de Dios, also an image in Almudena's church. In 1934 Doña Fortunata ordered the manufacture of the Virgen de Natividad's crown, for which, according to Don Manuel, "she melted down all her gold and silver jewelry." Finally, in 1956 the Velasco Quintanilla family again carried out the "Big Cargo" (the Cargo Grande), celebrated every September 8 in the neighborhood. That same year, the brothers Isaac and Manuel made the necessary administrative arrangements for the Virgin's inclusion in the Corpus Christi procession in June.[16]

Don Manuel recalls 1956 as a year of "great drought; there was nothing for the celebration, the fields were dry, the earth was cracked." That same year city authorities created the district of Santiago, which included the neighborhood of Almudena and its new urban settlements, which had previously been a part of an old neighborhood called Belén (Porcel et al., 1992: 18). To make Almudena comparable to this old barrio, which celebrated its patron saint, the Virgen de Belén, during Corpus Christi, the Velasco Quintanillas created a similar Corpus Christi mayordomía for the Nativity Virgin. Manuel Velasco Quintanilla said, "Until 1956 when we made our mayordomía, the fiesta was only here, in the neighborhood. We decided to make it larger, like the Virgen de Belén's, for all of Cuzco, not just for the people from Almudena . . . so that all of Cuzco would know us, would know that we can carry out a big cargo. So we had our cargo here in the neighborhood, and then we also took the Virgin to the Corpus." Their mother, Doña Fortunata was the center of the celebration, and to carry it out, the Velasco Quintanillas had to set all their social relationships in motion. They utilized the relationships in which they were patrons, those in which they were clients, and those in which they were equal to their guests in the festival. Don Manuel recalled:

> My mother had an *ahijado de matrimonio* (godson by marriage), a baker named Tomás, [who,] when he found out that we were going to carry out the cargo, came to offer us his services. "Mama, we have an oven, let's make the bread for our commitments [*compromisos*]," he told us. To request fine wines we went to Sr. Lambarri's store. He was Spanish, a friend of ours, he gave us wine, liquor, everything. . . . We asked Sr. Gárate, owner of the Puquín hacienda, for straw to make bonfires; we arranged with Sr. Cazorla who lived in the Cuesta de Santa Ana for the band for the procession. In the Corpus cargo we got the cooperation of almost all of the market vendors. Aaaahh, the mestizas never rejected us when we approached them with a request, they themselves offered their help. . . . Even the people of [the peasant community] of Chitapampa wanted to collaborate with corn, with potatoes, each one according to his ability gave us [things].

"The jurka lasted six months," continued Don Manuel, whose perception of social identities informed the ritual invitations. "The biggest breads" (an element of the jurka that the mayordomos have to give their future guests) "were for the first-class guests, and the smaller ones for the less important people." The mother, as a good mestiza, invited her godchildren from the countryside (the peasants from Chitapampa) who worked in the family's agricultural property. She also invited the market vendors who supplied Fortunata's picantería whenever the family's crops were insufficient. Manuel and Isaac — who were also musicians — invited the best-known bands through the jurka. Last but not least, to buy liquor, they obtained credit from Mr. Lámbarri, owner of one of the most important commercial establishments of the time and a well-known liberal politician. The way in which the Velasco Quintanilla brothers used the jurka illustrates the inclusive and differentiating aspects of the invitation, as well as the symbolic violence undergirding both the jurka and the mayordomía. These brother's cargo was an attempt to reaffirm and renew their ongoing social relations, and place their family at the head of the neighborhood's socially differentiated groups. According to Don Manuel, his family carried out the cargo to "demonstrate that we were equal to those of Belén and better than the rest in Almudena, we were the *antiguos* (the old-timers). We could do things in a big, grand way." Carrying the Virgin in the Plaza de Armas during the Corpus Christi procession added to the neighborhood prestige of this family, and, more important, to their own symbolic capital as it confirmed their long urban tradition and thus their higher status relative to the new barrio dwellers.

Like most cuzqueños interested in cultural production during the 1950s, the Velascos designed their mayordomía using the new neoindianist ideas. Manuel and Isaac approached the circle of intellectuals and told them about their intentions. Because it was coherent with their vision of mayordomías as folklore, several neoindianistas, notwithstanding their anticlericalism, encouraged the brothers. Andrés Alencastre, the elite poet and playwright who wrote in Quechua, dedicated a poem to the Virgin that the Velasco Quintanilla family included in their printed program. Horacio Villanueva, a historian and then member of the neoindianista group, allowed the reproduction in the same pamphlet of a piece of his work dealing with the history of the Almudena church, the image of the Virgin, and of the Bethlehemite friars. Most important, the intellectuals suggested the use of Quechua and "folk dances" during the religious events.

The brothers followed the advice and included Quechua and dance groups as central attractions of their mayordomía. Don Manuel explained to me that it was an attempt to emulate the staging of Cuzco Day. But there were subtle differences between this grassroots production and those of the cuzqueño elite. In the first chapter I related that in the 1920s elite intellectuals used Capac Simi, an invented purist sociolect, to set themselves apart from mestizo and Indian cuzqueños, who according to those same intellectuals spoke Runa Simi, an impure version of the imperial language, contaminated by borrowings from Spanish. Following these ideas, and contradicting in part the neoindianista mestizaje project, in the 1944 Inti Raymi, the "First Inca" used Capac Simi with its undergirding belief in "pure Quechua" to distinguish himself from "Inca people" [*el pueblo Incaico*], represented by peasants from the nearby villages. The Velasco Quintanillas did the opposite. Instead of using Quechua to exclude commoners from their sphere, they employed it to include people from the neighborhood (even those the brothers considered infe-rior) and to advertise the festival among them. They invited Father Zúñiga Cazorla, the playwright whom indigenistas despised in the 1920s and who had become a renowned Quechua specialist in the neoindianista era. His Quechua was far from Capac Simi. Instead, as Isaac's daughter Doña Berta, recounts: "We brought him because he could do everything in both Spanish and Quechua; he even mixed them, and he spoke beautifully. The prayers and songs were also in Quechua, and he composed music and words and made all the peo-ple sing. He also narrated the story of the Nativity Virgin in Que-chua. People felt at home [*como en su casa*]." Father Zúñiga's pres-ence in the Velasco's celebration raised the family's social reputation. Granted his Quechua appealed to commoners, but using it did not imply canceling neighborhood social hierarchies. "Feeling at home," as Doña Berta described the situation, also implies the sensation of everyone's being in their "proper" social place.

The use of "folk dances" by the Velasco brothers was immersed too in the inclusive yet differentiating dynamics that colored other aspects of the celebration. On explaining to me why he had used dances, Don Manuel mentioned that dances enticed his neighbors to participate since "they know how to dance." However, he also iden-tified several categories of dances that corresponded to the differenti-ated social identities of the dwellers of Almudena, all of whom were invited to participate. For example, the dance *Chilenos* represented "gentlemen with straw hats and leather boots," and according to Doña Berta was presented to her family by the more prestigious residents. The less reputable comparsa guests, by contrast, danced the *Sallqa Qolla* (the savage [*sallqa*] people of the *altiplano* [*qolla*]). Using the cultural paraphernalia proposed by neoindianismo, and adapting it to the feeling and experience of their old and new neigh-bors, the Velascos attracted cuzqueño dwellers' attention to the cele-bration of their own mayordomía and gained prestige in their neigh-borhood as the implementators of such a successful event. This undoubtedly accrued them symbolic capital while setting themselves apart from the recién bajados, who had undoubtedly contributed with their presence, labor, and gifts to the Velascos's cultural and ritual feat.

September 8
Mestizas, Discrimination, and Symbolic Capital

In 1957, the devotees split the responsibilities for the celebration of the Virgin of the Nativity. The residents of Almudena kept the September 8 mayordomía for themselves, while people living in the colonial urban perimeter of Cuzco (known as *el centro*) assumed the Corpus Christi cargo. To be their successor in the neighborhood celebration, the September 8 cargo, the Velasco Quintanillas chose, according to Don Manuel, "Miss Carmen Calvo, owner of a large grocery store on Hospital Street. She also had a very large house, where she rented out rooms." Two other mayordomos succeeded her: one "had a musical band," and the other was the "owner of a rural property in Puquín." These are the last male characters recalled in the neighborhood's oral history. Almudena neighbors and mayordomos remember that in 1960 a clear succession of carguyoq couples began, in which the wife — always a mestiza — was the salient figure of the celebration: "In 1960, Señora Ermila Leiva did the cargo, she was a meat seller, an old woman with a lace mantilla. . . . Her husband was a cattle dealer. Then came Señora Agripina Villafuerte, who had a picantería; then Leonor Paucar, also sold in the market, and then Simeona Inca Roca, a meat seller too."

The list of mestiza mayordomas continues until 1980. Besides meat sellers, the list includes *paperas* (vendors of potatoes), *verduleras* (of vegetables), and *fruteras* (of fruit). There are also *chicheras* and owners of restaurants and *picanterías*. Almost all lived on Hospital Street, close to the Camal (slaughterhouse), on Almudena Bridge, or in the streets adjacent to the bridge. Certainly, they had male partners (or they would not have been elected mayordomas); however, the men's names are not central in the neighborhood's memory.

Mestizas' power in the celebration of the mayordomías was built upon features of local popular culture that elites and working classes share. To me, the most obvious ones were the beliefs that cargos are for gente del pueblo and that women are more pious than men. Although these ideas subordinate mestizas as women and as commoners, in the case of mayordomas these assumptions have also been door-openers through which mestizas assertively entered the ritual public sphere. Once situated there, while the neoindianista version of cuzqueñismo exoticized them in their role as folk matriarchs, mestizas accumulated symbolic capital by demonstrating both their economic strength and their piety. To do so they became ritual specialists and created institutions to control the celebration. For example, Nicolasa Villafuerte, the owner of a "good restaurant," brought up one important innovation when she decided during her mayordomía in the mid-1960s "that women, and not only men, should carry the Virgin." Nicolasa's mayordomía was the first in which, after the Misa de Despierto — literally the "Wake-Up Mass," the ceremony that initiates the annual September 8 celebrations — the "market señoras carried the Virgin's litter to the market and back."[17] The inclusion of female litter-bearers in the celebration's opening rite was extremely important in marking the culmination of mestizas' appropriation of the festival. Nicolasa herself recalled, "Until that moment, only men carried the Virgin. That couldn't continue because the Mamita is ours." By the end of the 1960s, mestizas who had gone through former cargos (*pasado el cargo*) created the Association of Ex-Mayordomos, initially intended to supervise the church's maintenance. Belén Ramírez narrated,

> When the association started, the church was in need of everything; it didn't have light bulbs; there was no money to pay for the Virgin's candles, this church was totally abandoned. It didn't have benches, the walls were all cracked, the doors didn't have locks. . . . [When I did the mayordomía] the mayor of the city was restoring the colonial churches. . . . I found this out, and went to his house to plead him to remember Almudena. I told him we didn't even have a sacristry, everything was falling down, *así lo jurké para la reparación de la sacristía* [Thus I ritually invited him so that he'd restore the sacristy].

A few years later they had appropriated the right to decide who could be mayordomos by choosing the future carguyoq from among their female neighbors or their colleagues at work. By deciding who would be mayordomo and maintaining the church, mestizas secured their right to choose the ritual elements and etiquette that cargos should accomplish. During my fieldwork period in 1992, the Ex-

Mayordomos Association was still the institution that authorized mayordomías' new rites, and I had to get permission from them to observe and participate in their ceremonies. Mestizas continued to steer the association. Several male associates, who were also successful businessmen agreed that "the older señoras are the ones who know how to do things, anything. Everything we want to do, we have to consult with them about it; it's always been like that."

Controlling the mayordomías has certainly empowered mestizas vis-à-vis the parish priest, who is no longer able to control the celebration. It has also made them controversial figures in the barrio. From the association, the women penalize or reward former mayordomos and veto potential ones. In judging to whom they will "give" the cargo, they evaluate the candidates' reputation as a couple, their economic situation, and their potential capacity to accomplish the ritual protocol. Mestizas judge these qualifications according to the mayordomo candidate's social proximity to their own status, thus validating old neighborhood social hierarchies and sanctioning new ones, at least partially. A potato seller named Primitiva Alvarado who was a mayordoma in 1966 told me: "Now there are so many mayordomías that anyone can be mayordomo. It wasn't like that before. Before we only chose from among people like us. Now any *chutito* [a person with straight hair, an Indian], any mujercita, [i.e., female Indian] can carry out a mayordomía, they don't know anything about cargos. We were very careful, we didn't turn over the cargo to just anyone."

Primitiva is an old woman who no longer goes to the association much because, as she says, "Now I'm very tired of walking." She is the owner of a large house in one of the oldest streets in Cuzco and in spite of her age still runs her potato stand at the central market. There she has employees whom she considers "chutitos" or "mujercitas," labels which are less offensive than "indios" and which mestizas use colloquially to refer to those they consider "Indian." These terms (the same ones that Primitiva employed to describe the people the Association of Ex-Mayordomos used to veto) convey the superior status of mestizas. Primitiva's words emphasized the discriminatory dynamics that oil the inner workings of the ritual mayordomía, which are indeed reminiscent of the marketplace behavior. While mayordomos use jurkas to invite a socially differentiated crowd, each guest has a preassigned social place in the ritual that is marked according to their contribution. Additionally and obviously, not every guest was considered a potential mayordomo.

Lower-ranked inhabitants of Almudena, the new arrivals who live in the barrio hills, have moved to the city because their incomes from agriculture were decreasing or because they were attracted by the tourist boom. They have challenged mestizas' discrimination by creating their own mayordomías, one of which was the cargo for the P'asña Coyacha dancers. Although the title of their group literally means "young Inca princess," the dance is said to represent "the little men and women from the heights," a euphemism for "Indians." A P'asña Coyacha troupe joined the September 8 celebration for the first time in 1965, when they received an invitation from Vicentina Escalante, that year's mayordoma, who owned a prosperous brick-yard in Almudena. Traditionally the Mestiza Coyacha troupe had danced in this cargo. The Mestiza Coyacha — as its name suggests — represents the mestizas. Primitiva — and the association — considered the P'asña Coyacha dancing inappropriate for the Almudena celebration, and the following year (1966) they criticized the troupe members, both because they "represented Indians" and because they were not urban cuzqueños but ex-peasant migrants. The P'asña Coyacha dancers still recall resentfully "They didn't treat [us] well. They didn't give [us] any food, or chichita." To avoid further discrimination they created their own mayordomía. Along with tourism, neoindianismo, and commercial and demographic growth, incentives to create new mayordomías have resulted from discrimination within working-class groups, and the challenges to it. Many of the new mayordomías occupy a lower rung in the hierarchy of cargos, the apex of which is the Cargo Grande of September 8. On many occasions the market women that I talked to assessed this mayordomía as "mestiza," while evaluating some of the others (particularly the dance troupe ones) as "more Indian" or "less mestizo," and certainly "less magnificent" and "poorer."

Residents of Almudena comment that in order to set themselves apart from the less prestigious new mayordomías, the mestiza mayordomas keep the Big Cargo tradition secret. They communicate it only to the elected carguyoq during the celebration itself as he/she goes about developing his or her ritual, the neighbors of Almudena told me. Although it is certainly impossible to "keep the secret" of a ceremony in which several hundred people participate each year, by spreading the idea that they conceal the ritual routine, mestizas have created a specialized field of knowledge of their own. Mestizas use secrecy, a relatively common mechanism employed by ritual specialists in other societies (see Helms, 1988), to distinguish their group from others in the neighborhood and to choose the individuals that they want to include in their mayordomo group. Their secret ritual knowledge grants them possession of crucial secular aspects of the ceremony. It also establishes them as ritual specialists, with the right to evaluate the mayordomías' display. Their task can be highly discriminatory and violent (and indeed, not only symbolically so), as exemplified by the events that occurred during 1991, when the association severely criticized and offended that year's mayordoma, Alejandrina Sana. This woman was not properly informed by former mayordomas about the ritual procedures and failed her cargo. When I visited her months after the event she still felt unhappy about it, "Those mayordomas have made my heart hurt a lot. I spent the three days [of the cargo] crying. They insulted me, they told me that I didn't know how to do it right. . . . But it was their fault [because] instead of showing me how things could be done, they went away, they didn't tell me a thing." Justifying their attitude regarding Alejandrina, Salvador, one of the members of the Association of Ex-Mayordomos thought, "That happened to her because she did one of the worst mayordomías. Up until the last moment there wasn't even a band; we did really badly giving [the cargo] to that woman. It can't be given to people *who don't have money,* because they do it their own way. Now, for next year we have all decided to give it to Hermenegildo; he'll do it better."

The Association of Ex-Mayordomos currently represents a self-perpetuating working-class neighborhood elite, a nucleus of influence and even of power, who can publicly denigrate some individuals and endorse those they consider successful in reproducing their symbolic capital as a social group. One of their considerations in choosing a mayordomo is the requirement that the individual "have money," as Salvador's remarks indicate. But this is not only about money; it is also about the perception of the money-related activity and the family situation of the mayordomo. In other words, it is about respect. Alejandrina is a wholesaler who deals in fodder for guinea pigs; she owns a brick house and a car that she rents out as a taxi. In relative terms she "has money." However, selling guinea pig fodder is not good enough for a mayordomo because it does not provide "good acquaintances," those that are necessary in the accumulation of symbolic capital. "Everybody has guinea pigs, anybody can collect *pasto* [fodder]; you can do that by yourself, you don't need anything, or anybody." Worst of all in terms of the rules of respect, although Alejandrina carried out the cargo with her son, she did not have a spouse, who as she told me, "would have defended" her from the scorn of the association.

The case of Hermenegildo, one of the valued mayordomos, is different. The activities with which he obtains "money" are prestigious in the working-class scale. He is an extremely successful owner of a chain of restaurants that serve roast chicken, *pollerías*. He also owns a small local radio station, several pick-up trucks he uses for his businesses, and a house in one of the city's new working-class neighborhoods. Accordingly, "Everybody knows him, wants to be his friend." Thus he was able to extend "more than seven hundred jurkas," when he carried out his cargo in 1985. The gifts he got for the church included "a gold crown for the Virgin, two church benches, a large prayer table, two electric chandeliers," along with many other smaller things (Roca Walparimachi, 1992:18). Indeed, he has a female partner with whom he shared the cargo and with whom he runs the family's business.

Hermenegildo represents the new working-class businessmen, who are increasingly infiltrating the central stage in the Cargo Grande celebration and who have joined mestizas in the nucleus of the Association of Ex-Mayordomos. During his 1985 cargo, he was the fifth businessman to be mayordomo. The first was a grain merchant, while the second was a *camionero*, the owner of a truck. Individuals in this group are engaged in marketplace-related businesses, enjoy economic prosperity and working-class social prestige, and have family linkages with mestizas. Possibly, mestizas identified these groups of men as their successors when their own marketplace trade declined, starting in the late 1980s, as a consequence of the overall economic crisis in the country, which yielded among other things the decrease of urban middle-class income. Although they have, at least partially, transferred their representation in mayordomías, mestizas continue to control the ritual. According to the new mayordomos, the women currently "test them" first to see how they performed in the smaller rituals that are part of the Cargo Grande. "The women first observe who fulfills [the obligation] and then they choose him or her," Salvador, who had been a September 8 mayordomo, told me. Mayordomías are crucial in these individuals' accumulation of symbolic capital because, in addition to displaying generosity in the rituals and thus asserting their economic power, the Association of Ex-Mayordomos functions as a pool from which its members can draw the regional economic connections that they need for their businesses.

The current mayordomos are mostly chosen among working-class entrepreneurs. "Working-class entrepreneurs" may seem incongruous in orthodox class terms, but it does accurately characterize these individuals who self-identify as gente del pueblo and claim to be descendants of mestizas but possess (and flaunt) relatively large amounts of economic capital. Like mestizas they cannot enter decent social circles. Their jobs are prestigious among commoners, but from the elite perspective they are socially polluted by their direct daily interaction with cuzqueños of lower strata. Moreover, their lack of formal university education, added to their uncultivated manners, definitely place them among the working class, regardless of their "wealth."

The presence of this new group in the ritual has not been free of conflict. Before, when mestizas were unrivaled mayordomas, most of their jurkado guests were other marketplace women. During the two years that I participated in the celebration I sensed a tendency, coming from the new businessmen mayordomos, to deny access to the Cargo Grande (the September 8 celebration) to newer marketplace vendors. They accept former mestiza mayordomas' ritual authority because they need their patronage, but they tend to prevent new ones from entering their prestigious social circle. Arnaldo and his wife — owners of a *chicharronería* [fried pork restaurant] in the city's center — told me that for their mayordomía they had not "entered the market to invite those women because if we had, they would start complaining about us and would want to eat everything in exchange for the handful of potatoes or hominy that they give in the jurka." This couple might have been an exception among the September 8 mayordomos. But among the Corpus Christi mayordomos (those that celebrate the June mayordomía in the Plaza de Armas instead of the September barrio cargo), the norm is to scorn mestizas and call them cholas.

In chapter 1 I described how the elites, in order to distinguish themselves from mestizos, ignored their shared phenotype and emphasized instead the allegedly superior innate moral standards granted to them "in the cradle," through birth in decent families. Many (although certainly not all) of the Corpus Christi mayordomos that I interviewed reminded me of this elite maneuver. Like the market women and the working-class business men, they have common rural origins. However, unlike the September 8 mayordomos, whose ceremony proudly displays the markers of their relative highland mestizo identity, most members of the Corpus Christi group, instead emphasize their relative lowland markers. Spanish is the main language during their mayordomía; wine, beer, and pisco the common beverage; and women dress like ladies, in contrast with the mestiza attires of the September 8 mayordomas. Members of this social group locate themselves in between those they consider cholos (the mestizas' group) and gente decente. Like the latter they are ashamed of sharing spaces with marketplace characters during Corpus Christi rituals. Although they are also compelled by their sense of cuzqueñismo to do so, they make efforts to distinguish themselves from the "indecent throng," whom they deem "ignorant Indians."

We are Mestizos but not Cholos
The Racial/Cultural Margins of Class

In 1956 to insure the continuity of the participation of their Virgin in the central procession in the Plaza de Armas, the Velasco Quitanilla brothers made a *demanda* representing the Corpus Christi mayordomía of the Virgin of the Nativity. The demanda is a small image of the patron saint, and in any given mayordomía either member of the mayordomo couple holds the figurine that distinguishes them as sponsors of the celebration. Thus, after making the demanda, the Velasco Quintanilla brothers had to locate a mayordomo to succeed them in holding the figurine. They found Señorita Rosa Salazar, whom they described as "a faithful woman who had to sell all her things to carry out the cargo." She lived near Santa Catalina, close to the Plaza de Armas. From 1957 on, when there were two mayordomías to celebrate the Virgin of the Nativity, the Corpus Christi cargo represented downtown Cuzco dwellers, a shift that had clear identity-related implications.

Following a social map charged with historical and cultural meanings, living in the center of the city generally required and implied a higher status than living in Almudena. Yet this did not necessarily reflect a higher level of income. Señorita Rosa Salazar, for example, did not belong to the circle of decent cuzqueños, and had a meager income compared to many market women, but her social status was higher than that of the mestizas. In contrast to the September 8 celebration, the social space of the Corpus Christi mayordomía is now filled by cuzqueño commoners and immigrants who distance themselves from the indigenous mestizo lore and any of its menial signifiers. Their identity as "professionals" currently distinguishes the group that sponsors the Corpus Christi Nativity mayordomía, and sets them apart from all those who have not been "improved" by "enough" education. Although their jobs are not marketplace-related — and thus not polluted by dealings with the underclass, as explained in chapter 4 — their meager economies place these mayordomos close to working-class urban cuzqueños. Given their social proximity to those they despise, to accumulate symbolic capital through mayordomías they see it as necessary to make obvious their cultural/racial difference vis-à-vis the September 8 mayordomas.

In a successive discriminatory chain, while mestizas prevent recent rural migrants (whom they perceive as Indians) to celebrate the central September 8 Cargo, the Corpus Christi mayordomos elevate their status by discriminating against cuzqueño mestizas, labeling them "cholas" and so closer to Indian than they are themselves. Sponsors of this mayordomía use their lowland origins to deny any link to cultural features (usually clothing, familiarity with Quechua, and workplace) that they identify as highland and for that reason indigenous. One of the Corpus mayordomas told me, for example, that as a child she did not know how to speak Quechua but learned it as an adult. "That's why I don't speak it well," she said, adding that among her family members, "no one has ever worn a *pollera,* nor has [anyone] sold in the market." This woman makes her living running a small coffee shop, wears a knee-length skirt, has permed hair, and is proud of her son who "can speak English and is a movie actor." She certainly does not see herself fitting into the marketplace mestiza category. Yet based on where she lives, her low income, and even her place of origin, she could belong to the same social group as the mestizas. To avoid being in any way seen as mestiza, this woman highlights her nonindigenous background. In so doing she brings to the fore the cultural differences between her and cholos and uses these differences to mark her superiority, unconcerned that her income is second-rate compared to that of some cholos she scorns.

The woman is not an exception among the Corpus Christi mayordomos. One of them, a grocery merchant, earnestly complained that before they gave him the cargo, "[he] had never been in the festival for fear of being stuck with mestizas." When his *compadre* Lucio — "who is the proprietor of an electric appliance shop" — invited him, he realized that "people of good category also went to the festival." A schoolteacher, who was also a Corpus mayordoma, admitted that she felt superior to the market mestizas because "she has studied at the university and those women just barely have a primary [school education]." Being "mestizo but not cholo" means having shed a putative indigenous background and having in its place nonindigenous manners usually acquired by birth and always enhanced by some kind of post–high school education. "Mestizo," as this group uses it, refers to modern notions of racial mixture between indigenous and Spanish creoles and the alleged biocultural evolution to a superior type. "Cholo" refers to indigenous market women and their escorts, those "unrefined mestizos, these urban Indians, who speak as much Quechua as Spanish, and sometimes more Quechua," as Gloria (the cafeteria owner) sharply pointed out while making clear her own ignorance of Quechua.

Physical separation in public stages is an important component of the social distance that this group of cuzqueños implement vis-à-vis those they insultingly call "cholas mestizas." Not coincidentally, Corpus Christi mayordomas adamantly avoid including market women in their celebration. Gloria proudly told me, "Among my jurkados I have not had even one meat seller, nor any other kind of market chola. Instead, I've only had proprietors of grocery stores, so that they'd give me provisions, and many proprietors of souvenir stores." This group of devotees commonly avoids the market vendors, preferring to invite "*gente con mejor preparación*," literally "people with a better preparation," implying a better education or higher-ranking occupation. In general they are considered better people as Juan, the 1987 mayordomo and owner of a small store, described it to me: "About ten years or so ago [the cargo] began to circulate among better people. . . . Before, it was the women from the market and picanterías who celebrated it. Unfortunately this year [1991], once again it has fallen in the hands of *gente inculta* [uncultivated people], who behave like *recién llegados* [the recently arrived]."

Juan's grievance stemmed from the splitting of the cargo in 1990. In 1989 the carguyoq could not find a mayordomo for the following year's celebration. "There was no one to turn the demanda over to," he remembered. Faced with the possibility that the Corpus Christi mayordomía might disappear because of a lack of sponsor, the mayordomos from previous years decided to split the cargo into six mayordomías, one for each of the main days of the celebration. The expenses would thus be divided among six families, since each one would have to subsidize only a single day of festivities.[18] Several mestizo-but-not-cholo mayordomos considered this was a mistake, as it opened the mayordomía doors to "other kinds of people," those they consider cholos who, as owners of small gas stations or restaurants, did have the money and the clientele to sponsor the cargo. In 1992 the central Corpus Christi mayordomos, *los mayordomos centrales,* were a very young couple, Vicky and Lucho, who were neither professionals nor merchants. As in the case of Alejandrina, who was humiliated by the mestiza organizers of the September 8 cargo, Vicky and Lucho were victims of the verbal discriminatory violence displayed by the "mestizo but not cholo" mayordomos who were distressed by the potential bad reputation that the mayordomía could acquire. They insulted them with references to their alleged "hunger," an implicit allusion to the deficient respect, a marker of their indigenous background. On recalling the way the mestizo-but-not-cholo mayordomos insulted them, Lucho narrated, "The previous mayordomos have criticized us a lot, even though we gave them food and [invited] them to drink. . . . The morning of the *subida* [the ascent of the Virgin to the cathedral] they offended us verbally. They insulted us [calling us] 'hungry cholos,' and they told us that we were taking all of our cholo relatives to eat like animals. . . . They told us that we had to go, my wife and I, no one else, since we didn't know how to dress or drink like people do [*como la gente*]."

Vicky and Lucho received the mayordomía from Vicky's parents. They thought they were not "prepared" to be mayordomos since she did not have a steady income and he earned very little as a blue-collar employee of the municipality of Cuzco. With the help of Vicky's parents, they obtained the necessary money and products to "pass the cargo." Vicky's father owns a small gas station and her mother has a vegetable stand in a small marketplace. Although they were thus able to meet the mayordomía food and drink standards, they could not fulfill the ritual protocol. Lucho explained, "What happened is that no one oriented us because my mother-in-law didn't know anything. She didn't know anything because no one taught her either, and she has only carried out cargos here in Chocco. She's never done [it] in the Plaza de Armas. . . . That is why we just did it the Chocco way, I tried to improve it a little, but the former mayordomos criticized us anyway."

Chocco is a shantytown neighborhood located in the hills of Almudena. Most of the dwellers are migrants from the countryside, some of them peasants in highland communities, others small farmers or merchants in rural towns. Among them are some relatively prosperous families, such as Vicky's parents, who, besides the businesses mentioned above, own a large brick house. This couple's economic situation had allowed them to carry out cargos in Chocco, and in 1991 they were ready to accept the Corpus Christi mayordomía. The owner of a small neighborhood restaurant offered it to them. I did not attend Vicky's parents' mayordomía celebration and

1992 Corpus Christi mayordomos, Vicky Mojonero (with sunglasses) and her partner Lucho Chihuantito (to her left) receiving their ritual guests — their *jurkados* — in the atrium of the Almudena church. The woman with the flowers had contributed the fireworks, which she holds with her other hand. Photograph by author.

cannot narrate the conflicts that colored that occasion. In 1992, however this family's highland origins and the fact that they live in a shantytown identified with former rural inhabitants stigmatized Vicky and Lucho's mayordomía. Lucho's mother and aunt wearing polleras during the ceremony marked the young mayordomo couple and their relatives as cholos. Vicky and Lucho were said to be "hungry," not to imply they were literally poor but to indicate their lack of urban table manners and deficient knowledge of the ritual protocol. Vicky and Lucho certainly felt insulted and insecure as a result of these comments, but they were also pleased and even proud about their performance in their ritual. "What could we do? We did our best, but we were not prepared," Lucho told me, surrendering to the criticisms. However, he also challenged them by adding, "But it was our right to do it the way we did it, and to hell with them and their complaints [*que se vayan al diablo con sus quejas*]. If we are too low for them, they should be free not to come to our banquet. We did not need them, and everybody else liked it. There was more than enough food and drink." Accepting *and* challenging their relative inferiority is common among working-class cuzqueños, who thus reproduce their social position at one level and transform it at another one, while rendering hegemonic the images of regional hierarchies.

Being witness to this incident led me to ask if mestizo-but-not-cholo mayordomos identified the retinues of the many images of Corpus Christi with prevailing urban social hierarchies. I was not surprised by the response I received from a mayordomo member of the mestizo-but-not-cholo group: "We and La Linda — the Virgin that represents the cathedral in the procession — have the best people. Market women and chicheras accompany the Virgen de Belén, *cargadores* [i.e., marketplace porters] who don't even have houses accompany San Pedro. This year the mayordomo of the Virgen de los Remedios was a decent gentleman. They are improving their mayordomía. We were also improving ours until this year. . . . Now we have to see what we'll do to improve it again."

In this response "to improve" does not mean to increase the number of guests at the celebration or the quantity of food or drink or to introduce new rituals. Neither does it mean looking for mayordomos who enjoy a better economic situation. "To improve" means to keep the mayordomías from circulating among people whose indigenous origins are obvious as in Vicky and Lucho's case. Although mayordomías have traditionally been sponsored only "by individuals of the cholo and indigenous strata," as the cuzqueño historian José Tamayo Herrera reported, recently individuals reputed as members of decent families, moved by cuzqueñismo, have taken over such mayordomías as that of Cruz Velakuy, which venerates the Holy Cross. According to Tamayo Herrera, participation in it is reserved to "distinguished professionals, university professors, and members of the elites" (1992:859), thus confirming the inclusive and differentiating dynamics of mayordomías.

Conclusions

By implementing the discriminatory discourses that scorn Indianness and that are nested in cuzqueñista "cultural intimacy" (cf. Herzfeld,

1997), mayordomías function as one of the inner mechanisms of hegemonic cuzqueño racism. In a superb irony, the continuity of Corpus Christi, the emblematic representation of urban elite moral standards, and of cuzqueñismo, rests on market women, the incarnation of immorality (according to gente decente). By means of the mayordomías, mestizas and other working-class cuzqueños respond to this dominant belief and dignify their image by displaying their piety and economic well-being in their barrios and in the main streets of Cuzco. Moreover, contradicting the elite intellectuals' opinions, common cuzqueños consider that rather than being a waste of time or money mayordomías have tangible benefits in building business networks and in improving one's "credit rating" in the informal economy. But, shifting gears, these institutions do not only represent the victorious cuzqueño working-classes' response to elite beliefs. Mayordomías have a Janus-faced character: through the ritual invitation called *jurka* they include differentiated social sectors in the celebration while at the same time, they exclude certain jurkados from election as mayordomos. This is so because the symbolic capital achieved through mayordomías has as one of its preconditions the reproduction of dominant urban beliefs, which (drawing from the regional politics of place and the racialized geography of Cuzco) assert the inferiority of newcomers from the countryside and the highlands and the superiority of residents of the city and the lowlands. The former (considered relatively Indian), who are usually excluded from more prestigious mayordomías, seek to create their own ones and thus carve out an urban social space that allows them access to the respect they have been denied by superior members of the working class. In their own mayordomías, so-called newcomers (many of whom are already long-time residents of the hills that surround traditional Almudena) perform mestizo identity and eventually subordinate those they deem Indians. This dynamic, which recreates in the ritual sphere the multiple layers of relative Indianness and mestizoness that permeates indigenous Cuzqueños daily life, has undergirded the continuous creation of mayordomías.

The efficacy of the symbolic capital achieved through mayordomías is limited to the sphere of gente del pueblo. The gente decente consider these celebrations plebeian extravagances, and thus the expenses incurred in producing the abundance required in respectable mayordomías set commoners apart from the elite. Mayordomías, thus, also demonstrate that the ownership of economic capital is only one element in the definition of cuzqueño social identity and status. Features like place of origin and kind of education are just as important as signifiers of identities and are considered indicators of "wealth," which therefore transcends the economic sphere.

Residents of Almudena, most of whom straddle city and country, currently use in their mayordomías some elements that tourism and neoindianismo have revitalized as folklore. The most obvious ones are the typical Indian costume, the Quechua language, folk dances, typical food, and the image of mestizas as folk matriarchs. By using these cultural expressions, producers of mayordomías have created a space for the expression of a new urban indigenous culture proudly displayed by some members of the working classes, who consider themselves mestizos (because of their urban economic success and relatively highland original culture). This group includes so-called newcomers from the countryside, mestiza market women, and their plebeian businessmen acquaintances. What makes their mayordo-mías 'indigenous' is this group's conspicuous cultural political subor-dination to the elites, which derives from their identification with the kind of cuzqueño authenticity associated with the highlands, the alleged source of Andean culture. The mestizo-but-not-cholo mayor-domos, who mark their differences from market women by denying a background they deem indigenous, signal the always blurred and shifting line between indigenous and nonindigenous culture. These evidently interpenetrate each other, while creating and maintaining differences.

6

Respeto and Authenticity

Grassroots Intellectuals and De-Indianized

Indigenous Culture

In the 1950s the Velasco Quintanilla brothers engaged in the revitalization of the celebration of their patron saint, the Virgen de la
Natividad. "The fiesta was fading until we revived it, and boosting
the dances was very important," recalled Don Manuel Velasco, the
main creator of the mayordomía of the Virgen de la Natividad in its
present format. He also remembered: "At the time of our cargo the
dances attracted a lot of people, most of whom had just settled in
Almudena." Currently, during the celebration of the mayordomías
of the Virgen de la Natividad, dancing troupes (*comparsas*) assemble
in the atrium of Almudena's church escorted by their own mayordomos, who are in charge of providing food and drink to the dance
group. These particular mayordomías became a tourist attraction
shortly after the mid-century, and ever since travel agents and intellectuals, including the local parish priest, have stimulated the participation of the dancing troupes that accompany them. "Folkloric
dances" are an important component of regional popular culture
and a tourist attraction as signifiers of cuzqueñista authenticity.
Since dances came to the fore, motivated first by neoindianismo and
later by tourism, elite intellectuals and commoners have handled the
definition of "authenticity" and its potential association with Indianness in divergent ways.

In the 1930s, cultural authorities chose dances as the conduit connecting the artistic "essences" of official intellectuals and indigenous
cuzqueños. As tourism increased (starting in the 1950s and peaking
in the early seventies), elite intellectuals themselves produced and

danced indigenous choreographies. During the four decades 1930s–
1970s the dances were the most conspicuous "texts" from which
elite and grassroots intellectuals learned about each other's conception of regional social identities.[1] I conceive of this interaction as an
implicit dialogue that, while being laden with power imbalances, has
allowed for relatively autonomous interpretation and reformulation
of each other's texts and narratives.

Currently the grassroots troupes dance in *comparsas* while *conjuntos folklóricos* (folklore groups) are the dance groups led by official intellectuals belonging to differentiated economic sectors. One
of the usual differences between the associations is the type of spaces
where they perform. Generally folklore groups perform on theater-
like stages and make a clear distinction between themselves and their
audience, which may include foreigners as well as people from Lima.
Comparsas, on the other hand, perform in rituals such as patron
saint celebrations that are attended by common cuzqueños (and
some anthropologists); their dancers draw no distinction between
audience and performers, mingling with nondancer participants of
the celebration. In this sense, the contrast between comparsa and
folklore group performances demonstrate one of Victor Turner's
points about the differences between ritual and theater: "Ritual unlike theater does not distinguish between audience and performers"
(1982:112).

In a similar vein, comparsas and folklore groups have different
performing strategies. While the groups *imitate* the characters they
represent, comparsas *become* the characters they impersonate during the rituals. Another important difference is how the dancers
identify themselves in cuzqueño racial or cultural taxonomies. Members of folklore groups usually identify themselves as mestizos by
race, claim to be nonindigenous by culture, and conceive of folklore as the representation of racial/cultural indigenous individuals.
Dancers of comparsas also self-identify as mestizos. But "mestizo"
for them alludes to a social condition, which does not preclude the
practice of indigenous tradition, which they identify as *nuestra costumbre auténtica* (our authentic custom). The phrase refers to a nationwide subordinate culture that includes Indians, but is not exclusively Indian. Thus, while they do not consider themselves Indians,

this social condition intersects with the (indigenous) mestizo identity they claim for themselves, because both are included within the scope of their authentic custom, the rural-urban indigenous tradition that they also call *neta*. This is not the case of dancers in folklore groups, whose belief that they stage "authentic dances" is detached from their self-identity as (nonindigenous) mestizos. As a result of these differences, although the performances of folklore groups and comparsas seem alike, their dances may represent disputes about meanings of identity labels. In this chapter I identify two central disagreements between elite and grassroots dance interpreters. The first is the representation of indigenous sexuality, and the second is their divergent definition of authenticity.

Like the Inti Raymi discussed in chapter 3, dances are invented traditions; yet its creators consider them *costumbre*. This conflation of invention and custom questions Eric Hobsbawm's 1983 claim that invented traditions "must clearly be distinguished from 'custom' which dominates so-called traditional societies" (Hobsbawm and Ranger, 1983:2). This perspective, some of which Terence Ranger (1993) has revisited, denies individual authorship of "custom," and assumes that "genuine traditions" result from the inert works of (also inert, or at least unaware) producers of culture, who thus remain anonymous, invisible in the collectivity they inadvertently act for. An analysis of comparsas reveals, in fact, an alternative to Hobsbawm's definition. Comparsa leaders, called *caporales,* relentlessly invent traditions, and are indeed extremely vigilant of every detail of their creations, both because they are intentionally autoethnographic texts, and because of their desire as authors to claim the originality of their choreography. Like inventors of traditions they also root their creations in a "remote past." Marking a sharp contrast with dominant inventors of nationalist traditions, caporales do not perceive the past where they root their creations as an abstract source for a potential homogeneous national identity. Instead, the comparsa leaders that I interviewed rest their traditions in a past that they specifically connect with their own present, thus making it exclusively meaningful to them, and they use it to assist their indigenous authenticity, their *neto* identity.

Taking a Gramscian point of view, and obviously inspired by the activism of indigenous intellectuals in Guatemala, Colombia, Ecuador, Bolivia, and those academics who have written about them (NACLA, 1996; Warren, 1992, 1996; Ramón Valarezo, 1992; Rappaport, 1994), I take the producers of de-Indianized indigenous traditions to be grassroots intellectuals. Steven Feierman (1990) has been particularly inspiring about how to broaden the traditional notion of intellectuals to include producers of subjugated knowledges (cf. Foucault, 1980:82). Members of comparsas do not earn their living as intellectuals (a condition that official intellectuals in contemporary Cuzco and in Peru do not meet either). However, like official intellectuals, the comparsa dancers I met have "a conscious line of moral conduct and therefore contribute to sustain or modify a particular conception of the world" (Gramsci, 1987:9). As intellectuals, comparsa leaders (*caporales*) are permanent persuaders, directives, and agents who implement their particular point of view by means of their dances. Through dance (which is, in the Gramscian sense, a socially recognized organizational, educative, and expressive activity) caporales guide their dancers into joining the regional hegemonic feeling of cuzqueñismo. Through their performances, they connect their social sphere — that of common cuzqueños — with the dominant sphere and communicate in both directions the social meanings produced in each. In their capacity as intellectuals they have participated, for many years now, in an implicit dialogue with official intellectuals about regional identities and have created a regional heteroglossic lexicon (embedded in alternative conceptual frames) to identify cuzqueños of different paths of life.

Two caveats are in order to complete this line of thought. The first is that I do not define "grassroots intellectuals" with reference to an essential position in cuzqueño social structure or as members of a reified "Andean culture." Rather, I identify as grassroots intellectuals those people who have actively sought to dignify what they call "nuestra costumbre neta," which I am inclined to call indigenous traditions, for lack of a better term. In honoring their customs they have created a notion of authenticity and regional social identities that both participate in and depart from the dominant racial/cultural taxonomies. To dignify their identity and *costumbre,* or tradition, comparsa members define a *neto* (real, opposed to "spurious") cuzqueño culture, which—based on a "logic of coupling" (Hall, 1995:472; Strathern, 1995) rather than on binarisms—presents its rural origins *and* uses urban manners. From this perspective comparsa dancers and others like them are indigenous mestizos who live in the city but draw inspiration from their rural knowledge to produce, the neto authentic cuzqueño culture. They are not Indians because, like the mestiza market women and mayordomas, they dance with respeto, they have not lost their human dignity. Although their definition of authenticity is multivocal (in the sense that there are many ways in which comparsas prove their *neto* identity) most comparsas evoke a nonurban place of origin to legitimate their representations.[2]

The second caveat is that, as individuals, comparsa members usually participate in both indigenous and nonindigenous traditions, albeit with different emotional intensities, and maintaining the distinction between both. Some of them may even be both official and grassroots intellectuals and exercise these identities in different facets of their lives. Some university students, for example, participate in the sphere of official intellectuals; as members of comparsas, the same people are indigenous intellectuals. Indigenous mestizo cuzqueños inhabit a cultural space where the indigenous and nonindigenous interpenetrate each other rather than a borderland (Anzaldúa, 1987; García Canclini, 1995). The space they inhabit is not interstitial or marginal; instead, it is coterminous with Cuzco as a geographical region and with its hegemonic feeling, cuzqueñismo. Because they inhabit a space where the indigenous and nonindigenous interpenetrate, they are hybrids; but not in the static sense implied by the modern definition of that term, which opposes the rural indigenous individual to the urban mestizo and assumes an evolutionary terminal process from the former (conceived as an inferior stage of race/culture) to the latter (deemed a superior stage of race/culture). Rather, indigenous mestizos are endlessly processing their hybridity, constantly de-Indianizing and dignifying their practices by using what they consider the best and most *neto* from both rural and urban traditions. The indigenous tradition they produce is not "pure" as modern indigenista intellectuals imagined it, but it is "neto," authentic by indigenous intellectuals' definition and fiat.

Representing the Festive Indian Other
Neoindianistas Meet Tourism

As indicated in chapter 1, indigenistas defined Indians as a rural race/culture. Artists — writers and painters — portrayed them as melancholic, introverted peasants, possessing a gregarious, potentially irritable collective temperament. Years later the neoindianistas, with their focus on folklore, dismissed the earlier image and instead portrayed a "festive Indian." As tourism gained impetus, this image became a magnet for attracting foreign visitors. It was thought that Cuzco could compete as an archaeological site with cities already recognized as international tourist centers. But the so-called Rome of America harbored an additional attraction in its contemporary indigenous population. Granted, Indians were coarse, illiterate peasants, but they were also considered to be *instinctive* musicians, choreographers, and above all, dancers.

The festive Indian became symbolic of the revitalization of regional culture. "Many believe they are attending the death throes of the Indian, but the dances serve to demonstrate that the Indian is not dead," wrote an influential neoindianista authority in 1940.[3] But indigenous art, the product of coarse Indians, needed the supervision of specialists before being made public, as the following quote indicates: "Indians have to be adapted to the stage; they can't be presented as they themselves do in town plazas. . . . [They have to be presented] as artists, not as drunken Indians during days of debauchery. . . . It's urgent, although we don't want to stylize, that [the dances] are presented with a certain purity, with a little bit of smoothness. . . . The motif has to be interpreted."[4]

To prevent non-Cuzqueños from learning about the coarseness of folklore and therefore to keep this fact as a cultural intimacy (Herzfeld, 1997) while also uplifting indigenous art, Indian artists were trained in *conjuntos musicales*. These were musical ensembles led by neoindianista directors who were in charge of molding indigenous musical instincts and of crafting artists out of their Indian pupils. Among these, probably the most famous one featuring "*indios netos*" on stage was the "Conjunto Acomayo." They were considered an authentic orchestra, which met the requirements of good music.[5] Cuzqueño cultural critics considered that the secret to the success of this ensemble was its leader, an educated musician, and neoindianista intellectual. His name was Policarpo Caballero, born in a rural town to a small local landowner, yet a musician trained in Argentina. He "adapted" his Indian partners to the artistic scene, and his presence and knowledge guaranteed the good quality of the music. In the opinion of a cuzqueño music expert, Caballero's creations were "very technical, very Andean, very indigenous" (Ojeda Vizcarra, 1990:84). Musical groups of this type mushroomed during the initial years of neoindianismo.

By "uplifting" indigenous music and dances and controlling Indian performers during the period between the 1930s and 1940s, Cuzco official intellectuals forged folklore as a cultural enterprise strongly stimulated by and linked to tourism. In the 1940s the Cuzco branch of the National Tourism Corporation inaugurated a quasi-academic Department of Folklore where university professors organized a *fichero folklórico* (folklore index), essentially a catalogue of stories and legends, foods, festivals, music and dance from Cuzco's various provinces (Vidal de Milla, 1985:23). In a related venture, the corporation created its own Conjunto Folklórico, whose aim was "the advancement of Peruvian art [and] especially its choreographic, musical, and dramatic manifestations."[6]

If directors of musical ensembles controlled Indians' performance on stage, intellectuals used the Conjunto Folklórico of the National Tourism Corporation to produce folklore directly while refining and preserving its artistic potential. The first stage in the production of folklore was known as *captación* (capture), a term that alluded to the direct field collection of material culture to reproduce it. During this phase, which aimed to retrieve indigenous essence from the locations where it persisted, folklorists armed with pencil and paper traveled to the artistic "natural settings" — relatively distant villages — where they observed dances and music as they were performed by members of local comparsas.[7] The traveling aspect of this task was in fact not necessary, since dances were performed in the city itself. However, it was an academic requirement, conveying the chronological and geographic distance necessary in any acceptable definition of folklore (Fabian, 1983; Thompson, 1991; Cirese, 1982).

The second stage in the production of folklore was linked to the preservation of regional cultural intimacies, that is, the Cuzqueñista task of concealing the rusticity of regional indigenous art. It was described as *"depurar las danzas"* (to purify the dances), a *"depurar"* being the same verb that indigenistas used to describe their duty in regards to Quechua in the 1920s. The *depuración* (purification) of indigenous style implied its adaptation to the supposedly high cultural standards of urban audiences. The most frequent "impurities" were "discordant" musical rhythms, some "Western" instruments (the accordion was scorned, the violin and guitar admired); "improper attire" made of industrial fabric or strident colors; and "lack of choreography." During the purification stage a competent intellectual authority — called the choreographic director in most folklore groups — supervised the process in order to make sure that "the essence and intention of the dance were not altered."[8] Generally depuración required composing a symmetric choreography, either softening or exaggerating the movements of the dance while "preserving" references to what the nonindigenous folklorists defined as the main musical melody and argument of the dance. The person charged with this feat, the group's choreographer, was identified in urban intellectual circles as a kind of "author" and "owner" of the dance and received the title of *maestro*. This was indeed a reverential term, judging from the following remarks by Humberto Vidal Unda, a leader neoindianista folklorist: "The maestro Juan de Dios Aguirre has collected [*ha captado*] the *Chullchu Tusuy* dance from the folklore of Paruro, and has transformed it into a serious piece that has no need to envy those of other great authors."[9] Maestros could also arrange choreographies that were considered authentic; as reputed artists they even knew how to reproduce the indigenous essence. The title "maestro" became the vehicle to identify folklorists among gente decente, and thus distinguish them from the Indians and village mestizos who created and presented dances or music. The emphasis on folk dances, and the possibility of "authoring" them, opened up room for recognition of the work of a group of intermediate-level intellectuals who thrived producing *captaciones* and composing choreographies. Thus, also in this respect, indigenous dances were to neoindianistas what Quechua was to indigenistas: they were a source, the study and production of which could cast them as intellectuals.

The obvious ethnographic undertone of *captación* may have been inspired by the fieldwork practice that professors had promoted since the 1920s to complete the academic training of university students. In addition to distinguishing and distancing the folklore collectors from the Indians from whom it was collected (Fabian, 1983), the practice conferred on folklorist productions an academic recognition that culminated when the Cátedra de Folklore was established in 1943, thus endorsing maestro folklorists as traditional intellectuals. According to the historian of Cuzco, José Tamayo Herrera (1992:777), "Among the social sciences, folklore was the discipline that prevailed in the period between 1943 and 1957."

University professors, students of folklore, and self-taught musicians all gathered in the Conjunto Folklórico of the National Tourism Corporation and enacted dominant descriptions of Indians and mestizos in their public presentations. Indians were rural, instinctively ferocious, and capable of enduring hard conditions; mestizos were vulgar urbanites to be distinguished from gente decente. For example, a typical performance by the Conjunto Folklórico included the short sketch (*estampa*) "Impresiones de un Recluta" (Impressions of a Recruit), which presented a dumb Indian, recruited by the military and recently arrived in the city. Following the sketch was the dance "K'achampa," representing an agile and warrior Indian; a bucolic Indian appeared in "Tik'a Rantij" (Flower Buyer); and an Indian enduring inclement weather wandered onstage in the sketch "Pajonal" (barren land). Finally, a violent Indian appears as the central character in "Chearaje" (a ritual confrontation among indigenous communities) that came to be considered representative of the "violent High Provinces," the scene of the alleged 1920s Indian rebellions analyzed in chapter 2. Urban mestizos were not portrayed in dances, but usually through sketches depicting them as irreverent drunkards in their pagan-like celebration of mayordomías.[10]

Notwithstanding the disavowal of biological race, by essentializing what they perceived as symbols of indigenous tradition, midcentury cultural authorities racialized their images of folklore. Thus, for example, they decided that "authentic" dances had to have ritual character, teach a moral lesson, and depict agricultural or Inca scenes. In addition dancers were expected "to move like Indians" (stomping, jumping, quarreling) and to wear "actual indigenous garb." Also cherished as regional folklore from the neoindianista viewpoint were dances that did not meet any of the above requirements but were reminiscent of "classic antiquity." The Greek bacchantes, for example, were thought to show the connection between indigenous art and universal and timeless artistic canons.[11]

Folklore, along with Incaism, became a central piece of cuzqueñismo when tourism started to surge in the late 1950s. In January 1960 newspapers announced that more than 23,000 tourists had visited Cuzco in 1959; in a city with fewer than 150,000 inhabitants this was a high number. At this time intellectuals came together in a venture, that along with "sheltering indigenous art from distortion," supported the promotion of folklore for tourists. The celebration in 1961 of the fiftieth anniversary of the unearthing of Macchu Picchu by Hiram Bingham was the extraordinary occasion for implementing this venture. For this occasion the American Institute of Art, following its commitment to preserve the authenticity of the presentations (and linking "authenticity" to popular notions of racial proper places), suggested that indigenous folk dances should take place "in their natural environment and surroundings." In keeping with these ideas, they simultaneously suggested "tourist visits to the villages that surround Cuzco" where the dances took place. Additionally, and to extend this tour of "the authentic" to the city of Cuzco itself, the institute proposed that hotels and restaurants prepared "typical cuzqueños dishes and drinks" to be served to foreign visitors.[12]

The combination of economic thrust, cultural endeavor, and cuzqueñismo reached its highest manifestation with the formation of an artistic ensemble called Danzas del Tawantinsuyu. Directed by the entrepreneur Raúl Montesinos, the artistic advisors were Juan Bravo, an artist, and Ricardo Castro Pinto, a self-trained musician who had played the role of the Inca in the Inti Raymi performances several times since 1958. Supported by the ideology of cuzqueñismo, this trio brought about the emergence of tourist folklore as a new genre in which the value of dances derived from their visual attractiveness rather than from faithful reproduction.[13] For their masculine gaze, the participation of nonindigenous women wearing a vernacular version of mini-skirts (designed by Juan Bravo), twirling to show the upper legs, was necessary if the dances were to be considered attractive.[14] During their reign, Danzas del Tawantinsuyu linked the promotion of tourist folklore to what their directors imagined as "female beauty." Indian women, whom Danzas del Tawantinsuyu's leaders imagined as sexually insipid to male Western taste (given their flat chests and buttocks) were replaced on stage by "desirable" non-Indian women who showed their prominent buttocks and breasts as they danced to indigenous rhythms.

Included in the racialized and gendered exoticization of folklore was the presentation of the supposed exotic sexuality of Indians. As explained in earlier chapters, notions of Indians' sexual peculiarities were an important cornerstone in the culturalist definition of race that the first indigenista generation produced. One of its members, Luis Felipe Aguilar, a champion of Indians, wrote in the 1920s, "The Indian's eroticism includes brutal manifestations. To him pinching and kicking his beloved are equivalent to caresses; he makes the woman feel his infatuation by beating her without any cause" (1922:61). Such beliefs were persistent: in 1956 a student at the local university wrote a term paper in which he paraphrased Aguilar: "Kicking and pinching are included in the mute language of Indians' love" (Dueñas, 1956:16). Such images swiftly entered the representation of Indians presented for tourist audiences. In the 1960s, the program for the Danzas del Tawantinsuyu described the Combapata Carnival or "Pujllaitaki" as a performance in which "single cholos and cholas invade plazas and streets, dancing for eight days. Among their choreographies, the insistent punishment the cholas mete out to their suitors with their slingshots stands out. A bloody punishment that the cholo receives gladly and with manly aplomb: certainly a strange way of showing love."[15]

Mid-century folklorists colored the Andean image of the carnivalesque with references to Indians' sexual otherness. "Pujllaitaki" is a Quechua word with erotic connotations, as it relates dance to sexual play, and in their staging of it Danzas del Tawantinsuyu accentuated its potential eccentric aspects. Undoubtedly, the coupling of tourism and folklore made Indians visible in Cuzco, and modified their previous depictions as miserable victims. Instead, the Indian became a festive figure, decked out in rich, multicolored wool clothing. This figure, ubiquitous in photographs, movies, and tourist guides worldwide, was replete with exoticism: here were individuals with intensely instinctive sensual temperaments, which made them both natural artists and brutal sexual beings.

Grassroots choreographers have worked with elite productions since the first official Inti Raymi in 1944, when indigenous dance groups responded enthusiastically to official calls to participate and dance around the Inca stage. At the dawn of the tourist boom in 1959, as many as nineteen comparsas traveled from their rural pueblos to the city to participate in the Cuzco Week.[16] In letters to the organizers of Cuzco Day, indigenous literate leaders of comparsas remarked their dance's "antiquity," its Inca origins and originality, the elegance of the performers' apparel, and the high artistic quality of the dance. For example, in 1955 the caporal of a group from Acomayo described the dance he led as "a true Incaic representation [that] will be presented in Sacsayhuaman for the first time." José Victor Pitumarca, another dance leader, negotiated his group's participation by insisting: "They wear the best costumes in the region, which will be of much interest to the tourists."[17] As these statements show, in their dialogue indigenous leaders of comparsas knew and used dominant folklorist terms. However, the descriptions belie the idea that their productions were unrefined and in need of improvement.

In 1991, the urban dancers I followed told me that they represented "typical cuzqueño characters," and this meant Indians, mestizos, or gente decente. However, in sharp contrast with the elite producers of folklore, these grassroots artists do not only "reflect" either indigenous culture or the social identities of the region. Rather, they also make them through their performances (Michaels, 1992:683). And in doing so they de-Indianize their culture and distance themselves from Indians. While removing themselves from Indianness, the dancers also style themselves as foremost producers of "neto" and *legítima* (legitimate) regional culture. To illustrate this process, I analyze some aspects of one of the comparsas I followed, the comparsa Capac Qolla de Haukaypata del Cuzco.[18] Their dance depicts the journey of muleteers from the high region of Collao to

temperate valleys with the specific purpose of bartering their produce (wool, weavings, and meat) for the valley products that they do
not have, such as maize and bread.[19]

Representing the Inclusive Other
The Capac Qolla of Haukaypata

Usually *Capac Qolla* comparsas are composed of a team of ten or
twelve male dancers impersonating the *qollas,* or itinerant merchants from the highlands (one of them is the "chief of the qollas"), a
female dancer denominated the *imilla,* and a *chanasko,* or child.[20]
The distinctive feature of Capac Qollas is that they own llamas, the
animal that accompanies them during the trip, which marks them as
herders and contrasts them to agriculturalists. Some comparsas even
use live llamas in their presentations. In addition to these main characters, the Capac Qolla troupes, like most Cuzco comparsas, feature
pablitos, pauluchas or *ukukus*. These characters are indispensable to
the comparsa. They are in charge of serving the performers, dancers,
and guests during the lulls in the dance; they also maintain order and
at the same time make the audience laugh with jokes and standard
numbers that they perform in almost every dance.[21]

    According to an anthropologist from Paucartambo, the Capac
Qolla dance already existed in that province at the end of the nineteenth century, when it was performed by a group of men from the
Paucartambo elite (Villasante, 1975:79). Zoila Mendoza's recent
study of this same dance, in the version of the comparsa from the
town of San Jerónimo, suggests that the Capac Qolla dance evolved
from an earlier dance called the *Colla,* an allusion to the trading trips
(*trajines,* see Glave, 1989) of the altiplano llama herders. The contemporary version is a stylization produced by the Paucartambinos, who (perhaps intending to cleanse the dance from derogatory
connotations) added the adjective "*capac,*" Quechua for "rich" or
"chief" (Mendoza-Walker, 1993:196). Despite this transformation
(from simple *llameros* to prosperous muleteers), the dance still represents the *habitantes de las alturas* (inhabitants of the high-altitude
zones). Given the geographic relational quality of indigenous identi-

ties, regardless of their wealth, these dancers impersonate individuals who can be considered Indians.

The Cuzco tourist boom and its aftermath are closely related to this dance. In July, Paucartambinos celebrate the Fiesta de la Virgen del Carmen, the feast day of their patron saint, an important event of the tourist season that opens in June with Corpus Christi and Inti Raymi. Inspired by the contest-like participation of comparsas in the Fiesta de la Virgen del Carmen, tourist entrepreneurs organized *concursos folklóricos* (folklore contests) and nominated Paucartambo the folkloric capital of Cuzco. The Capac Qolla comparsas became popular in this context, and by the seventies the dance was widely known in the region.[22] Several members of the Capac Qolla de Haukaypata are street vendors of weavings and other crafts, a trade which also owes much to tourism and the presence of foreign visitors.

The version that this comparsa dances is the interpretation of Alejandro Condori, who directs the group as its caporal.[23] A son of peasants, he was born in the rural village of Llactapampa, in the province of Acomayo. I met him in 1991, when he was thirty-seven years old. He first danced Capac Qolla in his village at the age of ten, on the occasion of his aunt's mayordomía. At his mother's prompting, Alejandro danced as a *chanasko* — under the orders of a caporal who "had danced in Paucartambo."[24] Alejandro recalls that this man "named him caporal" and tells the members of his comparsa the following anecdote about his initiation as chief of the qollas: "When we stopped dancing that caporal told me 'You will always remember me. I'm going to make you caporal.' And giving me his hat [*montera*], his whip, and his llama he named me [*me ha nombrado*] caporal. I first danced as caporal the day of *cacharpari* [the last day]."[25]

For the comparsa members, Alejandro's initiation has mythical connotations, as it makes him a legitimate caporal and this gives the group its uniqueness by ensuring the ritual nature of their dance. It also makes them an authentic comparsa neta, different from many other cuzqueño groups. They "just copy the lyrics and steps, *without [ritually] learning* them," says Don Alejandro about those dancing groups. To guarantee that the Capac Qollas de Haukaypata learn the same "old" (*antiguos,* with a connotation of timelessness) songs and dance steps that the old caporal taught Don Alejo (as members of the comparsa refer to him), he tells a story about how at the time of his initiation, he "jotted down in a notebook all the lyrics and the numbers to remember and save them exactly as I had learned them *tal y como las sabía mi caporal* [exactly as my caporal knew them]." In certifying the authenticity of the dance through his references to a written document, Alejandro questions academic interpretations that underscore the role of orality in perpetuating local traditions (Thompson, 1991; Anderson, 1983). Such interpretations fail to consider the role of literacy in shaping identities, particularly the capacity of literacy to distribute power and authority among individuals in groups like comparsas, where traditions *may also* be transmitted orally. In this case, his being literate allowed Alejandro (who considers himself neto and has rural origins) to legitimately avoid the label "Indian." His mythical caporal appointment also certified him as a ritual dance specialist. Both characteristics — being not Indian but still an authentic practitioner and producer of neto dances — empower Alejandro and entitle him to exercise authority as caporal.

Authenticity, as implied by Alejandro and the comparsa members, connotes what I call "inclusive otherness," namely, setting some distance between oneself and Indians while reproducing indigenous culture or what Alejandro calls "our cultura *neta*." First, in Alejandro's version the ritual dance is authentic (*neta* or *legítima*) because in it the actors identify with the qollas. The comparsa has chosen the Capac Qolla dance because, in addition to their own highland rural origins, they define themselves as *ambulantes,* that is, street vendors, who seven days a week walk through the portales of Cuzco's Plaza de Armas selling tourists sweaters, knit in rustic workshops. From their perspective they are comparable to the itinerant highland merchants, the qollas. In keeping with that role, they go as a dancing troupe to the Sanctuary of our Lord of Coyllur Rit'i, which is the most famous pilgrimage in the southern Andes. Dancers of the Capac Qolla de Haukaypata identify their ritual journey to the sanctuary with their daily peddling their merchandise up and down the streets of the city of Cuzco. On explaining this aspect of their authenticity Alejandro said to me, "All that we represent is the truth. We go to the sanctuary once a year. We don't dance for people. We don't care if people look at us. For us there's no parade, there's no pageant. We represent the

The Capac Qolla comparsa performs a ritual dance before departing from Almudena to Coyllur Rit'i.
(Below) Fernando, a Capac Qolla dancer, university student, and librarian who introduced me to Don Alejo Condori, and guided me through my understanding of what it meant to be a *neto*, an indigenous mestizo like him. Both photographs by the author.

qollas, because they are like us, merchants, spinners. They're always walking and selling just like us. We are walkers, street merchants. We are comparable. They are walkers and merchants too."

As noted earlier, a wave of unionization hit the political panorama in Cuzco in the fifties. From this dance group I learned that unionization transcended traditional politics and even influenced rituals. For ritual aspects the Capac Qolla de Huakaypata consider themselves a *comparsa legitima* also because their group functions as an urban union and guild. As an urban merchants' guild, the Capac Qollas needed the sponsorship of a patron saint housed in a *parroquia* (parish) of the city of Cuzco, which could represent them.[26] Thus when in 1988 Don Alejandro heard rumors that the Nativity Virgin of the parish of Almudena was the "wool merchants' patron" (*patrona de los comerciantes de lanas*) he asked the parish priest to also sponsor the Capac Qolla de Haukaypata.[27] Following worker unions procedures Alejandro called an assembly of his dancers and told them, "They say the devotees of the Mamita Natividad are like us, they are merchants and work in weaving. Since as qollas we're all independent merchants and wool dealers, we should choose her as our patron." Similarly, mirroring the structure of Cuzco worker unions, the Asociación Capac Qolla de Haukaypata has a book of minutes (*libro de actas*) and a Board of Directors (*junta directiva*), and uses democratic balloting to solve conflicts or make decisions. Alejandro recalls all these details: "I invited all the participants to a meeting at my house. There we elected our board of directors [*hemos elegido nuestra junta directiva*] and became a legitimate comparsa with the name Asociación Capac Qolla de Haukaypata." But what above all gives this comparsa legitimacy is their pilgrimage to the sanctuary of Coyllur Rit'i, which ends with their participation in the urban Corpus Christi procession.

These two events are coordinated moveable feasts, which take place on a lunar calendar. They take place annually on different dates in the months of May and June and symbolize indigenous and Christian rituals respectively. Even the contrasting geographic locations where they are held are emblematic of racialized conceptions of geography and culture. The Coyllur Rit'i pilgrimage takes place in the region of Apu Ausangate (a snow-covered peak and an Andean protective deity); the celebration of Corpus Christi is in the Plaza de Armas in Cuzco. The participation of the Capac Qolla de Hau-kaypata in both rituals is an eloquent illustration of their logic of coupling rural and urban to both achieve authenticity and de-Indianize their performance. On their way back from Coyllur Rit'i, the Haukaypata Capac Qollas join up with the Corpus Christi pro-cession in the main streets of the city. In this encounter the Capac Qollas confirm their profound rurality and ability to perform and excel in the high, snow-covered peaks by openly displaying the big blocks of ice that they have hauled from the preeminent snow-covered Ausangate, the Apu, which symbolizes regional indigenous religiosity. Simultaneously, their name Haukaypata — the Quechua name of the Plaza de Armas — conveys that members of this com-parsa ascend to the peaks as representatives of this plaza, the urban heart of the Cuzco region. The presiding cathedral is the required final destination of the ritually hoarded ice; connecting it with Apu Ausangate is a main purpose of their pilgrimage.

When the Haukaypata dancers were returning from Ausangate during the 1992 Corpus Christi celebration, they were distressed by the news that the ecclesiastical authorities had banned the presence of comparsas in the Plaza de Armas. The implementation of the ban would have impeded the finale of their ritual. "*Por gusto hemos viajado* [we've traveled in vain]," they anxiously commented as they realized that their pilgrimage to Coyllur Rit'i would not be valid if they could not take their ice to the Plaza de Armas cathedral. To complete their ritual, Alejandro and the others managed to cir-cumvent the archbishop's prohibition. Removing their dancing cos-tumes, and replacing them with clean, freshly ironed shirts and trou-sers, they paraded in the Plaza de Armas with their ice block, thus carrying their ritual to an end.

Shattering modern binary oppositions between city and coun-tryside, the Haukaypata comparsa managed once again to juxtapose Corpus Christi and Coyllur Rit'i, and the Plaza de Armas with Aus-angate, as well as the urbanity and rurality that interpenetrate their identities.[28] Wagner (1991) and Abraham (1993) would characterize these identities as "fractal," which in this case, cancel the binary relation between the rural and the urban, while maintaining the dis-

Don Alejandro Condori, dressing as a Capac Qolla, on our return from Coyllur Rit'i. We are in front of the cathedral, waiting to complete the pilgrimage by depositing the ice hoarded from the Ausangate inside the temple.

(Below) Cornelio, one of the pablitos of the Capac Qolla comparsa, proudly posing with the ice he hoarded from the Ausangate. Both photographs by the author.

tinction between both. This interpenetration of urbanness and rurality is visible also in Alejandro's apparently contradictory efforts to de-Indianize those elements of their performance he considers "neto" — indigenous in my translation — in order to ensure the authenticity of his comparsa (*para que la comparsa sea legítima*). Although it may seem incongruous, it is not: in de-Indianizing the dance Alejandro produces a discourse that enables him to display what he considers authentic but respectful indigenous culture, *lo neto pero con respeto*. In what follows, I describe how Alejandro de-Indianizes his dance troupe.

Urban and Rural Indigenous Culture and De-Indianization

In keeping with his idea that the Capac Qolla de Haukaypata must represent their "true" identity, Alejandro has created verses that permit the dancers to verbally express the fusion of their rural origins with their urban occupation as merchants. The lyrics of their song narrate that they descend from the town of Paucarcolla, an invented place that represents the dancers' place of origin in "the highlands," to a town of valley mestizos, which represents the city of Cuzco. The name Paucarcolla presumably alludes both to *Paucartambo*, the valley town where Capac Qolla are famous, and Collao, the highland region that is home to the qolla merchants. The journey from the highlands to the valleys is difficult, and so is life in the unfamiliar urban town where the rural muleteers must learn a different lifestyle.

From my town of Paucarcolla,
I'm coming down to the valley town, to the town of the *canchis,*
Llaulli thorn, *pinina* thorn.
Don't enter my bare feet, don't get into my flesh.
Learn, learn, you'll find out, you'll find out.
If you don't learn what will your life be like, how we'll suffer.
What will my life be like, when will my life be.
In this strange land where I suffer, where I cry streams of tears,
Where will I pass through to reach my llama, to reach my rope?[29]

Explaining this part of the song, Alejandro said:[30] "All this that we sing is what happens when one goes to *chalar* [to trade]. . . . It is a reality, there is no untruth [in] what we sing. We sing that we are coming down from our town, and down there we encounter thorns, and since people from the country don't wear shoes we have to learn [to use them] in the city so the thorns don't pierce us. We have to learn what life is like, we don't know what's going to happen down there. This happened to all of us when we first came to the city." In Cuzco, the hispanicized Quechua word "chalar" carries two possible meanings, which Don Alejandro uses simultaneously to talk about his double identity as migrant and merchant. On the one hand, it means "exchanging one thing for another," that is, bartering or buying and selling, something that llameros and merchants do. It also means "to use something for the first time." In this case, it refers to a debut in a new place of residence, the city of Cuzco, the behaviors of which they have to learn from scratch, including how to wear shoes.

Using modern dichotomies that bound notions of culture/race to geography, the dominant *imagineros* ("imaginers," cf. Muratorio, 1994) of Indians have suggested since the 1920s indigenista period that migration to the city would transform Indians (defined as agriculturalists) into mestizos (mostly defined as merchants). This proposition also implies that the new urban knowledge will displace rural wisdom. The ritual performance of the Capac Qolla de Haukaypata contradicts this image, as in it the new urban knowledge that the capac qolla muleteers acquire does not replace but rather adds to their countryside experience. Demonstrating the latter, these newcomers to the city use what they call "dialects," which to them are a sine qua non feature of their sacred journey to Coyllur Rit'i. "There are many qollas now, more and more qolla comparsas appear every year, but they do not know the dialect [*el dialecto*]. . . . They see a dance group and like it and then they say 'I'd like to learn.' They rent the costume and just dance, but they don't know anything about the dialect. . . . You have to learn the dialects to be neto, to be authentic; when I learned them I didn't say anything, because if I ever do, they will copy me."[31]

A way of asserting the rural origins that authenticate their comparsa, the dialects are secret ritual behaviors and words that "not everyone understands even though they might know Quechua." The Capac Qolla de Haukaypata use dialects while they are in the sanctuary territory. This is the crucial stage of the pilgrimage and the point at which competition with other comparsas, rural and urban, comes to a head over proofs of authenticity. The Haukaypata comparsa members see themselves as the best and most legitimate because of their use of dialects. "From Mahuayani you have to call the demanda 'Apuyaya,'" Alejandro said instructing us before getting off the truck in Mahuayani, where the hike to the sanctuary begins. The demanda is the miniature image of patron saints owned by each comparsa. During the course of the pilgrimage, when we met up with other comparsas, and briefly exchanged the demandas, Alejandro used the dialect words, only allowing us to hear the greeting: *taytan wayran pustan* to the men, and *maman wayran pustan* to the women.[32]

Alejandro told us that he learned the secrets involved with this stage of the ritual from a *pablito,* the ubiquitous and multifaceted character present in almost every cuzqueño comparsa. Alejandro narrates that the pablito who instructed him "was *matrero* [a Spanish word that locally means 'old and expert'] in the rituals of Coyllur Rit'i." To certify the authenticity of his teacher's knowledge he also mentioned the pablito was from the "highlands of Paruro." On our trip to Ausangate he told me and the dancers:

> When I danced in my town I knew the whole dance, but I didn't understand anything about Coyllur Rit'i; my caporal did not teach me [about that]. . . . But I met that pablito, and he accompanied us three times to the peak. He came with us from the first time we made the pilgrimage; he taught me everything about the dialects. . . . He told me, "You're going to meet up with other qollas here and there, and you have to speak dialects. . . ." In the encounters with qollas, it is required to speak dialects. Pablitos come from the countryside. They come from the heights. They know more about the ancient dialects, so they know how to ask properly. They know how to greet us during the pilgrimage. Now I know, as the pablito has taught me, then I can answer properly, that is part of coming to Coyllur Rit'i.

As Alejandro describes, pablitos are associated with "the heights" and, therefore, generally considered the most Indian members of dancing troupes. As such they are assigned menial ritual tasks — they serve the dancers, carry loads, and hold the last turn in every routine — and hence some comparsas choose among the most uneducated and poor of its members for the role of pablito. Yet the pablitos that go to Coyllur Rit'i are also important specialists in this ritual, since they are in charge of safely bringing the sacred ice from assigned areas in the peak. This may be a lifelong ritual career, which usually starts as an apprenticeship with more experienced ice carriers. Thus, pablitos are the lowest ranked socially and at the same time highly valued authorities in Coyllur Rit'i.

Learning the so-called dialects from a pablito, Alejandro acquired the neto ritual knowledge that distinguishes him from "sham caporales who copy the dance and bring their groups to the snowy peak, without knowing any of the meanings of the dialects, who don't know how to respond [in dialect]." Yet mastering the dialects (like knowing the role) is perceived as an attribute of Indians and thus one of the dangers in using them is that it might incur disapproval for being rural, being Indian. To counteract this negative judgment, the Capac Qolla de Haukaypata emphasize what they see as the prime urban characteristics of their identity. Just as their songs reveal their rural origins, they also conspicuously explain that they are merchants coming from the "very center of the city, from Haukaypata in the Plaza de Armas." Although this interpretation of their personas juxtaposes rural knowledge and urban livelihood (and thus contradicts dominant binary oppositions), it continues to abide by dominant hierarchies inasmuch as it asserts urbanity to counteract negative aspects of ruralness which, supposedly, indicate Indianness.

For this comparsa, taking care of one's appearance in order to look "urban" is as rigid a rule as mastering "rural" dialects. Together, both are a source of distinction, markers of their authenticity as a ritual comparsa. On one occasion, when I was accompanying the comparsa, a new resident in Almudena parish asked to join the group. He was a monolingual Quechua speaker, whose demeanor indicated his recent arrival from the countryside to the city. The comparsa admitted him, but they made it clear that they, the Haukaypatas, represented the city among all the other Capac Qolla comparsas that go to Coyllur Rit'i. Therefore, before joining them, he had to bathe, comb his hair, clean his shoes, so he "wouldn't look rustic [Indian], like members of other comparsas." Besides being clean, Alejandro requires from his comparsa dancers, as he did from the newcomer, not to get drunk while performing the ritual (ever, and not only at Coyllur Rit'i), since for him this is irrefutably a trait of Indianness. "*Los borrachitos de las alturas*" (the little drunks from the highlands), is Alejandro's alternative way of saying "Indians," and it falls somewhere between affection and scorn. To further counteract allusions to Indianness, and enable the comparsa to proudly display symbols of their rural authenticity, Alejandro has eliminated the overt sexual connotations of characteristic parts of this dance. Alejandro thus distances his creation from dominant opinions regarding the deviant deportment of Indians, and in turn, he attempts to present what he considers appropriate standards of domestic behavior.

Hiding the Chinka-Chinka and Redefining the Indian's Exotic Sexuality

Almost all the Capac Qolla comparsas in the city of Cuzco and its vicinity have modeled their dance following the Paucartambo version, which emphasizes the bravado imputed to the *llameros'* (llama muleteer's) masculine identity. According to the Huakaypata dancers, many members of Capac Qolla comparsas attend the central festival in Paucartambo to observe the dance directly and take tape recorders with them in order to copy the lyrics. Consequently, the most common version of the dance follows the "Paucartambo style" (in Alejandro's words), which narrates the sexual vicissitudes of the male qollas as they arrive in unfamiliar places.[33] A very important part of the dance is called *chinka-chinka,* from the Quechua verb *chinkay,* which means "to get lost." In the context of these dance versions, it means hiding oneself in order to play around sexually. In this part of the dance, the qollas run into a woman, performed by the *imilla* (the woman who dances in the comparsa), who seduces them (or whom they seduce) and with whom they have sexual relations. Alejandro's modifications distinguish the Huakaypata group from these widespread versions. He proudly contradicts the trend: "We don't follow Paucartambo's style, but the manner of my home town. . . . We don't do the songs the same way. . . . We don't do the steps the same way either. . . . We dance *con ronda nomás* [in a circle, that's all]." Alejandro has specifically deleted the representation of sexual relationships between the imilla and the dancers, a central attraction in other comparsas.

Eliminating the sexual connotations of the dance Alejandro wants to preserve the respeto that he had been endowed with on his initiation and to protect his group from being associated with irreverent behavior that would diminish the comparsa's urbanity and approximate it to Indianness. He considers the versions that follow Paucartambo's model a "mockery of the imilla and a mockery of the *llamero* [the qolla merchant]." In keeping with the inclusive otherness of their neto authenticity, their ritual performance as llameros has to represent their veneration, as walking merchants, of the Lord of Coyllur Rit'i. Mocking the llamero's identity would mean mocking their own everyday identities. So, to avoid mockery, and since he cannot eliminate chinka-chinka (given its importance and distinctive melodies), Alejandro has modified it.

In Alejandro's version, chinka-chinka appears in a context in which the idea of "getting lost" (*chinkay*) lacks overt sexual connotations. Rather, it refers to the potential risks confronted by the rural migrant in the city, the traveling merchant, and the pilgrim to Coyllur Rit'i, that is, the risks to the Haukaypata group's "true" identity. In addition to modifying through songs the best-known meaning of chinka-chinka, the Haukaypata group has reduced the distinctive choreography of this part of the dance to a minimum: they make a circle (*ronda*) in which they enclose the imilla and the caporal. In the circle, the qollas sing:

Ay *chinka-chinka, ay chinka-chinka, ay chinka-chinka.*
[Getting lost, getting lost, getting lost.]
With my imilla [woman/wife] I get lost, lost.
With my *chanasko* [little boy/son] I get lost, lost.
With the old qolla [man] I get lost, lost.
With the old *qolla* [woman] I get lost, lost.

With my *taruka* [deer] I get lost, lost.
With my *vicuña* I get lost, lost.
I'm making a corral.
I'm making a corral.
To confine my old llama,
To touch him when he starts to fly.
A little corral I'm making,
To confine my old llama,
To hold him when he starts to fly.[34]

The majority of Capac Qolla comparsas accentuate the sexual allusions of the lyrics with choreography representing sexual intercourse between the caporal and the imilla, and even between the caporal and a llama. For example, describing this section as performed by the Capac Qollas from San Jerónimo, anthropologist Zoila Mendoza says:

When the caporal captures the imilla in the middle of the circle [that the other Qollas have made] . . . he twirls her to the music and they dance with their arms locked. The Qollas change their dance, breaking the circle by letting go of the other dancers. They bring their arms up and down, palms inward, their hands meeting in a quick clap. They move their legs in the same motion, lifting their knees in a high hop. This movement is supposed to celebrate the capture and, as the lyrics indicate, sexual pleasure in general. The Qollas sing: "Doing this gives me pleasure, doing this gives me pleasure, climbing to a rock peak, climbing over a bridge." (Mendoza, 1993:223)

The 1953 Paucartambo version has similar lines: "Doing this I'm getting pleasure, on the side of the mountain I'll carry you, over there on that side I'll carry you" (Villasante, 1975:85). Alejandro's interpretation, however, disengages his comparsa from these allusions. Members of the Haukaypata group interpret the lyrics and choreography of their own chinka chinka as follows: "When we arrive at the city or town we were traveling to, the *chanaskito* [small boy] gets lost, then the old qolla also gets lost in the city, with his wife. . . . We leave our children [the other dancers] at a temporary home, and we go out to see the city and get lost. . . . Afterward, the qolla children find us, they make a circle and enclose the two of us, the imilla, my wife, and me the old male, qolla, the caporal, so we won't go out and drink."

Alejandro is right when he says that he does not follow the Paucartambo version. He has refashioned the best-known story of the qollas, adapting it to their experiences as rural migrants in the city of Cuzco, emphasizing the representation of an established family. Obviously, just like any other interpreter, he is aware of the modifications he has introduced and of his reasons for doing so:

> In my town the chinka-chinka is done differently [from what we do here]. When a woman interests you, you want to follow through, you want to take her away from her father and her mother, the *machu qolla* and *paya qolla,* who are like Inca with *ñusta* (Inca princess). In my hometown the imilla and the caporal leave [the church where the comparsa has been dancing] when mass is over and in the doorway they imitate marriage [they form a circle and simulate sexual games]. . . . Now I'm getting rid of all that because when I do that they laugh, they lose respect. . . . But we continue dancing in the old way, I dance authentically, I haven't made changes, to be "nicer," when they tell me to change because something is nicer, I answer that we dance in the old way.

According to Alejandro, recontextualizing the dance and adapting it to the city is not equivalent to changing the dance. Rather than totally eliminating the allusions to sexuality, by continuing to dance the old way he has *hidden* them, compared to the openly burlesque Paucartambo style. His choreographic modifications have created double meanings in the lyrics of the song. Following his explanation, "to get lost" maintains its connotation of seeking privacy to carry out sexual play; the corral could be the place where the pair — the old male qolla and the old female qolla — can have sexual intercourse. The words "hold him when he starts to fly" could refer to the sexual caresses that result in the erection of the penis and then orgasm. But they do not do this overtly because Alejandro considers that it is disrespectful of their own identity and of the ritual in which they perform.

The hidden meanings of what Alejandro calls "dialects" are fundamental ritual aspects of the dance. For his own comparsa, he alone knows the majority of the dialects. For him, the hidden meaning of chinka-chinka has the same secret status as the dialects: they can only be revealed if stating them will not prompt the audience's scorn or mockery. The ritual secrecy of the meaning of dialects and of chinka-chinka creates a space of cultural intimacy that enables the comparsa members to proudly assert their indigenous ways while protecting themselves from public scorn as Indians. Thus, in order for their dance to be authentic and simultaneously project an urban identity *con respeto* (with respect), Alejandro has concealed the sexual connotations of the version of chinka-chinka that he originally danced. From his point of view, this version is not suitable for the city, where showing it would diminish his authority vis-à-vis the dancers, or lower the status of his comparsa relative to the other dance groups. Alejandro's modifications do not go unchallenged though. Even within his own dance group he has to confront prevailing ideas about indigenous identity encompassing brutality, drunkenness, and sexual exoticism.

De-Indianization
Respect and Masculinity

Alejandro's endeavor to clean his comparsa of stigmatizing aspects of Indianness is not free of conflict because the behavior that he demands from the male members of his comparsa as *"netos de respeto"* challenges dominant images of masculinity that individuals in his group may embrace. Another choreography that Alejandro has changed is the Yawar Mayu ("River of Blood" in Quechua).[35] This piece, which is also important to other comparsas, was originally performed by an all-men cast that participates in a whipping contest that takes place in the margins surrounding the dance performance. Contemporary ethnographers interpret the Yawar Mayu as a demonstration of masculinity (e.g., Allen, 1983). The observers that I interviewed concurred, saying that during the Yawar Mayu the pablitos challenge each other to a whipping contest to prove their courage. Intrepidly transforming the meaning of this number, Alejandro presents the Yawar Mayu as educational and analogous to an initiation rite. Through it, younger people, represented by the comparsa's pablitos and the chanasko, learn lessons of respect. The lyrics of their Yawar Mayu act are as follows:

Don't get frightened, little brother.
Seeing yourself in Yawar Mayu.
Even if the hail will come.
You don't see me getting scared.
My *huaraca* goes *kac-kac*.
My mirror shines *liuliu*.
My knife cuts *siusiu*.
My huaraca goes kac-kac.
Did you know, chanasko? Learn, chanasko.
You respect the young and the old.
You greet the young and the old.
Did you know pablito? Learn pablito.
You respect the young and the old.
You greet the young and the old.

Although I have obviously not observed every single Capac Qolla comparsa, I think that the allusions to respect throughout the song are emblematic of the Haukaypatas. Alejandro, its author, interprets them as follows: "When the child does not obey the father, the older brother has to punish him with his whip so that he learns good manners." The men administering the blows are the leaders of each row of dancers. These are also called caporales, and they follow Alejandro in a ranked order. According to Alejandro, the group of qollas represents a group of male siblings, the children of the older qolla whom he represents. These two caporales who follow Alejandro in hierarchy, are the "older children," and since this scene portrays an educational act and not a competition in masculinity, following the family hierarchies they are the ones in charge of the discipline of the rest when the father is absent. Similarly, to avoid references to violence, the whip lashes are feigned among the Haukaypatas. In contrast with the other dance groups that "hit each other until they draw blood, Alejandro doesn't want us to hit each other very much," one of the participants said, with a combination of relief and irritation in his tone of voice.[36] This assertion contained

an implicit complaint against Alejandro. If they are actually everything they enact, why can't they demonstrate their courage like other
comparsas do by actually using the whip? Continuing his quest for
respect, and implementing what can be interpreted as a moral, patriarchal version of Capac Qolla, Alejandro has eliminated several
other numbers that he considers contrary to his comparsa's character. One of these is the *Charki Tauka* (burden of dried meat), in
which the dancers lie face down, one crossed on top of the other.
When other Capac Qolla comparsas do this number, the chanasko
or the imilla sits or leaps down on top of the mound made up of the
rest of dancers. This provokes the laughter of the public, because
they expect the dancers to be crushed. Alejandro has also eliminated
the *Cuchi Taka* and the *Puka Cinta*. In the first one, pairs of dancers
hit each other with their shoulders, simulating a pig fight — which is
what "Cuchi Taka" literally means. During the second (which means
"Red Ribbon") one the dancers make a circle with their *wachalas,*
long multicolor ribbons. For Alejandro, the first two scenes are "very
brutal, and only serve to make people laugh." He has deleted the
third scene because, he says, it is "not masculine." According to
prevalent regional beliefs, brutality and lack of masculinity are characteristics of Indian identity. And these traits do provoke laughter
and scorn among the social sectors that define themselves in opposition to Indians. By eliminating these three numbers from his comparsa, Alejandro is claiming urbanity and "respect" for his dance.
But his modifications (which Alejandro implements without any
consultation) also risk making his comparsa "less attractive" than
others, representing a sober masculinity that is festively unattractive.
This indeed provokes conflict and fosters Alejandro's arbitrary behavior as the patriarch of the group.

While I still was accompanying the group, Alejandro expelled one
of the participants who questioned his authority by demanding the
reinclusion in the comparsa's repertoire of Charki Tauka. A few days
after the incident, one of the dancers explained to me that Zenón, the
expelled dancer, respected Alejandro because: "Don Alejo knows a
lot about the dance, the dialects, and the old things." And he added,
"But Zenón felt that he himself knew more about how the dance
should be in the city because he was more urban than Don Ale-

jandro." Being a ritual specialist endows Alejandro with authority; likewise being literate and urban identifies him as an indigenous mestizo, "mestizo neto" in local terms. Yet his relatively recent settlement in the city occasionally weakens his status vis-à-vis other individuals, who like Zenón participate in indigenous culture but consider themselves *mejores* (better, less Indian), because of their longer or deeper urban experience and higher level of formal education. Zenón's demands revealed that he had connected authenticity, masculinity, and respeto in a manner that was different from Alejandro's: he wanted to show courage rather than education and good manners. What will Zenón do now that Alejandro has expelled him?" I inquired. The answer, delivered in a manner that revealed my question was too naive, was, "He will join another comparsa that suits his ideas better than the Haukaypatas." This convinced me that although Alejandro's claim of authenticity did attract dancers to his comparsa, their membership was also contingent on how Alejandro represented the many aspects of their identity and, crucially, on how he negotiated his portrayal of the dancers' masculinity and non-Indianness. Striving to convince them of his position (and to keep them as dancers because he needed them), Alejandro argued that if they did the number Zenón promoted, the dance would lose respect and, along with it, their high ranking in Coyllur Rit'i, a very important motivation for the comparsa. He added that only the "new" (spurious) comparsas placed importance on the Charki Tauka and the Cuchi Taka. Authentic comparsas, old ones (*las antiguas*) like the Haukaypatas, were not interested in those numbers. He immediately suggested that those who wanted to perform that number should leave the comparsa and join another one. "Here we have to maintain that which is old, if not, we are going to lose it, and if I pay attention to these compañeros, [it'll be] worse. Without respect, we'll hit bottom [*en lo más bajo vamos a caer*]," he explained to me later. Although this time he faced only one defection, and did not yield, maybe on another occasion he will have to capitulate and satisfy, at least partially, the dancers' images of their masculinity, which are not affixed to images of any kind of essential authenticity. The negotiation between Alejandro and the dancers of the Capac Qolla de Haukaypata regarding the staging of their choreographies is integral

to the dialogic process through which grassroots intellectuals produce their identities. Interestingly, it reflects challenges as much as
agreements with dominant images of regional identities.

Conclusion

In discussing the need to produce an anthropology of Western hegemony, Talal Asad suggests that anthropologists should observe the
"role of Western technologies in transforming colonial subjects"
(1991:323). He gives as an example Terence Turner's study of the
Kayapos' utilization of video to represent their changing concept of
culture and accordingly, the ways they have transformed their views
of themselves (1991). In this chapter I have assigned tourist folklore
the role of a Western technology, which grassroots intellectuals like
the caporal Alejandro Condori have used in order to present dances
as autoethnographic texts that challenge the dominant perceptions
of indigenous cultural features and to present alternative ways of
self-styling as indigenous individuals deserving of respect.

In 1960, the repertoire of the Danzas del Tawantinsuyu (the
tourist-oriented folklore group that promoted the contests where
capac qolla comparsas became popular) defined the dance of the
qollas in the following terms: "A troupe of dancers that represents
groups of merchants from the region of Kollao arriving at the festivals of the Virgen del Carmen de Paucartambo. In it, the Quechua
Indian satirizes the inhabitant of the high plateau, whom he denomi-
nates qolla."[37]

Undoubtedly the Capac Qolla comparsas — and myriads of others — have profited from the neoindianistas' impulse of tourist folklore. Directly or indirectly, they have even borrowed elements of the
dances elites promoted. However, they did not exactly duplicate the
models that inspired them. The capac qolla directed by Alejandro
Condori is in no way a satire of the "inhabitant of the high plateau,"
as Danzas del Tawantinsuyu claimed in 1960.

One of the disagreements between the director of Danzas del Tawantinsuyu and the comparsa leaders is over the performances of
their respective dance troupes. For actors of folklore groups like

Danzas del Tawantinsuyu, the dances simply represent the "others" of the region, whom they call Indian or mestizos. For comparsa dancers, the dance and the ritual in which it is immersed link to their identity, in ways that can be subtle or obvious, shallow or deep. Exegesis of agreements or disagreements over the interpretations of the dance hinge on the way in which the images, choreography, and costumes express the identity the dancers wish to construct simultaneously for Indians and for themselves. This is so because when they represent "the Indian," or aspects of him/her, comparsa dancers include their own self-representation. This inclusive character of the performance is possible due to its ritual character, but it also stems from their lived identities as indigenous mestizos who are also relatively and occasionally Indians. This fractal relational condition emerges in comparsa dances, notwithstanding the elites' blindness to it, trapped as they are in conceptual binarisms. On performing the relativity of their identities, grassroots intellectuals abide by alternative taxonomies in which de-Indianization is key to the reproduction of indigenous culture in its dignified mestizo version.

Thus, far from lampooning or idealizing the neto identity, as some nonindigenous performers do, comparsas seek to elevate their representations by stressing what they call authenticity. Although this notion probably has as many definitions as there are comparsas, the dancers and members of the Capac Qolla de Haukaypata, agree that being neto is possible, because of their rural origins and ritual knowledge, uplifted by their present urbanity and the union-like character of the association. It requires a combination of rural and urban forms of knowledge in order to claim authenticity and legitimacy and certainly explodes the binary definition that assigns indigenous culture to the countryside and deletes urban mestizaje from it. However, this alternative position exists within the confines of regional hegemony inasmuch as it still identifies Indianness with primitive rurality. Alejandro, for example, emphatically denies, "We don't dance Salqa Qolla (Savage Qolla), we dance Capac Qolla." As the language Quechua has its alleged lofty version, Capac Simi, the version of the dance Alejandro wants to present must be of the highest standards. In this case, the adjective "capac" reflects the elevated, urban status of these qollas, vis-à-vis the sallqa version, which is rooted in the highest peaks and whose interpreters are supposedly ignorant of urban manners. Notwithstanding Don Alejo's claims to authenticity and his proud exhibition of neto rural knowledge, his version privileges the city over the countryside, and because of this Alejandro and others like him are working within hegemonic hierarchies. Instead of claiming Indianness, they silence it and restrict its meaning to a despicable condition, while opening up the notion of neto culture to include mestizos, an identity label they have appropriated and concomitantly reformulated.

Silencing Indianness is a signifier of respect, one that demonstrates the inclusive otherness pervading cuzqueño indigenous identities and the inferiority ascribed to exclusively rural identities. This allows the perception of discriminatory behavior to be seen as legitimate and as integral to the rules of respect, which follow sharp hierarchies. Gaining respect implies accepting social differences and behaving according to one's social position. Consequently, accepting one's inferiority is the path to improvement. Although this inferiority is perceived as relative rather than final, the behavior imposed by respect implies accepting humiliation. The case of the young monolingual Quechua speaker, obviously a recent emigrant from the country to the city, illustrates this view. When he tried to join the Capac Qolla de Haukaypata, the members ordered him first to clean his face and hands and shine his shoes because "now he was in the city." They assigned him a marginal role in the dance as *maqtacha* (youth), that they specially created for him and that more than reflecting his chronological age, reflected his social condition as an inferior urbanite relative to the other dancers of Capac Qolla, who knew more about the dance, but also who had polished their rural origins with urban knowledge. The fact that they included him in the comparsa, however, evinces that the differences that may exist between Indians (the maqtacha) and mestizos (the other Qolla dancers in the troupe), more than cultural distinctions, reflected differences in social conditions. In a few years, if he gets a job in the city and builds his external appearance accordingly, this maqtacha would probably ascend to the category of Qolla dancer within the comparsa, and although this transformation will reflect the changes in his social condition it will not signify cultural "passing."

7

Indigenous Mestizos,

De-Indianization, and Discrimination

Cultural Racism in Cuzco

Indians as an Essentially Illiterate Race/Culture

In late 1922, a journalist from the Cuzco newspaper *El Comercio* met Miguel Quispe, an indigenous leader from the district of Colquepata in the province of Paucartambo. The encounter took place at the office of the prefecto while both parties were waiting for a hearing with the representative of President Augusto B. Leguía in Cuzco. The 1920s were a particularly unstable period in Cuzco politics. The city was suffused with tensions arising from revived colonial fears about Indian rebellions and from painful urges to modernize the region. Two main elements underscored the tensions. First, indigenous leaders from rural provinces were channeling their complaints to state representatives in Cuzco. Although this was a customary practice, and one that local governments routinely ignored, in the 1920s the novelty was that the authorities were willing to negotiate an official remedy to the Indians' situation. Second, representatives of the local elite intelligentsia were crafting indigenismo — a modern and allegedly pro-Indian science — which later became a long-lasting and pervasive intellectual and political discourse in Peru.

The parties waiting for the prefect, Señor Godoy, represented both the indigenous leaders and the indigenistas Miguel Quispe was among the most famous and controversial indigenous leaders. A partisan of President Leguía, the Cuzco elite mockingly called him "the

Inca Quispe," yet at the same time they feared him. The journalist was an indigenista writer, who chose to remain anonymous. While they were waiting for the hearing, the latter approached Quispe. "Distrustful, with a feline look, like a wild beast lying in wait, the Great Emperor threw us a furtive glance of his tiny and deceptive eyes, in a mute inquiry as to what we wanted to say to him," wrote the journalist about the first glances he and Miguel Quispe exchanged. Then he arranged for an interview that later appeared in *El Comercio*.[1]

In his conversation with the journalist, Miguel Quispe denounced the depradations of hacendados against his ayllu, Sayllapata, and the endless tortures he endured as a result of his protests against his exploiters. He denied that he had proclaimed himself an Inca or that he had organized rebellions. Those were inventions of his enemies who did not hesitate to besmirch him, he said. Although the journalist might have believed these assertions, Quispe's deep and clear insights and the way he exposed them unsettled him and other indigenistas. The journalist began his account of the interview by expressing surprise at this Quispe's rhetoric. According to the journalist, Quispe "answers without the least trouble, with a tranquil mastery that *makes us doubt his condition as an illiterate Indian*. . . . His conversation is fluid, eloquent; he speaks Quechua very well, and at times, to give us a better sense of his ideas, he adds in a few Spanish words, of course poorly pronounced" (my emphasis). The article ended with the journalist showing his mistrust of "the Indian Miguel Quispe": "And here we must ask ourselves this disturbing question: Who is Miguel Quispe? Is he perchance a crafty, sly, pettifogging [*tinterillo*], calculating, treacherous Indian who pursues his interests while measuring his words, or is he as he claims the sad victim of the *misti*, educated through experience and adversity? We have no way of knowing."

Quispe's demeanor did not correspond to the journalist's definition of Indians. These, even from an indigenista viewpoint, were racial subjects with *embotamiento intelectual* (intellectual impediment) (Aguilar, 1922:49). An intelligent and articulate Indian politician like Miguel Quispe did not fit their conceptual racial framework. Indians who did not behave like "sad victims" were "astute liars." Miguel Quispe's informed opinions about Indian participation in solving the country's "Indian question," his declared patriotism, and his familiarity with the subterfuges of state institutions were certainly more than what the indigenista journalist was reasonably prepared to hear from "an Indian." After all, in the year of 1922, when the interview was taking place, dominant Peruvian politicians regretted the political failure to consolidate Peru as a nation and explained this situation as resulting, at least partially, from the significant presence of Indians, a backward race that represented an immense obstacle to progress and, indeed, to the desired national homogeneity. That year, when Miguel Quispe, a self-identified Indian, claimed his membership to the nation by telling the interviewer "You too are Peruvian, that is to say Indian. You are only different from me in your dress and education," he did not have a chance of being heard, much less acknowledged. To his interviewers, clothing and instruction were external manifestations of hereditary cultural differences that characterized "the Indian race." Surmounting these differences required changes, to be met through political processes led by liberal politicians educated in the needs of the country. Evidently Quispe was not racially/culturally endowed to be one of these leaders, and therefore his bid to alter the meaning of Indianness and to make Indian citizens through a literacy program led by the Tawantinsuyu Committee was doomed to failure.

Following culturalist definitions of race (and thus manufacturing their legacy of a racialized definition of "culture"), elite cuzqueños believed that natural evolutionary differences separated Indians from the rest of the nation, inasmuch as they represented a nonrational, essentially illiterate, and non-Spanish speaking racial/cultural group of rural, communitarian agriculturalists. Literate Indians like Miguel Quispe, whose demands were rational, were considered racial/cultural transvestites, ex-Indians who maintained the markers of their previous identity (like indigenous clothes) to manipulate actual (irrational) Indians. By maintaining Indian identity and being literate, Quispe represented a challenge to the dominant definition of Indianness. Similarly, Tawantinsuyu's proposal to grant citizenship to literate Indians challenged — even exceeded — the pro-Indian intellectuals' imagination. Citizenship required rationality, an advanced

Miguel Quispe, a follower of President Leguía, whom Indigenistas mistrusted. The original caption says: "The so-called New Inca, Miguel Quispe, of great influence among the indigenes." Photograph from the Lima magazine *Mundial*, July 1921.

stage in the evolution of the mind that Indians as a racial/cultural group had not reached. Given Indians' irrationality, pro-Indian intellectuals explained the series of rural disturbances that agitated Cuzco in the 1920s by benevolently acquitting Indians from guilt because, they said, their animal-like fury had been dangerously provoked either by non-Indian agitators or by local scourges, the gamonales. When the self-identified Indian leaders of the political disturbances were imprisoned and prosecuted, indigenista lawyers defended them by pointing out their irresponsibility as members of an ignorant, inferior race/culture. I argued in chapter 2 that this defense represented the defeat of the social movement that Tawantinsuyu led and that was a bid for Indian citizenship that did not require the transformation of Indians into mestizos. Not surprisingly, the racial/cultural notion of an inferior-but-redeemable-Indian that the indigenistas used to acquit Indians of crimes and to cancel their political responsibility had a broad appeal and became consensual among both conservative, official legislators, and radical, oppositional thinkers and politicians.

The historical conditions preventing a political alliance between indigenistas and Tawantinsuyu Committee were embedded in decencia, a moral class ideology shared by both progressive and conservative intellectuals and politicians. During indigenista times, combining decency with popular Lamarckian beliefs, and attracted to culturalist postulates about race, Cuzco intellectuals believed in the potential of education to uplift racial conditions. It followed, from this perspective, that cultural/racial hierarchies depended on the quality and quantity of formal education, which also reflected the moral status of an individual. These opinions implied that literacy transformed Indians into mestizos if they migrated to the cities or found a job away from agriculture. For those indigenistas who, like Valcárcel, advocated for racial/cultural purity and believed in "racial proper places," cuzqueño mestizos symbolized degeneration, while the same cuzqueño mestizos represented the ideal national type in the eyes of neoindianista, who championed constructive miscegenation. Both groups shared a view of actual living Indians as a wretched racial/cultural group, made what they were by years of colonial subjugation. This image was strengthened as indigenista beliefs in the preeminence of racial/cultural purity and the abhorrence of mestizaje faded and were replaced by populist advocacy for regional mestizaje. In 1959 a well known neoindianista intellectual taught a course in human geography at the local university. Depicting the Indians from Ccolquepata, the district where Miguel Quispe was born, a student in that class wrote: "Like all Indians, [the Ccolquepata Indian] is timid and skeptical; he expects nothing of anyone, and distrusts everything and everybody. . . . The Indians live dispersed in communities called 'ayllus'; their huts are distant from each other, are unhygienic and very primitive. They do not use beds, or if they do these are made of some filthy llama and sheep hides. . . . The Indians have not formed neighborhoods, much less small towns. Their isolation contributes considerably to their unsociability and makes for a sullen character."[2]

Indians as an Essentially Illiterate Class/Culture

Starting in the late 1930s—and after being defeated in their endeavor for Indian citizenship and consequently in their attempt to redefine Indianness as a literate condition—indigenous leaders shifted the focus of their struggle. The new focus was *sindicalización*, which consisted in organizing peasant unions (sindicatos campesinos) that handled legal claims against hacendados through the Federación de Trabajadores del Cuzco (FTC), the Cuzco Federation of Workers. In the 1950s the FTC thrived as the organization for both urban and rural regional working classes. Led by urban workers and with the legal advice of intellectuals, many of whom belonged to the Communist Party, the FTC replaced indigenistas as the urban-based political allies of indigenous peasants. Although communists and other leftist leaders (inspired by Marxist-Leninist manifestos declaring the dictatorship of the proletariat) subordinated peasants to urban workers, rural unions and their indigenous organizers became the key leaders of the political turmoil that hit Cuzco beginning in the late 1950s, eventually precipitating in the 1970s the long-awaited agrarian reform. Avoiding self-reference as Indians became an implicit point in the indigenous agenda for an empowered identity. During this period, rural leaders identified themselves as peasants and called each other "compañero," which became a common label that continues to be used even in religious rituals. The violence conveyed by the word "Indian" led to the silencing of this word, but this attitude, in turn, implied the consensual acceptance of the inferior social condition of those meriting such a name.

Some years ago, in theorizing about the political dimensions of ethnicity, John Comaroff asked if there was a moment when ethnic ideologies broke down and gave place to class consciousness instead. He also asked if the reasons that provoked such circumstances could be identified (1987:319). In Cuzco, the spread of class rhetoric among so-called Indians, and probably of class consciousness too, did not imply the breaking down of ethnic ideologies nor the cancellation of racial/cultural hierarchical feelings and structures. Instead, one of its causes was the political defeat (at the hands of liberal indigenistas) of the political project that Tawantinsuyu had raised, which rested on racial/cultural agendas to promote indigenous citizenship and to de-stigmatize Indianness and thus emancipate Indians from images of racial inferiority. Starting in the 1950s Marxist oppositional politics emerged as an alternative to the racial/cultural path to emancipation, wielding a class rhetoric that relegated "culture" to the realm of false consciousness. However, the identity labels then popular, such as "peasant," "worker," or "classist intellectual," were laden with references to evolutionary stages that were explicitly evaluated according to the person's potential to develop "class consciousness" and to lead the revolutionary process; yet they were also implicitly colored with beliefs in racial/cultural differences. The "peasants" (definitely a gloss for Indians) occupied the lowest ranks in leftist groups. "For the transformation of rebellions into revolution, peasants require the leadership of other classes," proclaimed a leftist lawyer in the 1980s, who justified his declaration by stating that because peasants believed that the Pachamama guided their own land seizures, they not be real political leaders (García Sayán, 1982:211–212). The implicit, yet obvious, idea was that peasants were only motivated by superstitions that belonged to prerational, inferior stages of knowledge. Thus the leftist deployment of "class" continued to rely on the earlier race/culture evolutionary assumptions. Most intellectuals believed, as did Aníbal Quijano (1978), that Indians were unable to create their own leadership; "peasant leaders" were those that had superseded the cultural stage of Indianness and had become cholos.

Following a common pattern of reasoning that was used by Marxists theorizing about subaltern identities during those years, these ideas conflated economicist definitions of "class" with an obviously evolutionary notion of "culture," still inspired by racialized notions of inherited and geographically bounded traditions and transmitted to mid-century leftist thinkers by means of their unimaginative readings of José Carlos Mariátegui. In the 1920s, the period of high racial thought, the leftist thinker José Carlos Mariátegui joined the trend to define race in cultural terms and thus countered dominant European inclinations to racial pessimism. In so doing, he denied the fixed nature of races as well as the preeminence of biological determinism and proposed, like many others, that surrounding conditions (which in Marxist fashion he called "productive forces") were crucial in determining races. Similarly, following the antiracist trend, he outlined an environmental definition of race, which included economic and cultural elements (1981:21–33). Inspired by indigenista readings of Luis E. Valcárcel and José Antonio Encinas, he asserted: "The indigenous race is a race of agriculturalists. The Inca people were a peasant people dedicated to agriculture and herding" (1968:45). But even more important (probably inspired also in this by Valcárcel), Mariátegui followed notions of "racial proper places" to articulate his proposals. Accordingly, he stated that the task of improving the Indian race had to be accomplished by preserving its historical/cultural symbiosis with the land and asserted "to remove the Indian from the land is to vary profoundly and possibly dangerously the race's ancestral tendencies" (1968:33).

The 1960s leftist politicians adopted Mariátegui's thought. But by then race had been internationally dismissed as a scientific concept, thus rendering superfluous and even racist the culturalist definition of race that undergirded Mariátegui's reflections about the "indigenous question." Thus the unquestioned adoption of Mariátegui's definition of Indians as "peasants" essentialized indigenous Peruvians as agriculturalists, fixed them to the countryside, and in anachronistic conceptual fashion, extended Mariátegui's culturalist definition of race into the class rhetoric that prevailed in the sixties. Unscrutinized by those who implemented it, indigenista cultural fundamentalism thus survived in the leftist political and academic sphere, which in many cases overlapped. Currently, this view still legitimates notions of a primitive Indianness, rooted in an imagined Andean culture that is fixed in the mountains and incapable of dealing with modernization. Mario Vargas Llosa's statements, which I used in the introduction of this book, are a perfect example of the currency of indigenista racialized notions of culture. Anachronistically — and worst of all, unknowingly — assisted by the legacy of early twentieth-century indigenismo, Vargas Llosa made his cultural fundamentalist pronouncements on the occasion of the Quincentennial of the Spanish Conquest of America. In it he chose to make a bid for "modernization," and invoked the incompatibility between modern and indigenous Peru, which he deemed archaic (Vargas Llosa, 1990b:50).

Ironically, Vargas Llosa, a right-wing proponent of neoliberalism, had the same beliefs — which I repeat derived from Valcárcel's and Mariátegui's teachings — as Antonio Díaz Martínez, one of the leaders of the Maoist Shining Path. Díaz Martínez also used a geographically determined racialized conflation of culture and class to define peasants as those agriculturalists who felt such "love, attachment and gratitude for the Pacha Mama that they were unable to break their ties with her." In a conceptual tone like that of Vargas Llosa, Díaz Martínez believed that "the clash between the westernized cities and the indigenous communities . . . prevented the technological modernization of the community, which [instead] resorted to the magical and conventional principles of its own culture" (1969:249). So, at the turn of the twentieth century, the intellectual leadership of the Shining Path and Mario Vargas Llosa — the two extremes of the Peruvian political spectrum — shared a crude racial/cultural evolutionism that posited incommensurable differences between "indigenous society" (terminally defined as premodern, illiterate, magical, and backward) and nonindigenous Peru, defined as modern, literate, rational, and with a potential for (communist or neoliberal) progress.

Prior to the 1969 agrarian reform, landowners used the expression "*Indio leído, Indio perdido*" (A literate Indian is a lost Indian). Using it, they referred either to the fact that literate Indians did not want to work as peons and migrated to the cities or to the idea that literacy transformed Indians from passive victims of abuses into stubborn producers of written denunciations against it. The same saying — which in its mildest version means that a literate Indian is not an Indian anymore — is implicit in the common definition of Indianness, and with marginal exceptions it reflects a belief that traverses the country. Still drawing on racial/cultural fundamentalism, this expression defines Indians as so essentially opposed to literacy and to urban ways that if they learn to read and write or migrate to the city, they are no longer Indians but racial/cultural mestizos.

De-Indianizing Indigenous Culture: Education and Respeto

Since the turn of the century indigenous leaders (including Miguel Quispe and the Tawantinsuyu organizers) have shared with domi-

nant politicians a belief in the redemptive powers of literacy. However, while for the conservative and progressive official intellectuals,
the effect that literacy had on Indians was to gradually cleanse them
from their original race/culture, for indigenous leaders, literacy had
different effects. For Mariano Turpo, a prominent leader of the hacienda Lauramarca, for example, literacy was empowering; yet, as
illustrated by his own life, it did not imply "cultural passing" to a
nonindigenous status. When he started his career as a unionist in the
1940s, one of his first goals was to get permission from the state to
build a school in the hacienda against the wishes of the hacendados.
In the late fifties, Turpo's profound knowledge of legal concepts
yielded the first successful verdict from the state in support of the
immediate expropriation of Lauramarca. In 1975 he continued to be
an important local leader and was reputed to be a *paqo* (a diviner)
and even an *altomisa* (the highest ritual specialist in the zone) with
the ability to communicate directly with the Apus, the great indigenous protective deities (Gow, 1982:213–215).

Although Alejandro Condori, the urban choreographer of the Capac Qolla de Haukaypata, is not as prominent a politician as Turpo,
he is a respected leader in his own terms. This street vendor believes
in the power of Ausangate, the indigenous regional Apu, and takes
his dancing troupe in an annual pilgrimage to honor him during the
celebration of Our Lord of Coyllur Rit'i. Like Turpo, he derives his
leadership from being both literate and an indigenous ritual specialist. Additionally, and probably as in Turpo's case, Alejandro's literacy has removed him from Indianness, a social condition that he
does not consider to be coterminous with indigenous culture. Rather,
Alejandro considers himself and his production as neto (indigenous)
inasmuch as he draws inspiration for his choreography from his
rural background, and also as mestizo because he colors it with what
he considers urban manners. Coupling rural and urban practices
(instead of opposing binary racialized notions of culture that assign practices either to the city or to the countryside but not both)
some indigenous grassroots creators have opened up the possibility
of redefining dominant evolutionary notions of mestizaje while de-
Indianizing cultural identities and the productions they designate as
"authentically" cuzqueño. Dominant intellectuals and politicians
define indigenous culture—the neta, regional "Andean" and, yes,

subordinate culture—as exclusively rural, essentially backward, irrational and illiterate. The grassroots indigenous intellectuals with whom I interacted have redefined it (mainly through their productions, but also in their daily lives) as both rural and urban and compatible not only with literacy but also with progress and even academic education. They see indigenous culture as being like this while retaining—many times purposefully—its distinctiveness within the national formation rather than simply being "assimilated" into it.

To draw analytical cultural boundaries (no matter how fluid) between present-day Indians and mestizos is to abide by only one definition of indigenous culture and, indeed, the dominant one. Significantly, in doing so, one dismisses the crucial detail that from some cuzqueño grassroots viewpoints, indigenous culture exceeds the scope of Indianness and includes subordinate definitions of the mestizo/a. Included in the grassroots definition of indigenous culture are definitions of Indian and mestizo as relative social conditions. From this standpoint calling someone mestizo/a (or Indian) is fixing momentarily a point of reference inherently related to that which is Indian (or mestizo/a). Similarly, becoming mestizo implies distancing oneself from the Indian social condition and thus de-Indianizing. But it does not mean "disappearing" into a national, gradually homogenizing culture. In Cuzco, from the viewpoint of those grassroots intellectuals who allowed me to participate in some aspects of their lives, de-Indianization is the process of empowering indigenous (neto) identities through economic and educational achievement *and* proudly displaying these identities in regional events of popular culture promoted by cuzqueñismo.

The notion of indigenous mestizaje is also evident in everyday subordinate discourses and is concretely embodied in the figure of mestiza market women. They fuse the dominant rural-urban divide, and the elite would not hesitate to call them "uppity" Indians. Their gendered identity, which slipped through the grasp of class rhetoric and continues to defy decencia, connotes a notion of mestizaje that runs counter to its dominant definition. I see mestizas as Andean indigenous individuals, mostly non-Indian, yet occasionally and relatively Indians, whose identities combine the endless motion between contestation and acquiescence suggested by the notion of hegemony, with the inherently relational dynamic, of the kind implied in the concept of fractal identities (Wagner, 1991). Contemporary indigenous mestiza/os *may seem* an anomaly when seen from the perspective of taxonomies built upon classificatory notions defined in the nineteenth and early twentieth centuries, which, allowing no room for uncertainties, rigidly moved between purity and impurity, city and country, literacy and illiteracy, and thus yielded "mestizaje" as a concept inserted in the dichotomies. Instead, the cuzqueño mestiza identity does not refer to the culturally or racially "evolving" mixed individual implied in modern taxonomies. By calling themselves mestizas/os and silencing Indianness, urban indigenous cuzqueños rebuke stigmas of all sorts and proceed to de-Indianization, which consists of (among other things) producing, celebrating, and staging a very "impure" indigenous culture, which is empowering because it has been stripped of such elements of Indianness as illiteracy, poverty, exclusive rurality, and urban defeat. In individuals, de-Indianization refers to the process of moving up through indigenous ranks. These harbor inherently relative Indian and mestizo identities that connote the educational and economic achievements of the individuals involved in the interactions. Far from representing flawless stories of subaltern resistance and success, these achievements represent differentiating mechanisms and legitimize daily life and ritual discriminatory behavior among indigenous cuzqueños. Notwithstanding its potential for contradiction, the subordinate notion of mestizaje not only contests certain aspects of its dominant counterpart but also represents an empowering alternative for the expression of indigenous identities.

Fractal Ethnicity and Subordinate Meanings of Mestizaje

Klor de Alva has suggested that "resulting from the variety of processes it has stood for, Latin America 'mestizaje' has a chameleonic nature that allows it to be western *in the presence of Europeans,* indigenous *in the native villages,* and Indian-like *in contemporary United States barrios*" (1995:243, my emphasis). While I agree with this heteroglossic nature of mestizaje, I differ from Klor de Alva in another respect. I think that the different meanings of mestizaje represent competing and situated political statements that dominant and subordinate individuals make about the national place of subaltern identities, rather than only reflecting a chameleon nature that unproblematically changes colors with different interlocutors. Thus viewed, "mestizaje" is not a meeting ground—the Latin American melting pot—as the Mexican dominant view bequeathed from Vasconcelos (1925) proposed. Rather, it is a terrain of political contestation and dialogic reformulation in which elite and grassroot intellectuals dispute meanings of identity labels and rights to equal citizenship.[3]

Drawing on Paul Gilroy (1993:2), I think that creolization, *métissage,* mestizaje, and hybridity derive from turn-of-the-century formulations and thus are rather unsatisfactory ways of naming identity processes that exceed the bounds of binary discourses of race and ethnicity. The indigenous mestizos from Cuzco, who are dialogically exposed to the dominant evolutionary notion of mestizaje that would make them incomplete participants in two discrete cultural formations, advance a different notion of hybridity: one that "continually breaks down the unitary aspect of each culture" (Anzaldúa, 1987:80)[4] thus allowing them to *completely* participate in both. Working-class cuzqueños taught me about a kind of hybridity that was not meant to be solved in the manner of "either/or" choices, but rather to assert that they were different from Indians yet also like them. This notion of hybridity connects with Roy Wagner's concept of fractals as "something as different from a sum as it is from an individual part" (1991:164)[5] as well as with Robert Young's interpretation of Bakhtinian hybridity as bringing "difference into sameness, and sameness into difference but in a way that makes the same no longer the same and the different no longer simply different" (1995:26).[6] Adriana and Isabel, the two young women whom I quoted in the introduction, translated this into their words when they said that they were both different from *and* like Indians, and that they were different from *and* like me: "Some mestizos like us are also indigenous, aborigenes, *oriundos,* because of our (neto) beliefs, others are only mestizos like you."

These two women, and many other people whom I befriended in

the process of doing this research, taught me another important distinction: indigenous culture and Indianness are not synonyms. This distinction is conceptually significant, as it opens up the notion of indigenous culture to include these mestizos who like Adriana and others, share neto beliefs yet are literate, earn an urban salary, and have what they consider to be "refined" manners. By including these mestizos, the grassroots intellectuals' definition of indigenous culture displaces the conceptual binarism of traditional intellectual narratives that fix the indigenous as one discrete colonized pole, subject to liberation only through wholesale rejection of its cultural markers in favor of others that mark the other discrete pole, which may be referred to as Hispanic, white, or coastal. Rather than signifying innate traits, the definition of culture underlying fractal hybridity highlights the capacity of individuals *to achieve*. Concomitantly, their acquisition of empowering knowledge (ranging from university education to the beginnings of literacy) is not underpinned by the "antinomy of loss" of indigenous culture (cf. Harris, 1995). Likewise, because achievements are calculated individually, rather than collectively, this definition of culture does not connote groups, let alone rank them. It does, however, rank individuals.

Grassroots intellectuals who use this definition of culture deessentialize dominant racial/ethnic identity categories and formulate prismatic ethnic taxonomies. I call them prismatic because they are shaped from infinite relational observation-points, which are agreed upon in each interaction only after taking account of the achieved culture, gender, and age of the persons involved.[7] Phrases such as "I owe Juan respect because he is more educated than me, but Cornelio has to respect me because my manners are refined and his are not," result from such prismatic and relational indigenous constructions of Indian and mestizo identities in Cuzco, in which self-subordination and superordination are in constant flux. Rankings are therefore perceived as valid, deriving from common sense.

Fixing the observation point in each interaction is a conflict-laden process, because, like their dominant equivalents, alternative prismatic taxonomies privilege urban formal education over countryside knowledge, and "Indianness" persists as the archetypal inferior social condition, a combination of poverty, illiteracy, powerlessness, and rural coarseness. Thus even as Indianness and mestizoness emerge from interactions rather than from fixed evolutionary features, on implementing these reformulated taxonomies, subordinate cuzqueños reproduce some aspects of the dominant classifications. At the same time, they contest others, as indicated by their own gendered and geographically formulated interests and their possibilities to make them prevail. From this perspective, de-Indianization in Cuzco is a process of empowering indigenous identities and cultures by redefining the dominant social classification, yet it is itself built upon unchallenged hierarchies that legitimize power differences and discrimination among indigenous cuzqueños. This identity-making process consists in the appropriation of the term "mestizo" and its redefinition to include powerful, successful urban indigenous individuals positioned in hierarchical opposition to "ignorant" rural Indians.

De-Indianization, Dominant Mestizo Nations, and Indigenous Social Movements

I would venture that de-Indianization, defined as the struggle against the wretchedness implicit in the dominant definition of Indianness, is an ongoing process in other Latin American indigenous projects, such as those occurring among the Aymara or Maya, for example. Kay Warren reported that Maya leaders, fearing that youths might "abandon their ethnicity and use their education to disappear into Ladino society," are looking to modernize Maya culture and thus make it more attractive to new people (1989:200). Likewise, in a conference in 1995 Rigoberta Menchú told how her young nephews and nieces still living in Guatemala responded to people who called them Indians, by answering, "We are not Indians, we are Mayas."[8] Thomas Abercrombie (1991) has also reported indigenous Bolivians' refusal to identify themselves as "Indians," and their choice instead of the term "Aymara." Such proud assertions of indigenous identities as Maya or Aymara (rather than Indian) suggest processes of de-Indianization.[9] Yet, it is striking how, unlike the Peruvian case, neither in Guatemala or in Bolivia does de-Indianization imply the indigenous appropriation of the label "mestizo" or in the case of

Guatemala, "ladino." Moreover, according to Brooke Larson, indigenous social movements in Bolivia reject mestizaje as a requirement to participate in a "national culture" imagined by a small creole elite in an attempt to claim hegemony by defining indigenous cultures within the nation-state as obstacles to national development and integration (1998:333).

The cuzqueño redefinition and appropriation of the category of "mestizo" to connote indigenous identities — and the current absence in Peru of indigenous social movements that raise ethnic banners — attests that contemporary indigenous social movements in Latin America are not only the result of the colonial definition of Indianness. On the contrary, they have been strongly influenced by the conflict-laden, implicit or explicit dialogue between the dominant nation-builders and grassroots intellectuals who have shaped images of the nation since the late nineteenth century. In this dialogue, which is still ongoing, hierarchies and taxonomies have been racially defined and then, since mid-century, given new terminologies in ethnic or class lexicons. During the initial years of the national period, Latin American elites also negotiated their own identities in racial terms. In Peru, indigenismo was — among other things — the project that made intellectuals from the sierra comparable to those from the coast. Through culturalist concepts of race, serranos negotiated their geographically defined racial inferiority with formulations and practices that reinforced the superiority of their honorable manliness and lofty intellectual qualities. Implicit in the casting of their own racial identity was the rejection of the "mestizo" label for themselves and, additionally, the stigmatization of mestizos as immoral. This apparently marginal result of the dominant indigenismo of the 1920s (namely, the defeat of mestizaje as a national project) forcefully colored images of the Peruvian nation and made it an exception among other Latin American countries, in which mestizaje was a nation-building goal. Leading the process, Mexicans have cast mestizaje as the paradigmatic identity of their nation since the nineteenth century. After the Revolution, and particularly — but not only — under Lázaro Cárdenas, the Mexican state set about creating *la raza cósmica* and at promoting its image as a mestizo nation (Mallon, 1995; Becker, 1995). The case of Bolivia was less straightforward and turn-of-the-century rulers constructed a "cult of antimestizaje" (cf. Larson, forthcoming), but later a mid-century nationalist revolution altered this attitude. Starting in 1952, and after decades of racial pessimism and white supremacist thought (during which Indians were kept back and "educated" in crafts but prevented from becoming literate), the state mounted a pomp-filled celebration of mestizaje in quintessential populist nation-building fashion (Gotkowitz, 1998). Following their own path, Ecuadoran elites made Indians invisible to national audiences in the nineteenth century while exporting idealized images of their "disappearing" native populations to international expositions (Guerrero, 1994; Muratorio, 1994). Not surprisingly, by the mid-twentieth century, Ecuadoran rulers were using the rhetoric of national mestizaje to express cultural "whitening" ideals (Stutzman, 1981). In Guatemala violence against "Indians" was as ruthless as it was in the other countries, but it was also blatantly undisguised. The proposals for national "ladinization" — the Guatemalan word for mestizaje — were brutally scornful of anything indigenous. In the introduction I quoted the analogy drawn by Guatemalan Miguel Angel Asturias between Indians and animals, which he used to promote biological eugenics to improve "the Indian race" (1923). That Asturias was considered an indigenista writer illustrates the inchoate nature of Latin American indigenismo. Official brutality in that country was curbed in the 1940s, as a reformist government took strides to reduce indigenous exploitation. Under the leadership of President Arévalo, the newly founded Instituto Indigenista de Guatemala aimed at implementing a policy of indigenous assimilation similar to Mexico's (Smith, 1995). This attempt did not last long, and ladinoization prevailed, not only in the format of assimilation but as a genocidal war led by the military against indigenous communities since the 1960s. This was complemented by a savage eugenicist ideology prevalent among the dominant classes, which I want to illustrate with the following unabashed and relatively recent confession by a Guatemalan landowner: "The only solution for Guatemala is to improve the race, to bring in Aryan seed to improve it. On my *finca* I had a German administrator for many years, and for every Indian woman he got pregnant I would pay him an extra fifty dollars" (Casaus Arzú, 1992:289). Not surprisingly, according to the Guatemalan Mayan intellectual Demetrio Cojtí Cuxil "assimilation" in his country was the label for the policies by which "the ladino prescribes the Maya's death in order to solve the 'Indian problem' of the 'ladino's country'" (1997:21).[10] Mayan intellectuals have articulated heterogenous responses that range from political organizing to intellectual self-representation and include strategic essentialisms to define (and thus defend) themselves from brutal attempts to homogeneity. As in Guatemala, Ecuador, Bolivia, and Mexico since January 1994 (after the indigenous resurgence in Chiapas), indigenous social movements have raised ethnic banners as political forces that challenge prevalent "mestizo" national images.

Within the current context Peru represents an exception. Not only do indigenous grassroots intellectuals appropriate the label "mestizo" for self-identification, but crucially, no indigenous social movement exists currently in Peru that rallies around ethnic identities. Peruvians were conspicuously absent from the 1991 meeting in Quetzaltenango protesting the Spanish Conquest (Hale, 1994). While I do not consider that the absence of indigenous ethnic movements in Peru is irreversible, I do not think it is a mere coincidence either.[11] Peru already represented an exceptional case during the peak period of Latin American populism, when, unlike in the aforementioned countries, "mestizaje" did not become a state-sponsored image. Purist indigenistas, including the leftist José Carlos Mariátegui, rejected it flatly, and actual proposals for mestizaje never achieved consensus, probably because they represented diverse and at times even antagonistic political tendencies. One such proposal was the aristocratic project of Víctor Andrés Belaúnde and José de la Riva Aguero (identified as hispanismo), which proposed mestizaje as a nation-building alternative and viewed it as spiritual "whitening": converted into Catholicism, Indians would be integrated into the Peruvian nation. Another was the largely anticlerical, populist definition of mestizaje that the Apra and the Communist Party advanced from the 1930s, which was populist, procholo, and colored by working-class ideals. Although these proposals occupied long hours of political debate in mid-century, neither became official state politics, and while conservative hispanismo faded, populist mestizo projects remained confined to regional orbits (as in the case of neoindianismo) or to the realm of oppositional politics, as with the Apra. Evidently, the Peruvian state did not represent the Latin American pro-Indian vanguard. However, unlike in Mexico and Guatemala, because mestizaje never became an explicit and official nation-building project in Peru, the state did not sponsor Spanish as the official national language, nor did "integration" or "assimilation" ever explicitly and officially signify a bid for the disappearance of "Indians."

Although purist indigenismo à la Valcárcel may have been inconspicuous, its diffusion from the Ministry of Education after the 1940s reduced the influence of assimilationist projects in Peru, while similar programs spread to the rest of Latin America from the Inter-American Indigenista Institute created in the same decade and which had its headquarters in Mexico. During the peak period of inter-American indigenismo (roughly 1940 to early 1960s), state-sponsored Peruvian educational policies, under the leadership of Valcárcel (with the aid of José María Arguedas), advocated bilingual Quechua and Spanish literacy campaigns, for which they promoted the training of Quechua-speaking rural teachers (Contreras, 1996). Meanwhile, during the same period, Mexico, Bolivia, Guatemala, and Ecuador implemented educational policies emphasizing Spanish literacy and promoting the elimination of vernacular languages.[12] It is no accident that in those countries, indigenous intellectuals emerged during the same years to reject forced assimilationist ambitions and launch projects that prominently asserted indigenous identity and rejected national mestizaje projects. Significantly, the indigenous emergence in Guatemala and Bolivia, for example, initially centered around an academic-type of revival of indigenous languages (Smith, 1990; Albó, 1987). A recent study on Mayan cultural activism notes that language is central to Guatemalan indigenous social movements and an important marker of indigenous identity (Fischer and McKenna Brown, 1997:5). Likewise, in Mexico, until the recent adoption of ethnic self-identification on national censuses, speaking an indigenous language was the ultimate marker of Indianness (Gerardo Rénique, personal communication). Similarly, while the Mexican and Bolivian states (backed by either the memory or the implementation of their respective populist revolutions) developed assimilationist policies to solve "the Indian problem," the Peruvian Ministry of Education promoted purist manifestations of "indigenous folklore," policy that was complemented by the absence of a state-promoted mestizo nation against which to assert indigenous identities. Why these efforts did not result in indigenous movements of "ethnic pride" in Peru is explained by the fact that these projects were led by elite intellectuals, who saw themselves as salvaging and uplifting a tradition encroached upon by modernization and despised by Hispanization. A second important element in the explanation is the political experience of the indigenous leadership, who since the defeat of the Tawantinsuyu project in the 1920s, had successfully joined the increasing, leftist, organized opposition that was dismissive of the "culturalist" political activism sponsored by the state. Not surprisingly, indigenous leaders participated in political movements as "peasants" not as "Indians." Confirming the tendency to assume class identities rather than culturalist ones in political projects, the 1969 leftist-inclined military government decreed that the label "Indian" would be banned from official state rhetoric and replaced with "peasant," which by then (and speaking to the ways in which Mariátegui's and Valcárcel's teachings had become part of intellectual and political culture) conveyed images of Indianness. Asserting its propeasant vocation, the same military junta made bilingual (Quechua/Spanish) education official and used indigenous symbols to promote their agrarian reform. All these elements help explain the current absence in Peru of a social movement led under the banner of indigenous ethnic nationalism. Likewise, they help understand the indigenous appropriation of the term "mestizo" and its redefinition to develop de-Indianization as a decolonizing indigenous strategy. Ignored by the state, the label "mestizo" was not charged with the same anti-indigenous culture emotion that the term (and its equivalent, "ladino") carried in Ecuador, Mexico, Guatemala, and Bolivia.

Evidently, neither the absence of self-identified Indian intellectuals nor de-Indianization implies that "the Peruvian peasantry did not succeed in incorporating anti-colonial and ethnic dimensions into its struggle to any real extent" or that among indigenous rural migrants to the cities, "actual ethnic suppression is the norm," as Silvia Rivera, a Bolivian intellectual, has asserted (1993:83, 85). This interpretation, which only too easily equates the process of accepting the stigma adhered to "Indianness" (and therefore silencing the label) with the suppression of indigenous ethnicity, privileges the academic concepts defined by elite intellectuals while ignoring the discourses of grassroots producers of meanings. This kind of analysis also privileges politics defined as overt ideological oral, or written speeches (and thus the politicians who deliver them) while dismissing the manifestations of politics in daily life and those who practice them. But what most prompts my rejection of Rivera's argument is that it seemingly assumes that there is universal value in the cultural/ethnic politics as they currently exist in Bolivia, and that the same cultural political strategy ought to apply in other Andean regions. My analysis instead shows that the conditions in Peru are different for historical reasons, and hence, the political-cultural strategy has been different. After the defeat of Tawantinsuyu's cultural/racial project, indigenous culture along with its emblems and symbols became subordinate practices in explicit political speeches. But, obviously, Andean culture did not disappear from everyday politics. Andean practices — such as being a ritual diviner, or *paqo* — were important in legitimating indigenous leaders, such as Turpo from Lauramarca, to name but one, even during the period when class struggle prevailed and "culture" was not a consideration of the country's Marxist leaders. Quechua, the indigenous language, was used in massive demonstrations in Cuzco's Plaza de Armas, which, during such events, was blanketed with ponchos and chullos, the clothes that express indigenous identity and that were specially and symbolically worn for those occasions. The absence of culturalist (or ethnic) political slogans among the people during that period, rather than a failure to incorporate anticolonial or ethnic rhetoric, represented both a historical shift and political strategy resulting from the earlier defeat of the indigenous movement led by Tawantinsuyu and from the need to distance themselves from state-sponsored indigenismo and its culturalist oral and written language. In earlier chapters I have explained that instead of using modern dichotomies and making "either/or" choices, people like Alejandro Condori or Lucrecia Carmandona use a logic of coupling "rural" and "urban" that cancels the dominant opposition by which indigenous culture is fixed to the countryside. Similarly, in the sixties, indigenous politicians fused cultural symbols and class rhetoric. The huge political demonstrations that they organized in the Plaza de Armas del Cuzco expressed a hybrid political discourse that was not *either* ethnic *or* classist. Instead, it coupled both. During this period the absence of "Indianness" and the assertion of peasant identity were gestures to empower the prevalent indigenous crusade, which in mid-century was for agrarian reform. In addition to what I have mentioned, my study has also shed light over other minor — yet also historically produced — reasons that endorsed the avoidance of indigenous ethnic labels as an efficient political strategy: Indianness was consensually deemed inferior, and Quechua was not synonymous with Indianness, as the elites used the language too. Neither of these trends however led to ethnic suppression. The case of Cuzco shows that the endurance of indigenous practices and discourses are not to be proven or refuted as a function of indigenous verbal compliance with the dominant lexicon, be it racial, ethnic, or classist. The suppression of certain labels and the enhancement of others does not automatically reflect the suppression and enhancement of "the culture" that the dominant meanings of those labels connote, or of "ethnicity" as prescribed in dominant scripts. Quite the opposite: the suppression of Indianness from subaltern practices meant the subaltern rewriting of dominant definitions of indigenous culture to include mestizo identities that exalt rather than extinguish their "authenticity."

Appropriating the term "mestizo," and silencing Indianness has allowed indigenous intellectuals to thrive as cultural producers, free of the geographical, economic, and social boundaries that the label "indio" imposed on them. But, most important, by rejecting self-ascribed Indianness, they have been able to produce dignified lives and indigenous practices. Currently, as a result of de-Indianization, indigenous culture is neither specific to the countryside nor to the urban poor. It is as ubiquitous and heterogeneous as the comparsa dance groups in which street vendors accompanied by university students journey throughout the region's peasant communities and towns, connecting such urban and "decent" icons as the Plaza de Armas with rural and Indian ones, such as the Ausangate Apu, where indigenous ceremonies include both Indian and mestizo participants.

In present-day Cuzco, elite intellectuals have acquiesced to silence

Indianness in their practice of cuzqueñismo. Although — not surprisingly — the local commemoration of the 1992 Quincentennial of the Spanish Conquest went almost unnoticed, one of the celebratory events that the leftist municipal authorities implemented was to replace the Spanish name of the city (with the Quechua "Qosqo," because, according to them "such was the name of the Inca city." Along with this, they coined the word *Qosqoruna,* an all-encompassing label that includes all the inhabitants of the region. It means "person of Cuzco." According to some anthropologists (e.g., Allen, 1988) *runa* is the term that monolingual indigenous peasants use in the countryside to refer to fellow *comuneros* and is thus used instead of "Indian." "Qosqoruna," as coined by the municipal authorities would have the same application, noticeably avoiding allusions to Incaness.

De-Indianization and Discrimination
The Hegemony of Education and the Silencing of Racism

It would be a simplification to present de-Indianization as a successful story of political resistance, moved by feelings of harmony and equality. In fact de-Indianization also reveals complicity between dominant and subaltern groups in identifying "Indians" as the most contemptible members of society. Moreover, this complicity constitutes one basis for the hegemony of Peruvian racism and is located — to use a phrase of Michael Taussig's — in that "sweaty warm space between the arse of he who rides and the back of him who carries" (1987:288). Constructed following the dominant racial interpretation of the regional geography, the conundrum of the cuzqueño subaltern definition of mestizaje that undergirds de-Indianization, is that although it values rural practices, it also accepts the preeminence of urban knowledge and its male (or masculinized) representatives. In spite of its empowering potential, the alternative definition of mestizas/os does not negate their subordination to "gente decente," which they accept even if insolently so. Mestizas represent economically successful indigenous women and occupy an important place among cuzqueño plebeian sectors, as is obvious in major urban religious rituals. Yet they also occupy the social space where "trato" signals the difference between indigenous mestizos from nonindigenous mestizos, or "whites." Moreover, rules for trato are grounded on norms of respect, which contest dominant propositions to evaluate identities based on ascribed features, yet which perceive social hierarchies as legitimate if they reflect educational and economic differences. They thus converge with dominant discrimination even if the latter orders hierarchies according to racial criteria. This convergence makes racism a hegemonic practice, as widespread discrimination measured by educational achievement takes place in the midst of decaying ascribed racial singularities, and even as indigenous mestizos themselves challenge cultural fundamentalism.

At the turn of the century, as Valcárcel (1914) admitted, a university degree could erase the stigma of nondecent origins. Considered proof of an individual's intellectual capacity and moral quality, university education erased stigmas of origin and could lift nonaristocrat middle classes to a higher social status, allowing them to join the cuzqueño elite as gente decente. Notwithstanding the important regional political changes, throughout the century the promise of an academic degree has always been able to raise an individual's social status, even if this transformation was not perceived in racial terms anymore. Adriana's words, quoted in the introduction ("En nuestro pais la raza ya no manda, ahora manda la intelligencia, la educación") reflect how education has maintained its discriminatory potential. Formal education — better yet, university education — is among the few experiences by which an individual can overcome the stigma of lower-class origins. It can take an individual from earning a livelihood in the marketplace — or similar environment — and "promote" him or her to work in an office job, a hospital, a primary school, or a childcare center.[13]

Mid-century intellectuals were thinking simply — or only academically and not politically — when they proposed that the replacement of the concept of race by one of ethnicity would eradicate racial discrimination. The conceptual shifts to "culture" (or ethnic groups) in the 1930s and to "class" rhetoric and "peasant" identity a little later preserved former discriminatory feelings and continued to legitimate them by resorting to the turn-of-the-century cultural fundamentalism that, while originally antiracist, legitimated ideas about the inferiority of "Indians." Obviously, the conceptual shifts to culture and class did not mean the end of discrimination. Moving away from biological notions of race has provided for a comfortable self-absolution of racist guilt, without eradicating culturalist notions of race, which now cohabit with gender, class, ethnic, and geographic discrimination. The hegemonic acceptance of the "legitimate" hierarchies produced by education accommodates the relationship between the dominant and subordinate forms of discrimination. This hegemony of educational hierarchies makes dominant culturalist racism not only possible but apparently unquestionable and thus all the more formidable.

Notes

Introduction

1 Mario Vargas Llosa has articulated his position in his fictional and nonfictional writing. Among his fiction see, for example, *Death in the Andes* (1996), and among what he would consider nonfiction see "Questions of Conquest" (1990b:45–46), and his very consequential "Informe sobre Uchuraccay" (especially 110–114) (1990a:79–114).

2 Such ambiguities in the definition of race disappeared as class, gender, and geography increasingly structured racial relationships and consolidated individual racial labels.

3 Besides Gramsci (1987), the works of Williams (1977); Hall (1986); Laclau and Mouffe (1985); and Mallon (1995), have inspired my treatment of the aspects of hegemony relevant to my study. I thank Florencia Mallon for illuminating discussions and inspiration on this topic.

4 This paraphrases Caryl Emerson and Michael Holquist, "Glossary," in Bakhtin, 1990:427.

5 In Cuzco, for example, dominant male intellectuals performed self-representations within a gendered racial discourse that contested their subordination vis-à-vis dominant Lima intellectuals while deploying discourses that subordinated regional "inferior" others. This process repeated itself at other levels, where subordinate cuzqueño men and women became the superordinators of even more "inferior" others.

6 Other scholars agree on the point. See Stepan, 1982; Barkan, 1992.

7 Paraphrased in Stoler, 1995:72; and Poole, 1997:212.

8 About race as a politically defined notion see Omi and Winant, 1986; Gilroy, 1987; Frankenberg, 1993; Anthias and Yuval-Davis, 1992; Goldberg, 1993; among others.

9 Knox, 1862:497, quoted in Young, 1995:17.

10 Knox published in 1862; Broca in 1864; Spencer from 1864 to 1867 (see Young, 1995; Stepan, 1982).

11 Clemente Palma was a limeño Le Bonian, who denied the possibility of racial improvement by means of formal instruction. He followed the European thinker's belief that "racial souls" could not be

transformed and believed, as did his inspirer, that only eugenic interbreeding between compatible races would improve the Peruvian racial situation. He championed the mixture of coastal inhabitants
with superior races, particularly Germans, whose immigration, he
thought, the government should promote. For Palma the Indian was
a lost cause: "The Indian never attempts to assimilate the progressive
elements of superior men. . . . The Indian race is not and will not be
adaptable to the civilized life of Indo-European races because, as
every other inferior race, the indigenous race has the innate tendency
to isolation, and to reject the ideals, the psychic and the even marital
life of foreigners" (1897:10).

12 Le Bon's influence was also controversial in Mexico. Mexican intellectuals' reactions to Le Bonian theories against miscegenation were
one of the pieces in the construction of mestizaje as the paradigmatic
nation-building process (Hale, 1986:404).

13 Contreras (1994, 1996) makes references to "autogenia." Further
conversations with him led me to Graña's (1908) text, for which I am
very grateful.

14 Gonzales Prada, for example, wrote: "We are always running into
Chinamen who dress, eat, and think like the silk-stocking, suave
gentlemen of Lima. We see Indians in the legislatures, town halls,
courthouses, universities and academies, where they reveal neither
more corruption nor more ignorance than other races. There is such
promiscuity of bloods and colors, each individual represents so many
licit and illicit mixtures, that in the presence of many Peruvians we
could be totally unable to determine the doses of black or yellow
races their organisms contain: nobody deserves qualification as 'pure
white,' not even if they are blue-eyed and have blond hair" (1904:
180–181).

15 The modern conflation of culture and blood had an antecedent in the
colonial principle of "purity of blood," *limpieza de sangre,* which
referred to the heritable transmission of Christian religious traditions
within a family lineage (Gose, 1996; Stolcke [Martínez Alier], 1974).
This principle extended beyond religion to become part of the daily
politics of race and lasted to color academic discourses in early
twentieth-century Peru. But the influence of colonial limpieza de sangre went beyond a mere juxtaposition. In colonial times, the racial-
cum-religious law had included "conversion" as the mechanism to
overcome religious differences and to eventually "purify" a family
lineage after several generations of Christianity. "Old Christians" did
not self-identify as mestizos or mulattos, even if they were biological
hybrids (from our own current viewpoint), regardless of their skin
color. In colonial Peru, the term "mestizo" was reserved for new

converts, or for individuals whose low-class standing made them suspect of having non-Christian origins (Gose, 1996; Schwartz and Salomon, forthcoming).

16 For example, Carlos Wiesse, a positivist geographer, defined race as the assortment of "somatic features (and) some qualities that have later penetrated the organism and have modified its temperament, and above all, the structure of the brain, and have then been transmitted by inheritance, accumulating in its descendants" (1909:252).

17 According to Jorge Basadre Limeño, elite men "dressed in black frock coats and the most fashionable trousers, made by French tailors in the capital, and lived in a happy world, interconnected by marriages within their groups" (Basadre, 1964, 11:127).

18 Transects were made academically popular by Alexander von Humboldt, Antonio Raimondi, and other European travelers (Poole, 1997; Pratt, 1992).

19 Cuzqueñismo was phrased in cultural and political terms. A contemporary historian, whom I consider Cuzco's official historian, defined it as follows: "Cuzqueñismo was the exaltation of everything that was local, including cuzqueño political values, at a moment when the limeños were attempting to coopt the representation of Cuzco in Congress, by taking advantage of their location in the capital and systematically excluding cholos serranos. Cuzqueñismo is a concept and an emotion, a 'feeling' [in English]" (Tamayo, 1992:860).

20 Certainly, indigenismo was neither a twentieth-century creation nor exclusively cuzqueño. In the nineteenth century, indigenista politicians and intellectuals were active in Lima and in the highland departments of Ayacucho and Puno (Gootenberg, 1993; Tamayo, 1982). Likewise, "defending Indians" or claiming Incan legacy to assert regional status were not infrequent practices during colonial times (Walker, 1993; Mannheim, 1984, 1991).

21 This line of thought was close to the Boasian tradition, although Valcárcel did not separate race from culture as Boas did.

22 Brooke Larson (1997) analyzes an equivalent case for Bolivia. There, during a period of "agonizing national-self examination," as she describes the first decade of the twentieth century, the small group that formed the intelligentsia in La Paz constructed a "cult" of anti-mestizaje, and blamed mestizos of every national ill. However, influential individuals among the group of Bolivian thinkers that Larson studies were ready for eugenic solutions aimed at "whitening" their country. This marks an interesting contrast with antimestizo cuzqueños and with promestizo limeños, who favored education to solve the "racial problem." While foreign immigration was indeed promoted in Peru, it was not perceived as an effective means to "improve

the Peruvian race." The reason was, not surprisingly, a racial one: the sexual temperament of Indians, it was claimed, was not compatible with that of Europeans. I explain this in more detail in chapters 1 and 4.

23 Indeed, some limeños would have agreed with Valcárcel in his anti-mestizo feelings. However, the tendency among limeño conservatives was to envision mestizaje (albeit spiritual in kind) as the future of Peru as a nation. The exemplary promestizo proposal came from Víctor Andrés Belaúnde, who proposed a form of cultural mestizaje guided by the precepts of Catholicism (Belaúnde, 1931).

24 Belaúnde identified biological notions of race with "modern bio-logisms" — *biologismos modernos* — and related them to imperialism (1991:53).

25 In this sense, two frequently cited works are Friedlander, 1975 and Bonfil, 1996.

26 It is also a far cry from scholarly definitions of de-Indianization such as the one implied by Guillermo Bonfil Batalla, a Mexican scholar. He criticizes de-Indianization (and thus defines it) as "a historical process through which populations that originally possessed a partic-ular and distinctive identity, based upon their own culture, are forced to renounce to that identity, with all the consequent changes in their social organization and culture" (1996:17). I do not want to criticize a notion of culture that was a product of his times. Neither do I want to raise a superficial critique of a work produced upon a historically constructed vocabulary. However, and though I cannot address the Mexican intellectuals' case ethnographically, I do suggest that one of the problems with his view, no matter how critical it is of dominant mestizaje, is that it continued to (blindly) reproduce the dominant perspective, which assumed the monolithical univocity of the term "mestizo" and identified indigenous culture with Indianness. Delving into alternative meanings of mestizaje, and of the term "mestizo" may also shed light into alternative definitions of indigenous culture and de-Indianization.

27 The popular culture that cuzqueñismo expresses is different from Joseph and Nugent's definition of popular culture as "the symbols and mechanisms embedded in the day-to-day practices of subordi-nated groups" (1994:17). Because this definition appears to be lim-ited to subordinate sectors, if applied to Cuzco, it would obscure the elite's shameful but nevertheless existing practice of judging what they deem proper of the common people. The fact that cuzqueñismo is shared by the grassroots as well as the elite is crucial for the analysis of a popular culture whose peculiarity is the constant struggle over meanings of regional identities.

28 In 1912, this occupational category comprised almost 27 percent of the working population (Giesecke, 1913:30–31). See also Kruggeler, 1993 on artisans.

29 Humberto Luna recorded that the houses located "at the edges of the Huatanay and Chunchulmayo river [had] the worst sanitary conditions" (1913:11). In 1926 these same streets were still considered the "dirtiest zones" (El Sol, March 6, 1926, p. 2).

30 Archivo Historico Municipal del Cuzco, Matrícula de Patentes, Legajo 176, 1906.

31 On shared domestic spaces see Gutiérrez, 1981 and Hardoy, 1983.

32 I thank Isabel Hurtado for this information.

33 According to Milla Batres, 105.6771 kilometers square (1995:285).

34 Omi and Winant (1986) and Stolcke (1993) illustrate similar processes in the United States and Europe respectively.

35 I have borrowed Mary Louise Pratt's notion of "autoethnography." However, while she defines it as "instances in which colonized subjects undertake to represent themselves in ways that engage with the colonizers own terms" (1992:7), I emphasize its relational perspective by referring to the constant dialogue that cuts across multilayered structures of subordination and domination.

36 Because of my limited knowledge of Quechua, I have limited my study to the aspects opened to me through Spanish.

1 Decency in 1920 Urban Cuzco
The Cradle of the Indigenistas

1 For a general overview about colonial disputes on the definition of race or ethnicity, see Kusnesof, 1995; Schwartz and Salomon, forthcoming; Minchom, 1994; Barragán, 1991; Silverblatt, 1995.

2 Although this was the dominant cuzqueño proposal in the 1920s, it was by no means undisputed. Uriel García proposed mestizaje, yet he had to wait for a lull in the regionalism versus centralism debate to do so. This lull came, as I shall explain in chapter 3, in the 1930s.

3 Similar ideas combining equality and distinction were present among modern European elites as well. See Nye, 1993; Bourdieu, 1984; Mosse, 1985.

4 Archivo Historico Municipal del Cuzco, Matrículas de Rentas, Legajo 174, 1906. Matrículas de Rentas were annual records kept for tax purposes. Declarations were required from individuals earning income from property owners, self-employed merchants, and professionals. The large number of informal and transient workers, such as servants, apprentices, and street vendors, were not recorded in

the Matrículas. These workers were certainly considered gente del pueblo.

5   It could well have been that these professionals "devalued" their incomes so as to decrease their annual contribution. However, if this was the case, there is no reason to think why the rest of the workers mentioned above did not do the same.

6   Funeral of Dr. Antonio Lorena, Dr. Luis E. Saldívar (1932:5).

7   *Mozo* was the term used to describe the male mestizo servants (or workers) on a hacienda (Archivo del Fuero Agrario, Documentación Ccapana, letter from Juliana Garmendia [widow of] Herrera to Manuel Navarro, November 14, 1902; December 2, 1903. Quoted in Flores Galindo A. and M. Burga 1980:28.

8   In many other Latin American cities caballeros behaved similarly. About gentlemen of La Paz, for example, Lesley Gill wrote that their "shortcomings would be excused and even admired as long as they did not become indiscreet" (1993:74).

9   "Corona fúnebre de Romualdo Aguilar," Biblioteca Centro de Estudios Regionales Andinos Las Casas (Cuzco: n.p., 1924).

10 *El Sol,* April 16, 1923, p. 2; December 18, 1925, p. 2.

11 Elite funerals contrasted with those of gente del pueblo. A visitor to Cuzco, Hildebrando Fuentes, wrote: "I have observed how Indians bury their dead. They walk inebriated, crying and singing the qualities the deceased had while he or [she] lived. After the last dirt is shoveled, they go to the door of the cemetry and squat [*en cuclillas*] in a circle and continue drinking liquor [aguardiente] to the point that it comes out of their eyes like tears. The gente decente carry their corpses solemnly and pompously. Since there are no carriages [*carrozas*] or public cars, the cortege walks: men on one side of the street, women on the other, because Cuzco is peculiar in that women [*el bello sexo*] also escort the deceased to their final dwelling" (1905:75).

12 In February 1921, a duel took place between José Ignacio Ferro and José L. Mercado. Ferro's sponsors were Jorge G. Ugarte and Alberto Pacheco Concha; Mercado was supported by Manuel M. Chávez Fernández and Mateo Gonzales. The duel was controlled by two physicians: Ferro's was Luis A. Arguedas, while Mercado retained Domingo Guevara. All of these men were wealthy cuzqueños. Ferro himself was a member of an affluent merchant family; Ugarte numbered among the richest urban and rural landowners; Guevara owned the largest hacienda in the surroundings of the city. Indeed, he owned several other estates. Luis A. Arguedas was the owner of the best house in the city and hosted the presidential family in 1928. Several of these men — if not all — held public posts at the moment of the duel (*El Sol,* "Lance de Honor Ferro-Mercado," February 28, 1921, p. 2).

Similar events are described in Valcárcel 1981:202. See also *El Sol,*
February 10, 1914, p. 3; February 16, 1914, p. 3.

13   "La verdad sobre el hecho desgraciado de la Calle Aronés," *El Sol,*
January 18, 1921, p. 3.

14   Patricia Oliart (1994) studied a similar aspect of male limeños self-
representation.

15   Archivo General de la Nación, Ministerio del Interior Book, 237,
December 1923.

16   Several of this woman's male peers — including Julio G. Gutiérrez —
narrated the story to me. I believe she was not the only one. The circle
of young communists was animated by the presence of some women
who might have shared the same ideas.

17   The news was published under the title "Crónicas Sensacionales."
The two men who had tried to rescue Señorita Yépez described her as
"a young lady whose manners and way of dressing clearly indicated
that she belonged to a decent family" (*El Sol,* February 26, 1925,
p. 3).

18   I have obtained information about receptions from *El Sol* (several
dates ranging from 1914 to 1927) from invitation cards and printed
menus housed in the Centro de Estudios Regionales Andinos Las
Casas, and from the private family archives of someone who asked to
remain anonymous.

19   *El Sol,* January 12, 1921, p. 2; January 18, 1921, p. 3.

20   On university reform, see Rénique, 1991; Tamayo Herrera, 1980,
1992; and Valcárcel, 1981.

21   In "Sepelio del Dr. Antonio Lorena: Dr. Luis E. Saldívar" (1932:6).

22   Lorena, 1891, quoted in Rénique, 1991:44. On the importance of
Lorena, see also Basadre, 1964, 10:4575.

23   On colonial indigenismo see Tamayo Herrera, 1980; Cornejo Polar,
1980.

24   Fuentes, 1867, quoted in Poole, 1997; Portocarrero, 1995; and
Oliart, 1994. But see also Palma, 1897. See my introduction to this
book for details.

25   Illustrative of this is the remark of Carl O. Sauer, a U.S.-based geographer who visited Cuzco in the 1940s, and upon meeting Federico
Ponce de León, a lawyer and a botanist, who was then the dean of the
university — a gentleman, and obviously gente decente — described
him as a "Quechua Indian" (Sauer, 1942:76). Ponce de León would
have been appalled had he read this description.

26   About Arguedas, Brooke Larson recently wrote: "Obviously *au cou-
rant* in international racial discourses, Arguedas drew inspiration
from a wide circle of European and Latin American race theorists,
ranging from Gustave Le Bon and Count de Gobineau, to Euclides da

Cunha and Carlos Ocavio Bunge. As much as anyone, it was the conservative Argentine writer, Bunge, who provided Arguedas with the theoretical premises and metaphor of social illness to use in his own study of Bolivia's bio-moral pathology." And she adds about him, "More than biology, history and social conditions, the mountains molded the physical and psychological character of Bolivia's Quechua and Aymara races" (1997:6, 7). No one has yet compared racial thought among the elites of Andean countries. So far, it is significant to notice a common pattern, that I would briefly characterize as the incoherent scientific borrowing of racial ideas, articulated by the elite's coherent political project of removing themselves from the possibility of being mestizos and thus potentially degenerate. Once situated in a racial sanctuary as gente decente, they could join "white" nation-builders in their use of race as the springboard to power. (This might not have been the case of Bunge, nor of Euclides da Cunha, who could safely self-identify as "white.") Argentina and Brazil, unlike Peru, implemented intense eugenic political programs, which may have been related to international evaluation of the national elites' identities.

27 See also Valcárcel's opinions in *El Sol,* July 28, 1920, p. 6.

28 *El Sol,* March 6, 1926, p. 3.

29 The most frequent epidemics included smallpox, typhus, scarlet fever, and measles. See Archivo Histórico Municipal del Cuzco, Legajo 22, 1901; Legajo 24, 1902; Archivo Departamental del Cuzco (hereafter ADC), Prefectura, Legajo 2, 1920–1922. See also Cueto, 1997.

30 Dr. Arguedas publicized his clinic in a commercial announcement published in *El Sol,* July 28, 1927, p. 2. About his participation in the Partido Liberal see *El Sol,* February 10, 1914. Brief biographic data are in Arguedas 1928.

31 *El Sol,* March 2, 1926, p. 3.

32 For the indigenista endeavor to "clean Indians" see Cueto, 1991, 1997.

33 Limeños had similarly protected their health by banning black water carriers (Oliart, 1994).

34 Cutting women's braids was also a part of the agenda of the Sanitary Brigade of Puno (Cueto, 1991:37).

35 Luis A. Arguedas, *El Sol,* June 2, 1926, p. 3.

36 *El Sol,* September 8, 1926, p. 3.

37 About measures against *chicherías* see *El Sol,* April 7, 1913; July 12, 1918; November 3, 1914; September 10, 1914; December 4, 1917; August 7, 1920, among numerous other sources.

38 César Itier has written extensively about Inca theater in Cuzco. I owe

him special gratitude for sharing with me information, conversation, and ideas. His doctoral dissertation has been particularly useful. See Itier, 1990. On theater in Quechua and in Cuzco, see also Mannheim 1984.

39 *El Sol,* January 7, 1914, p. 2.

40 Among the stagings of daily life figured the *Awaj-Kuna* (the Weavers). The scene was described as follows: "Men and women carry out their separate harmonic labors [and] work and sing. Such is the life in Tawantinsuyu: art accompanies it at all times." One of the dances they represented was tika kaswa (Dance of the Flower), described in the program as follows: "In the great rural festivals . . . there existed among the Incas beautiful games and joyful dances that crowned the agricultural tasks" (from the *Programas* of the representations in Buenos Aires and La Paz (personal archive of Ricardo Castro Pinto). The program reflected the influence of Valcárcel's ideas in the representations. In his academic writings he pronounced: "Agrarianism absorbs all their activities and impregnates their existence with love for the land" and "[The] *kaswas* [dances] convoked the entire ayllu to celebrate . . . the triumph of the harvest" (1925:89, 97).

41 Reproduced from the Buenos Aires newspaper *La Prensa* by *El Sol,* November 21, 1923, p. 3.

42 *El Sol,* October 25, 1953, p. 2. Juan Manuel Figueroa Aznar was from Ancash, a highland department north of Lima. Yet his marriage to Ubaldina Yabar linked him to a prominent landholding family. On Figueroa's works and his interpretation of modernism, see Poole, 1992.

43 Connecting language and race was a widespread practice and by no means exclusive to Cuzco. See Appiah, 1992; Young, 1995.

44 Contemporary linguists defined Capac Simi as a colonial hispanicized Quechua sociolect. See several authors in Godenzzi, 1992.

45 *El Sol,* January 7, 1914, p. 2.

46 *El Sol,* May 8, 1926, p. 5.

47 José Lucas Caparo Muñiz, senator, district mayor, director of welfare, dean of the College of Lawyers, wrote a Quechua *zarzuela* (light opera) called *Inti Raimi.* Roberto Barrionuevo, member of a wealthy landowning family from Quispicanchis, performed in *Usca Paucar* in 1914; he also formed part of the Compañía Dramática Incaica that Valcárcel directed. In 1919 he acted in *Yawar Waqaq,* by Félix Silva, another well-known playwright and, indeed, member of a prominent family. Angel Colunge, member of the superior court of Abancay, acted in a work called *Chuqui Illa* (Itier 1995).

48 *El Sol,* January 14, 1926, p. 3. César Itier, a cuzqueño gentleman and contemporary of Zúñiga Cazorla, described him in 1990 as "rather

odd [*medio raro*], vulgar; he didn't know how to treat educated people" (Itier, personal communication).

49 Announcement published in *El Sol*, July 21, 1921, p. 2.

50 *El Sol*, January 12, 1921, p. 2.

51 *El Sol*, September 14, 1921, p. 2.

52 In 1914 for example the staging of *Usca Mayta*, written by Canónigo Rodríguez, was a fund-raiser for repairs to the church of San Pedro (*El Sol*, August 15, 1912, p. 2).

53 "One man's story," unpublished ms., p. 60 (personal archives of Albert Giesecke). I thank Cecilia Israel de Giesecke for allowing me to consult the archive.

54 *El Sol*, January 12, 1921, p. 2; November 17, 1921, p. 2.

55 *El Sol*, June 31, 1922, p. 3.

56 *El Sol*, October 28, 1922, p. 3.

57 *El Sol*, March 9, 1922, p. 3.

58 For an analysis of similar discourses in non-Latin American contexts, see Breman, 1990:123–152. Of particular interest is the section titled "Ethical Policies Combined with Racism" (134–140), which describes a colonial Dutch project similar to indigenismo, also developed during the first two decades of the twentieth century.

2 Liberal Indigenistas versus Tawantinsuyu
The Making of the Indian

1 See Deustua and Rénique, 1984; Rénique, 1991; Davies, 1974; Burga, 1986; Kapsoli, 1977; Flores and Burga, 1980; Glave, 1992; Reátegui, 1978; Hazen, 1974.

2 The law read: "The Nation recognizes the legal existence of the indigenous communities and the law will declare the rights which belong to them." Article 58, Constitution of 1919, p. 357, 1821–1919, *Constituciones Políticas del Peru* (Lima: Imprenta Torres Aguirre, 1922).

3 According to Hipólito Pévez, a peasant born in the coastal department of Ica and one of its initiators, the Comité Pro-Derecho Indígena Tawantinsuyu was founded by members of the Asociación Pro-Indígena. The Asociación had functioned in Lima from 1906 to 1916, and its members were urban intellectuals and rural leaders from several parts of the country, including Lima, Puno, and Cuzco (Pévez 1983). About the Asociación Pro-Indígena see Kapsoli, 1980.

4 According to Pévez, José Carlos Mariátegui had instructed him to twist the president's arm regarding "the Indian problem." In a conversation, the founder of the Peruvian Communist Party had told Pévez: "As secretary [*Secretario de Actas*] you should ask that the

government, which had offered to help raise the condition of the
Indian race from that of slaves, sponsor this Congress" (quoted in
Kapsoli, 1984:294).

5 Hipólito Pévez (probably the only organizer of the event who was
still alive in the 1980s) recalled: "[The Indian delegates] had nothing
to eat, and Leguía gave orders to contract two restaurants for those
who were really hungry, and I remember that they ate there. When
the Congress ended, we also went to explain that they had no return
tickets. So he ordered they be given credits. They received a pass
which they showed on the train or boat, and it was paid for by the
treasury of the respective province or port town. Leguía gave them
substantial credits" (quoted in Kapsoli, 1984:206).

6 *El Tawantinsuyu,* July 28, 1921; quoted in Kapsoli, 1984:251.

7 *Declaración de Principios o Estatutos del Comité Central Pro-
Derecho Indígena Tawantinsuyu.* Published in Pévez, 1983:353–
358.

8 Memorial sent by Ezequiel Urviola and other peasants from Puno to
the parliament on October 12, 1922; quoted in Kapsoli and Reátegui, 1972:125.

9 See *Declaración de Principios,* chapter 12, in Pévez, 1983:357–358.

10 The cuzqueño delegation to the first congress requested that the government build a monument to Manco Cápac, the mythic first Inca
sovereign. Puno delegates insisted that congresses take place during
the last week of August, to commemorate the death of "the last Inca
Atahualpa at the hands of Francisco Pizarro, the Spanish conqueror"
(Pévez 1983:150). Following a congress agreement in August 1922,
"ten thousand Indians gathered in the main square of Puno to commemorate another centennial of the Inca's [Atahualpa's] death," *El
Sol,* August 31, 1922, p. 2.

11 Generally, the delegations of the southern departments of Cuzco and
Puno were the most numerous. Pévez recalled that since the news
about the organization of the first congress was heard in the countryside, "many delegates . . . [went to the association site] to get
information about the congress. . . . They wanted written details
about it, they wanted to know what their role in the congress would
be" (1983:147–148).

12 *La Prensa,* September 10, 1921; quoted in Kapsoli and Reátegui,
1972:182.

13 *El Comercio* (Lima), April 23, 1921, p. 4; quoted in Pévez, 1983:142.

14 *El Comercio,* the *civilista* newspaper, linked the "movements concerned with Indian redemption" to attempts to annex the southern
department of Puno to Bolivia (April 23, 1921, p. 4; quoted in Pévez,
1983:143). One month later, *La Crónica,* a *leguiísta* newspaper, re-

ported that a commission had found Bolivian weaponry in Puno (*La Crónica*, May 26, 1921, no page; quoted in Pévez, 1983:144).

15   *La Crónica*, June 9, 1922, p. 11; quoted in Pévez, 1983:154–5.

16   *El Sol*, October 3, 1922, p. 3.

17   Kapsoli, 1984:237. Kapsoli's information comes from a newspaper published by the committee, *El Tawantinsuyu*, no. 5 (1921), p. 2.

18   Kapsoli, 1984:210–211.

19   *El Sol*, October 22, 1921, p. 3.

20   Office of the Comité Departmental Indígena to the Sub-Prefect of the Province of Canchis, November 1921, Archivo Histórico Municipal del Cuzco, Legajo 85, 1925.

21   *El Sol*, August 2, 1922, p. 3.

22   *El Sol*, August 5, 1922, p. 2.

23   *El Sol*, August 3, 1922, p. 3.

24   Archivo General de la Nación, Ministerio del Interior, Legajo 237, 1923.

25   *El Heraldo*, August 1927; quoted in Kapsoli, 1984:243–244.

26   *La Prensa* (Lima), February 19, 1930; quoted in Hazen, 1974:196. (I have taken it from Collins and Painter, 1990:23.)

27   This of course did not mean the end of gamonalismo as a system in which abusing power was a frequent, and unpunished, practice of local powerful cliques, usually (but not necessarily) connected to state representation. See Paponnet-Cantat, 1994; Poole, 1988.

28   *El Sol*, May 4, 1921, p. 3.

29   *El Sol*, June 2, 1921, p. 3.

30   *El Sol*, June 27, 1921, p. 1.

31   Archivo Departamental del Cuzco, Corte Superior de Justicia, Legajo 90, 1921.

32   Ibid.

33   *El Sol*, July 6, 1921, p. 1.

34   *El Sol*, July 5, 1921, p. 3.

35   *El Sol*, July 4, 1921, p. 2.

36   *El Sol*, July 20, 1921, p. 2.

37   *El Sol*, July 1, 1921, p. 2; July 6, 1921, p. 1; July 21, 1921, p. 2.

38   *El Comercio* (Lima), March 21, 1921, p. 3.

39   *El Sol*, July 7, 1921, p. 4; July 8, 1921, p. 2; July 21, 1921, p. 2; July 23, 1921, p. 3; July 27, 1921, p. 2.

40   *El Sol*, July 21, 1921, p. 2. According to Luis Miguel Glave, Domingo Huarca and Nazario Zaico belonged to the better-off families of Espinar (1992:240–242).

41   *El Sol*, August 9, 1921, p. 3.

42   Ricardo Quiñones, Benancio Arias, Hipólito Nina, Silvano Chuilquetuma, and Manuel López signed it as "Indígenas de Livitaca" (*El Sol*, July 21, 1921, p. 2).

43   *El Sol,* September 24, 1921, p. 2.
44   Archivo General de la Nación, Ministerio del Interior, Cuzco, Legajo 219; also quoted in Burga, 1986:482.
45   *El Sol,* October 10, 1921, p. 2.
46   Archivo General de la Nación, Ministerio del Interior, Legajo 227, 1922.
47   Ibid. As a hypothesis for future research, I want to suggest that the close relationship between the Tawantinsuyu Committee and the prefect might have been at least partially motivated by the fact that Cuzco was a stronghold of antileguiísmo. Significantly, Luis Miguel Sánchez Cerro, the military officer who ousted President Leguía in 1930, was in the early 1920s assigned to the Cuzco military headquarters. Strong antileguiísmo also came from civilians like Víctor Guevara. In the 1930s, Guevara, accompanied by Luis E. Valcárcel, figured among the most active supporters of the ousting of Leguía. The prefects' alliance with some leaders of Tawantinsuyu, might have — at least to some extent — responded to the need to coopt indigenous forces as allies and use them as a threat against the president's foes.
48   *El Sol,* December 14, 1922, p. 3.
49   During his antileguiísta period, early in 1921 José Angel Escalante (who would soon become an ardent leguiísta and Congress representative of his hometown Acomayo) was also accused of organizing a "revolution" against the president and proclaiming himself "the Sultan of Tawantinsuyu." Apparently, the accusation had been forged by a judge who held a longstanding conflict with Escalante's brother. Being a well-known and powerful antileguiísta also made him a good target for these kinds of accusations. *El Sol,* October 21, 1921, p. 2.
50   *El Sol,* September 26, 1922, p. 2.
51   *El Sol,* November 3, 1922, p. 2.
52   Ibid.
53   *El Sol,* December 1, 1922, p. 1.
54   *El Comercio* (Cuzco), December 1, 1922, p. 2.
55   *El Sol,* January 24, 1922, p. 4.
56   *El Sol,* October 30, 1922, p. 2.
57   *El Sol,* March 9, 1922, p. 3.
58   *El Sol,* October 30, 1922, p. 2.
59   *El Sol,* October 31, 1922, p. 2.
60   Ibid. In 1980, José Tamayo Herrera, the writer of the definitive history of Cuzco, said about Luis Felipe Aguilar, "He was the first one to write a book about the Indian in Cuzco and perhaps the only one in whose work one can find the direct version of an existential experience, acquired from reality and not from books" (1980:214).
61   The debate took place in the pages of *El Sol.* See August 7, 1922, p. 2;

August 8, 1922, p. 2; August 9, 1922, p. 2; August 10, 1922, p. 2; October 24, 1922, p. 2; October 30, 1922, p. 2.

62 *El Sol,* August 8, 1922, p. 3; October 31, 1922, p. 2.

63 *El Sol,* August 8, 1922, p. 3.

64 *El Sol,* July 21, 1923, p. 2.

65 Luis Felipe Aguilar in *El Sol,* October 31, 1923, p. 2.

66 About the liaisons between Ayllu *estancieros* and Tawantinsuyu see *El Comercio* (Cuzco), February 15, 1923, no page number; quoted in Deustua, 1984:86.

67 Archivo Departamental del Cuzco, Fondo Oscar Zambrano (hereafter ADC, OZ), Legajo 188, 1923.

68 *El Sol,* February 15, 1922, p. 2 and Archivo Corte Superior de Justicia del Cuzco (hereafter ACSJC), Causa 1054, 1922. "Denunciando atropellos y explotaciones piden garantías." Signed by Crisóstomo Molina, Vicente Huillca, Andrés Alvis, Teodoro Kula, Leandro Alvis, Estevan Masi, and Jacinto Gómez. (Document transcribed and published in Valderrama and Escalante, 1981:35–37.) Although in this communication Alvis (who was also a lieutenant governor from Quinota) self-identified as indigenous, in the future trial against the alleged assassins he would claim mestizo identity, thus revealing the protean quality of regional identities (ADC, OZ, Legajo 188, 1923).

69 Natividad Huilcapacco, Esteban's daughter, denounced the crime in a communication to the judges from Cuzco. In it she declared the local authorities accomplices in her father's death. ACSJC, Causa 648, 1922. "Pide juez y comisión ad-hoc." (Published in Valderrama and Escalante, 1981:45).

70 *El Sol,* June 28, 1922, p. 2.

71 *El Comercio* (Cuzco), January 27, 1923, p. 3; February 15, 1923, p. 3. Quoted in Deustua, 1984:82. See also ACSJC, Causa 15, 1923, "Contra Pedro Cruz, Manuel Layme, y otros por motín, asonada y ataque a mano armada en Haquira," in Valderrama and Escalante, 1981:21.

72 ADC, OZ, Legajo 188, 1923.

73 Ibid.

74 Ibid.

75 Ibid.

76 The document "Denuncian la comisión de varios atroces crímenes" was signed by Mendoza and sent to the Corte Superior in Cuzco. (In Valderrama and Escalante, 1981:38–44.)

77 The letter was published by *El Sol,* December 7, 1923, p. 3 and *El Comercio,* December 19, 1923 (the latter quoted in Deustua, 1984:84).

78 *El Sol,* December 17, 1923, p. 3; *El Comercio,* December 19, 1923, quoted in Deustua, 1984:84.

79 *El Sol*, August 8, 1922, p. 3.

80 On March 9, 1926, Félix Cosio cautioned in favor of Mariano Quispe; he did the same in August 1926 for Carlos Mollco; Nicanor A. Dueñas cautioned Mariano Huillca on August 16, 1926; the next week Alberto A. Salas did the same for Agustín Gómez; Luis Felipe Paredes cautioned Crisóstomo Molina and his wife on November 12, 1926. These men and women had been accused of Berveño's murder. (*Fianzas* in ADC, OZ, Legajo 195, 1926.)

81 Letter from Félix Cosio to the Tribunal Correccional, 5/14/26 in ADC, OZ, Legajo 195, 1926. Two years earlier this lawyer had been appointed as the official judge in the episodes in which Huarca and Alencastre died. Given the unclear circumstances of both deaths, Cosio did not accept the appointment and was lauded for his "humanitarian ideas and [for being] a magnificent and impeccable judge." *El Sol*, October 19, 1921, p. 2.

82 Luis E. Valcárcel wrote a short story ("Ensañamiento") that seems to me to be based on accounts of Berveño's murder. The writer's narrative bears many similarities — if it is not exact — with the information I gathered from the "criminal cause" described in ADC, OZ, Legajo 188, 1923, and Legajo 195, 1926. The story ends by implicitly justifying the crime of a gamonal who had killed Indians to increase his property and wealth. (See Valcárcel, 1975:68–70.)

83 The reasoning was that although the offenders were "semicivilized and illiterate Indians," the infractions were serious, had been "deliberately planned," and revealed the ferocious and socially dangerous nature of the agents of the crimes. *Sentence and Conclusions*, ADC, OZ, Legajo 195, 1926.

84 Signed by the defendants, Leoncio Olázabal, César A. Muñiz, and Luis Sueldo Guevara (ADC, OZ, Legajo 195, 1926).

85 *El Sol*, July 28, 1929, p. 2.

86 *Defensa de Lucas e Ignacio Gómez*, April 2, 1928; *Queja de la sentencia*, April 4, 1928, in ADC, OZ, Legajo 195, 1926.

87 *Código penal*, article 45, p. 15. Positive criminology (Criminología Positiva) was not exclusively an indigenista interest. In 1925, the cuzqueño *hacendado*, anti-indigenista, and lawyer Victor J. Guevara called for a new Civil Code that would consider the special condition of the "illiterate Indian . . . who given his present idiosyncrasy is an incomplete *persona jurídica*, whose deficiency should be considered by the Civil Code to protect him against mistakes and pains . . . just as in the case of legal minors" (de la misma manera que se hace con el menor de edad). *El Sol*, December 5, 1925, p. 3.

88 The example was used by Fernando de Trazegnies (1993:13–57).

89 Piel, 1967:377. It surprised him, he said, that these events had never been studied and attributed this to the "fact" that the actors of re-

bellions were Indians and that the sources were scant or simply inexistent. The lack of sources prompted him to travel to Tocroyoc to collect local memories about the 1921 events. Additionally, he mentioned *El Sol* and *El Comercio*, the two cuzqueño newspapers, as sources of his study (1967:385). He did not quote them, though. Related to the lack of previous studies, it astonished him, Piel said, that the important historian Jorge Basadre devoted only three lines of his production to the analysis of "rebellions" (1967:377). Later, Basadre would reply, in another context, that an explanation for this historiographic void might have been the fact that the events were not important enough, maybe not even rebellions — and therefore were ignored even by local historians such as Luis E. Valcárcel (in Cuzco) or Emilio Romero (in Puno) (Basadre, 1971:20). In an interesting historical twist, the political events of the 1960s and 1970s would grant the 1920s "rebellions" their importance.

90 One of the latest interpretations opposing modern politics and Andean messianic ideologies comes from the prolific historian Luis M. Glave. Analyzing the Tocroyoc case, he states: "The peasants acted within a behavior pattern ruled by symbolism and messianic ideologies expressed through rituals rather than through political or military expressions" (1992:246–47).

91 Cuzqueño members of the Communist Party were urban radical intellectuals who (unlike Mariátegui) had in the previous years distanced themselves from liberal indigenista rhetoric (Gutierrez, 1986). This, and the initial leguiísmo of the Tawantinsuyu Committee may explain the absence of cuzqueño official intellectuals among its urban-based leadership in the early 1920s, when these radicals started their political activities. Some became active in the neoindianista intellectual movement that superseded indigenismo. I will elaborate on this in the next chapter.

92 ADC, Prefectura, Legajo 6, 1931.

93 Mariano Turpo to Gregorio Cayllay, September 1, 1933. Mariano Turpo's personal archive. I thank Aroma de la Cadena and Eloy Neira for allowing me access to Turpo's archive.

3 Class, Masculinity, and Mestizaje
New Incas and Old Indians

1 This book, first published in 1942, represented a synthesis of his previous writings such as *La Realidad Nacional* (1931) and *Meditaciones Peruanas* (1932).

2 Itier, 1995:22.

3 *El Sol,* July 28, 1934, p. 1.

4   Itier, 1995; *El Sol,* September 1, 1937, p. 2.

5   Itier makes a similar remark (1995:40–41).

6   *El Sol,* September 3, 1942, p. 2.

7   *El Sol,* October 6, 1930, p. 4.

8   *El Sol,* July 20, 1946, p. 3.

9   Cuzqueño specialists would appreciate that among them were Julio J. Gutiérrez, Sergio Caller, and Luis Nieto. Their names that are definitely part of the leftist resistance in Cuzco. See *El Sol,* April 5, 1940, p. 2; January 27, 1942, p. 4; September 15, 1943, p. 2; November 11, 1944, p. 2; on Bustamente see *El Sol,* August 8, 1945, p. 4.

10 *Vilcanota,* October 1945, nos. 4 and 5, p. 23.

11 *El Sol,* July 10, 1937, p. 3.

12 *Guía General del Cuzco* (Herscht and Flores, 1937), 28.

13 Thomas Krugeler indicates that "although many masters tried to modernize their enterprises and invested some money into their workshops, these efforts took place in a rather modest scale" (1993:191).

14 This information comes from *El Sol,* July 10, 1937, pp. 5–6 and *Guía General del Cuzco,* pp. 26–27.

15 *El Sol,* August 6, 1937, and personal archive of Humberto Vidal Unda.

16 See Aragón, 1983. In 1992, Radio Tawantinsuyu boasted one of the largest listening audiences of Cuzco.

17 See *El Sol,* February 2, 1915, p. 2; July 9, 1921, p. 2; May 7, 1925, p. 3; February 16, 1921, p. 2. By the end of the decade, in October 1929, Darío F. Eguren Larrea presented the tourist attractions of Cuzco at the Congreso Turístico Suramericano in Lima. He wrote a tourist guide (Larrea, 1929). It was not the first, and would not be the last.

18 Archivo Departamental del Cuzco, Prefectura, Legajo 15, 1940–41, from José Gabriel Cosio to Department Prefect, May 1, 1940.

19 *El Sol,* June 22, 1943, p. 2; March 29, 1949, p. 2.

20 *El Sol,* January 13, 1960, p. 4.

21 *El Sol,* January 22, 1945, p. 2.

22 During the same years, Brazilian intellectuals also asserted the powerful future of their mixed race (see Skidmore, 1993; Stepan, 1991). However, their desire to "whiten" black Brazilians seems to conflict with the nationalist Peruvians' viewpoint. Peruvians might have perceived Brazilians' whitening efforts as yielding to the imperialist racial hierarchies of the United States, and of northern countries in general. On "mestizaje" as a nationalist, anti-imperialist ideology in Nicaragua during the same period, see Gould, 1996, 1998.

23 All citations are in Vasconcelos, 1957:906–942; quoted in Haddox, 1989.

24 On "indología" as Latin American culture, see Vasconcelos, 1926.

The Argentinian thinker Ricardo Rojas had proposed in the 1920s a similar version of trans-Americanism, although politically it could not be articulated as anti-imperialism, given its tendency to include in what he called Eurindia the Hispanic legacy, along with indigenous American legacies. Yet, like Vasconcelos, he proposed mestizaje and opposed purist nation-building programs. He coined the famous statement: *"Ni lo Indio, ni lo gaucho, ni lo español separadamente tiene todo el espíritu nacional"* ("Separately, neither the Indian, nor the Gaucho, nor the Spanish contain all of our national spirit"; quoted in Sánchez, "Colofón," in Valcárcel, 1927:177).

25 Sivirichi, "Prólogo," in Vargas Fano, 1940.

26 See Salazar Bondy, 1954:79–80.

27 My depiction of this group summarizes information presented by Gutiérrez, 1986:12–47.

28 They called the oral periodical *Pututo,* after a wind instrument made from a shell indigenous to the Andes. The pamphlets also had Quechua names: *Kosko* and *Kuntur* (Gutiérrez, 1986).

29 For more on the disputes, see Gutiérrez, 1986:42.

30 García, 1937, "Preface to the Second Edition."

31 Lecture by Francisco Ponce de León, on April 12, 1937. Personal archive of Humberto Vidal Unda.

32 Archive of the Instituto Americano de Arte, Libro de Actas, May 10, 1937, pp. 1–6.

33 Navarro del Aguila, 1945. One of the most influential North American promoters of folklore was Ralph Steele Boggs, who was a member of the Asociación Folklórica de Buenos Aires and of Mexico. Following his suggestion, the neoindianista cuzqueño founded the Sociedad Folklórica del Cuzco in 1944 (*El Sol,* September 1, 1944, p. 2).

34 Personal archive of Humberto Vidal Unda; several documents related to the celebration of the Día del Cuzco, inaugurated in 1944.

35 Julio G. Gutiérrez, personal interview. This man was one of the founders of the cuzqueño branch of the Communist Party.

36 Delia Vidal de Milla, one of the few women who publicly supported neo-indianism remembered: "When I was a kid we spoke Quechua *a escondidas* (we had to hide to do so). My mother did not like it . . . we were ashamed of using a poncho, of dancing and singing *huaynos.* . . . We could do all of that in the hacienda, not when we came back to the city. . . . All that changed years later" (personal communication, August 1991).

37 E. K'allata, pseudonym of Román Saavedra, Cuzco, 1936 (personal archive of Humberto Vidal Unda). He referred to this group as "ladylike men who lack substance and get their inspiration from

ladies' fashion catalogues. They like to hang out and listen to jazz bands" (*El Sol*, July 28, 1930, p. 3).

38 See Handler, 1986, for ideas about the linkages between "sincerity" and "authenticity" in the construction of national traditions in Western countries.

39 *El Sol*, June 11, 1946, p. 3.

40 *El Sol*, April 3, 1942, p. 2. "Recital del música neo-indiana en el municipal" was the title of the article.

41 *El Sol*, January 27, 1948, p. 2. Other quotes about Gomez Negrón: October 8, 1946, p. 3; April 3, 1942, p. 2.

42 Personal archive of Humberto Vidal Unda, radio program for *La hora del charango*, April 1937.

43 The first station, Radio Cuzco, was inaugurated in April 1936. Local civilian, military, and ecclesiastic authorities were all present to celebrate this important civic event. Later, in 1948, the second station was inaugurated, christened Radio Rural, which afterward changed its name to Radio Tawantinsuyu. (See Aragón, 1983:139–143). In 1991–1992 the latter boasted one of the highest audiences of Cuzco.

44 Several ms. documents, August 1938, personal archive of Humberto Vidal Unda.

45 Editorial, *La hora del charango*, September 7, 1937, personal archive of Humberto Vidal Unda.

46 See Itier, 1990:108 for a description of the drama. On dramatizations of el Challakuy, see *El Sol*, August 10, 1941, p. 1.

47 *El Sol*, July 21, 1934, p. 3; July 11, 1934, p. 4; July 28, 1934, p. 1.

48 Humberto Vidal Unda, ms. of speech delivered on seventeenth anniversary of the Día del Cuzco, June 24, 1961, personal archive of Humberto Vidal Unda.

49 Interview with his sister, Delia Vidal de Milla (August 1992).

50 *El Sol*, March 3, 1944, p. 3.

51 *El Comercio* (Cuzco), March 3, 1944; and Vidal de Milla 1985:28.

52 Humberto Vidal Unda, ms. of speech delivered on seventeenth anniversary of Cuzco Day.

53 Both phrases from *El Sol*, March 9, 1944, p. 4.

54 All quotes from the *Revista de la Semana del Cuzco*, 1 (no. 1, 1945): 15–41.

55 Vidal Unda, 1944. The following month, when he was commissioned by the city council to deliver a speech on the fifth anniversary of Prado's government, he said: "Doctor Prado has a clear statesman vision, which allows him to understand the serious responsibility endowed to him as a ruler, to protect our territorial integrity. He has intelligently solved our old quarrel with the northern republic after a series of shameful treaties that were dismembering our sacred terri-

tory." "Discurso en el Municipio," ms. July 1944, personal archive of Humberto Vidal Unda.

56 The Protocol of Río de Janeiro, defining the borders between both countries, had been settled in 1942. In January 1944, the new Ecuadoran president, Velasco Ibarra, and Manuel Prado ratified the treaty (Barrenechea et al., 1978).

57 On occasion of the second celebration of Inti Raymi the following year, a newspaper article pronounced: "Cuzqueñidad is the highest and most noble definition of Peruvianness. Cuzco has led Peru, since the cosmogonic Pirhuas and Amautas, since the times of the Sinchis and the Incas, until the initial years of foreign domination; when Cuzco was denied its leading role, Peru fragmented into pieces and the process of *desperuanización* began. . . . The *peruanización* of Peru, a program and plan for a true national independence, includes — along with a return to the sources of our tradition and of history — the recovery of its primordial territory" (*El Sol,* June 23, 1945, p. 2).

58 *Revista de la Semana del Cuzco* 1 (no. 1, 1945): 13–14.

59 *El Sol,* June 24, 1944, p. 1.

60 Faustino Espinoza Navarro, personal communication. He was the first person to perform the role of the Inca.

61 Vidal de Milla, 1985:33–34.

62 Ms. August 1938, personal archive of Humberto Vidal Unda.

63 *El Sol,* March 6, 1944, p. 2; also several documents in personal archive of Humberto Vidal Unda.

64 *El Sol,* June 24, 1944, p. 4.

65 This account was written by Julio G. Gutiérrez, one of the founders of the Communist Party in Cuzco. He published it in *Revista de la Semana del Cuzco* (1946), under the title "Evocación del Inti Raymi," pp. 71–76.

66 Navarro del Aguila 1946:80.

67 Faustino Espinoza Navarro, personal communication. See also *El Sol,* June 26, 1944, p. 2.

68 The title of the article was "La evocación de la fiesta del Inti Raymi en la capital arqueológica de América," *El Sol,* January 1, 1946, p. 3.

69 Faustino Espinoza Navarro, personal communication.

70 A respected academic folklorist, Víctor Navarro del Aguila, explained the social categories that prevailed in 1945: "In Cuzco the aristocracy are known as 'decent people' or 'cultured'; the same can be said for the middle class. . . . Members of the lower classes are known as *chusma,* ignorant, or indecent" (*El Sol,* July 28, 1945, p. 6).

71 Valcárcel, 1944; quoted in Varallanos, 1962.

72 In fact, when he made these confessions Valcárcel was the first president of the Peruvian branch of the Instituto Indigenista Interamericano, which had its headquarters in Mexico and was created in 1941 by the U.S.-sponsored Pan American Union.

73 See Vargas Llosa, 1990a and Martínez, 1969. The former founded a right-wing political movement in the nineties, while the latter was a leader of the fanatical leftist group Shining Path. About the ironical coincidences between both extremes see De la Cadena, 1998, in Stern 1998.

74 I have carefully read his *Memorias* in an unsuccessful bid to find any indication of his participation in the Inti Raymi. As minister of education he was interested in implementing Quechua literacy campaigns and development projects in indigenous communities. Both aimed at preventing peasant migration to cities, thus restricting the campesino population to their "natural environment." See Valcárcel, 1981.

75 José María Arguedas in *La Prensa*, November 19, 1944; later published in Arguedas, 1976:233–234.

76 *Actas del Comité de la Semana del Cuzco*, May 13, 1952, no page number. Personal archive of Humberto Vidal Unda.

77 Ibid.

78 Several documents, personal archive of Humberto Vidal Unda.

79 The commission that wrote the 1952 *guión oficial* consisted of archaeologists Manuel Chávez Ballón and Luis A. Pardo; anthropologist Oscar Núñez del Prado; ethnomusicologist Josafat Roel Pineda; and painters Mariano Fuentes Lira and Juan Bravo. *Actas del Comité*, May 13, 1952.

80 "Guión General de la Ceremonia de Inti Raymi" in Vidal 1985:50–54.

81 Clippings from *La Prensa* (Lima), June 29, 1952, p. 13. Personal archive of Ricardo Castro Pinto.

82 Ibid., p. 12.

83 Clippings from *La Prensa*, June 26, 1958, p. 12. Another comment, from the prominent playwright Sebastián Salazar Bondy, reads: "The recreation of the Inca feast by the actor Faustino Espinoza was exactly what Dr. Josafat Roel Pineda had announced it would be; a painful mockery. It would have been desirable instead that it were a well-directed spectacle. [What has been presented] undermines historical values . . . [and] uproots the mythical concepts that the masses have about the remote part of our country" *La Prensa*, June 26, 1958, p. 12.

84 The local press from Cuzco said: "The repeated calls and even begging from Cuzco to prevent such a crime against history were not heard, the early warning issued by Josafat Roel Pineda, an expert on

the issue and a representative of the Dirección de Educación Artística was not taken into account. An important aspect of Peruvian history and the current life of the social dynamics of the Indian people has been destroyed." Clippings from *El Comercio* (Cuzco), June 27, 1958, p. 2. Personal archive of Ricardo Castro Pinto.

85 Clippings from *La Prensa* (Lima), June 27, 1958. Personal archive of Ricardo Castro Pinto.

86 Interview with Ricardo Castro Pinto.

87 Speech by Humberto Vidal Unda. No title, September 1944. Personal archive of Humberto Vidal Unda.

88 The nomination was made at a Congreso Nacional de Turismo that met in the city of Cuzco. The idea's promoter was none other than the champion of Inti Raymi, Humberto Vidal Unda (Vidal de Milla, 1985:22).

89 See, for example, Humberto Vidal Unda, 1958; and Yépez, 1965.

90 *Libro de Actas de la Academia de la Lengua Quechua* (no page number, session of May 7, 1960). I thank Mercedes Nino-Murcia for giving me a copy of this document.

4 Insolent Mestizas and Respeto
The Redefinition of Mestizaje

1 *Bases para el Concurso de Belleza Autóctona Departmental,* April 1957, personal archive of Juan Bravo Vizcarra, president of the contest's organizing committee. I thank Juan Bravo, an iconoclastic painter with a long artistic career in Cuzco, for all the help he gave me, patiently accepting me in his own house, where for many hours he recounted stories of the neoindianista counterculture to which he had belonged and shared with me visual and literary material from his personal archive. I recall him as an impassioned cuzqueñista (passion is the characteristic that cuzqueño authorities typically demand with greatest fervor of their constituents) and at the same time as one of the most energetic critics "of the chauvinism of [his] fellow townsmen" (*el chovinismo de mis paisanos*). I discussed with him my own opinions regarding the beauty pageant, disagreed with him, and requested his permission to cite him in my analysis, which he granted.

2 About the use of images of indigenous women in beauty pageants in Guatemala, see Hendrickson, 1991.

3 *Bases para el Concurso de Belleza Autóctona Departmental.*

4 Market women evoke images of power and struggle everywhere. See Babb 1989; Clark, 1994; Horn, 1994; House-Midambe and Ekechi, 1995.

5 *Cuzco Actual, 1953–1954* (Cuzco: Editorial Noticias e Informaciones, 1954), no page number.

6 Ibid.; and Legajo 156 (1952) in Archivo Histórico Municipal del Cuzco (hereafter AHMC).

7 According to an evaluation of the growth of new neighborhoods, "the urban settlements of Dolorespata, Coripata Sur, and Zarzuela appeared between 1958 and 1960; the hills of Puquín and Picchu were starting in 1967; immigrants occupied the right bank of the Watanay River between 1967 and 1973, and created the settlements of General Ollanta, Manco Cápac, and Viva el Perú, among others" (Porcel et al., 1992:18).

8 *Cuzco Actual*, no page number.

9 It was a record of municipality-owned kiosks rented to small-scale merchants called *Censo de Kioskos de Alquiler Municipal de la Plaza San Francisco* (AHMC, Legajo 156, 1952).

10 Immediately after the earthquake the local chamber of commerce took actions intended "to resolve the housing problem, keeping in mind that the sector most affected by the quake had been those serving our businesses, of which 90% have lost their shelter" (AHMC, Legajo 144, 1950).

11 *Cuzco Actual*, no page number.

12 Tax rates did not vary greatly. See Ruiz Bravo, 1983.

13 "Landed properties" became the most important source of municipal income after 1956. In that year a *cabildo abierto* demanded more municipal rents from the central government in Lima. Responding to the request, President Manuel Prado transformed the *impuesto predial*, from a prectural income to a municipal one. See AHMC, Legajo 166 (1956): from the Alcaldía del Cuzco to Manuel Prado, President of the Republic. On the infrastructure of the marketplace, see AHMC, Legajo 168 (1957); Legajo 170 (1959).

14 *El Sol*, March 27, 1923, p. 2.

15 On the emergence of populist parties in Peru see Stein, 1980.

16 *El Sol*, November 24, 1930, p. 2.

17 Ibid.

18 Mariano Turpo to Gregorio Cayllay, September 1, 1933, personal archive of Mariano Turpo. I thank Aroma de la Cadena and Eloy Neira for allowing me access to this archive.

19 Such was the case of the Peru-Cornell Project, which began in 1952. See Osterling and Martínez, 1983.

20 Although the Oxford English Dictionary records the first usage of the noun "ethnicity" in 1953 (Tonkin et al., 1989:14–15; quoted in Stolcke, 1993:24), this concept did not flourish in Peruvian anthropology until the late 1980s, when "class" rhetoric fell in disgrace

as a consequence of the bloody civil war led by the terrorist group Shining Path.

21 In J. L. Rénique, 1991:173; quoted from "La situación revolucionaria en el Perú y las tareas del PCP," in Kapsoli, 1977.

22 AHMC, Legajo 144 (1950), "Temario del primer Congreso Obrero Departamental del Cuzco," April 1950.

23 *El Cuzco,* October 11, 1962; quoted in Rénique, 1991:221.

24 When, as part of the "rural development" state agenda an indigenista commission arrived in Cuzco in April 1958, a group of Lauramarca leaders met them at the airport to talk to them, before the hacendados did. Likewise, they also participated in the communist leagues (Patch, 1958).

25 Eloy Neira, a cuzqueño who worked for a nongovernmental organization in the zone where Lauramarca is located, confirmed this information. Another indigenous leader, Mariano Mamani, Turpo's political successor and himself active since the 1950s, trusted Eloy Neira that he also sought advice for his political actions from local ritual specialists. "When the hacienda manager was hit by the lightning, Mamani interpreted it as a signal favorable to their struggle against Lauramarca landowners," Neira informed me. He also mentioned that Mariano Mamani addressed him as *compañero.*

26 *El Sol,* February 14, 1946, p. 1.

27 "Federación de Trabajadores del Cuzco: Temario del Primer Congreso Obrero Departamental," AHMC, Legajo 144 (1950).

28 Under the title "Cori Ocllo," Roberto F. Garmendia (hacendado, lawyer, and congressman) wrote a newspaper article portraying this woman as exemplary and called her a "Cuzco heroine" (*El Sol,* July 28, 1921, p. 3). The priest and playwright N. Zúñiga Cazorla, author of Inca dramas, wrote the play *Tika Hina* (Like a Flower), in which the argument is the punishment of the Indian woman who falls in love with a foreigner (César Itier, personal communication).

29 References to this theme are recurrent and not the prerogative of Cuzco intellectuals. Antero Peralta, a well-known poet from Arequipa, published in *Amauta,* the prestigious leftist newspaper published in Lima: "[The Indian] . . . is cold, indifferent, inexpressive in his sexual relations. . . . One can observe [in him] a tenuous amorous key, strange, somewhat primitive, essentially instinctive, almost animal. . . . The Indian surely conceives a type of love — difficult for Europeanized mentalities to comprehend — that harmonizes with the metric proportions of his race. . . . The Indians' type of love does not fit within any classification. . . . It approaches the form of love of the 'serious autistics' (cold men, absorbed or withdrawn inside themselves) of which Ernst Kretschner speaks" (Peralta, 1924:29).

30   *El Sol,* March 13, 1926, p. 3.

31   *El Sol,* April 3, 1926, p. 4.

32   *El Sol,* February 13, 1926, p. 3.

33   See Segundo Jara Eguileta, 1936. Also "A mi chola Eduviges" (1944). The *huayno* (a local musical melody) "Valicha" dates from the same period (Tamayo, 1992:861). It is a famous song, absolutely familiar to any cuzqueño, narrating the predicaments of its composer when he fell in love with a mestiza.

34   A lady of Cuzco who enthusiastically participated in the neo-indianist movement told me, "Bohemian men were *choleros,* they liked cholas because they [the men] were eccentric. . . . We believed in folklore, but we did not go to chicherías. . . . That was fine for the cholas but not for *señoritas decentes* [decent young ladies]."

35   *El Sol,* June 7, 1944, p. 2.

36   See among many others *El Sol,* December 12, 1934, p. 3; September 13, 1937, p. 6; February 10, 1944, p. 4; May 9, 1952, p. 5; October 8, 1956, p. 4; May 7, 1956, p. 4; June 8, 1957, p. 5; May 5, 1959, p. 3; December 8, 1961, p. 4.

37   *El Sol,* November 29, 1938, p. 4.

38   *El Sol,* August 9, 1936, p. 3.

39   *El Sol,* January 17, 1930, p. 1.

40   *El Sol,* March 24, 1922, p. 1.

41   For example, when the license of Evarista Loayza, a market butcher, was suspended "for ten days without work." She arranged with the market inspector to pay a fine of seventy soles in order to cancel the suspension and return to her stall immediately (AHMC, Legajo 167, August 8, 1957).

42   AHMC, Legajo 153, July 12, 1951, report from the municipal police officer to the Housing Inspector (*Del vigilante al Inspector de Inquilinato*).

43   In Cuzco anybody could request from the market authority any market woman's "certificate of conduct." The person requesting it could use it as evidence in favor of or against the woman in judicial transactions. Physical and verbal aggressions against municipal market guards were severe offenses that had negative consequences on the "certificate of conduct." AHMC, Legajo 153 (1951), January 25, 1952.

44   See various documents in AHMC, Legajo 93 (1931–1932); 154 (1952); 159 (1953).

45   AHMC, Legajo 114 (1941), May 16, 1941; Legajo 119 (1942), October 28, 1941; Legajo 157 (1953), May 6, 1953; Legajo 165 (1956).

46   AHMC, Legajo 157 (1953), September 17, 1953 and May 26, 1953.

47   AHMC, Legajo 169 (1958), May 9, 1958.

48   AHMC, Legajo 156 (1952), July 15, 1952, letter to the Prefect of the

Department from Paula Castillo, Gregoria de Sueldo, Vicentina Far-
fán, Luisa Vera de Bazán, Honorata Béjar [widow] de Palma, and
others.

49 See various documents from Legajo 119 (1942) to Legajo 167 (1957).

50 AHMC, Legajo 157 (1953), October 28, 1953.

51 AHMC, Legajo 90 (1929–1930).

52 Comunicado de Prensa del Sindicato de Mercados Unidos, Cuzco,
February 18, 1961, personal archive of Agustin Mamani and Lucrecia Carmandona de Mamani.

53 Agustín Mamani and Lucrecia Carmandona de Mamani, personal
communication. Agustín Mamani was the secretary general of the
United Markets Union and organization secretary of the Federación
de Trabajadores del Cuzco. The successful outcome of the strike that
had already caused injuries and one death was largely due to Mamani. He kidnapped the general in charge of the troops of Cuzco and
forced him to halt the repression against the working people of
Cuzco. On other aspects of this strike see Sotomayor Pérez, 1984.

54 AHMC, Legajo 167 (1957), December 16, 1958.

55 AHMC, Legajo 170 (1959), February 2, 1960, *letter from the United
Markets Union to the mayor.*

56 AHMC, Legajo 170 (1959), February 25, 1960, *from the President of
the Butchers Guild to the mayor.*

57 AHMC, Legajo 111 (1940).

58 AHMC, Legajo 167 (1957), April 26, 1958.

59 AHMC, Legajo 119 (1942), September 16, 1942, *request from the
market place women to the mayor.*

60 In 1950 a student of the University of Cuzco wrote, "Mestizo women
dress in pleated skirts and jackets adorned with lace. They use large
heavy shawls that cover their breasts. They wear stiff straw hats,
boot-like shoes. . . . Indian women dress in handwoven skirts, they
only wear small shawls or *llicllas* covering their backs. Their hats
are *monteras* that indicate the region they belong to. Many Indian
women, especially those of the city, are beginning to use a kind of
cheap cotton fabric and felt hats" (Escobar Moscoso, 1950:8). The
historian José Tamayo, following the cultural norms of Cuzco, says
in his latest book: "The women of Qosqo who use Castillian skirts,
a white hat, embroidered shawls and worked in the market were
called, or are called, mestizas" (1992:815).

61 According to a locally produced monograph from the fifties, male
buyers are classified as "decent gentlemen, cholos, and Indians. The
first act superior to the vendor: they do not bargain, but they complain; the cholo is the vendor's equal: they swear if they are not in
agreement"; and finally, "the Indian is treated the worst: he suffers

the abuse of the vendors, even if they themselves are Indians" (Escobar, 1950:5).

62 Teófila classifies wholesale intermediaries as Indians, "puneños" (or *arequipeños*), "gentlemen," and "señoras." The first sell animal products (tripe, lamb heads), vegetables, fresh herbs, coca, and annatto seeds and are peasants from nearby communities; middlemen from Puno and Arequipa — the highest in Teófila's hierarchy — sell "coastal fruit." "Gentlemen" wear "hat and leather jackets" and sell "good beef meat." "Señoras" — like Dionicia — sell tomatoes, potatoes, and other vegetables.

63 Archivo Departamental del Cuzco (ADC), Oscar Zambrano, Legajo 209 (1934).

64 AHMC, Legajo 167 (1957), November 2, 1957.

65 The most popular image of a "buena mestiza" has her wearing fine shawls held by silver pins (*tupu*), gold earrings, and calf-high leather boots. However, Lucrecia is considered a "good mestiza" although she does not dress this way. She has earned the title because of her excellent reputation as a politician.

66 AHMC, Legajo 167 (1957), September 19, 1958.

67 However, mestiza women can also be considered abusive in relation to "little men," or Indians. Once, when a señora dropped her wallet in front of a meat stall, a porter who was standing nearby picked it up with the intention of keeping it. Unfortunately for him, a carnicera had also seen the wallet. She ran out from behind her table and grabbed it from the porter, when he was already opening it. The surrounding vendors deemed the mestiza "abusive."

5 Cuzqueñismo, Respeto, and Social Discrimination
The Mayordomías of Almudena

1 David Cahill (1996:70) presents a good summary of the schedule of the contemporary festival: "The cuzqueño Corpus Christi . . . involves fourteen patron saints, who are carried to the cathedral, where they remain for eight days. The saints commence their *bajada* [descent] on 25 May, and enter the cathedral on June 4 (the *entrada*). Corpus Christi itself begins on 5 June, with the octave of Corpus running 6–12 June, the departure (*salida*) on 13 June."

2 There are usually fifteen participating saint images, each corresponding to a local parish. See Huayhuaca, 1988 for a complete list and description of the participating images and parishes to which they belong.

3 Elite intellectuals have long acknowledged that Corpus Christi is a

festival shared by all cuzqueños. Uriel García, for example, wrote: "Landowners from the nobility together with humble peasants, vain bureaucrats pressed up against mestizo artisans, bejeweled ladies wearing silk beside Indian women, no less decked out in their best polychrome outfits observe or follow the path of the images" (1949: 138). Another cuzqueño intellectual, paraphrasing García reports: "[During Corpus Christi] one finds bejeweled, coifed ladies next to Indian women no less turned-out in eye-catching outfits . . . artisans of modest economic condition dispute the best spot with gentlemen in suits and ties" (Huayhuaca, 1988:118).

4 Newspapers articles reporting the coincidence usually read like this one from *El Sol:* "Corpus is the new cuzqueño Pascua [Easter], the new transformed Inti Raymi of the great crowds of the empire of the children of the sun. . . . The ancient Incaic ayllus were reduced to parishes, which instead of the mummified *mallquis* [ancestors] of the emperors, recreated their totems in the icons and saints of Catholicism" (*El Sol,* June 2, 1945, p. 2).

5 In the *Calendario Turístico del Departamento del Cuzco,* "Programa de Festejos del Cuzco 1982." Quoted in Huayhuaca, 1988:40.

6 *Carguyoq* is a combination of the Spanish "cargo" (duty or task) and the Quechua suffix "yoq" (the person who has something). *Carguyoq* thus means "duty holder." Carguyoq or mayordomos are couples — a man and a woman, generally husband and wife, but also father and daughter, mother and son — charged with giving the festival in honor of a parish's patron saint.

7 The geographical assignment of status and of culture is not exclusive to the Andes. Brackette Williams found something similar in Guyana where "the link between status and locality is often conflated with the relationship between geography and spatial distribution of ethnically identified persons" (1991:71).

8 *El Sol,* July 28, 1945, p. 6. The author of this statement was Víctor Navarro del Aguila, a reputed folklorist.

9 Nancy Scheper-Hughes (1992) makes a similar observation about northeastern Brazil. There, shantytown dwellers classify people according to degrees of poverty, and the lowest ranked are those who have to beg to survive. Stephen (1991) and Stern (1995) also refer briefly to "respeto" as a social category among rural working classes in Mexico.

10 *El Sol,* August 10, 1939, p. 5. In general the press shared the opinion. (See *El Sol,* August 28, 1928, p. 4; July 19, 1938, p. 3; May 21, 1941, p. 2). Intellectuals had copiously contributed to this idea since the early twentieth century. Consider the following quotes: "The religious cargoes are principal sources of the poverty and the alcoholism

that prevail in the indigenous race, and even of the consequences that produce them. In these cargos, great quantities of liquor are consumed and therein the Indian has to sacrifice all his income to fulfill the cargo, which has been imposed beforehand by the parish priest [who teaches] catechism" (Sueldo Guevara, 1921:11). Years later a graduate at the university repeated the idea: "[The cargos] are orders and stipulations that are imposed on the indigenous people, who, because of the very backwardness in which they live, are the most easily influenced" (Rodríguez, 1949:233).

11 On the neighborhood of Almudena, see Villanueva, 1948; Roca Walparimachi, 1992; Flores Ochoa and Flores Nájar, 1992.

12 Several documents, from the Archivo Departamental del Cuzco, Judicial Civil, Legajo 36 (1905).

13 Ibid., Legajo 38 (1907–1912).

14 Ibid., OZ, Legajo 175, 1913.

15 Jorge Flores Ochoa believes that Almudena became a strategic space for the muleteers because one of the commercial routes uniting Cuzco and Chumbivilcas started there: "It was the route to Chumbivilcas, [and] other cuzqueño, apurimeño, and arequipeño provinces" (1992:283).

16 The 1956 participation of the Virgen de Almudena at Corpus Christi was an occasion that cuzqueño university students noticed. "Last year, the Virgen de Almudena appeared," reported one of them (Paredes, 1957:5).

17 La Misa de Despierto takes place in the early morning on August 29. It is the first mass of the novena that initiates the annual celebration. Mass is followed by a procession that serves as a sign to the residents of the streets through which the procession passes that the Virgin's novena has begun.

18 The six mayordomías that were created were Bajada de Trono (descent of the throne), Bajada (descent), Día Central de Corpus (central day of Corpus), Bendición or Octava (benediction or octave), Subida (ascent), and Subida de Trono (ascent of the throne). Each one is celebrated on a specific day; the most important mayordomía is Día Central, followed by the Bendición. Then come the mayordomías of Bajada and Subida, which enact the moments when the Virgin "descends" to the cathedral from Almudena and then "ascends" in the opposite direction. These processions take place the first and last day of Corpus, respectively. The less important mayordomías are Bajada and Subida de Trono. In these ceremonies — which only take place in the Almudenas church — the mayordomos move the image of the Virgin from the pedestal on which she stands during the year (the throne) to the litter that she will use for the procession, and back

again. These ceremonies are on the first and last day of the festival, respectively.

6 *Respeto* and Authenticity
Grassroots Intellectuals and De-Indianized Indigenous Culture

1 As is the case in other places, in Cuzco, dances have been vehicles for the expression of social identities. Anthropological studies of dance as an expressive vehicle of identities is not new. See Mitchell, 1956; Ranger, 1975; Cowan, 1990. Regarding dances in Cuzco see Poole, 1991; Sallnow, 1991; Mendoza-Walker, 1993 and 1994; Cánepa, 1993.
2 Thus most *comparsas* claim origins away from the city of Cuzco, the only real urban center in the region.
3 See Jorge A. Lira, in *El Sol,* April 11, 1940, p. 2; October 10, 1940, p. 2; November 16, 1940, p. 3. In their choice of dance as representative of Indianness, cuzqueños showed strong similarities with Mexican indigenistas of the same period. According to Mexicanist historian, Marjorie Becker, a quote in a pamphlet that circulated among rural school teachers in 1933 read: "Indians have an intelligence which they demonstrate in their artistic efforts, their music, dance, songs, handwork, and plastic arts." From "El Internado Indigena en Matagolpa" in *El Maestro Rural* (1933), quoted in Marjorie Becker, 1995:70.
4 *El Sol,* March 6, 1930, p. 4.
5 Ibid.
6 "Reglamento Interno del Conjunto Folklórico," in the personal archive of Humberto Vidal Unda (APHVU). The Conjunto Folklórico was preceded by the Centro Qosqo de Arte Nativo, which was still active in 1997. Inaugurated in 1924, it was reorganized several times until it assumed the form it now has as one of the most important groups in the diffusion of tourist folklore. In the 1940s, the Centro Qosqo underwent one of many organizational crises and was briefly replaced by the Conjunto Folklórico. This disappeared in the mid-fifties and was replaced by a group of artists, intellectuals, and self-trained Quechua specialists (*quechuistas*), who later reclaimed the name Centro Qosqo de Arte Nativo.
7 With tape recorders, photography equipment, and in some cases camcorders, this is the same procedure that folklore groups use today to copy dances. The word "captación" is still used to refer to the process.
8 "Reglamento Interno del Conjunto Folklórico," article 1, no date (APHVU).

9 Humberto Vidal Unda, message in radio program "La Hora del Charango" (1938) (APHVU).

10 "Distribución del Personal y Programa del Conjunto Folklórico de la Corporación de Turismo." Stock numbers for other folklore groups (such as the Centro Qosqo de Arte Nativo) presenting shows for tourists was similar (APHVU).

11 Propuesta de Reglas de Concursos Folklóricos, 1954 (APHVU).

12 Libro de Actas, Instituto Americano de Arte (2A), March 9, 1961, session.

13 Interviews with Ricardo Castro Pinto and Juan Bravo. See also *El Comercio* (Cuzco), July 14, 1961; newspaper clippings in the personal archive of Ricardo Castro Pinto.

14 So much so that journalists complained that Danzas del Tawantin- suyu had exaggerated the twirlings, and shortened the skirts too much (*El Sol,* July 3, 1961, p. 3).

15 Personal archive of Raúl Montesinos. Program from Danzas del Tawantinsuyu, no date [ca. 1963].

16 "Planilla General de Gastos que el Instituto Americano presenta al Comité de la Semana del Cuzco," *Revista del Instituto Americano de Arte* 9:298–299 (1959).

17 From Eulogio Tapia to the Comité Pro-Semana del Cuzco, July 7, 1955; and from Víctor Pitumarca to Humberto Vidal Unda, June 23, 1955, respectively. Jacinto D. Flores, representing another comparsa, stated: "Our comparsa has merited the praises [it has received] be- cause of its eye-catching costumes, and its unequaled dance, which is nothing but the Andean expression of our land in which the incandes- cent ondulation of our legendary lake is presented" (letter to Hum- berto Vidal Unda, June 7, 1954; APHVU, various documents).

18 The Capac Qolla comparsa alludes to the commercial, social, and cul- tural exchange between the inhabitants of the highest zones (known as *punas,* normally located above 2,000 meters above sea level), and the valleys, also known as *quebradas* or *quechua* (located between 1,200 and 2,200 meters above sea level). For several decades anthro- pologists and historians of the Andes produced innumerable inter- pretations of these interactions which, under the influence of John V. Murra, became an obsession of Andeanists in the 1970s. See John, 1975; and Duviols' classic article (1973). Also Alberti and Mayer, 1974. *Haukaypata* is the Quechua name for the Plaza de Armas in the city of Cuzco.

19 *Collao* is the region of the altiplano that stretches toward the south- east of the department of Cuzco. It occupies the territories of Puno and a large part of Bolivia, and in general is located at a higher altitude above sea level than the principal cities of Peru.

20   *Imilla* is the Aymara word for girl, and *chanasko* refers to the "small-est" of a group.

21   For an extended interpretation of *pablitos* see Allen, 1983.

22   Several documents (1960–1972), personal archive of Raúl Mon-tesinos.

23   Alejandro Condori studied primary school in his town. He is a bi-lingual Quechua/Spanish speaker, the latter of which he speaks with a strong Quechua accent.

24   It is possible that the caporal who initiated Don Alejandro had not danced in the principal Capac Qolla comparsa of Paucartambo, since it is reserved for the most important people of the province. Nonethe-less, in the districts of that province other Capac Qolla groups exist, and his caporal could have belonged to one of them.

25   The *montera, wichicho,* and *llama* are three characteristic elements of this dance. "Montera" refers to a flat rectangular hat, with crushed brims on the sides, which typifies the qollas. The "wichicho" is a small doll dressed like the qollas, which, according to Alejandro, personifies the authority of the caporal. The "llama" in this particular case is a real dead fetus, which carried on the back. Other comparsas carry a live llama. See Mendoza-Walker, 1993.

26   This practice is linked to the cuzqueño celebration of Corpus Christi. Traditionally, each saint that participates in the procession is spon-sored by a workers' guild.

27   I never certified the rumors, but suspect that these were related to the participation of puneños in the mayordomías offered to the Virgen de Natividad.

28   I have borrowed the expression from a metaphor by Ralph Abraham: "Ocean and land are not divided by the coast in a binary fashion, they interpenetrate in a fractal geometry" (1993). I thank Penelope Har-vey for providing this reference.

29   Alejandro, another dancer named Fernando, and I wrote down the verses in a session in which we carefully listened to a tape on which we had recorded the comparsa's song. The lyrics are in Quechua. We translated the words to Spanish in an ensuing session. The English version is mine.

30   Alejandro explained this (and other aspects of the Capac Qolla's per-formance) both to me and to the rest of the dancers while they were practicing or when he was solving a problem in the comparsa. Don Alejandro also answered many of my questions about the meanings.

31   Alejandro explained to me that for the same reason he could not teach me the "dialects" he used.

32   *Pustan* was one of the dialect words that I could not translate, and it remained untranslated as neither the dancers nor Alejandro did it for

me. According to a bilingual teacher (Margarita Huayhua), the word may refer to a calf whose growth is truncated without any apparent reason. She suggested that *taytan wayran pustan* could be translated as "the small wind of the father, the small father of the wind" and *maman wayran pustan* as "the small wind of the mother, the small mother of the wind." The phrases, however, are ambiguous enough in meaning that Alejandro could interpret them differently without necessarily being arbitrary.

33 My "sample" of these qolla comparsas is limited to three versions. In addition to the Haukaypata one, I followed the performance of the Capac Qolla de Ttiobamba del Puente de Ejército. My familiarity with the third version comes from Mendoza-Walker's analysis (1993). This comparsa dances in San Jerónimo, a district near Cuzco. Alejandro is familiar with the San Jerónimo version, which he criticizes. "In the beginning they sing about the imilla, making fun of the imilla, [saying] that they are going to exchange the imilla for products. They should not do that," he says.

34 I have left words in Quechua that Alejandro Condori did not translate into Cuzco Spanish. *Chanasko* is the youngest in a group of brothers and sisters. Alejandro explained that the *imilla* was not just any woman, but the caporal's wife. Likewise, the chanasko was their son.

35 The first account of Yawar Mayu that I have been able to find goes back to the neoindianista era (Alencastre and Dumézil, 1953). It describes a ritual confrontation among several peasant villages located in the province of Canas. It is known as Chiaraque, and starts with a song, performed by the single women of the villages, whose lyrics are similar to the first three verses used in the Yawar Mayu act by the various Capac Qolla comparsas that I am familiar with. The ritual of Chiaraque is sometimes used by Andeanists to refer to the Indians' "secular violence."

36 The lyrics to Yawar Mayu differ in other comparsas. For example, the San Jerónimo version of this number includes these characteristic lines: "I'm not going to cry, even though they see me [covered] with blood, like water, even though they see me in blood, like a river." These lyrics are similar to those sung by the Capac Qolla comparsa of Ttiobamba: "I'm hardly scared, really, seeing me in streams of blood, seeing me in towns with unfamiliar people, seeing streams of blood running. You have to say it's water from the airampo cactus." Both sets of lyrics belittle dangers. I wish to thank Zoila Mendoza for giving me a copy of the complete lyrics from the San Jerónimo Capac Qolla comparsa.

37 Program of Danzas del Tawantinsuyu, no date [ca. 1963], personal archive of Ricardo Montesinos.

7　Indigenous Mestizos, De-Indianization, and Discrimination
Cultural Racism in Cuzco

1　*El Comercio,* December 1, 1922, p. 1.
2　Abril, 1959.
3　Hale, Gould, and Smith (1994) also analyze "mestizaje" from a perspective that takes into account its multiple and competing meanings. They define it as "the outcome of an individual or collective shift away from strong identification with indigenous culture and to the myth of cultural homogeneity which elites imposed from above as a standard part of their repertoire of nation-building." And, crucially, they add: "Most simply, mestizo is a 'mixed race' identity category, and mestizaje refers to the process through which that category is created. But the culturally elaborated content and meaning of the identity varies widely — from the complete suppression of Indianness such that it remains only a distant memory; to a superficial acceptance of the dominant society as a facade, behind which a deep adherence to Indian culture persists; to a simultaneous affinity with multiple cultural traditions not completely compatible with each other." I understand the need to cautiously stress the potential incompatibility of different cultural traditions, and agree with their definition of mestizaje and their political position toward indigenous cultural struggles. However, to avoid slippages à la Vargas Llosa (see the first epigraph in the introduction), I want to make an obvious, yet also cautious remark: this supposed incompatibility of cultural traditions is not inevitable. Among other factors, it depends on the manner in which dominant politicians formulated "mestizaje" as a nation-building project and on mestizaje's impact on indigenous struggles for citizenship, or even survival. Indeed, cultural extermination, as in Nicaragua (Gould, 1998), or physical massacres, as in El Salvador or in Guatemala (Carmack, 1988; Falla, 1994), can be carried out under the banner of national "mestizaje," thus making factual the incompatibility between nonindigenous and indigenous traditions. The popular and subordinate politics of "mestizaje" in Cuzco, however, express an alternative of compatibility with dominant ways, one that does not reflect superficial acceptances of façades, yet also does not imply shedding indigenous ways. As I have explained in the last three chapters, this alternative is not free of friction or contradiction. A similar situation apparently exists in Cochabamba (Bolivia), where, according to Brooke Larson, the subaltern mestizo political culture is characterized by a "fluid in-betweenness" that undermines preconceived dichotomies (between rural/urban,

peasant/laborer, Indian/mestizo), with compatible, yet still conflict-laden articulations between indigenous and nonindigenous cultural traditions (1998:349–353).

4 I find Anzaldúa's work in *Borderlands* enormously inspirational as a new way of writing, thinking, and feeling. Yet in some of her work, I still get a sense of a lingering binarism, that sometimes gets to be surprisingly positivistic. This tone is evident in phrases such as "As a culture, we call ourselves Spanish when referring to ourselves as a linguistic group, and when copping out. It is then that we forget our predominant Indian genes. We are 70–80% Indian." She weights "syncretism" similarly: "The *indio* and the *mestizo* continue to worship the *old* spirit entities (including Guadalupe) and their supernatural power, under the *guise* of Christian Saints" (1987:31, my emphasis). Her apparent leaning toward genetic Indianness (as in the first statement) or cultural essences (as in the second) may be a strategic position (Spivak, 1988b), but I find it difficult nevertheless to reconcile the rigidity they imply with the fluidity of her own notion of "being a crossroads" (195) that explodes binarisms, syncretism, and essentialized hybridities splendidly.

5 I thank Penelope Harvey for having suggested the notion of fractal identities, as well as for having called Roy Wagner's article to my attention.

6 This is not how García Canclini (1995) defines hybridity. I think, as Rosaldo does (1995), that he continues to imply a space between two *discrete* cultural entities, thus maintaining the idea of "purity" and "impurity" initially entailed by modern notions of hybridity (Young, 1995).

7 Although I do not use it in its original sense, I have borrowed the expression "observation point" from Michel Foucault's essay "The Eye of Power." He proposes that the exercise of power needs a center, which he calls an "observation point," which is also the place from which knowledge is registered (1980:148). Although among cuzqueño commoners the act of fixing an observation point implies itself the exercise of power, the observation points are multiple, and this allows for constantly challenging dominant assignments of univocal identities.

8 Rigoberta Menchú, speech at the Latin American and Iberian Studies Program, Distinguished Lecturers Series, October 10, 1995, Madison, Wisconsin.

9 A similar move is illustrated by the proposal of Bolivian indigenous intellectuals to use the term "originario" in an attempt to get away from degrading categories (Sinclair Thomson, personal communication).

10 See also Trujillo, 1993; Barragán, 1992; Smith, 1990; Knight, 1990.

11 In fact there are some attempts to politicize overtly indigenous identities. However many of these are still marginal and mostly promoted
by intellectuals who have not — as of yet — self-identified as indigenous. An exception is the nongovernmental organization Chira-
paq Centro de Culturas Indias (in Lima), which is directed by a female grassroots intellectual, Tarcila Rivera, who self-identifies as
indigenous.

12 According to Carol Smith, many of the first generation of Guatemalan anthropologists supported the Instituto Indigenista in Guatemala, also established in 1945. They aimed at implementing a policy
of indigenous assimilation like Mexico's (Smith, 1995:14). In the case
of Mexico, according to Nancy Leys Stepan, Indians were admitted
into the mestizaje process only if "they adopted the rationalism and
materialism of the Mexican state. . . . The eugenic goal was not to
give value to the variety of biological and cultural types that made up
the nation, but to eliminate heterogeneity in favor of a new homogeneity, the Europeanized mestizo" (1991:15; also in Smith, 1995:32).

13 Not surprisingly the number of university students increased from
215 in 1925 (a little over 1 percent, when the city housed not more
than 20,000 dwellers) to 18,511 in 1988, almost 10 percent in a city
close to 200,000 inhabitants (Tamayo Herrera, 1992:769).

Bibliography

Abercrombie, Thomas. 1991. "To Be Indian to Be Bolivian: 'Ethnic' and 'National' Discourses of Identity." In Greg Urban and Joel Sherzer, eds., *Nation-States and Indians in Latin America.* Austin: Texas University Press. 95–130.

Abraham, Ralph. 1993. "Human Fractals." *Visual Anthropology Review* 9 (1): 52–56.

Abril, Victor. 1959. "El Indio de Colquepata." Unpublished manuscript. Quoted in Catherine Allen, *The Hold Life Has: Coca and Cultural Identity in an Andean Community.* Washington, D.C.: Smithsonian Institution Press, 1988. 27–28.

Adorno, Rolena. 1991. "Images of *Indios ladinos* in Early Colonial Peru." In Kenneth J. Adrien and Rolena Adorno, eds., *Transatlantic Encounters: Europeans and Andeans in the Sixteenth Century.* Berkeley: University of California Press. 232–270.

Aguilar, Luis Felipe. 1922. *Cuestiones indígenas.* Cuzco: Imprenta El Comercio.

Aguilar, Rafael. 1934. "Doctor Cosme Pacheco." *Revista Universitaria* 69: 12–16.

Alberti, Giorgio, and Enrique Mayer. 1974. *Reciprocidad e intercambio en los Andes peruanos.* Lima: Instituto de Estudios Peruanos, 1974.

Albó, Xavier. 1987. "From MNRistas to Kataristas to Katari." In Steve J. Stern, ed., *Resistance, Rebellion, and Consciousness in the Andean Peasant World.* Madison: University of Wisconsin Press. 379–419.

Albó, Xavier, Tomás Greaves, and Godofredo Sandoval. 1983. *Chuquiago: La cara Aymara de La Paz.* La Paz: Centro de Investigación y Promoción Campesina.

Alencastre, Andrés. ca. 1940. "El Challakuy." In *Dramas Del Ande.* Cuzco: n.p.

Alencastre, Andrés, and Georges Dumézil. 1953. "Fêtes et usages des indiens de Langui." *Journal de la Societé des Americanistes* 42: 1–118.

Alencastre, Jaime. 1957. "Los levantamientos indígenas de la provincia de Canas." Unpublished manuscript. In Archivo Departamental del Cuzco, Monografías de Geografía Humana. Vol. 10.

Allen, Catherine. 1983. "Of Bear-Men and He-Men: Bear Metaphors and Male Self-Perception in a Peruvian Community." *Latin American Indian Literatures* 7 (1): 38–51.

——. 1988. *The Hold Life Has: Coca and Cultural Identity in an Andean Community.* Washington, D.C.: Smithsonian Institution Press.

Almanza, Antonio. 1930. *Tambien el indio ruge.* Cuzco: Rozas.

Alonso, Ana. 1994. "The Politics of Space, Time and Subsistance: State Formation, Nationalism and Ethnicity." *Annual Review of Anthropology* 23: 379–405.

Alvarez, Angélica. 1925. "Ayllu Ankcoccahua." *Revista Universitaria* 47: 15–26.

Angeles Caballero, César A. "Los estudios folklóricos peruanos en el último decenio, 1942–1952." *Revista tradición* 6 (15): 12–28.

Anderson, Benedict. 1993. *Imagined Communities: Reflections on the Origin and Spread of Nationalism.* London: Verso.

Anonymous. "A mi chola Eduviges." 1944. *Revista Waman Poma* 3 (16).

Anthias, Floya, and Yuval-Davis Nira. 1992. *Racialized Boundaries: Race, Nation, Gender, Colour and Class and the Anti-Racist Struggle.* London: Routledge.

Anzaldúa, Gloria. 1987. *Borderlands La Frontera: The New Mestiza.* San Francisco: Spinsters/Aunt Lute.

Aparicio Vega, Manuel Jesús. 1970. "Apuntes para el estudio del Corpus Christi cuzqueño." *Revista Wayka* 2: 38–44.

——. 1994. "A los cincuenta años del Inti Raymi." *Revista del Instituto Americano de Arte* 14: 32–40.

Appiah, Kwame Anthony. 1992. *In My Father's House: Africa in the Philosophy of Culture.* New York: Oxford University Press.

Aragón, Luis Angel. 1983. *Historia del periodismo cuzqueño, 1822–1983.* Cuzco: Idea Editores.

Aramburú, Clemencia, and Pilar Remy. 1986. *La población del cuzco colonial: Siglos XVI–XVIII.* Lima: Instituto Andino de Población y Desarrollo.

Aranda, Arturo, and María Escalante. 1978. *Lucha de clases en el movimiento sindical cusqueño, 1927–1965.* Lima: G. Herrera.

Arguedas, José María. 1976. *Señores e indios: Acerca de la cultura quechua.* Montevideo: Calicanto.

Arguedas, José María, et al. 1985. *He vivido en vano? Mesa redonda sobre "Todas las sangres."* Lima: Instituto de Estudios Peruanos.

Arguedas, Luis Alberto. 1928. "Las necesidades sanitarias del Cuzco." *Mundial: Revista Semana Illustrada* (December).

——. 1930. "La mancha azul mongólica: Su existencia entre los peruanos." *Revista Universitaria* 14 (1): 136–147.

Arnold, Bettina. 1990. "The Past as Propaganda: Totalitarian Archaeology in Nazi Germany." *Antiquity* 64: 464–478.

Asad, Talal. 1991. "Afterword." In George Stocking Jr., ed., *Colonial Situations: Essays on the Contextualization of Ethnographic Knowledge*. Madison: Wisconsin University Press. 314–324.

Asturias, Miguel Angel. 1923. *Sociología guatemalteca: El problema social del indio*. Guatemala: Tipografía Sánchez y de Guise.

Avendaño, Angel. 1980. *Cusco: Crónica de una pasión*. Lima: Antarki.

Babb, Florence. 1989. *Between Field and Cooking Pot: The Political Economy of Marketwomen in Peru*. Austin: University of Texas Press.

Bakhtin, Mikhail. 1984. *Rabelais and His World*. Bloomington: Indiana University Press.

———. 1990. *The Dialogic Imagination: Four Essays*. Austin: University of Texas Press.

Balibar, Etienne. 1988. "¿Existe un nuevo racismo?" In Etienne Balibar and Immanuel Wallerstein, eds., *Raza, nación y clase*. Madrid: IEPALA. 31–48.

Banks, Marcus. 1996. *Ethnicity: Anthropological Constructions*. London: Routledge.

Barkan, Elazar. 1992. *The Retreat of Scientific Racism: Changing Concepts of Race in Britain and the U.S. between the World Wars*. Cambridge: Cambridge University Press.

Barker, Martin. 1982. *The New Racism: Conservatives and the Ideology of the Tribe*. Frederick, Md.: Aletheia Books.

Barragán, Rossana. 1991. "Aproximaciones al mundo 'Chhulu' y 'Huayqui.'" *Estado y Sociedad* (La Paz) 8: 68–88.

———. 1992. "Identidades indias y mestizas: Una intervención al debate." *Autodeterminación* 10: 17–43.

———. 1998. *Tramas de la identidad, 1825–1880*. Paper presented at the Race and Gender in Latin America Conference, Cuernavaca, Mexico, June.

Basadre, Jorge. 1961–1964. *Historia de la República del Perú*. 16 volumes. Lima: Ediciones Historia.

———. 1971. *Introducción a las bases documentales para lo historia del Perú*. Lima: P. L. Villanueva.

———. 1978. *Perú: Problema y posibilidad*. Lima: Banco Internacional del Peru.

Barrionuevo, Roberto. 1921. "La provincia de Quispicanchi: Estudio presentado para el doctorado en jurisprudencia." Cuzco: H. G. Rozas.

Becker, Marjorie. 1995. *Setting the Virgin on Fire: Lázaro Cárdenas, Michoacán Peasants, and the Redemption of the Mexican Revolution*. Berkeley: University of California Press.

Beezley, William H., Cheryl English Martin, and William E. French. 1994. *Rituals of Rule, Rituals of Resistance: Public Celebrations and Popular Culture in Mexico*. Wilmington, Del.: SR Books.

Belaúnde, Víctor Andrés. 1932. *Meditaciones peruanas*. Lima: Impresiones y Publicidad.
———. 1940. *La crisis presente, 1914–1939*. Lima: Mercurio Peruano.
———. 1962. *Memorias: Planteamiento del problema nacional*. Lima: Mercurio Peruano.
———. 1965 [1942]. *Peruanidad*. Lima: Librería Studium.
———. 1991 [1931]. *La realidad nacional*. Lima: Editorial Horizonte.
Benavente, Adelma. 1992. "Nishiyama: 50 años de mirar." *Revista del Instituto Americano de Arte* 13: 145–146.
Blanco, José María. 1957. *Cuzco*. Cuzco: Instituto Interamericano de Arte.
Blanco, Hugo. 1972. *Land or Death: The Peasant Struggle in Peru*. New York: Pathfinder.
Bonfil Batalla, Guillermo. 1990. *México profundo: Reclaiming a Civilization*. Austin: Texas University Press.
Bonilla, Heraclio. 1987. "The Indian Peasantry and 'Peru' during the War with Chile." In Steve J. Stern, ed., *Resistance, Rebellion, and Consciousness in the Andean Peasant World*. Madison: University of Wisconsin Press.
Bourdieu, Pierre. 1991. *Distinction: A Social Critique of the Judgement of Taste*. Cambridge, Mass.: Harvard University Press.
———. 1993 [1977]. *Outline for a Theory of Practice*. Cambridge: Cambridge University Press.
Brading, David A. 1984. *Prophecy and Myth in Mexican History*. Cambridge: Latin American Studies.
———. 1991. *The First America: The Spanish Monarchy, Creole Patriots, and the Liberal State, 1492–1867*. London: Cambridge University Press.
Brass, Tom. 1924. "Cargos and Conflict: The Fiesta System and Capitalist Development in Eastern Peru." *Journal of Peasant Studies* 13 (3): 45–60.
Breman, Jan. 1990. "The Civilization of Racism: Colonial and Post-Colonial Development Policies." In Jan Breman, ed., *Imperial Monkey Business: Racial Supremacy in Social Darwinist Theory and Colonial Practice*. Amsterdam: Vrije Universiteit Press. 123–152.
Broca, Paul. 1864. *On the Phenomenon of Hybridity in the Genus Homo*. London: Anthropological Society.
Burga, Manuel. 1986. "Los profetas de la rebelión." In J. P. Deler and Y. Saint Geours, eds. *Estados y naciones en los Andes*. Lima: Instituto de Estudios Peruanos. 467–517.
———. 1988. *Nacimiento de una utopía: Muerte y resurrección de los incas*. Lima: Instituto de Apoyo Agrario.
Burga, Manuel, and Wilson Reátegui. 1981. *Lanas y capital mercantil en el sur*. Lima: Instituto de Estudios Peruanos.

Burns, Kathryn. 1999. *Colonial Habits: Convents and the Spiritual Economy of Cuzco, Peru.* Durham: Duke University Press.

Caballero, Policarpo. 1959. "Auqa Tusuy." *Revista Universitaria* 117: 84–93.

Cahill, David. 1996. "Popular Religion and Appropriation: The Example of Corpus Christi in Eighteenth-Century Cuzco." *Latin American Research Review* 31 (2): 67–75.

Callaway, Hellen. 1993. "Purity and Exotica in Legitimating the Empire: Cultural Constructions of Gender, Sexuality and Race." In Terence Ranger and Olufemi Vaughan, eds., *Legitimacy and the State in Twentieth Century Africa.* Oxford: Macmillan. 31–61.

Campbell, Howard. 1994. *Zapotec Renaissance: Ethnic Politics and Cultural Revivalism in Southern Mexico.* Albuquerque: University of New Mexico Press.

Cancian, Frank. 1905. *Economics and Prestige in a Maya Community: The Religious Cargo System in Zinacantan.* California: Stanford University Press.

Cánepa Koch, Gisela. 1993. "Máscara y transformación: La construcción de la identidad en la fiesta de la Virgen del Carmen en Paucartambo." In R. Romero, ed., *Música, danzas y máscaras en los Andes.* Lima: Universidad Católica.

Carmack, Robert, ed. 1988. *Harvest of Violence: The Maya Indians and the Guatemala Crisis.* Norman: University of Oklahoma Press.

Casaús Arzú, Marta. 1992. *Guatemala: Linaje y Racismo.* San José, Costa Rica: Facultad Latinoamericane de Ciencias Sociales.

Chance, John K., and William B. Taylor. 1985. "Cofradias and Cargos: An Historical Perspective on the Mesoamerican Civil-Religious Hierarchy." *American Ethnologist* 12 (1): 1–26.

Chattarjee, Partha. 1986. *Nationalist Thought and the Colonial World: A Derivative Discourse?* London: Zed Books.

———. 1990. "The Nationalist Resolution of the Women's Question." In Sangari Kukum and Sudesh Vaid, eds., *Recasting Women: Essays in Indian Colonial History.* Rutgers: Rutgers University Press. 233–254.

Chávez Ballón, Manuel. 1955. "Inti Raymi, fiesta del Sol." Cuzco: n.p.

Chevalier, François. 1970. "Official indigenismo in Peru: Origins, Significance and Socioeconomic Scope." In Magnus Morner, ed., *Race and Class in Latin America.* New York: Columbia University Press. 185–196.

Cirese, Alberto M. 1982. "Gramsci's Observation on Folklore." In Anne Showstack Sassoon, ed., *Approaches to Gramsci.* London: Writers and Readers.

Clark, Gracia. 1994. *Onions are My Husband: Survival and Accumulation by West African Market Women.* Chicago: University of Chicago Press.

Clifford, James. 1988. *The Predicament of Culture: Twentieth-Century Ethnography, Literature and Art*. Cambridge, Mass.: Harvard University Press.

Coatsworth, John. 1988. "Patterns of Rural Rebellion in Latin America: Mexico in Comparative Perspective." In Friedrich Katz, ed., *Riot, Rebellion and Revolution: Rural Social Conflict in Mexico*. Princeton: Princeton University Press.

Código penal, Ley 4868: Edición Oficial. 1924. Lima: E. Moreno.

Coello, José M. 1906. "Descripción de los Indígenas de Panti Pata." *Boletín del Centro Científico del Cusco* (11, April).

Cojtí Cuxil, Demetrio. 1997. "The Politics of Maya Reivindication." In Edward F. Fischer and R. McKenna Brown, eds., *Maya Cultural Activism in Guatemala* Austin: Texas University Press. 19–50.

Collins, Jane, and Michael Painter. 1990. "Reconstructing Ethnicity as Class: The Tawantinsuyu Uprising of Southern Peru." *Florida Journal of Anthropology* 6: 21–28.

Comaroff, Jean, and John L. Comaroff. 1991. *Of Revelation and Revolution: Christianity, Colonialism, and Consciousness in South Africa*. Chicago: University of Chicago Press.

Comaroff, John L. 1987. "Of Totemism and Ethnicity: Consciousness, Practice and the Signs of Inequality." *Ethnos* 52 (3–4): 301–323.

Constituciones políticas de Perú, 1821–1919. 1922. Lima: Torres Aguirre.

Contreras, Carlos. 1994. "Sobre los orígenes de la explosión demográfia en el Perú." Documento de trabajo no. 61. Lima: Instituto de Estudios Peruanos.

———. 1996. "Maestros, mistis y campesinos en el Perú rural del siglo XX." Documento de trabajo no. 80. Lima: Instituto de Estudios Peruanos.

Cornejo Bouroncle, Jorge. 1949a. "Los indios." *Revista Universitaria* 96: 155–162.

———. 1949b. *Sangre andina: Diez mujeres cuzqueñas*. Cuzco: H. G. Rozas.

Cornejo Polar, Antonio. 1980. *Literatura y sociedad en el Peru: La novela indigenista*. Lima: Las Ontay.

Corona fúnebre de Romualdo Aguilar. Biblioteca Centro Regional de Estudios Andinos Las Casas. Cuzco: n.p., 1924.

Cosio, Félix. 1916–1917. "La persona jurídica." Archivo Departamental del Cusco, Book 11.

———. 1921. "La universidad ante el problema indígena." *Revista Universitaria* 35: 53–59.

———. 1922. "La misión social de la Universidad del Cuzco." *Revista Universitaria* 36: 3–42.

Cosio, José Gabriel. 1925. *Cuzco histórico y monumental*. Lima: Editorial Incazteca.

Cossio del Pomar, Felipe. 1935. *Cuzco imperial.* Paraguay: Guaranía.

Cowan, Jane. 1990. *Dance and the Body Political in Northern Greece.* Princeton: Princeton University Press.

Crandon-Malamud, Lisbbet. 1993. "Blessings of the Virgin in Capitalist Society: The Transforming of a Rural Bolivian Fiesta." *American Ethnologist* 95 (3): 574–595.

Crumrine, Ross N., and Alan Morinis, eds. 1991. *Pilgrimage in Latin America.* New York: Greenwood Press.

Cueto, Marcos. 1989. "Andean Biology in Peru: Scientific Styles on the Periphery." *ISIS* 80: 640–658.

———. 1991. "*Indigenismo* and Rural Medicine in Peru: The Indian Sanitary Brigade and Manuel Nuñez Butrón." *Bulletin of the History of Medicine* 65 (1): 22–41.

———. 1997. *El regreso de las epidemias: Salud y sociedad en el Perú del siglo XX.* Lima: Instituto de Estudios Peruanos.

Curcio-Nagy, Linda A. "Giants and Gipsies: Corpus Christi in Colonial Mexico." In William H. Beezley, Cheryl English Martin, William E. French, eds., *Rituals of Rule, Rituals of Resistance: Public Celebrations and Popular Culture in Mexico.* Wilmington, Del.: SR Books. 1–26.

Cuzco Actual. 1953–1954. Cuzco: Editorial Noticias e Informaciones.

Da Cunha, Euclides. 1944 [1902]. *Rebellion in the Backlands (Os Sertões)* Chicago: Chicago University Press.

Dandler, Jorge, and Fernando Calderón, eds. 1986. *Bolivia: La fuerza histórica del campesinado.* La Paz: Centro de Estudios Regionales Sociales.

Dávalos, Benjamin. 1904. "La despoblación del Cuzco." *Boletín del Centro Científico del Cuzco* 8 (8).

Davies, Thomas, Jr. 1974. *Indian Integration in Peru: A Half Century Experience, 1900–1948.* Lincoln: University of Nebraska Press.

Davis, P. 1979. *The Normands and Their Myths.* London: Thames and Hudson.

Dean, Carolyn S. 1993. "Ethnic Conflict and Corpus Christi in Colonial Cuzco." *Colonial Latin American Review* 2 (1–2): 93–120.

De la Cadena, Marisol. 1995. "Women Are More Indian: Gender and Ethnicity in a Community in Cuzco." In Larson Brooke and Olivia Harris, eds., with E. Tandeter, *Ethnicity, Markets, and Migration in the Andes: At the Crossroads of History and Anthropology.* Durham: Duke University Press.

———. 1998a. "Silent Racism and Intellectual Superiority in Peru." *Bulletin of Latin American Research* 17 (2): 143–164.

———. 1998b. "From Race to Class: Insurgent Intellectuals *de provincia* in Peru, 1910–1970." In Steve J. Stern, ed., *Shining and Other Paths: War and Society in Peru 1980–1995.* Durham: Duke University Press. 22–59.

Deler, Jean Paul, and Yves Saint Geours, eds. 1986. *Estados y naciones en los Andes*. Lima: Instituto de Estudios Peruanos.

Delgado Zamalloa, Humberto. 1909. "Apuntes etnográficos de los aborígenes del pueblo de Acomayo." *Revista Universitaria* 1: 21–28.

Degregori, Carlos Iván. 1995. "El estudio del otro: Cambios en los análisis sobre etnicidad en el Perú." In Julio Cotler, ed., *Perú, 1964–1994: Economía, sociedad y política*. Lima: Instituto de Estudios Peruanos. 303–332.

De Ipola, Emilio. 1982. *Ideología y discurso populista*. Mexico City: Folios.

De Lauretis, Teresa. 1987. *Technologies of Gender*. Bloomington: Indiana University Press.

De la Vega, Garcilaso. 1991. *Comentarios reales de los Incas*. Lima: Fondo de Cultura Económica.

Del Pino, J. J. 1909. "Psicología de la mujer india." *Contemporáneos* 344–349.

Demelas, Marie-Danièle. 1981. "Darwinismo a la criolla: El darwinismo social en Bolivia." *Historia Boliviana* 1 (2): 17–36.

De Trazegnies, Fernando. "Pluralismo jurídico: posibilidades, necesidad y límites." In Fernando de Trazegnies, ed. *Comunidades campesinas y nativas en el nuevo contexto nacional*. Lima: CAAAP. 13–57.

Deustua, Alejandro. 1941. "Introducción." In Javier Prado, ed., *Estado social del Peru durante la dominación española*. Lima: Imprenta Gil.

Deustua, José. 1984. "Indigenistas y movimientos campesinos en el Cusco, 1918–1923." In José Deustua and J. L. Rénique, eds., *Intelectuales, indigenismo y descentralismo en el Perú, 1897–1931*. Cuzco: Centro de Estudios Regionales Andinos. Las Casas. 69–96.

Diario de los Debates del Congreso Regional del Sur Legislatura de 1919. 1919. Vol. 1. Lima: Imprenta El Comercio.

Díaz Martínez, Antonio. 1969. *Ayacucho: Hambre y esperanza*. Ayacucho: Ediciones Guamán Poma.

Dietler, Michael. 1994. "Our Ancestors the Gauls: Archaeology, Ethnic Nationalism, and the Manipulation of Celtic Identity in Modern Europe." *American Anthropology* 96 (3): 584–605.

Dore, E., and M. Molyneux. Forthcoming. *The Hidden Histories of Gender and the State in Latin America*.

Drake, Paul. 1978. *Socialism and Populism in Chile, 1932–1952*. Urbana: University of Illinois Press.

DuBois, William Edward Burghardt. 1953. *The Souls of Black Folk: Essays and Sketches*. Greenwich, Conn.: Fawcett Publications.

———. 1996. "The Conservation of Races" [1897]. In Eric J. Sundquist, ed., *The Oxford DuBois Reader*. New York: Oxford University Press. 38–47; 101–107.

Dueñas, M. 1956. "Descripción psicológica del indio." 1956. Unpublished manuscript, Archivo Departamental del Cuzco, Monografías de Geografíe Humana. Vol. 10.

Duviols, Pierre. 1973. "Huari y Llacuaz, Agricultores y Pastores: Un dualismo pre-hispánico de oposición y complementareidad." *Revista del Museo Nacional* 39: 153–191.

Eguren Larrea, Darío F. 1929. *El Cuzco: Su espíritu, su vida, sus maravillas.* Lima: Edit Excelsior.

"El Internado Indígena en Matagalpa." In *El Maestro Rural,* July 1933. Cited in Marjorie Becker (1995), *Setting the Virgin on Fire: Lázaro Cárdenas, Michoacán Peasants, and the Redemption of the Mexican Revolution.* Berkeley: University of California Press.

Encinas, José Antonio. 1920. *Contribución a una legislación tutelar indígena.* Lima: Casa Editora E. K. Villarán.

Escalante, José Angel. 1910. "Apuntes acerca del problema de la inmigración europea en el Perú." Archivo Departamental del Cusco, Universidad Nacional San Antonio Abad del Cusco, Book 9-G.

———. 1922. "Cuestiones indígenas." In Luis Felipe Aguilar, ed., *Cuestiones indígenas.* Cuzco: Imprenta El Comercio.

———. 1976. "Nosotros los indios." In Manuel Aquézolo, ed., *La polémica del indigenismo.* Lima: Mosca Azul.

Escobar Moscoso, Mario. 1950. "Ensayos de interpretación de los aspectos sociales y geografía del Cuzco a través del Mercado Central. Archivo Departamental del Cusco, Monografías de Geografía Humana. Volume 8.

Espinoza Navarro, Faustino. 1977. *Guión del Inti Raymi.* Cusco: n.p.

Fabian, Johannes. 1983. *Time and the Other: How Anthropology Makes Its Object.* New York: Columbia University Press.

Falla, Ricardo. 1994. *Massacres in the Jungle.* Boulder: Westview Press.

Fanon, Frantz. 1967. *The Wretched of the Earth.* New York: Grove Press.

Feierman, Steven. 1990. *Peasant Intellectuals: Anthropology and History in Tanzania.* Madison: University of Wisconsin.

Ferri, Enrico. 1911. "Various Short Contributions to a Criminal Sociology." Report 7. *Internationaler Kongress der Kriminalanthropologie.* 49–55, 138–139.

Findlay, Eilleen. 2000. *Hidden Stains: The Politics of Sexuality and Race in Puerto Rico, 1870–1920.* Durham: Duke University Press.

Fischer, Edward F., and R. McKenna Brown, eds. 1997. *Maya Cultural Activism in Guatemala.* Austin: Texas University Press.

Fioravanti, Eduardo. 1974. *Latifundismo y sindicalismo agrario en el Peru: El caso de los valles de La Convención y Lares (1958–1964).* Lima: Instituto de Estudios Peruanos.

Flores Ayala, Timoteo. 1913. "Estudio Sicológico del Sentimiento Indígena." Archivo Departamental del Cusco, Universidad Nacional San
Antonio Abad del Cusco, Book 12.

Flores Galindo, Alberto. 1977. *Arequipa y el sur andino: Ensayo de historia regional (siglos XVIII–XX).* Lima: Editorial Horizonte.

———. 1986a. *Buscando un Inca. Identidad y Utopía en los Andes.* Cuba:
Casa de las America.

———. 1986b. *Violencia y campesinado.* Lima: Instituto Agrario Andino.

Flores Galindo, Alberto, and Manuel Burga. 1980. *Apogeo y crisis de la
República Aristocrática: Oligarquía, aprismo, y comunismo en el
Perú.* Lima: Ediciones Rikchay.

Flores Ochoa, Jorge. 1990. *El Cuzco: Resistencia y continuidad.* Cusco:
Editorial Andina.

Flores Ochoa, Jorge, and Eldi Flores Nájar. 1992. "Mamacha nati,
Mamita Nati: Devoción intercultural a la Virgen Natividad." In
Hiroyasu Tomoeda and Jorge Flores Ochoa, eds., *El Qosqo:
Antropología de la ciudad.* Cuzco: Japanese Ministry of Education,
CEAC. 277–308.

Foster, George. 1953. "What is Folk Culture?" *American Anthropologist*
55 (2): 159–173.

Foucault, Michel. 1980. "The Eye of Power." In *Power/Knowledge: Selected Interviews and Other Writings, 1972–1977,* ed. Colin Gordon.
New York: Pantheon Books. 146–165.

Fowler, Don D. 1987. "Uses of the Past: Archaeology in the Service of
the State." *American Antiquity* 52 (2): 229–248.

Frankenberg, Ruth. 1993. *The Social Construction of Whiteness: White
Women, Race Matters.* Minneapolis: University of Minnesota Press.

Friedlander, Judith. 1975. *Being Indian in Huayepán: A Study of Forced
Identity in Contemporary Mexico.* New York: St. Martin's Press.

Friedrich, Paul. 1977. *Agrarian Revolt in a Mexican Village.* Chicago:
University of Chicago Press.

Frisancho, Manuel. 1918. "Memoria presentada por el señor alcalde
provincial del Cercado del Cuzco Dr. Manuel S. Frisancho, de su ad-
ministración durante el año de 1917." *Boletín Municipal, Organo del
Concejo Provincial del Cuzco* (4) 1–8. Cuzco: Imprenta H. G. Rozas.

Frye, David. 1996. *Indians into Mexicans.* Austin: University of Texas
Press.

Fuentes, Hildebrando. 1905. *El Cuzco y sus ruinas.* Lima: Imprenta del
Estado.

Fuentes, Manuel Atanasio. 1867. *Lima: Esquisses historiques, statisti-
ques, administratives, comerciales et morales.* Paris: Fermin Didot.

Fuenzalida, Fernando. 1970. "Poder, raza y etnia en el Perú contemporáneo." In F. Fuenzalida et al., eds., *El indio y el poder en el Peru.*
Lima: Instituto de Estudios Peruanos. 15–87.

——. 1971. "Poder, etnia y estratificacion social en el Perú rural." In José Matos Mar et al., eds., *Perú hoy.* Mexico: Siglo Veintiuno. 8–86.

García, Uriel. 1937 [1930]. *El nuevo indio.* 2nd ed. Cuzco: H. G. Rozas.

——. 1948. "Ensayo sobre el cholo." *Peruanidad* 2 (3): 210–212.

——. 1949. *Pueblos y paisajes sud-peruanos.* Lima: Cultura Antártica.

García, Uriel, and Albert Giesecke. 1925. *Guia histórica y artística del Cuzco.* Cuzco: Editorial Garcilaso.

García Calderón, Ventura. 1986. "Nosotros." In Luis A. Sánchez, ed., *Obras escogidas.* Ediciones Edubanco.

García Canclini, Néstor. 1993. *Transforming Modernity: Popular Culture in Mexico.* Austin: University of Texas Press.

——. 1995. *Hybrid Cultures: Strategies for Entering and Leaving Modernity.* Minneapolis: University of Minnesota Press.

García Sayán, Diego. 1982. *Tomas de Tierras en el Perú.* Lima: Desco.

Garmendia, Roberto F. [1940]. "Al pueblo del Cuzco." Lima: n.p.

Gerbi, Antonello. 1988. *Il mito del Peru.* Milano: Franco Angeli.

Giesecke, Albert. 1912. "Memoria leída en el acta de clausura de la Universidad del Cuzco en el año 1912." *Revista Universitaria* 3: 26–45.

——. 1913. "Informe sobre el Censo del Cuzco." *Revista Universitaria,* 4: 2–45.

——. 1915. "Memoria del señor rector de la Universidad del Cuzco, Alberto A. Giesecke, correspondiente al año académico de 1915." *Revista Universitaria* 14: 6–11.

——. 1916. "Memoria del señor rector de la universidad, doctor don Alberto A. Giesecke, leída en la clausura del año académico de 1916." *Revista Universitaria* 18: 5–7.

——. 1917. "Marcha de la universidad en 1917." *Revista Universitaria* 22: 5–9.

Gill, Leslie. 1993. " 'Proper Women' and City Pleasures: Gender, Class, and Contested Meanings in La Paz." *American Ethnologist* 20 (1): 72–88.

——. 1994. *Precarious Dependencies: Gender, Class, and Domestic Service in Bolivia.* New York: Columbia University Press.

Gilroy, Paul. 1987. *There Ain't No Black in the Union Jack: The Cultural Politics of Race and Nation.* Chicago: Chicago University Press.

——. 1991. "La Fin de l'antiracisme." *Les Temps modernes* 46 (540–541): 186–187.

——. 1990. "One Nation under a Grove: The Cultural Politics of 'Race' and Racism in Britain." In Theo Goldberg, ed., *Anatomy of Racism.* Minneapolis: University of Minnesota Press. 263–282.

——. 1993. *The Black Atlantic: Modernity and Double Consciousness.* Cambridge, Mass.: Harvard University Press.

Glave, Luis Miguel. 1989. *Trajinantes: Caminos indígenas en la sociedad colonial, siglos XVI–XVII.* Lima: Instituto de Apoyo Agrario.

———. 1992. *Vida, símbolos y batallas: Creación y recreación de la comunidad indígena, Cusco, siglos XVI–XX*. Buenos Aires: Fondo de Cultura Económica.

———. 1996. "Imágenes del tiempo: De historia e historiadores en el Perú contemporáneo." Working paper. Lima: IEP.

Gobineau, Arthur, comte de. 1915. *The Inequality of Human Races*. London: William Heinemann.

Godenzzi, Juan Carlos, ed. 1992. *El quechua en debate: Ideología, normalización y enseñanza*. Cuzco: Centro de Estudios Regionales Andinos Las Casas.

Godelier, Maurice. 1991. *Big Men and Great Men: Personifications of Power in Melanesia*. Cambridge: Cambridge University Press.

Goffmann, Erving. 1959. *The Presentation of Self in Everyday Life*. New York: Bantam Doubleday.

Goldberg, Theo, ed. 1990. *Anatomy of Racism*. Minneapolis: University of Minnesota Press.

———. 1993. *Racist Culture: Philosophy and the Politics of Meaning*. Cambridge, Mass.: Blackwell.

González Prada, Manuel. 1982 [1904]. "Nuestros indios." In Jorge Ruedas de la Serna, ed., *Manuel González Prada: Una antología general*. Mexico City: SEP. 171–183.

Gootenberg, Paul. 1993. *Imagining Development: Economic Development in Peru's Fictitious Prosperity of Guano, 1840–1880*. Berkeley: University of California Press.

Gose, Peter. 1994. *Deathly Waters and Hungry Mountains: Agrarian Ritual and Class Formation in an Andean Town*. Toronto: University of Toronto Press.

———. 1996. "The Inquisitional Construction of Race: *Limpieza de Sangre* and Racial Slurs in 17th-Century Lima." Paper presented at the annual meeting of the American Anthropological Association, San Francisco.

Gotkowitz, Laura. 1998. *Within the Boundaries of Equality: Race, Gender, and Citizenship in Bolivia (Cochabamba, 1880–1953)*. Ph.D. diss. University of Chicago.

———. Forthcoming. "Commemorating the Heroínas: Gender and Civic Ritual in Early Twentieth-Century Bolivia." In E. Dore and M. Molyneux, eds., *The Hidden Histories of Gender and the State in Latin America*.

Gould, Jeffrey. 1996. "Gender, Politics and the Triumph of *Mestizaje* in Early 20th Century Nicaragua." *Journal of Latin American Anthropology* 2 (1): 4–33.

———. 1998. *To Die in This Way: Nicaraguan Indians and the Myth of Mestizaje, 1880–1965*. Durham: Duke University Press.

Gould, Jeffrey, Charles R. Hale, and Carol A. Smith. 1994. "Memories of *Mestizaje:* Cultural Politics in Latin America since the 1920s." Unpublished ms.

Gould, Stephen J. 1985. *The Flamingo Smile: Reflections in Natural History.* New York: Norton.

———. 1996 [1981]. *The Mismeasure of Man.* New York: Norton.

Gow, Rosalind. 1981. "Yawar Mayu: Revolution in the Southern Andes, 1860–1980." Ph.D. dissertation, University of Wisconsin–Madison.

———. 1982. "Inkarri and Revolutionary Leadership in the Southern Andes." *Journal of Latin American Lore* 8 (2): 197–223.

Graham, Richard, ed. 1990. *The Idea of Race in Latin America, 1870–1940.* Austin: University of Texas Press.

Gramsci, Antonio. 1987 [1971]. *Selections from the Prison Notebooks.* Ed. and trans. Quintin Hoare and Geoffrey Nowell Smith. New York: International Publishers.

Graña, Francisco. 1908. *El problema de la población en el Perú: Inmigración y autogenia.* Lima: El Lucero.

Gregory, Steven. "Race, Rubbish, and Resistance: Empowering Difference in Community Politics." *Cultural Anthropology* 8 (1): 24–48.

Gregory, Steven, and Roger Sanjek, eds. 1994. *Race.* New Brunswick: Rutgers University Press.

Guerrero, Andrés. 1994. "Una imagen ventrílocua: El discurso liberal de la desgraciada raza indígena a fines del siglo XIX." In *Imágenes e imagineros: Representaciones de los indígenas ecuatorianos, siglos XIX y XX.* Quito: Flacso. 197–252.

Guevara, Guillermo. 1959. *La rebelión de los provincianos.* Lima: Ediciones Folklore.

Guía general del Cuzco, 1937. 1937. Cuzco: Herscht and Florez.

Guía para la recolección de material folkórico. 1952. Cuzco: Universidad Nacional del Cuzco.

Guillamón, Javier. 1981. *Honor y honra en la España del siglo XVIII.* Madrid: Department of Modern History, Universidad Complutense.

Guha, Ranajit. 1983. *Elementary Aspects of Peasant Insurgency in Colonial India.* Delhi: Oxford University Press.

Gupta, Akhil, and James Ferguson. 1992. "Beyond 'Culture': Space, Identity, and the Politics of Difference." *Cultural Anthropology* 7 (1): 6–22.

Gutiérrez, Julio G. 1946. "Evocación del Inti Raymi." *Revista de la semana del Cuzco,* 71–76.

———. 1986. *Así nació el Cuzco rojo: Contribución a su historia política, 1924–1934.* Cuzco: Derechos Reservados.

Gutiérrez, Ramón. 1981. *La casa cuzqueña.* Corrientes: Universidad del Nordeste.

Guy, Donna. 1991. *Sex and Danger in Buenos Aires: Prostitution, Family and Danger in Argentina*. Lincoln: University of Nebraska Press.

Haddox, John H. 1989. "La influencia de José Vasconcelos en Victor Raúl Haya de la Torre." In Heraclio Bonilla and Paul Drake, eds., *El APRA de la ideología a la praxis*. Lima: Idesi. 135–160.

Hale, Charles A. 1986. "Political and Social Ideas in Latin America, 1870–1930." In Leslie Bethel, ed., *The Cambridge History of Latin America* 4. Cambridge: Cambridge University Press. 367–442.

Hale, Charles R. 1994. "Between Che Guevara and the Pachamama. Mestizos: Indians and Identity Politics in the Anti-Quincentanary Campaign." *Critique of Anthropology* 14 (1): 9–39.

Hall, Stuart. 1986. "Gramsci's Relevance for the Study of Ethnicity." *Journal of Communication Inquiry* 10: 5–27.

——. 1991a. "The Local and the Global." In Anthony D. King, ed., *Culture, Globalization and the World System: Contemporary Conditions for the Representations of Identity*. New York: State University of New York at Binghamton. 19–39.

——. 1991b. "Old and New Identities, Old and New Ethnicities." In Anthony D. King, ed., *Culture, Globalization and the World System: Contemporary Conditions for the Representations of Identity*. New York: State University of New York at Binghamton. 41–68.

——. 1992. "New Ethnicities." In James Donald and Ali Rattani, eds., *Race, Culture, Difference*. New York: Sage Books. 252–259.

——. 1993. "What Is This 'Black' in Black Popular Culture?" *Social Justice* 20 (1–2): 104–114.

——. 1995. "Negotiating Caribbean Identities." *New Left Review* 209: 3–14.

Hall, Stuart, Chas Critcher, Tony Jefferson, John Clarke, and Brian Roberts. 1978. *Policing the Crisis: Mugging the State, Law and Order*. London: Macmillan.

Hall, Stuart, and T. Jefferson. 1975. *Resistance through Rituals*. London: Hutchinson.

Handelman, Howard. 1975. *Struggle in the Andes: Peasant Political Mobilization in Peru*. Austin: University of Texas Press.

Handler, Richard. 1986. "Authenticity." *Anthropology Today* 2 (1): 2–6.

Hardoy, Jorge Enrique. 1983. *El centro histórico del Cuzco: Introducción al problema de su preservación y desarrollo*. Lima: Banco Industrial del Perú.

Harris, Olivia. 1995. "Knowing the Past: Plural Identities and the Antinomies of Loss in Highland Bolivia." In Richard Fardon, ed., *Counterworks: Managing the Diversity of Knowledge*. London: Routledge. 105–123.

Harrison, Faye. 1995. "The Persistent Power of 'Race' in the Cultural and Political Economy of Racism." *Annual Review of Anthropology* 24: 47–74.

Harvey, Penelope. 1993. "Género, comunidad y confrontación: Relaciones de poder en la embriaguez en Ocongate, Perú." In Tierry Saignes, ed., *Borrachera y memoria: La experiencia de lo sagrado en los Andes*. La Paz: Hisbol, Instituto Francés de Estudios Andinos. 113–136.

———. 1994. "Bilingualism and the Consumption of Ethnic Dichotomies in Contemporary Southern Peru." Paper presented at the annual meeting of the American Ethnological Society, Santa Monica, California.

Haya de la Torre, Víctor Raúl. 1935. *¿A dónde va Indoamérica?* Santiago de Chile: Ercilla.

Hazen, Dan. 1974. "The Awakening of Puno: Government Policy and the Indian." Ph.D. dissertation, Yale University.

Helms, Mary W. 1988. *Ulysses' Sail: An Ethnographic Odyssey of Power, Knowledge and Geographical Distance*. Princeton: Princeton University Press.

Hendrickson, Carol. "Images of the Indian in Guatemala: The Role of Indigenous Dress in Indian and Ladino Constructions." In Greg Urban and Joel Sherzer, eds., *Nation-States and Indians in Latin America*. Austin: University of Texas Press. 286–306.

Hernández, Max. 1993. *Memoria del bien perdido: Conflicto, identidad y nostalgia en el Inca Garcilaso de la Vega*. Lima: Instituto de Estudios Peruanos.

Herrera, Fortunato L. 1902. "Chinchereños." *Boletín del Centro Científico del Cuzco* 5 (1–2).

Herzfeld, Michael. 1986. *Ours Once More: Folklore, Ideology, and the Making of Modern Greece*. New York: Pella.

———. 1997. *Cultural Intimacy: Social Poetics in the Nation-State*. New York: Routledge.

Hobsbawm, Eric. 1959. *Primitive Rebels: Studies in Archaic Forms of Social Movements in the 19th and 20th centuries*. Manchester: Manchester University Press.

———. 1990. *Nations and Nationalism since 1780*. Cambridge: Canto.

Hobsbawm, Eric, and Terence Ranger, eds. 1983. *The Invention of Tradition*. London: Cambridge University Press.

Horn, Nancy E. 1994. *Cultivating Customers: Market Women in Harare, Zimbabwe*. Boulder: Lynne Rienner.

House-Midambe, Bassie, and Felix K. Ekechi. 1995. *African Market Women and Economic Power: The Role of Women in African Development*. Westport: Greenwood Press.

Huayhuaca, Luis A. Villasante. 1988. *La festividad del Corpus Christi del Cusco*. Cuzco: n.p.

Instituto Nacional de Estadística e Informática. [INEI] 1994. *Censos nacionales 1993: IX de población, IV de vivienda. Resultados definitivos a nivel provincial y distrital.* Lima: Instituto Nacional de Estadistica.

Isbell, Billie Jean. 1978. *To Defend Ourselves: Ecology and Ritual in an Andean Village.* Austin: University of Texas Press.

Itier, César. 1990. "Le théâthre moderne en quechua á Cuzco (1885–1950)." Thèse du doctorat de nouveau régime. Aix-en-Provence: Université de Provence.

———. 1995. *El teatro quechua en el Cuzco.* Lima: Instituto Francés de Estudios Andinos/Centro de Estudios Regionales Andinos Las Casas.

Jacobsen, Nils. 1993. *Miracles of Transition: The Peruvian Altiplano, 1780–1930.* Berkeley: University of California Press.

Jara Eguileta, Segundo. 1936. "Choladas." *Alma Quechua* 12: 7.

Joseph, Gilbert. 1990. "On the Trail of Latin American Bandits: A Reexamination of Peasant Resistance." *Latin American Research Review* 25 (3): 7–54.

Joseph, Gilbert, and Daniel Nugent. 1994. "Popular Culture and State Formation in Revolutionary Mexico." In Gilbert Joseph and Daniel Nugent, eds., *Everyday Forms of State Formation: Revolution and the Negotiation of Rule in Modern Mexico.* Durham: Duke University Press. 3–23.

Joseph, Gilbert, and Daniel Nugent, eds. 1994. *Everyday Forms of State Formation. Revolution and the Negotiation of Rule in Modern Mexico.* Durham: Duke University Press. 3–23.

Kaplan, Temma. 1992. *Red City, Blue Period: Social Movements in Picasso's Barcelona.* Berkeley: University of California Press.

Kapsoli, Wilfredo. 1977. *Los movimientos campesinos en el Perú, 1879–1965.* Lima: Delva.

———. 1978. *Partido Comunista Peruano: Documentos para su historia, 1931–1934.* Lima: Ediciones Documentos.

———. 1980. *El pensamiento de la Asociación Pro-Indígena.* Cuzco: Las Casas.

———. 1984. *Ayllus del sol: Anarquismo y utopía andina.* Lima: Tarea.

Kapsoli, Wilfredo, and Wilson Reátegui. 1972. *Situacion economico-social del campesinado peruano, 1919–1930.* Lima: Universidad Nacional Mayor de San Marcos.

Katz, Friedrich, ed. 1988. *Riot, Rebellion and Revolution: Rural Social Conflict in Mexico.* New Jersey: Princeton University Press.

Kearney, Michael. 1996. *Reconceptualizing the Peasantry: Anthropology in Global Perspective.* Boulder: Westview Press.

Kertzer, David. 1988. *Rituals, Politics and Power.* New Haven: Yale University Press.

Klaren, Peter. 1986. "The Origins of Modern Peru." In Leslie Bethel, ed., *The Cambridge History of Latin America* 1. Cambridge: Cambridge University Press. 587–640.

Klor de Alva, Jorge J. 1995. "The Postcolonization of the (Latin American) Experience: A Reconsideration of 'Colonialism,' 'Postcolonialism,' and 'Mestizaje.' " In Gyan Prakash, ed., *After Colonialism: Imperial Histories and Postcolonial Displacements*. Princeton: Princeton University Press. 241–275.

Knight, Alan. 1990. "Racism, Revolution and *Indigenismo*: Mexico, 1910–1940." In Richard Graham, ed., *The Idea of Race in Latin America, 1870–1940*. Austin: University of Texas Press.

———. 1994. "Popular Culture and the Revolutionary State in Mexico, 1910–1940." *Hispanic American Historical Review* 74 (3): 393–444.

Knox, Robert. 1862. *The Races of Men: A Philosophical Inquiry into the Influence of Race over the Destinies of Nations*. London: Renshaw.

Kruggeler, Thomas. 1993. "Unreliable Drunkards or Honorable Citizens? Artisans in Search of Their Place in the Cuzco Society, 1825–1930." Ph.D. dissertation, University of Illinois at Urbana-Champaign.

Kusnesof, Elizabeth Anne. 1995. "Ethnic and Gender Influences on 'Spanish' Creole Society in Colonial Spanish America." *Colonial Latin American Review* 4 (1): 153–202.

Laclau, Ernesto. 1977. *Politics and Ideology in Marxist Theory: Capitalism, Fascism, and Populism*. London: New Left Books.

Laclau, Ernesto, and Chantal Mouffe. 1985. *Hegemony and Socialist Strategy: Towards a Radical Democratic Politics*. London: Verso.

Landes, Joan B. 1988. *Women and the Public Sphere in the Age of the French Revolution*. Ithaca: Cornell University Press.

Larson, Brooke. 1997. "Redeemed Indians, Barbarianized Cholos: The Cultural Politics of Nation Making in Bolivia, 1900–1910." Paper presented at the 20th annual meeting of Latin American Studies Association, Guadalajara, Mexico.

———. 1998 [1988]. *Cochabamba, 1550–1900: Colonialism and Agrarian Transformation in Bolivia*. Durham: Duke University Press.

———. Forthcoming. "Andean Highland Peasants and the Trials of Nation-Making during the Nineteenth Century." In S. Schwartz and F. Salomon, eds., *The Cambridge History of Native American Peoples: South America*.

Le Bon, Gustave. 1979 [1913]. "Aphorisms of Present Times" and "The Psychology of Revolutions." In Alice Widener, ed., *Gustave Le Bon: The Man and His Works*. Indianapolis: Liberty Press. 269–304, 229–266.

Lienhard, Martin. 1992. *Testimonios, cartas y manifiestos indígenas (desde la Conquista hasta comienzos del s. XX)*. Venezuela: Biblioteca Ayacucho.

Lira, Jorge A. 1960. "La mujer andina y la biblia." *Revista del Instituto Americano de Arte* 10: 111–117.

Longsdale, John. 1989. *Wealth, Power, and Civic Virtue in Kikuyu Political Thought*. Oxford: Oxford University Press.

Loreno, Antonio. 1905. "Discurso del catedrático Dr. D. Antonio Lorena." *Velada Literario-Musical celebrada en Honor de S.E. el Presidente de la República D. D. José Pardo*. Cuzco: Imprenta Minotauro.

———. 1931 [1908]. "Materiales para la antropología del Cuzco." *Revista Universitaria* 2: 17–27.

———. 1932 [1891]. "Estado social del Cuzco (abril 1891)." *Revista Universitaria* 21: 37–51.

Lovón Zavala, Gerardo, and Rocío Moscoso Blanco. 1981. *Investigación sobre desarrollo regional, Cusco, 1950–1980. Informe: Sector turismo*. Cusco: Centro de Estudios Regionales Andinos Las Casas.

Luna, Humberto. 1913. "Paidología del Niño del Cuzco." *Revista Universitaria* 7: 3–22.

———. 1919. "Observaciones criminológicas." Unpublished manuscript. Archivo Departamental del Cusco, Book 12.

Lynch, John. 1992. *Caudillos in Spanish America, 1800–1850*. Oxford: Clarendon Press.

McClintock, Anne. 1995. *Imperial Leather: Race, Gender and Sexuality in the Colonial Contest*. New York: Routledge.

Macera, Pablo. 1977. *Trabajos de historia 4*. Lima: Instituto Nacional de Cultura.

———. 1988. *Rebelión india*. Lima: Ediciones Rikchay.

Mallon, Florencia. 1995. *Peasant and Nation: The Making of Postcolonial Mexico and Peru*. Berkeley: University of California Press.

Mannheim, Bruce. 1984. "*Una nación acorralada*: Southern Peruvian Quechua Language Planning and Policies in Historical Perspective." *Language and Society* 13: 291–309.

Mannheim, Bruce. 1991. *The Language of the Inca since the European Invasion*. Austin: University of Texas Press.

Manrique, Nelson. 1981. *Las guerrillas indígenas en la guerra con Chile: Campesinado y nación*. Lima: Centro de Investigaciones Campesinas.

———. 1988. *Yawar Mayu: Sociedades terratenientes serranas, 1879–1910*. Lima: Instituto Francés de Estudios Andinos, DESCO.

Maraval, José. 1979. *Poder, honor y Élites en el siglo XVII*. Madrid: siglo XXI.

Marco, Asunción. 1989. "La historia que no fue contada." *Crónicas Urbanas* 1: 6–19.

Marcoy, Paul. 1961. "Viajes a través de la América del Sur." In Porras Barrenechea Raúl, ed., *Antología del Cuzco*. Lima: Librería Internacional.

Mariscal, Rosendo. 1918. "Condición jurídica y social del indio." Unpublished manuscript, Archivo Departamental del Cusco, Book 12.

Mariátegui, José Carlos. 1929. "Civilización y Feudalidad." *Mundial* 467, May 31.

———. 1968 [1928]. *Siete ensayos de interpretación de la realidad peruana*. Lima: Amauta.

———. 1981 [1929]. "El problema de las razas en América latina." In *Ideología y Política*. Lima: Amauta.

Marret, C., and C. Leggon. 1985. *Research in Race and Ethnic Relations: A Research Annual*. Greenwich, Conn.: JAI Press.

Martínez Peláez, Severo. 1970. *La patria del criollo: Ensayo de interpretación de la realidad colonial guatemalteca*. Guatemala: Editorial Universitaria.

Masís, Horacio (pseudonym). 1927. "Las walkirias del Ande." *La Sierra* 2: 7.

Mathews, Holly. 1985. " 'We Are Mayordomo': A Reinterpretation of Women's Role in the Mexican Cargo System." *American Ethnologist* 17: 285–301.

Mayer, Dora. 1921. *El indígena peruano, a los cien años de república libre e independiente*. Lima: n.p.

Mayer, Enrique. 1970. "Mestizo e indio: El contexto social de las relaciones interétnicas." In Fernando Fuenzalida et al., eds., *El indio y el poder en el Peru*. Lima: Instituto de Estudios Peruanos.

Mendoza-Walker, Zoila. 1993. "Shaping Society through Dance: Mestizo Ritual Performance in the Southern Peruvian Andes." Ph.D. dissertation, University of Chicago.

———. 1994. "Contesting Identities through Dance: Mestizo Performance in the Southern Andes of Peru." *Repercussions* 50–80.

Meyers, Albert, and Diane Hopkins, eds. 1988. *Manipulating the Saints: Religious Brotherhoods and Social Integration in Post-Conquest Latin America*. Hamburg: Wayasbah.

Michaels, Walter Benn. 1992. "Race into Culture: A Critical Genealogy of Cultural Identity." *Critical Inquiry* 18 (4): 655–685.

Milla Batres, Carlos. 1995. *Atlas geográfico y documental del Perú*. Lima: Milla Batres.

Minchom, Martin. 1994. *The People of Quito, 1690–1810: Change and Unrest in the Underclass*. Boulder: Westview Press.

Mishkin, Bernard. 1916. "The Contemporary Quechua." In Julian Steward, ed., *Handbook of South American Indians* 2. Washington: Bureau of American Ethnology. 411–470.

Mitchell, Clyde. 1956. *The Kalela Dance: Aspects of Social Relationships among Urban Africans in Northern Rhodesia*. Manchester: Manchester University Press.

Montagu, Ashley. 1962. "The Concept of Race," *American Anthropologist* 64 (5): 919–928.

Moore, Sally Falk, and Barbara Myerhoff, eds. 1977. *Secular Ritual*. Amsterdam: Van Jorcum.

More, Ernesto. 1960. *Reportajes con radar*. Lima: Minerva.

Morell, Jack, and Arnold Tackeray. 1981. *Gentlemen of Science: Early Years of the British Association for the Advancement of Science*. New York: Oxford University Press.

Moreno Yanez, Segundo. 1992. *El levantamiento indigena del Inti Raymi de 1990*. Quito: Abya-Yala.

Morner, Magnus. 1979. *Notas sobre el comercio y los comerciantes del Cuzco desde fines de la Colonia hasta 1930*. Lima: Instituto de Estudios Peruanos.

Morner, Magnus, ed. 1970. *Race and Class in Latin America*. New York: Columbia University Press.

Morote Best, Efraín. 1988. *Aldeas sumergidas*. Cusco: Centro de Estudios Regionales Andinos Las Casas.

Mosse, George. 1978. *Toward the Final Solution: A History of European Racism*. New York: Howard Fertig.

———. 1985. *Nationalism and Sexuality: Respectability and Abnormal Sexuality in Modern Europe*. New York: Howard Fertig.

Mukerii, Chandra, and M. Schudson. 1991. *Rethinking Popular Culture: Contemporary Perspectives in Cultural Studies*. Berkeley: University of California Press.

Muratorio, Blanca. 1994. "Nación, identidad y etnicidad: Imágenes de los indios ecuatorianos y sus imagineros a fines del siglo XIX." In *Imágénes e imagineros: Representaciones de los indígenas ecuatorianos, siglos XIX y XX*. Quito: Flacso. 109–196.

Murra, John. 1975. *Formaciones económicas y políticas del mundo andino*. Lima: Instituto de Estudios Peruanos.

Murra, John V., and Mercedes López-Baralt, eds. 1996. *Las cartas de Arguedas*. Lima: Pontificià Universidad Católica.

National Congress on Latin America. *Report on the Americas: Gaining Ground. The Indigenous Movement in Latin America* 19 (5).

Navarro del Aguila, Víctor. 1943a. "Las danzas populares en el Perú." *Revista del Instituto Americano de Arte* 1 (2): 24–44.

———. 1943b. "Entrevista con José Gabriel Cossio." *Waman Puma* 3 (15): 2–8.

———. 1944. "Calendario de fiestas populares del departamento de Cuzco." *Revista del Instituto Americano de Arte* 1 (3): 37–80.

——. 1945. "Cartilla de la ciencia del folklore." *El Ayllu* 1 (1–2): 20–22.

——. 1946. "Muestrario de algunas expresiones indígenas." *Revista de la Semana del Cuzco.* 77–82.

Neira, Hugo, ed. 1975. *Huillca: Habla un campesino peruano.* Buenos Aires: Corregidor.

Nieto, Luis. 1942. "Romance de la Barbaracha." *Revista del Instituto Americano de Arte* 1 (1): 25.

Nieto Degregori, Luis. 1997. "Visión de progreso de las élites políticas e intelectuales cusqueñas." Inés Fernández Baca and Luis Nieto Degregori, eds. In *Nosotros los cusqueños: visión de progreso del poblador urbano del Cusco.* Cusco: Centro de Educación y Comunicación Guamán Poma de Ayala.

Niño-Murcia, Mercedes. 1997. "Linguistic Purism in Cuzco, Peru: A Historical Perspective." *Language Problems and Language Planning* 21 (2): 134–161.

Núñez del Prado, Oscar. 1945. "Folklore." *Revista Vilcanota* 4: 7–11.

Núñez del Prado, Juan Víctor, and Marco Bonino. 1969. "Una celebración mestiza del Cruz-Velakuy en el Cuzco." *Revista Allpanchis* 1: 12–22.

Nye, Robert. 1993. *Masculinity and Male Codes of Honor in Modern France.* New York: Oxford University Press.

Ojeda Vizcarra, Pablo. 1990. *Importancia de la música cusqueña.* Cuzco: Municipalidad del Qosqo.

Oliart, Patricia. 1994. "Images of Gender and Race: The View from Above in Turn-of-the-Century Lima." Master's thesis, University of Texas at Austin.

Omi, Michael, and Howard Winant. 1986. *Racial Formation in the United States: From the 1960s to the 1980s.* New York: Routledge.

Orlove, Benjamin. 1977. *Alpacas, Sheep, and Men: The Wool Export Economy and Regional Society in Southern Peru.* New York: Academic Press.

——. 1990. "Rebels and Theorists: An Examination of Peasant Uprisings in Southern Peru." *Research in Social Movements, Conflict and Change* 12: 138–187.

——. 1993a. "The Dead Policemen Speak: Power, Fear, and Narrative in the 1931 Molloccahua Killings (Cusco)." In Deborah Poole, ed., *Unruly Order: Violence, Power, and Cultural Identity in the High Provinces of Southern Peru.* Boulder: Westview Press. 63–96.

——. 1993b. "Putting Race in its Place: Order in Colonial and Postcolonial Peruvian Geography." *Social Research* 60 (2): 301–336.

Ortner, Sherry. 1979. *Sherpas through Their Rituals.* Cambridge: Cambridge University Press.

Ossio, Juan. 1992. *Parentesco, reciprocidad y jerarquía en los Andes: Una aproximacion a la organizacion social de la comunidad de Andamarca*. Lima: Universidad Católica.

———. 1994. *Las paradojas del Perú oficial: Indigenismo, democracia y crisis estructural*. Lima: Universidad Católica.

Osterling, Jorge P., and Héctor Martínez. 1983. "Notes for a History of Peruvian Social Anthropology." *Current Anthropology* 24 (3): 342–360.

Pagden, Anthony. 1992. "Fabricating Identity in Spanish America." *History Today* (May): 44–49.

Palma, Clemente. 1897. *El porvenir de las razas en el Perú*. Lima: Imprenta Torres Aguirre.

Paponnet-Cantat, Christiane. 1994. "*Gamonalismo* after the Challenge of the Agrarian Reform: The Case of Capacmarca in Chumbivilcas." In D. Poole, ed., *Unruly Order: Violence, Power and Cultural Identity in the High Provinces of Southern Peru*. Boulder: Westview Press. 199–222.

Paredes, Saturnino. 1976. *El trabajo en el frente campesino*. Lima: Ediciones Trabajo y Lucha.

Paredes Tresierra, Juan. 1957. "Las fiestas religiosas de la ciudad del Cuzco." Archivo Departamental del Cusco Monografías de Geografía, Volume 19.

Parker, Andrew, Doris Sommers, and Patricia Yaeger. 1992. *Nationalisms and Sexualities*. New York: Routledge.

Patch, Richard W. 1958. Working paper. "The Indian Emergence in Cuzco: A Letter from Richard W. Patch." New York: American Universities Field Staff.

Paz Soldán, Mariano. 1862. *Geografía del Perú*. París: Imprenta de Fermin Didot.

Peralta, Antero. 1924. "Amor de indio." *Amauta* 11: 29.

Pévez, Hipólito. 1983. *Memorias de un viejo luchador campesino*. Lima: Tarea.

Piel, Jean. 1967. "A propos d'un soulevement rural Péruvien au début de vingtième siècle: Tocroyoc 1921." *Revue d'histoire moderne et contemporaine* 14: 375–405.

Pitt-Rivers, Julian. 1977. *The Fate of the Shechem; Or the Politics of Sex: Essays in the Anthropology of the Mediterranean*. Cambridge: Cambridge University Press.

Poole, Deborah. 1988. "Landscapes of Power in a Cattle Rustling Culture of Southern Andean Peru." *Dialectical Anthropology* 12: 367–398.

———. 1990. "Accommodation and Resistance in Andean Ritual Dance." *Drama Review* 34 (2): 98–126.

———. 1991. "Rituals of Movement, Rites of Transformation: Pilgrimage and Dance in the Highlands of Cuzco, Peru." In Ross N. Crumrine and Alan Morinis, eds., *Pilgrimage in Latin America.* New York: Greenwood Press.

———. 1992. "Figueroa Aznar and the Cusco *Indigenistas:* Photography and Modernism in Early Twentieth-Century Peru." *Representations* 38: 39–76.

———. 1994. "Performance, Domination, and Identity in the *Tierras Bravas* of Chumbivilcas." In D. Poole, ed., *Unruly Order: Violence, Power and Cultural Identity in the High Provinces of Southern Peru.* Boulder: Westview Press. 97–134.

———. 1997. *Vision, Race, and Modernity: A Political Economy of Andean Photography.* Princeton: Princeton University Press.

Porcel, Binolia, Eduardo Contreras, and Zaniel Tapia. 1992. *Plan de desarrollo del distrito de Santiago.* Cuzco: CERA Las Casas.

Porras Barrenechea, Raúl. 1961. *Antología del Cuzco.* Lima: Librería Internacional.

———. 1978. *Historia de los límites del Perú.* Lima: Editorial Universitaria.

Portocarrero, Gonzalo. 1990. "El Apra y el Congreso Económico Nacional." In Alberto Adrianzén, ed., *El Pensamiento Político Peruano.* Lima: Desco. 113–130.

———. 1995. "El fundamento invisible." In Aldo Panfichi and Felipe Portocarrero, eds., *Mundos Interiores: Lima, 1850–1950.* Lima: Centro de Investigación de la Universidad del Pacifico. 219–259.

Prado, Javier. 1891. *Evolución de la idea filosófica en la historia.* Lima: Imprenta Torres Aguirre.

———. 1909. "Memoria del decano de letras del Año 1908." *Revista Universitaria de San Marcos* (Lima, Universidad de San Marcos): 50–56.

Pratt, Mary Louise. 1992. *Imperial Eyes: Travel Writing and Transculturation.* New York: Routledge.

Price, Sally. 1989. *Primitive Art in Civilized Places.* Chicago: University of Chicago Press.

Quijano, Aníbal. 1978 [1965]. *Problema agrario y movimiento campesino.* Lima: Mosca Azul.

Rama, Angel. 1996. *The Lettered City.* Durham: Duke University Press.

Ramón Valarezo, Galo. 1992. "Ese secreto poder de la escritura." In I. Almeida et al., eds., *Indios.* Quito: Ildis and Ediciones Abya-Yala.

Ranger, Terence. 1975. *Dance and Society in Eastern Africa, 1890–1970: The Beni Ngoma.* London: Heinemann Educational.

———. 1993. "The Invention of Tradition Revisited: The Case of Colonial Africa." In T. Ranger and O. Vaughan, eds., *Legitimacy and the State in Twentieth-Century Africa.* Oxford: Macmillan Press.

Rappapport, Joanne. 1994. *Cumbe Reborn: An Andean Ethnography of History.* Chicago: University of Chicago Press.

Rasnake, Roger. 1988. *Domination and Cultural Resistance: Authority and Power among an Andean People.* Durham: Duke University Press.

Reátegui Chávez, Wilson. 1977. "Breve descripción de las acciones de los campesinos de la hacienda Lauramarca." In Wilfredo Kapsoli, ed., *Los movimientos campesinos en el Perú, 1879–1965.* Lima: Delva.

———. 1978. *Documentos para la historia del campesinado peruano.* Lima: Ediciones Kallpa.

Redfield, Robert. 1941. *The Folk Culture of Yucatan.* Chicago: University of Chicago Press.

Rengifo, Antonio. 1977. "Semblanza del Mayor de Caballería Teodomiro A. Gutierrez Cuevas: Defensor calificado de los indios y enemigo de los gamonales." Unpublished manuscript, Lima.

Rénique, José Luis. 1991. *Los sueños de la sierra: Cusco en el siglo XX.* Lima: Cepes.

Riva Aguero, José. 1995 [1912]. *Paisajes Peruanos.* Lima: Pontificia Universidad Catolica del Peru.

Rivera, Silvia. 1984. *Oprimidos pero no vencidos: Luchas del campesinado aymara y quechwa de Bolivia.* La Paz: Hisbol.

———. 1993. "Anthropology and Society in the Andes." *Critique of Anthropology* 13 (1): 77–96.

Robledo, José María. "La vía fluvial del Urubamba." 1899. *Boletín del Centro Científico del Cuzco.* 3.

Roca, José Gerardo. 1922. "Estudio socio-económico de la provincia del Cuzco." *Revista universitaria* 37: 32–50.

Roca Walparimachi, Demetrio. 1992. *Fiesta de la Natividad de la Almudena.* Cuzco: Universidad Nacional de San Antonio Abad del Cuzco.

Rodríguez Usandivaras, Junia O. 1949. "Los cargos religiosos y diferentes aspectos del problema indígena." *Revista universitaria* 97: 233–264.

Roel Pineda, Josafat. 1950. "La danza de los 'C'uncos' de Paucartambo." *Revista Tradición* 1 (1): 59–70.

Rojas Díaz, Benjamín. 1935. "Estudio etnográfico del indio quechua." *Revista universitaria* 70: 49–96.

Romero, Raúl, ed. 1993. *Música, danzas y máscaras en los Andes.* Lima: Pontificià Universidad Católica del Perú.

Rosaldo, Renato. 1993. *Culture and Truth: The Remaking of Social Analysis.* Boston: Beacon Press.

———. 1995. "Introduction." In García Canclini Néstor, ed., *Hybrid Cultures: Strategies for Entering and Leaving Modernity.* Minneapolis: University of Minnesota Press.

Rowe, John H. 1944. "Métodos y fines del estudio del folklore." *Waman Puma* 3 (16): 21–27.

Rowe, William, and Vivian Schelling. 1991. *Memory and Modernity: Popular Culture in Latin America*. London: Verso.

Ruedas de la Serna, Jorge. 1982. *Manuel Gonzáles Prada: Textos. Una antología general*. México: SEP/UNAM.

Ruiz Bravo, Patricia, and Carlos Monge. 1983. *Cusco: Ciudad y mercado*. Cusco: Centro de Estudios Regionales Andinos Las Casas.

Saavedra, Román. 1967. "La intelectualidad cuzqueña." *Revista del Instituto Americano de Arte* 12: 241–244.

Sacks, Karen Brodkin. 1994. "How Did the Jews Become White Folks? In Sanjek Roger and Gregory Steven, eds., *Race*. New Brunswick: Rutgers University Press. 78–102.

Sáenz, Moisés. 1933. *Sobre el indio peruano y su incorporación al medio nacional*. Mexico: Publicaciones de la Secretaría de Educación Pública.

Saignes, Tierry, ed. 1993. *Borrachera y memoria: La experiencia de los sagrado en los Andes*. La Paz: Hisbol, Instituto Francés de Estudios Andinos.

Salazar Bondy, Augusto. 1954. *La filosofía en el Perú: Panorama histórico*. Washington, D.C.: Union Panamericana.

Saldivar, Luis E. 1932. "Discurso del Sr. Catedratico de la Facultad de Ciencias Naturales." *Revista universitaria* 21: 6–11.

Sallnow, Michael. 1987. *Pilgrims of the Andes: Regional Cults in Cuzco*. Washington, D.C.: Smithsonian Institution Press.

———. 1991. "Dual Cosmology and Ethnic Divisions in an Andean Pilgrimage Cult." In Ross N. Crumrine and A. Morinis, eds., *Pilgrimage in Latin America*. New York: Greenwood Press. 281–306.

Salomon, Frank. 1981. "Killing the Yumbo." In Norman E. Whitten Jr., ed., *Cultural Transformation and Ethnicity in Modern Ecuador*. Urbana: University of Illinois. 162–208.

Sánchez, Luis Alberto. 1927. "Colofón." In Luis Eduardo Valcárcel, ed., *Tempestad en los Andes*. Lima: Amauta. 177–183.

———. 1985. *Conservador, no, reaccionario sí: Notas sobre la vida, obra y proyecciones de don José de la Riva Aguero y Osma, marqués de Montealegre y Aulestia*. Lima: Mosca Azul.

Sangari, Kukum, and Sudesh Vaid. 1990. *Recasting Women: Essays in Indian Colonial History*. Rutgers: Rutgers University Press.

Sarmiento, Faustino. 1966. *Civilización y barbarie: Vida de Juan Facundo Quiroga*. Mexico: Editorial Porrúa.

Sassoon, Anne Showstack, ed. 1982. *Approaches to Gramsci*. London: Writers and Readers.

Sauer, Carl O. 1982 [1942]. "Letter 15. The Peruvian Highlands:

Cuzco" (March 24). In Robert C. West, ed., *Andean Reflections: Letters from Carl O. Sauer while on a South American Trip under a Grant from the Rockefeller Foundation, 1942.* Boulder: Westview Press. 75–77.

Scheper-Hughes, Nancy. 1992. *Death without Weeping.* Berkeley: University of California Press.

Schwartz, Stuart B., and Frank Salomon. Forthcoming. "New Peoples and New Kinds of People: Adaptation, Readjustment, and Ethnogenesis in South American Indigenous Societies (Colonial Era). In *Cambridge History of the Native Peoples of the Americas* Part 3: *South America.* New York: Cambridge University Press.

Silverblatt, Irene. 1995. "Becoming Indian in the Central Andes of Seventeenth-Century Peru." In Gyan Prakash, ed., *After Colonialism.* Princeton: Princeton University Press. 279–298.

Sivirichi, Atilio. 1937. "El contenido espiritual del movimiento indigenista." *Revista Universitaria* 76: 1–23.

———. 1940. "Prólogo." In Américo Vargas Fano, *Mestizaje.* Lima: Linotipia Guadalupe.

Skar, Sarah Lund. 1994. *Lives Together—Worlds Apart: Quechua Colonization in Jungle and City.* Oslo: Scandinavian University Press.

Skidmore, Thomas E. 1993 [1976]. *Black into White: Race and Nationality in Brazilian Thought.* Durham: Duke University Press.

Smith, Carol. 1995. "A Critical Geneology on North American Treatments of Race and Racism in the Social Analysis of Guatemala." Paper presented at annual meeting of Latin American Studies Association, Washington, D.C.

Smith, Carol, ed. 1990. *Guatemalan Indians and the State: 1540–1988.* Austin: University of Texas Press.

Spivak, Gayatri C. 1988a. "Can the Subaltern Speak?" In Cary Nelson and Lawrence Grossberg, eds., *Marxism and the Interpretation of Culture.* Urbana: University of Illinois Press. 271–313.

———. 1988b. "Subaltern Studies: Deconstructing Historiography." In Ranajit Guha and Gayatri C. Spivak, eds., *Selected Subaltern Studies.* New York: Oxford University Press. 3–34.

Sollors, Werner. 1989. "Introduction." In W. Sollors, ed., *The Invention of Ethnicity.* New York: Oxford University Press. ix–xx.

Sotomayor Pérez, José. 1984. *Cuzco 1958: Análisis testimonial de un movimiento urbano.* Cuzco: Centro de Estudios Regionales Andinos Las Casas.

Spalding, Karen. 1974. *De indio a campesino.* Lima: Instituto de Estudios Peruanos.

Squier, George E. 1974 [1877]. *Un viaje por tierras incaica: Crónicas de una expedicion arqueológica.* Lima: San Marcos–United States Embassy.

Stallybrass, Peter, and Allon White. 1986. *The Politics and Poetics of Trangression*. Ithaca: Cornell University Press.

Starfield, J. 1985. "Theoretical and Ideological Barriers to the Study of Race Making." In Marret C. and C. Leggon, eds., *Research in Race and Ethnic Relations: A Research Annual*. Greenwich, Conn.: JAI Press. 161–181.

Stein, Steve. 1980. *Populism in Peru: The Emergence of the Masses and the Politics of Social Control*. Madison: University of Wisconsin Press.

Stepan, Nancy Leys. 1982. *The Idea of Race in Science: Great Britain, 1800–1960*. Hamden, Conn.: Archon Books.

——. 1985. "Biological Degeneration: Races and Proper Places." In Chamberlin J. Edward and Sander L. Gilma, eds., *Degeneration: The Dark Side of Progress*. New York: Columbia University Press. 97–120.

——. 1991. *The Hour of Eugenics: Race, Gender and Nation in Latin America*. Ithaca: Cornell University Press.

Stepan, Nancy Leys, and Sander L. Gilman. 1991. "Appropriating the Idioms of Science: The Rejection of Scientific Racism." In Dominick La Capra, ed., *The Bounds of Race: Perspectives on Hegemony and Resistance*. Ithaca: Cornell University Press. 72–103.

Stephen, Lynn. 1991. *Zapotec Women*. Austin: University of Texas Press.

Stephen, Lynn, and James Dow. 1990. *Class, Politics, and Popular Religion: Religious Change in Mexico and Central America*. Washington, D.C.: American Anthropological Association.

Stern, Steve J. 1982. *Peru's Indigenous Peoples and the Challenge of Spanish Conquest: Huamanga to 1640*. Madison: University of Wisconsin Press.

——. 1987. "Introduction." In *Resistance, Rebellion, and Consciousness in the Andean Peasant World*. Madison: University of Wisconsin Press. 1–25.

——. 1995. *The Secret History of Gender: Women, Men, and Power in Late Colonial Mexico*. Chapel Hill: University of North Carolina Press.

Steward, Julian, ed. 1946. *Handbook of South American Indians 2*. Washington, D.C.: Bureau of American Ethnology.

Stocking, George. 1968. *Race, Culture, and Evolution: Essays in the History of Anthropology*. Toronto: Collier-Macmillan.

——., ed. 1991. *Colonial Situations: Essays on the Contextualization of Ethnographic Knowledge*. Madison: University of Wisconsin Press.

——. 1994. "The Turn-of-the-Century Concept of Race." *Modernism/modernity* 1 (1): 4–16.

Stolcke, Verena. 1974. *Marriage, Class and Colour in Nineteenth-*

Century Cuba: A Study of Racial Attitudes and Sexual Values in a Slave Society. London: Cambridge University Press.

——. 1993. "Is Sex to Gender Like Race Is to Ethnicity?" In Teresa del Valle, ed., *Gendered Anthropology.* London: Routledge. 17–37.

——. 1995. "Talking Culture. New Boundaries, New Rhetorics of Exclusion in Europe." *Current Anthropology* 36 (1): 1–24.

Stoler, Ann. 1989. "Making the Empire Respectable: The Politics of Race and Sexual Morality in 20th-Century Colonial Cultures." *American Ethnologist* 16 (4): 634–660.

——. 1995. *Race and the Education of Desire: Foucault's* History of Sexuality and the Colonial Order of Things. Durham: Duke University Press.

Strathern, Marilyn. 1991. *Partial connections.* Savage, Md.: Rowman and Littlefield.

——. 1995. "Comments." In V. Stolcke "Talking Culture: New Boundaries, New Rhetorics of Exclusion in Europe." *Current Anthropology* 36 (1): 1–24.

Stutzman, Ronald. 1981. "*El Mestizaje:* An All-Inclusive Ideology of Exclusion." In Norman Whitten, ed., *Cultural Transformations and Ethnicity in Modern Ecuador.* Urbana: University of Illinois Press.

Sueldo Guevara, Luis. 1921. "Las Fiestas Religiosas." Unpublished manuscript. Archivo Departamental del Cusco, Book 15.

Szeminski, Jan. 1987. "Why Kill the Spaniard? New Perspectives on Andean Insurrectionary Ideology in the 18th Century." In Steve J. Stern, ed., *Resistance, Rebellion and Consciousness in the Andean Peasant World.* Madison: University of Wisconsin Press. 166–192.

Taguieff, Pierre-André. 1987. *La Force du préjugé: Essai sur le racisme et ses doubles.* Paris: Editions La Découverte.

——. 1990. "The New Cultural Racism in France." *Telos* 83: 109–122.

Tamayo Herrera, José. 1980. *Historia del indigenismo cuzqueño, siglos XIV–XIV–XX.* Lima: Instituto Nacional de Cultura.

——. 1981. *Historia social del Cuzco republicano.* Lima: Universo.

——. 1982. *Historia social e indigenismo en el Altiplano.* Lima: Ediciones treintaitrés.

——. 1992. *Historia general del Qosqo: Una historia regional desde el período lítico hasta el año 2000.* Cuzco: Municipalidad del Qosqo.

Tauro, Alberto. 1988. *Enciclopedia ilustrada del Peru 2.* Lima: Peisa.

Taussig, Michael. 1987. *Shamanism, Colonialism, and the Wild Man: A Study in Terror and Healing.* Chicago: University of Chicago Press.

Tax, Sol. 1953. *Penny Capitalism: A Guatemalan Indian Economy.* Washington, D.C.: U.S. Government Printing Office.

Tealdo, Alfonso. 1947. "Interview. Luis E. Valcárcel." *Boletín Indigenista.* 7 (3): 260–272.

Thompson, E. P. 1991. *Customs in Common.* London: Merlin.

Thomson, Sinclair. 1988. "La cuestión india en Bolivia a comienzos de siglo: El caso de Rigoberto Paredes." *Autodeterminación* (La Paz) 4: 83–116.

———. 1996. "Colonialism, Community, and Revolution: Aymara Politics in the Age of Insurrection (La Paz, 1740–1809)." Ph.D. dissertation, University of Wisconsin–Madison.

Tomoeda, Hiroyasu, and Jorge Flores Ochoa, eds. 1992. *El Qosqo: Antropología de la ciudad.* Cuzco: Ministerio de Educación de Japón, CEAC.

Tonkin, E., M. McDonald, and M. Champman, eds. 1989. *History and Ethnicity.* London: Routledge.

Tord, Luis Enrique. 1978. *El indio en los ensayistas peruanos: 1848–1948.* Lima: Editoriales Unidas.

Trujillo, Jorge, ed. 1993. *Indianistas, indianófilos e indigenistas: Entre el enigma y la fascinación.* Quito: Ildis Aya-Yala.

Turner, Terence. 1991. "Representing, Resisting, Rethinking: Historical Transformations of Kayapo Culture and Anthropological Consciousness." In *Colonial Situations: Essays on the Contextualization of Ethnographic Knowledge.* Madison: University of Wisconsin Press. 285–313.

Turner, Victor. 1982. *From Ritual to Theatre: The Human Seriousness of Play.* New York: Performing Arts Journal Publications.

Unanue, Hipólito. 1940 [1806]. *Observaciones sobre el clima de Lima y su influencia en los seres organizados en especial el hombre.* Lima; Comisión Nacional Peruana de Cooperación Intelectual.

Urban, Greg, and Joel Sherzer, eds. 1991. *Nation-States and Indians in Latin America.* Austin: University of Texas Press.

Urquiaga, José. 1977. *Indios: Puno–1916.* Lima: Universidad Nacional Mayor de San Marcos.

Vail, Leroy. "Introduction." In L. Vail, ed., *The Creation of Tribalism in Southern Africa.* Berkeley: University of California Press. 1–19.

Valcárcel, Luis Eduardo. 1914. "La cuestion agraria." *Revista universitaria* 9: 16–38.

———. 1916. "Los Problemas Actuales." Cuzco: Imprenta El Trabajo.

———. 1925. *De la vida Inkaika: Algunas captaciones del espíritu que la animó.* Cuzco: Editorial Garcilaso.

———. 1937 [1931]. *Mirador indio.* Cuzco: Ed. Garcilaso.

———. 1944. "Nuevo significado del Cuzco." In *Hora del Hombre.* Lima: n.p.

———. 1945. *Ruta cultural del Perú.* Mexico: Editorial Gráfica Panamericana.

———. 1946. *Historia del Perú antiguo.* Lima: Editorial Juan Mejía Baca.

———. 1972. "Autobiografía." *Revista del Museo Nacional* 31: 10–14.

———. 1981. *Memorias*. Lima: Instituto de Estudios Peruanos.

———. 1978 [1927]. "El mito de Kori Ojllo." In *Tempestad en los Andes*. Lima: Editorial Universo.

Valderrama, Ricardo, and Carmen Escalante. 1981. *Los levantamientos indígenas de Haquira y Quiñota (1922–1924/Apurímac, Cuzco)*. Lima: Universidad Nacional Mayor de San Marcos.

Van den Berghe, Pierre, and George Primov. 1977. *Inequality in the Peruvian Andes: Class and Ethnicity in Cuzco*. Columbia: University of Missouri Press.

Varallanos, José. 1962. *El cholo en el Perú: Introducción al estudio sociólogico del hombre y un pueblo mestizos y su destino cultural*. Buenos Aires: Imprenta López.

Vargas Llosa, Mario. 1990a. "Informe sobre Uchuraccay." In *Contra viento y marea*. Lima: Peisa. 79–114.

———. 1990b. "Questions of Conquest: What Columbus Wrote and What He Did Not." *Harper's* (December): 45–53.

———. 1996. *Death in the Andes*. New York: Farrar, Strauss and Giroux.

Vasconcelos, José. 1925. *La Raza Cósmica: Misión de la raza Iberoamericana. Notas de viaje por la América del Sur*. Barcelona: Agencia Mundial de Librería. Reprinted in *Obras completas*. 2 (México: Libreros Mexicanos Unidos), 906–942.

———. 1926. *Indología: Una interpretación de la cultura Iberoamericana*. Barcelona: Agencia Mundial de Librería.

———. 1937. *Bolivarismo y Monroísmo*. Santiago de Chile: Eds. Ercilla.

Vega Centeno, Máximo. 1925. "La personalidad jurídica." Unpublished manuscript. Archivo Departmental del Cusco, Book 17.

Veil, Leroy, ed. 1989. *The Creation of Tribalism in Southern Africa*. Berkeley: University of California Press.

Verger, Pierre. 1945. *Fiestas y danzas en el Cuzco y en los Andes*. Buenos Aires: Ed. Sudamericana.

Very, Francis G. 1962. *The Spanish Corpus Christi Procession: A Literary and Folkloric Study*. Valencia: Tipografía Moderna.

Vidal de Milla, Delia. 1985. "Humberto Vidal Unda: Su pensamiento, su obra, su Pasión. El Cusco." Cuzco: n.p.

Vidal Unda, Humberto. 1938. *Hacia un nuevo arte peruano*. Cuzco: Tipografía La Económica.

———. 1940. "El problema del indio y el indigenismo." *Revista Universitaria* 78: 73–93.

———. 1944. "Discurso del Dr. Humberto Vidal en la velada de gala del Cine Colón." In *Revista del Instituto American de Arte,* Año III, Vol. 1, 144–146.

———. 1958. *Visión del Cuzco*. Cuzco: n.p.

Villanueva, Horacio. 1948. "Historia de la fundación del Hospital y Convento de Nuestra Señora de la Almudena." *Revista Universitaria* 94: 53–74.

Villanueva, Víctor. 1973. *Ejército peruano: Del caudillaje anárquico al militarismo reformista.* Lima: Editorial Mejía Baca.

Villasante Ortiz, Segundo. 1975. *Paucartambo: Provincia folklórica.* Cuzco: Ed. León.

Wade, Peter. 1993. *Blackness and Race Mixture: The Dynamics of Racial Identity in Colombia.* Baltimore: Johns Hopkins University Press.

———. *Race and Ethnicity in Latin America.* 1997. Chicago: Pluto Press.

Wagley, Charles. 1965. "On the Concept of Social Race in the Americas." In Dwight B. Heath and Richard N. Adams, eds., *Contemporary Cultures and Societies in Latin America.* New York: Random House.

Wagner, Roy. 1991. "The Fractal Person." In Maurice Godelier and Marilyn Strathern, eds., *Big Men and Great Men: Personifications of Power in Melanesia.* Cambridge: Cambridge University Press. 159–174.

Walker, Charles. 1992. "Peasants, Caudillos, and the State in Peru: Cusco in the Transition from Colony to Republic, 1780–1840." Ph.D. dissertation, University of Chicago.

———. 1993. "Voces discordantes: El discurso sobre el indio a fines de la Colonia." Paper presented at the fifth annual colloquium, "El siglo XVIII en los Andes" of Centro Latino Americano de Ciencias Sociales—Centro de Estudios Regionales Andinos Las Casas, Paris.

Warren, Kay B. 1989. *The Symbolism of Subordination: Indian Identity in a Guatemalan Town.* Austin: University of Texas Press.

———. 1992. "Transforming Memories and Histories: The Meanings of Ethnic Resurgence for Maya Indians." In Alfred Stepan, ed., *Americas: New Interpretive Essays.* New York: Oxford University Press. 189–219.

———. 1996. "Reading History as Resistance: Maya Public Intellectuals in Guatemala." In E. Fischer and R. McKenna Brown, eds., *Maya Cultural Activism in Guatemala.* Austin: University of Texas Press. 89–106.

———. 1998. "Indigenous Movements as a Challenge to the Unified Social Movement Paradigm for Guatemala." In Sonia Alvarez, Evelina Dagnino, and Arturo Escobar, eds., *Cultures of Politics, Politics of Cultures: Re-Visioning Latin American Social Movements.* Boulder: Westview Press. 165–191.

———. 1998. *Indigenous Movements and Their Critics. Pan-Maya Activism in Guatemala.* Princeton, N.J.: Princeton University Press.

White, Hayden. 1982. "The Forms of Wildness: Archaeology of an Idea." In *Tropics of Discourse: Essays in Cultural Criticism.* Baltimore: Johns Hopkins University Press. 150–182.

Wiener, Charles. 1880. *Pérou et Bolivie: Récit de voyage*. Paris: Librairie Hachette.

Wiesse, Carlos. 1902. *Lecciones de geografía del Perú: Estudio político, económico-industrial, administrativo*. Lima: Editorial Rosay.

———. 1909. "Los hechos históricos y el factor étnico." *Contemporáneos* (June 15): 249–253.

Williams, Brackette. 1989. "A Class Act: Anthropology and the Race to Nation across Ethnic Terrain." *Annual Review of Anthropology* 18: 401–444.

———. 1991. *Stains on My Name, War in My Veins: Guyana and the Politics of Cultural Struggle*. Durham: Duke University Press.

Williams, Raymond. 1977. *Marxism and Literature*. New York: Oxford University Press.

Wolf, Eric. 1994. "Perilous Ideas: Race, Culture, People." *Current Anthropology* 35 (1): 1–12.

Yépez Miranda, Alfredo. 1945. "Cuzco, emblema de Peruanidad." *Revista de la Semana del Cuzco* 1 (1): 25–30.

———. 1965. *Cuzco eterno*. Cuzco: n.p.

Young, Robert C. 1995. *Colonial Desire: Hybridity in Theory, Culture and Race*. New York: Routledge.

Zamosc, Leon. 1995. "Agrarian Protest and the Indian Movement in the Ecuadorian Highlands." *Latin American Research Review* 23 (3): 37–68.

Index

Marisol de la Cadena is Assistant Professor
in the Department of Anthropology at the University of
North Carolina, Chapel Hill.

Library of Congress Cataloging-in-Publication Data

de la Cadena, Marisol.
Indigenous Mestizos: Race and the politics of representation in
Cuzco, 1919–1991 / by Marisol de la Cadena.
p.   cm. — (Latin America otherwise)
Includes bibliographical references and index.
ISBN 0-8223-2385-0 (cloth : alk. paper) — ISBN 0-8223-2420-2
(pbk. : alk. paper)
1. Mestizos — Peru — Cuzco — Social conditions. 2. Indians of South
America — Mixed descent — Peru — Cuzco. 3. Racism — Peru —
Cuzco. 4. Cuzco (Peru) — Social conditions. I. Title. II. Series.
F3429.3.M63C33 2000
306'.0985'37 — dc21   99-37470
                                                              CIP